Naked Tropics

New World in the Atlantic World
Jack P. Greene and Amy Turner Bushnell, Series Editors

Naked Tropics

Essays on Empire and Other Rogues

Kenneth Maxwell

ROUTLEDGE

NEW YORK AND LONDON

Published in 2003 by
Routledge
29 West 35th Street
New York, NY 10001
www.routledge-ny.com

Published in Great Britain by
Routledge
11 New Fetter Lane
London EC4P 4EE
www.routledge.co.uk

Routledge is an imprint of the Taylor & Francis Group.
Printed in the United States of America on acid-free paper.

10 9 8 7 6 5 4 3 2 1

Library of Congress Cataloging-in-Publication Data

Maxwell, Kenneth, 1941–
    Naked tropics : essays on empire and other rogues / by Kenneth Maxwell.
        p. cm. — (New World in the Atlantic world)
    Includes index.
    ISBN 0-415-94576-3 (hb) — ISBN 0-415-94577-1 (pbk.)
      1. Brazil—History.   2. Portuguese—Foreign countries.   3. Portugal—Relations—
    Foreign countries.   I. Title.   II. Series.

F2521.M495 2003
981—dc21

                                                                                2003043129

For Stanley J. Stein and Barbara Hadley Stein

The empires of our time were short lived, but they have altered the world forever; their passing away is their least significant feature.
V. S. Naipaul, *The Mimic Men*

Contents

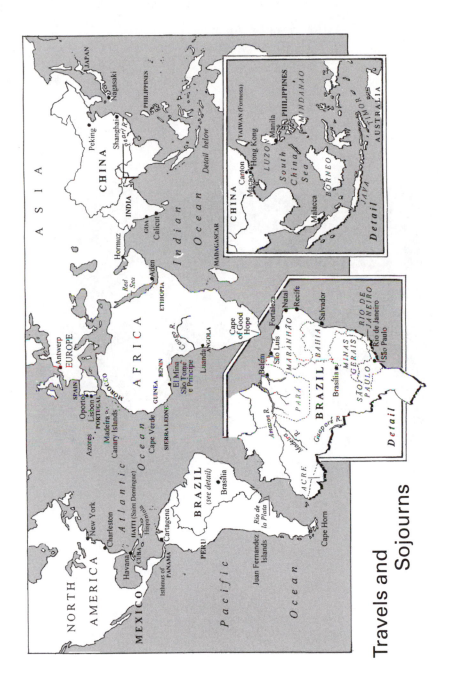

Travels and Sojourns

ENTRANCE TO THE HARBOR OF RIO.

Foreword—Blame It on Rio
The Historical Vocation of Kenneth Maxwell

In one of his arresting and subtle works, *Finding the Center* (1984), V. S. Naipaul writes of the promptings of his craft and offers a narrative of his literary beginnings—a narrative intended to "admit the reader to the process of writing." By now we know the themes and the methods of that writer: the journey from his small birthplace in Trinidad to the metropolitan center, the panic of arrival, the wanderlust that took him to distant lands in a world beginning to shake off its colonial heritage. There was glamour in the travel, and knowledge, the gathering together of the strands of a man's life and background. In these pages by the gifted historian Kenneth Maxwell, we are "admitted" into the process of writing as well. A historian of great talent, working at the peak of his powers, takes us into the promptings of his own vocation. Piece by exquisite piece in this book, we see the historian's method and the concerns that have been the driving passions of his life for four decades now: the peopling of the Americas, the shaking up of continents, the spirit that took a "precocious" Portugal into its imperial venture, the play between Portugal's extensive imperial reach into Africa and Asia and the Americas, and the limits of its own demography and abilities, the rise of Brazil and its tumultuous history.

The direction of Professor Maxwell's journey reverses Naipaul's, though. With the historian, it is the pushing outward of a child of the empire, a young man at Cambridge venturing into the tropics. Born in 1941, Maxwell belonged to a generation that was hanging on with its fingernails to the old imperial order. On a "misty, cold, damp, and dreary East Anglian evening," in an old picture palace that had reinvented itself as an "art theater," Maxwell had seen Marcel Camus's film *Black Orpheus*. It "could not have been a greater revelation," he writes. The ancient story set against the tropical background, the color and the vibrancy of that background, hooked him. "I determined immediately that Brazil, and above all, Rio de Janeiro, was somewhere I had to go." He went there via Lisbon, and in that great Luso-Brazilian world he was to find his material, and his range, and they are on full display here. This "material" could have supplied great fiction or travel writing: Maxwell himself, as these beautiful pieces demonstrate, with their love of color, with their ability to conjure up a forlorn colonial outpost on the South China Sea (Macao), or the teeming streets of Brazil's cities, or the life and murder of a rubber tapper, a union activist, in the hinterland of Brazil by a violent clan of ranchers, could have pulled it off and produced that sort of literary work. But he is a historian of ideas, and of social and economic life, and his insatiable, boundless curiosity infuses this work with an energy and a life all its own.

Edward Gibbon, as we learn from the late historian John Clive's loving tribute to the reading and writing of history, *Not by Fact Alone* (1989), once called the historian's first person "the most disgusting of pronouns." Gibbon was giving voice to an ambivalence, for the historian's "I" was there in his work, in his footnotes, in the text itself, the writer's personality and attitudes toward the subjects at hand. Macaulay, too, used his first person to convey to his readers a sense of immediacy, of places seen and oral histories he had collected. So did Tocqueville who had his own way of taking the reader into his confidence, of letting the reader know what that liberal aristocratic historian thought of revolutionary violence and pretensions, Clive tells us. The narrator's "I" gives this work by Maxwell its unique place in what this prolific historian has produced. We saw precious little (directly, that is) of Maxwell when he produced his seminal biography of Portugal's leading eighteenth-century statesman, Marquês de Pombal, and his attempt at a revolution from above, *Pombal: Paradox of the Enlightenment* (1995). Nor would we have surmised much about the historian had we read his definitive accounts of the Portuguese Revolution of 1974, or of the political traffic between Portugal and Brazil in the second half of the eighteenth century. This work is different: we are truly taken into the narrator's confidence, admitted into the craft of writing. The personal pronoun is never intrusive though. There is a kind of trust between historian and reader, an illicit pact of sorts.

We know and trust this historian: we are eager to travel with him to Macao or the Amazon forests; we are eager for him to tell us about other historians and chroniclers. We pick up his trail—and his likes and dislikes, for that matter. When he writes that Carlos Fuentes is "never one to use two words if more will do," and that that Mexican writer in one of his works throws at the reader "every stereotype of *hispanidad* propaganda (Bulls, Virgins, Tangos, Gauchos, Don Quixote)," he gives voice to his readers' verdict (most of them, I hazard to guess) on that exhibitionist writer. "My Portuguese was the swallowed nasal Portuguese of Lisbon, and I was utterly unprepared for the musicality, rhythm, and softness of Brazilian speech," he writes on the occasion of meeting his first Brazilian in his academic supervisor's office at Princeton. Until then his Brazil had been "entirely phantasmogorical," he adds, the stuff of books and films. The historian's trail, and the anxiety of the first probings of an alien world: they come together for us in that episode. And we don't have to search for the historian's pride in the world he had come to adopt in the Americas. It is there in Maxwell's sense of exasperation with the "provincialism" of Europe. The Old World may have "discovered" and disrupted the New World, but the latter remade the Old Continent, he reminds us. The educated Europeans may have been fixated on classical literature and Renaissance cosmology. But they did so, he adds, while "drinking their American-produced coffee, smoking American-produced tobacco, binding their texts between American leather hides, and enjoying the leisure that the dividends from overseas investments made possible."

At the heart of this book, its binding if you will, is of course Portugal's imperial journey: it is the historian's beat and his pride. It was the Portuguese, he reminds us, who linked the Atlantic to the Indian Ocean, who mapped the coastline of Asia, and explored the African coastline from Cape Verde in the West to the mouth of the Red Sea in the East. In one of those mysterious spurts that enable a particular people to do stunning, surprising feats, the Portuguese recast and revisioned the world. Their advantage, we learn, was less navigational than conceptual: their cartography enabled them to arrive at a "new graphic conception of global space." The Portuguese broke the monopoly of the trans-Saharan trade route between West Africa and the southern shores of the Mediterranean. In less than two decades after Vasco da Gama's voyage of discovery of 1497–1498, Portugal had claimed a vast dominion: Brazil in 1500, Goa in 1510, Malacca in 1511, Hormuz in 1515, and so on. Portugal aimed for the passageways of trade, the "choke points" of international trade: Hormuz at the mouth of the Persian Gulf, Mombassa and Mozambique, Malacca, the Azores, Macao at the mouth of the Pearl River in China, Cape Verde. The Portuguese must have intuited their own weakness. Portugal, Maxwell reminds us, was after all, a "small country with a large empire." No wonder the Portuguese hugged the coasts—and stayed aloof from the interior of the worlds they probed and ventured into.

Weakness—and backwardness—stalked the imperial push. The nemesis was not far behind. In the span of a few decades after that remarkable spurt, Portugal itself slipped under Castilian hegemony in 1580. A deranged monarch had taken the country and its nobility on a quixotic crusade into North Africa; the venture had issued in tragedy and the decimation of the country's nobility. Philip II had offered a traumatized Portugal rescue. But an absentee, semi-alien monarch would not do. Portugal was to recover its independence in 1640, but the imperial thrust was broken. There would be no Portuguese empire in the Orient. The very national epic of Portugal's voyages of discovery, *The Lusiads*, by the great poet Luís Vaz de Camões, published in 1572, was a lament for what might have been. There was patriotism aplenty in Camões, and there was national pride, to be sure. The poet, who had spent seventeen of his adult years as a sailor and soldier in Goa, Cochin, and Macao, praised Portugal's urge to "discover the sun's very cradle in the East." But Camões himself was a child of disappointment. The trajectory of his country—the early success, then the steady retreat from progress, and Castilian rule—brackets his life. He was born the year Vasco da Gama died, in 1524; he died in 1580, right as his country was slipping under the Castilian noose. Portugal succumbed to despondency, and the sorrow is there in *The Lusiads*, and a knowledge of the heartache that came with the imperial temptation. In Canto IV, a wise old man comes to the shore to bid farewell to the voyagers and to weep for his country, and for the sorrow that imperial appetite heaped upon her:

> Oh craving of command! Oh vain Desire!
> Oh vainest vanity man miscalleth Fame!
> Oh fraudulent gust, so easy fanned to fire
> By breath of vulgar, aping Honour's name!
> What just and dreadful judgement deals
>   thine ire,
> To seely souls who overlove thy claim!
> What deaths, what direful risks, what
>   agonies
> Wherewith thou guerdonest them, thy
>   fitting prize!
>
> What new disaster dost thou here design?
> What horror of our realm and race invent?
> What unheard dangers or what deaths
>   condign,
> Veiled by some name that soundeth
>   excellent?

What bribe of gorgeous reign, and golden
    mine,
Whose ready offer is so rarely meant?
What fame hast promised them? What
    pride of story?
What palms? What triumphs? What
    victorious glory?

That sorrow and despondency of Portugal—and the urge for reform and repair—are caught in Maxwell's pages. But that despondency that until recent years hovered over Portugal, a steady shadow and companion, did not travel to Brazil. The tropics worked their will here. Indeed, it is doubtful, I would think, that a child of an empire in decline (Britain) of Maxwell's temperament would have been hooked on another somber land. There may have been troubles in Brazil, but the history was one of tumult and possibilities. In that Luso-Brazilian encounter, the issue, the child of the encounter, bounced with greater freedom, had less burden to carry than the motherland. In its passage from colony to imperial center (the monarchy had quit Portugal for Brazil in the wake of Napoleon Bonaparte's armies' invasion of Portugal in 1807) to independent nationhood in 1822, Brazil charted its own course; Portugal had for all practical purposes become a dependency of Brazil.

A central theme of Brazil's history, and a theme that Maxwell handles with amazing skill, concerns the tension between liberty and order in Brazilian history. In a land where the whites constituted a distinct minority, the revolution that held the attention of the oligarchs and the elite of the land was not the American Revolution in 1776 but the Haitian slave revolt. In Haiti's fire, in the success of its rebels, the Brazilian elite saw the specter of its own undoing. There was fear of revolutionary "contagion" and a recognition that a society that would give unfettered run to the idea of "equality" in a land "ordered by racial as much as by social hierarchy" would be torn asunder. Progress in this outwardly flamboyant land was tethered to order.

Nor was the American republic, for that matter, so keen on seeing its liberty replicated in the South American landscape. In a characteristic bit of homage to liberty's reach, Thomas Jefferson, in 1820, had written to a Portuguese-born friend, Abbé Corrêa da Serra, in praise of a new world in the Americas free of the curse of Europe's wars, of a day over the horizon when the fleets of Brazil and the United States would ride together "as brethren of the same family and pursuing the same object." Jefferson was in retirement in Monticello then. As Maxwell reminds us, the decisive American voice on the independent nations of South America belonged to John

Quincy Adams both as secretary of state between 1817 and 1825 and as president in the four crucial years that followed. Adams was bereft of tropical romance. "He saw South Americans as irredeemably corrupted by the Roman Catholic religion, Iberian tradition, and the tropical climate." Brazil had to find its own mix of liberty and racial assimilation. Maxwell allows Brazil its final flourish and vindication, a signature of its own on this great quest: the seminal, great figure of its independence, Jose Bonifácio, was a metallurgist. He aimed for a Brazilian race that would "amalgamate" all the diverse "metals" of Brazil, blend them into a common national identity.

* * *

Now a word about the "introducer's" personal pronoun. My knowledge of the Americas is rather scant, of the Iberian world a bit better. My authority for writing these brief pages of appreciation I owe to Kenneth Maxwell's flattering and surprising invitation. I couldn't have declined the honor, though undeserved. Circles are closed and connections are made in these pages. It was at Princeton where Maxwell met his first Brazilian, as we were told. It was there, on the same campus, a decade later, where I met Professor Maxwell. We are roughly the same age; he had grabbed the colonial drama of the time, Portugal's struggle with its last African colonies and Portugal's struggle at home with its rebellious young officers who had had their fill with imperial burden. It was with excitement that I can still call up that I read his magnificent depiction of the Portuguese Revolution of 1974, and my admiration of his craft has never ceased.

My second claim is given me by the work itself. Maxwell writes of broken worlds and "hollow empires." A child and a chronicler of matters and lands Islamic and Arab, I know something of that malady and of the trajectory of civilizations that rise on impulse, draw on mysterious energy, and then succumb to despondency. I may be unfamiliar with the settings of Professor Maxwell's work, but the themes are innately, painfully, familiar. The very first time I came upon fado music and songs, I understood not a word, but I intuitively, readily, caught the themes and the mood—love and loss and lament. I had no difficulty "entering" the haunting songs of the great Amália Rodrigues: we have her peer in the legendary Egyptian woman singer Umm Kulthum, who must be reckoned the twentieth century's greatest Arabic singer, and whose themes and tone were evocations of loss and sorrow. The "fado" in the Portuguese fragments by Maxwell is familiar to me in the same way. Of all of Maxwell's work, this work is meant for the general reader (hence my casting) who wants to know about the history of chocolate, or the voyages of discovery that have remade our world, or the true historical sociology of pirates and piracy.

Our towering historians are few and far between. In the age of the 24/7 cable channels and the gabfest and the instant analysts, those historians are sure to become rarer still. Attribution, rigor, fidelity to sources, once the assumed tools and ways of the craft, are flung on the sidelines. Behold in these pages this distinguished historian, the (younger) peer of Bernard Lewis on Islam and C. Vann Woodward on Southern history and Arthur Schlesinger on the American experience and David Landes on economic history. In these pages we are in the hands of a guide who truly owns his field, and roams its expanses with easy authority and a genuine wonder at the ways of our world.

Fouad Ajami

Acknowledgments

First my thanks to Tomás Amorim who is a valued colleague at the Council on Foreign Relations and as my research associate from 1999 to 2002 has been instrumental to seeing this selection of essays prepared for publication. I am grateful to him for his care and attention to detail and for his patience with my endless reworkings of the texts. The Council has provided me with a stimulating environment for work, and I appreciate the great latitude they have allowed me over the years to pursue my interests in history as well as public policy. I owe much to its president, Leslie H. Gelb, for his encouragement and support, and not least appointing me in 1995 as first holder of the Nelson and David Rockefeller Chair. Peter Tarnoff and Nicholas X. Rizopoulos invited me to join the Council in 1989, and for this I am much in their debt. I have had the great privilege of working with fine editors such as Bob Silvers of the *New York Review of Books*, James Chace and Linda Wrigley of the *World Policy Journal*, Helder Macedo and Toni Huberman of *Portuguese Studies*, and Steven Lagerfeld of the *Wilson Quarterly*, as well as Dauril Alden, Marcos Sá Corrêa, Flávio Pinheiro, Pedro Doria, Adriano Schwartz, and Marcos Flamínio Peres. All held me to the highest standards. It is a special pleasure to appear in the Routledge Series New World in the Atlantic World, edited by Jack Greene and Amy Bushnell. Both have been pioneers in the field of cross-cultural Atlantic studies, long an orphan, but now at long last receiving due attention by their colleagues, and they have always understood the interconnectedness of the Americas and the value of comparative approaches to histories which remain too often parochial and compartmentalized. I am especially grateful to Jack since he has long kept me linked to the historical profession despite my wanderings (or, as Albert Hirschman calls it, "trespassing") between various disciplinary fields. For this I am ever grateful. John Coatsworth, director of the David Rockefeller Center at Harvard, and James Dunkerley, director of the Institute of Latin American Studies at the University of London, read the whole manuscript, and I was encouraged to go forth with their support. And not least, my thanks to Fouad Ajami for his splendid if undeserved foreword.

Kenneth Maxwell
New York City, March 2003

Illustrations

All illustrations are from *The Boy Travellers in South America: Adventures of Two Youths in a Journey through Ecuador, Peru, Bolivia, Brazil, Paraguay, Argentine Republic, and Chili, with Descriptions of Patagonia and Tierra del Fuego, and Voyages upon the Amazon and La Plata Rivers*, by Thomas W. Knox (New York: Harper & Brothers, Franklin Square, 1886).

SURVEYING UNDER DIFFICULTIES.

First Encounters

"Brazil is not for beginners."
—Antonio Carlos Jobim

I do not remember exactly when I became conscious of Brazil, but I distinctly remember how and where. I was in my second or third year as an undergraduate at Cambridge. At the time, diversions were limited. The curriculum in history never seemed to get beyond the Tudors and Stuarts, and I was heartily tired of them. The continent of Europe appeared rarely in it; the Americas never. The wider world was pretty much limited to the gaudy Indian and Chinese restaurants in town, which compensated for the dreary food and very formal dining in the grand old sixteenth-century college hall. Life for a twenty-year-old at Cambridge was then still recognizably monastic. Undergraduates in the early sixties were required to dress in academic gowns at all times, and toward the end of my period at Cambridge in 1963 the dean of my college, the Reverend Doctor Bessant, mumbled his displeasure one evening, after the interminable Latin grace was concluded and before we could sit down, that a young gentleman had been observed dressed in workmen's clothes. This, the dean admonished us, was a shocking offense to the decency at the college, which he hoped would not be repeated. He was referring to the first appearance of blue jeans in that hallowed place.

The Indian restaurants in Cambridge were infamous for notes on the tables which read: "plates only come with meals." At first sight it was an odd statement of the obvious, but was intended to intimidate undergraduates who might request four plates for one meal which they would then share, not an economical outcome as far as the restaurant owner was concerned. In Rio I learned that Brazilian students were well ahead in this game. They took care to strategically seat themselves toward the periphery of an open-air cafe. After enjoying a *churrasco* (steak) and *batatas fritas* (french fries) and several excellent *chopes* (draft beer), on a signal they would all rise en masse and run away at great speed before the bill could be presented. I am not sure that such guerrilla tactics would have worked in a small town like Cambridge, though Cambridge did have its own form of genteel robbery. Aspiring aristocrats at the time still believed it good form to run up bills they had no intention of paying with the local haberdashers and tailors. But like so much else of that epoch in Britain—the somewhat threadbare tail end of an old world kept alive well beyond its useful life— this was all for show. Unbeknownst to the debtors the merchants had extended credit in the full knowledge that fathers would eventually honor their sons' debts, just as their own fathers had honored theirs with the same tailors and haberdashers a generation before; thus the artifice of aristocratic nonchalance and merchant thrift could both be safeguarded without loss of face.

The expedition to the "flicks" was the real highlight each week. We bicycled out, gowns and all, to a vast barnlike and decrepit old picture palace on the outskirts of town which had kept in business by reinventing itself as an "art theater." It was there I saw Marcel Camus's *Black Orpheus.* Set against a spectacular tropical landscape, this ancient story erupted from the screen magnificently with drama, color, and extraordinary music. At least that is how it hit me at the time. On a misty, cold, damp, and dreary East Anglian evening it could not have been a greater revelation. I determined immediately that Brazil, and above all Rio de Janeiro, was somewhere I had to go.

I

The route to Brazil, however, took me on a detour through Lisbon and Princeton. I suppose it was typical of my generation that we did not see education as leading to anything in particular, or ever gave much thought to the fact that at the end of it all we might need to get a job. So I graduated from Cambridge in 1963 without any real sense of what I wanted to do. I had traveled a lot as a student; by train from Berlin to Warsaw, Moscow, and on to Leningrad, today once more known as St. Petersburg, a turn of history which in 1961 seemed totally impossible. Later I took the sad remnant of the Orient Express (by then basically a third-class carriage attached at each frontier to other trains) as it made its way down the Rhine Valley through Austria and the Balkans into Greece. I crossed the Mediterranean to Crete and Cyprus by ship and worked on an Israeli kibbutz north of the sea of Galilee. I spent a lazy marvelous summer in Florence where Harold Acton, the last of the eccentric 1920s esthetes, took me around the haunts of Byron and his friends; and then in Normandy where my host had the only Lagonda in the region in which we raced around shouting, "Vive de Gaulle," between the Basilica of Our Lady of Lisieux, the beaches and race-tracks of Dauville, Camembert factories and illegal *calvados* stills where the red-nosed proprietor would proudly display the helmets of the German soldiers he had killed (he said) during the Allied Normandy landing.

So to take a year off in Europe seemed a sensible thing to do when nothing else very attractive beckoned. I went to Madrid for six months where I lived just off the Puerta del Sol and attended lectures I barely understood at the university, and then took the Lusitanian Express to Lisbon. I did think travel should have a purpose, so mine was to learn the languages. I financed my stay by writing articles for a regional English newspaper, the *Western Morning News*, on such topics as "Galicia: Spain's Forgotten Corner" and "Lisbon: City Built on an Earthquake's Ruins" and a comparison of Spain and Portugal which came down to the fact that in Spain the women were beautiful and men ugly whereas in Portugal the opposite was true, and for these articles I received five guineas a time, enough then to live in a modest *pensão* (boarding house) for a month.

Unbeknownst to me, my tutor at Cambridge had written to the Gulbenkian Foundation in Lisbon to say I was there, and I was called in one day to see the head of the International Division, Dr. Ayala Monteiro. He said that Gulbenkian would like to help me in my studies and I should submit a budget to him. I did so by itemizing what I was actually spending. Ayala Monteiro laughed uproariously on seeing it—no one could survive on such a sum he said—and he wrote the budget for me. For the rest of my time in Lisbon, I received a very welcome check each month from Gulbenkian. Lisbon was then full of conscripted soldiers on their way to fight in Africa, and I found the absence of Brazil from the discourse on colonies very odd. After all Brazil had gained independence from Portugal over a century before, yet Brazil was held up as the origin of the ideology of Luso-tropicalism by which the Salazar regime sought to perpetuate its colonies in Africa, not liberate them.

Of course my Brazil was still entirely phantasmogorical. I had yet to meet a real Brazilian. England at the time offered very few prospects as far as Latin American studies was concerned. The two or three British "Latin Americanists" had not been to Latin America at all, and they had written their books entirely based on the archives in London. They looked across the Atlantic "by spyglass," it was said. The best of them, John Parry, had written a report for the government recommending a major investment in the field but had then himself taken off immediately for Harvard. So I looked at what the various American universities might offer, and came across a marvelous book by Stanley Stein on the Brazilian coffee-producing town of Vassouras in the Paraíba Valley, a rich microstudy that described intimately a whole community in transition. I applied to Princeton where Stanley Stein taught, and much to my delight was accepted with a modest stipend. Stein was a marvelous tutor; he accepted few doctoral students but gave them demanding attention. I was not of course then aware of how peculiar a place Princeton was, with its mock English architecture and odd self-contained provincialism, or fully aware of how lucky I was to have landed fortuitously at a university where students mattered. I loved the place and was only slightly disoriented by the bits of Oxford and Cambridge Colleges which appeared juxtaposed in the wrong order.

Stein called me in one day to meet my first Brazilian. It was Sérgio Buarque de Holanda traveling with his teenage son; I assumed later on that it must have been the young Chico, a radiantly beautiful youth who sat quietly in the corner.[1] My Portuguese was the swallowed nasal Portuguese of Lisbon, and I was utterly unprepared for the musicality, rhythm, and softness of Brazilian speech. I barely caught most of the pearls of wisdom the great Sérgio launched forth over the next two hours in Stanley Stein's office that afternoon.

Professor Stein recommended I apply without delay to the metropolitan graduate training program which was administered by Columbia University. It would take me to Brazil for the long summer vacation. It seemed too good to be true. I had only just stepped foot in the United States and here I was being sent to Brazil with all expenses paid. Actually Columbia, I gathered later, was only too glad to have someone from Princeton among the fifteen or so graduate students sent out to Latin America that summer because the program was intended to be both interuniversity and interdisciplinary, but in fact was dominated by Columbia anthropologists. So I suppose I was a shoo-in, even if most Columbia students regarded Princeton as irredeemably snobbish, waspish, and worst of all "southern"—a code word for racist, anti-Semitic, and such bad things. In fact when I first went up to Columbia and was asked where I was from and said Princeton, I was immediately ostracized. My Columbia classmates assumed my accent was affected. I should have just said that I came from England and left it at that.

The program had a Brazilian coordinator, the anthropologist Thales de Azevedo in Bahia, and we were given very few coordinates, none at all in fact that I can remember now. It was intimated that it might be a good idea to check in with Professor Azevedo on our arrival. Mr. Brazil of the Prince-

---

[1]Sérgio Buarque de Holanda was one of Brazil's foremost historians. His works, however, have still not been translated into English. See especially: *Raízes do Brasil* (Rio de Janeiro: J. Olympio, 1936); *Caminhos e fronteiras* (Rio de Janeiro: J. Olympio, 1957); and *Visão do paraíso: os motivos edênicos no descobrimento e colonização do Brasil* (Rio de Janeiro: J. Olympio, 1959). His then young son Chico Buarque went on to be an early star of Brazilian pop music, or MPB (*música popular brasileira*). He remains a renowned figure in Brazilian music and is one of the country's greatest singer-songwriters.

ton travel agency—his real name strange as it may seem—was contracted by the Columbia program to make my travel arrangements. He booked me on a flight from Miami to Belém. Then I was to pick up a plane there for São Luiz, Fortaleza, Natal, Recife, and Salvador da Bahia. Mr. Brazil apparently knew little of Brazil, but his itinerary had the advantage of making my first landfall in Brazil an Amazonian one; not that I got to see much of Belém. I was, it turned out, the only international passenger to deplane at Belém Airport on what was intended to be a refueling stop. The airport authorities, or rather "the" authority, a sallow air force officer much put out at having to deal with such unexpected business in the middle of the night when no immigration or customs officials were present, decided I was "in transit" and confined me to the airport until my connecting flight arrived whenever that might be (no one seemed sure). So I settled down more or less alone in what looked to me at the time like a large tin hanger in the middle of the jungle.

Daylight arrived coincidentally with a small rotund figure furiously mopping his bald head with a large red handkerchief and carrying a battered suitcase. He was not as I first thought a fellow traveler, but the concessionaire of the airport newsstand. Very carefully and very very slowly he took out twelve or so dog-eared foreign magazines (perhaps he had heard I was there and they were intended for me) which he arranged with great delicacy as though they were diamonds on his counter. This took him an hour at least before he was satisfied. While I was there, which was most of that day, I saw no one so much as look at them, so I assume he packed them all away again in their suitcase that evening as carefully as he had unpacked them that morning.

By midday at the far end of the terminal a shutter rolled up to reveal a café. An enormous figure (in girth, that is, for certainly he was wide as he was tall, chest puffed forward in self-importance, dressed in a white suit and sporting a large white hat, and whose skin was the palest pink I had ever seen) appeared from nowhere and made his way toward the café. Behind him followed a diminutive Indian, head bowed, who was pulling a two-handled trolley-type conveyance on which lay the smallest carpetbag I had ever seen. Later on in Rio, I came across a picture by the early nineteenth-century artist Jean-Baptiste Debret with a scene that was strikingly reminiscent. But the plane did arrive, a French-built Caravelle, an appropriate name I thought for a traveler to Brazil, and eventually with my entry permit stamped into my passport, and now "officially" admitted into Brazil, I was ushered onto it and up front as befitted the only international passenger. As the Caravelle made its way around the Brazilian coastline, at each stop a new crowd of passengers surged on board, and a new round of drinks and meals was proffered—including to the pilots, I noted from my front seat vantage point, who became, as I did, increasingly jolly as we approached our destination of Bahia.

I had no idea where in Salvador, capital of the state of Bahia, I might stay, so I followed some passengers onto the Volkswagen *kombi* minivan for the trip into the city, having decided I would go wherever they went since presumably they knew where they were going if I did not. We seemed to glide along the edge of a moonlit beach which stretched effortlessly into a deep purple sea. Clumps of tall palm trees and the occasional small shack stood at the beach's edge. Lovers sat together embracing and looking out at the ocean. Perhaps I was drunk, but it was a magical arrival. We bumped up a cobbled street into the city, and I followed my fellow passengers into their hotel and checked in. The next morning I awoke in darkness and made my way over to the windows and threw open the shutters. Below me was an astonishing city, colonial church towers, yellow and green peeling walls, squares bustling with people of all colors, and, just at that moment, appearing on the far horizon of a great shining bay, small white sails, a few of them at first, then it seemed hundreds, coming slowly toward me into the port below.

At lunch the waiters at the hotel seemed to think I was Portuguese and insisted that I eat codfish. When I tried to protest by pointing out a picture of the Beatles in the local newspaper and insisting they and not Camões were my fellow countrymen it got me nowhere; but when I asked for a *garoto* (in Lisbon a coffee with milk, but also in Portuguese the word for a boy) they knew at once where I was from, and said I should go next time to the restaurant in the square down the block where such requests might be more discreetly accommodated. I did in fact eat out after that, and my first real Bahian shrimp was so spicy that I had to drink four large old-fashioned Antarctica bottles of beer to get through it.

Since I had come to Bahia to call on Professor Azevedo and find out what it was I was supposed to do, I set out to visit him. I remember the brightness of the day, the glorious colors of the foliage in the gardens along the way and the odd little white painted moats around the plants to protect them from insects. But my arrival caused great consternation. I was ushered quickly into the kitchen where three large black ladies in white aprons busied themselves with pots while eyeing me curiously. It was some years before I realized how significant it was to be ushered into the kitchen. I assumed this is where Brazilians always received their visitors.

I suppose the metropolitan training program role was just another emolument for Professor Azevedo unconnected to any duties, and that students stood somewhere with household servants in the anthropological order of things. I waited, but Professor Azevedo never received me. I think it was this experience which led me later on very rarely to call on Brazilian professors and instead get on with my own thing. I was used to this from Portugal, and in any case, with the political police and informers everywhere, it was never wise to say exactly what one was studying. Strangely I returned that day to my hotel to find the honorary British consul waiting to take me out for a drink. News about strangers spread quickly in those days. He looked as if he had stepped out of a Graham Greene novel. I most vividly remember his very bloodshot eyes and rumpled linen suit. But he was more than gracious and wanted me very much to meet an Oxford student in town, a John Russell-Wood.[2] But I never got to see Russell-Wood either. Perhaps the honorary consul should have known that the last thing most Englishmen want to do is to meet other Englishmen in tropical places. But as Professor Azevedo apparently had no instructions for me, and it seemed I was on my own, I made for Rio, which was where, ever since seeing *Black Orpheus* on that misty night in Cambridge, I most wanted to be.

I arrived in Rio at the Santos Dumont Airport and asked the airline clerk if he could recommend a hotel. He looked at several cards in his pocket and sent me off to a hotel on Rua Riachuelo, up beyond the old eighteenth-century aqueduct over which the ancient trams so prominently featured in *Black Orpheus* rumbled to and fro, and beyond the jumble of shops and houses that then crowded the area. The hotel seemed fine until I tried to sleep that night, only to find myself attacked by bedbugs and disturbed by prowling rats, while on the corner outside the local prostitutes chatted noisily. So the next day, I took myself off to the British Embassy and asked a somewhat bemused official if he had a better recommendation. He did; it was the "Grande Hotel of Copacabana" as the embassy called it, in fact the apartment of one Maitê Bertrand, situated on the street beside the Copacabana Palace Hotel. Maitê Bertrand had apparently at some point in her long life helped the British in some way by hiding something or someone somewhere; it was never made clear where or when (Shanghai was mentioned), but for this service she had earned the gratitude of the British diplomatic service, and any respectable person seeking a respectable place to stay was directed by the embassy to Maitê.

Her apartment was on the top floor, it was close to the beach, and I found it quite delightful. Maitê ran a sort of informal *pensão* (boarding house) with several long-term residents, among them an ancient Greek who had fled from Alexandria when King Farouk was overthrown and Gamal Abdel Nasser took over the Egyptian government, two somewhat prim English lady teachers at the Cultura Inglesa (which was and remains a redoubtable bastion of British language instruction), a mechanic for Air

---

[2]A. J. R. Russell-Wood was to become a prolific scholar on things Brazilian and Luso-Brazilian. His most recent book is *The Portuguese Empire, 1415–1808: A World on the Move* (Baltimore: Johns Hopkins University Press, 1998).

France who supervised the maintenance of the Air France jet that came through every other week on the round-trip between Paris and Santiago, Chile, and the French pilots, who also stayed at regular intervals but dined separately from us so as not to have to eat at the same table as the mechanic, or so he claimed vociferously each time when they were gone. The Air France crowd, however, was Maitê's bread and butter. She charged the rest of us a very modest fee which for me included a small room with its own external door, a bathroom, and dinner each evening. We ate as a group unless Maitê was entertaining her own friends, or the Air France pilots were in town, in which case she had a special table set up for herself and her guests by the window.

II

And Rio? Well Rio was breathtaking to me. More than my mind and eyes had anticipated. In those days the native cariocas sometimes made fun of the wan Europeans standing spellbound before Rio's sheer natural majesty. I surely must have been one such. I would walk early each morning from one end of the Avenida Atlântica to the other and back along the Avenida Nossa Senhora de Copacabana, stopping at the coffee stands for a *cafézinho* (espresso-sized dark coffee) every few blocks, it seemed, joining the afternoon sunbathers on the beach outside the Copacabana Hotel, taking the funicular up the Sugar Loaf Mountain and to the top of Corcovado, and eventually getting my identity card for the National Library and starting to explore its books and archival holdings, while escaping across the road to the weird and wonderful world of "Cinelândia" for a *queijo quente* (grilled cheese sandwhich) and *chope* each lunchtime.

Two of Maitê's guests each week at the special table by the window were a silver-haired Swiss businessman, probably somewhere in his early sixties, and a very beautiful Brazilian student, Julio, who must have been about my own age. I was more than intrigued by this couple, and I guess they must have been fascinated, Julio certainly, by me. In any case, one evening after dinner Maitê invited me to stay for a coffee and cognac so that Julio could then take me off to a movie in the neighborhood of Flamengo. I was not prepared for the directness of Brazilian sexuality. The supposed conditioning of English boarding schools in such matters is much exaggerated. I was entirely naive. Poor Julio must have thought he had made a terrible misjudgment, but we became the best of friends, never out of each other's sight if we could help it, and while our relationship remained almost entirely platonic, we fell deeply and obsessively in love.

Julio was a student, though he never seemed to attend classes or study that I could see. Ralph, the Swiss businessman, had a penthouse apartment at the far end of Copacabana at Posto 6 with panoramic views over the beach and the Forte de Copacabana. And as Ralph spent much of the time traveling, this became our base. Arpoador beach was a short distance. At the corner of his block were the early studios of TV Globo, the doors open so we could drop in to see the strange variety of shows that Globo then broadcast. We went twice a week to join a *escola de samba* (samba school) where after some hesitation and amid much hilarity I shed my inhibitions and began to dance. We went out to sit quietly and reverently at Macumba ceremonies. We dropped in at the Teatro Jovem where Francisco Pereira da Silva's *O Chão dos Penitentes* (The penitents' ground) was playing and drank beer at the café in Ipanema where Tom Jobim and various luminaries of the Cinema Novo held court. I would go back to Maitê's for dinner, get a couple of hours' sleep, and then slip out at midnight so Julio and I could spend the nights in the *boates* (night clubs) of Copacabana where with grand political neutrality we would sip Cuba libres while listening to "Hello Dolly," walking home along the Avenida Atlântica as the sun was rising over the mouth of Guanabara Bay.

A week before I was due to return to Princeton, all hell broke loose at Maitê Bertrand's. The Air France pilots, it turned out, had been using Maitê's as a safe house for smuggling something or other. The mechanic had disappeared. Maitê had been tipped off she was about to be raided. Since her "Grande Hotel" was entirely unauthorized and she paid no taxes on her earnings from her guests, we were all required to leave that very evening. Fortunately the two prim English teachers at the Cultura Inglesa, or at least one of them, had fallen in love with a Brazilian journalist and she was finding Maitê's quarters more restrictive than I had as a base for my nocturnal wanderings. She had just taken an apartment overlooking Leblon, and was happy to have me stay there over my few last days in Rio. We never saw Maitê again, or the old Greek, and we were strictly enjoined not to go near the Copacabana Palace Hotel again until the crisis, whatever the crisis was, wound down.

I arrived in Princeton that September, brown as a berry and with some work accomplished. I had not ceased to go to the National Library each day despite my other perambulations, and had accumulated a formidable stack of index cards full of notations. I was intending at the time to write a dissertation on Brazilian decolonization in the early nineteenth century, an idea inspired in part by my Lisbon sojourn. But academic work was not my preeminent Brazilian experience of that first encounter. In early November 1965, the Columbia organizers of the training program called us up to New York to report on our summer accomplishments. I was loath to be entirely honest and said to Professor Charles Wagley, the director of the program, that although I had indeed done some work, I had also had a very good time at the beach. I was really not sure what if anything had been expected of me because in effect I had been dropped in Brazil without any real orientation and with no one much concerned about what if anything I did there. "But that was the whole point," he said, smiling. "We want to hook people to Brazil. It is cheaper for us to throw you out with a summer's support to sink or swim, rather than to commit ourselves for three years' dissertation work only to find you hate the country and cannot cope with living there." It was a marvelous revelation, and it was a strategy that had certainly worked with me. I did not sink. I had fallen in love. I was hooked. More so perhaps than Charles Wagley realized, though he probably guessed, wise old man that he was. I could not wait to get back.[3]

---

[3]The historian István Jancsó felt I had been disrespectful to Professor Thales de Azevedo (1915–1995) and responded in a subsequent edition of *Folha*'s MAIS! where this chapter first appeared. See István Jancsó, "O professor Azevedo e as andanças do jovem Maxwell" (Professor Azevedo and the journeys of young Maxwell), *Folha de São Paulo* (January 25, 1998), MAIS!

MARCHING THROUGH THE FOREST.

CHAPTER 2

¡Adiós Columbus!

"Plausible impossibilities should be preferred to unconvincing possibilities."
—Aristotle, *Poetics 24*

Columbus was mugged on the way to his own party. The American quincentennial year of 1992 drew to a close with barely a mention of the Admiral of the Ocean Sea and would-be "Viceroy of India." Even the advertising agencies found him too hot a potato (the potato of course being one of Europe's more useful American acquisitions resulting from Spain's conquests in the New World). By October Columbus had become what advertisers dislike most, especially when they are promoting department store sales on family holidays: he had become controversial.

I

Kirkpatrick Sale made a preemptive strike against Columbus as a destructive colonizer in *The Conquest of Paradise*, and in spite of criticism of Sale for tendentiousness, the wave of subsequent publications could not erase the initial tone he had set.[1] The great birthday therefore passed with barely a murmur of national celebration. Two multimillion-dollar movies about Columbus came and went, largely unattended. Carlos Fuentes presented several hours of televised historical travelogue in Europe and the Americas, ending predictably at the U.S.-Mexican border, where he asserted (at least culturally speaking) Mexico's claim to the lost northern territories, an

---

[1]Kirkpatrick Sale, *The Conquest of Paradise: Christopher Columbus and the Columbian Legacy* (New York: Knopf, 1990).

irredentism President Salinas must have found singularly ill timed as the debate over NAFTA heated up.

Fuentes's book *The Buried Mirror*, like much of its bibliography, in fact appears firmly stuck in the 1960s.[2] His presence seemed intrusive in the otherwise well-filmed and constructed television series with the same title, which would have been much better had it made more use of the originator of the idea, Peggy Liss, a distinguished historian of Spain and Spanish America and author of an excellent new biography of Columbus's sponsor, Queen Isabella. Fuentes, never one to use two words if more will do, throws in virtually every stereotype of *hispanidad* propaganda (Bulls, Virgins, Tangos, Gauchos, Don Quixote) while adding little that is distinctive of his own. Latin America, mired in disaster, is somehow to be "rescued by culture." His book looks attractive, as do parts of the television series in which he appeared, and we are given good views of the crossing of the Andes by San Martín, of the baroque churches of Mexico and Peru, and of paintings by Velázquez and Goya. Such skillful and expensive packaging is not an uncommon characteristic of the quincentennial year, where the wine is often less impressive than its container.

The Spanish government had earlier set store by the quincentennial (and had subsidized the Fuentes undertaking along with the many other projects, books, and exhibitions in the quincentennial cause); but it virtually banished Columbus's name from the great Seville exposition as soon as the organizers began to realize that Spain risked alienating Jews, Muslims, and much of Latin America by too direct a celebration of Columbus's accomplishments. As for the pope, in the arranging of his long-planned visit to Hispaniola in commemoration of the evangelization of the New World, some last-minute rescheduling was needed so that he might avoid the controversy surrounding the inauguration of the giant "lighthouse" constructed in Columbus's memory by the Dominican Republic's blind president to illuminate the evening sky with an ethereal cross.

What remains of this curious, diverse, and singularly unenlightening year? The most curious thing about the mountain of books the quincentennial produced is how little they tell us about the significance of what Columbus did in his own time, and how little they reflect the rich scholarship on Latin America of the past two decades. Some of the better books published during the quincentennial year, like Anthony Grafton's *New Worlds, Ancient Texts*, deal more with the intellectual imagining of Amer-

---

[2]Carlos Fuentes, *The Buried Mirror: Reflections on Spain and the New World* (Boston: Houghton Mifflin, 1992).

ica than with its social reality.[3] Grafton's book has in fact a much broader scope than its quincentennial timing would imply, and Columbus himself is disposed of in a few brief if instructive pages.

Grafton's intention is to look at the long, convoluted, and contradictory process by which European scholars absorbed and dealt with the experiences forced on them by the existence of a New World unforeseen in the intellectual tradition they had inherited. "Ancient texts did rise like revenants around them," Professor Grafton writes in his epilogue,

> paradoxically providing the language and images that enabled them to explain away a fact unknown to the classical writers they revered. A potentially revolutionary discovery was given a noble name, a biblical pedigree, a place in existing geographies and ethnographies; much of its sting was thus removed.

Grafton follows the revisionist argument of J. H. Elliott's brilliant book *The Old World and the New,* that the European discovery of the New World had very little impact on European thought (or at least much less impact than had been claimed by the Enlightenment).[4] This is all very well so far as it goes, but unlike Elliott, who never lost sight of the wider world, Grafton takes a view that at times seems antiquarian, and tells us very little about the real consequences for most people outside the print shop or the academic cloister of Columbus's arrival in the Caribbean. Grafton says little about the establishment of European hegemony over large parts of the globe, which was the most lasting result of Columbus's stumbling into the New World in 1492; and he gives no clear sense of the broader movement of the European overseas expansion, of which the Columbus voyages were part. Visitors to the 1992 New York Public Library exhibition which was the occasion for Grafton's book hardly appreciated the vast shaking up of the world that occurred as a result of the voyage of 1492, with consequences that deeply affect the life of New York City today.

II

A major point that was largely ignored in 1992, although it has been demonstrated by a quarter century of historical research, is that the European discovery of America in 1492 was not an isolated event. This is very well

---

[3]Anthony Grafton, with April Shelford and Nancy Siraisi, *New Worlds, Ancient Texts: The Power of Tradition and the Shock of Discovery* (Cambridge: Harvard University Press, 1992).
[4]J. H. (John Huxtable) Elliott, *The Old World and the New, 1492–1650* (Cambridge: Cambridge University Press, 1970).

demonstrated in the excellent *Times Atlas of World Exploration*, edited by a group of scholars under the direction of Felipe Fernández-Armesto.[5] The voyage of Christopher Columbus was in many respects an offshoot of an oceanic system of commerce and navigation which preceded and outlived the epoch of Columbus; the speed and success with which Spanish rule was imposed in the Caribbean and later on the mainland are in large part explained by this broader process.

It was the great innovation of the fifteenth-century mariners and entrepreneurs, among whom the Portuguese were the most precocious, to learn how the winds and currents of the Atlantic Ocean could be used to make travel among the continents possible. They perfected navigational instruments, in particular the astrolabe and the quadrant, which enabled them to take accurate readings on the celestial bodies in order to find their latitude when on the high seas.

The Portuguese also made their audacious Atlantic explorations a profitable enterprise. As with all great revolutions, the discovery of how the ocean could be conquered by sail was a revolution of perception: the recognition of patterns of nature which before had been only imperfectly comprehended. For centuries European sailors had seen only the edges of an oceanic world; in a mere two decades, they were able to discern its totality. Hence, quite suddenly and with spectacular consequences, the Atlantic Ocean, which for millennia had been the great divider between continents, became the means of intercontinental contact, the pathway to new continents in the West and to empires in the East.

The Atlantic commercial system evolved around two intersecting ellipses of seaborne communications, one in the North Atlantic and the other in the South Atlantic. The trajectory of each was governed by the prevailing winds and ocean currents. These two Atlantic ellipses could finally be traced and mastered because of the collective experience gained from the voyages of oceanic exploration. Bartoloméu Dias in 1488, encountering contrary winds and currents on the southwest African coast, had swung out in a wide circle to round the Cape of Good Hope, thus demonstrating the possibility of sailing from the Atlantic into the Indian Ocean. By reaching the greater Antilles in 1492, Christopher Columbus showed the outbound and the inbound route between America and Europe.

Five years later, Vasco da Gama, leaving Portugal in 1497, was the first to trace the wide arc of wind systems of the South Atlantic (he was ninety-three days out of sight of land compared with the thirty-three days of

---

[5]Felipe Fernández-Armesto, ed., *The Times Atlas of World Exploration: 3,000 Years of Exploring, Explorers, and Mapmaking* (New York: HarperCollins Publishers, 1991).

Columbus), thereby making it possible to sail into the Indian Ocean, where he was able to draw upon Arab navigational experience to reach Calicut in 1498 and return to Lisbon in 1499. The elliptical routes, and hence the trajectory of all subsequent wind power navigation, were discovered during a remarkably short period between 1492 and 1500.

Skillful navigation meant very little in itself. The North Atlantic had been crossed before 1492 by the Vikings, who had established colonies in Iceland and Greenland. In the early fourteenth century, merchant adventurers from Barcelona had gone at least as far as the Canary Islands. These achievements, however, had little long-term effect. What mattered was the ability to take advantage of the opportunities oceanic exploration opened up and to sustain them within a network of commerce and regular communications.

The second great achievement of the fifteenth century was to make sailing on the Atlantic routes profitable for many years to come.[6] The first steps, again, had been taken by the Portuguese when they established the maritime connection between Europe and the West African coast. Their principal aim had been to tap the supply of African gold which had previously reached Europe by means of the camel caravans that provided a trans-Saharan trade connection between West Africa and the southern shore of the Mediterranean. Beginning in 1443, the Portuguese broke the monopoly of the Saharan land route and established a string of trading posts (their so-called *feitorias*) along the West African coast, at Argium, then Sierra Leone, Cantor, and, eventually, in 1482, at the great fort of São Jorge da Mina on the Gold Coast.

By outflanking the long-established Arabic trans-Saharan trade connections between Guinea and North Africa, the Portuguese succeeded in capturing a part of the landborne commerce of West Africa for the new European-dominated sea route. The caravel—a fast, small ship adapted by the Portuguese from the Arab and Mediterranean vessels and used for voyages to West Africa—effectively competed with camel caravans. The Portuguese exchanged cloth, carpets, silks, brassware, and trinkets for gold, slaves, and "grains of paradise" (malaguetta pepper), sometimes through intermediaries or by direct bargaining at the fairs in the West African interior. Portuguese domination of the African coast, such as it was, remained essentially commercial. They never became involved directly in West

---

[6]Fundamental to the reinterpretation of early Atlantic history are the three great works by Pierre Chaunu, Vitorino Magalhães Godinho, and Frédéric Mauro; Pierre Chaunu, *Séville et l'Atlantique, 1504–1650*, 12 vols. (Paris: SEVPEN, 1955–1960); Vitorino Magalhães Godinho, *L'économie de l'empire Portugais aux XVe et XVIe siècles* (Paris: SEVPEN, 1969); and Frédéric Mauro, *Le Portugal et l'Atlantique au XVIIe siècle, 1570–1670; étude économique* (Paris: SEVPEN, 1960).

African gold mining. All this is clearly and beautifully laid out in *The Times Atlas of World Exploration.*

With a prosperous seagoing link established between West Africa and Lisbon, control of the offshore archipelagoes, of the Canary Islands, of Madeira, and the Azores became the next and inevitable order of business. Incorporating these Atlantic islands into the expanding network of commerce, initially as sources of water and supplies, coincided with the establishment of the seaborne routes between West Africa and Europe. But the islands soon produced valuable return cargoes in their own right. The settlement by Portugal of the uninhabited archipelagoes of Madeira (1420–1425) and the Azores (1427–1439) and the gradual decimation and enslavement by Spain of the Guanches—settlers probably of Berber origin—who inhabited the Canaries (1483–1500) were followed by the introduction into the islands, by the early European settlers, of sugarcane from the Mediterranean.

The sugarcane from the Atlantic islands soon found ready markets from the Baltic to the Italian port cities, and the wide distribution of Atlantic island sugar in Europe dramatically brought down its price. Sugar consumption was also apparently stimulated, for sugarcane production expanded quickly in the Cape Verde archipelago and later, by 1490, to the islands of São Tomé e Príncipe in the Gulf of Guinea off the African coast. The tropical soils and climate of São Tomé e Príncipe in particular provided an ideal environment. African slave labor was soon imported from the nearby mainland.[7]

The experience in Madeira, Porto Santo, and the Canaries was important for other reasons. As Professor Alfred Crosby has shown in several original and fascinating books, particularly *Ecological Imperialism: The Biological Expansion of Europe, 900–1900,* the Europeans tried to make use of the landscape, flora, and fauna.[8] Bartoloméu Perestrello, future father-in-law of Columbus, set loose a female rabbit and her offspring in Porto Santo, the latter born on the voyage from Europe. The rabbits reproduced so rapidly as to "overspread the land, so that our men could sow nothing

---

[7]For the Atlantic islands, see Luís de Albuquerque and Alberto Vieira, *The Archipelago of Madeira in the Fifteenth Century* (Madeira: Centro de Estudos de História do Atlântico, 1984); Virginia Rau and Jorge de Macedo, *O açúcar da Madeira nos fins do século XV: Problemas de produção e comércio* (Madeira: Junta-Geral do Distrito Autónomo do Funchal, 1962); Felipe Fernández-Armesto, *Before Columbus: Exploration and Colonization from the Mediterranean to the Atlantic, 1229–1492* (Philadelphia: University of Pennsylvania Press, 1987); and Alberto Vieira, *O comércio inter-insular nos séculos XV e XVI: Madeira, Açores e Canárias* (Madeira: Centro de Estudos de História do Atlântico, 1987).

[8]Alfred Crosby, *Ecological Imperialism: The Biological Expansion of Europe, 900–1900* (Cambridge and New York: Cambridge University Press, 1986).

that was not destroyed by them." The settlers in fact were forced to retreat to the larger island of Madeira nearby. They returned, but rabbits remained a problem for crop growers, not to mention for the indigenous plants and animals.

Madeira and Porto Santo had been previously uninhabited by human beings. The Canaries had not; and as Professor Crosby demonstrates, the fate of the Guanches there also prefigured later experience. In particular, the Europeans brought with them "their extended family of plants, animals, and microlife," as Crosby puts it. He observes, "Very few experiences are as dangerous to a people's survival as the passage from isolation to membership in the worldwide community that included European sailors, soldiers, and settlers"—carriers of parasites and pathogens to which isolated people would be susceptible. The experiences of the Atlantic islands thus taught two lessons: that Europeans, and their plants and animals, could do quite well in new lands; and the indigenous population, though numerous and brave, could be conquered, and could indeed disappear, to be replaced by laborers imported from Europe and Africa.

The evolving Atlantic commercial and maritime complex was also linked to a broader network.[9] The Portuguese, by developing the seaborne route between Europe and West Africa, were establishing new connections between known sources of supply for products such as sugar and existing markets.

Lisbon and Seville both benefited from the new oceanic commerce and seaborne traffic. These ancient Atlantic port cities possessed long-standing trading connections with the Muslim world, especially in North Africa, and their traders had long been aware of the existence of West African spices and gold. Their ports were favorably placed geographically for the mariners using them to take advantage of the currents and winds for the run to the Canary Islands, Madeira, and the African coast. Both Lisbon and Seville were situated at the edge of fertile valleys, rich in olives, vines, and fruit, with access to nearby salt pans, vital for the preservation of meat and fish.

But, above all, Lisbon and Seville had attracted large colonies of Italian traders who used both ports as way stations in their commercial dealings in the Iberian Peninsula and as ports of call for their shipping between the Eastern Mediterranean and northwestern Europe. Genoese merchants, in particular, contributed their commercial sophistication. They were skilled at bills

---

[9]See Charles Verlinden, *The Beginnings of Modern Colonization* (Ithaca, N.Y.: Cornell University Press, 1970); Herman Van der Wee, *The Growth of the Antwerp Market and the European Economy, Fourteenth to Sixteenth Centuries,* 3 vols. (The Hague: Martinus Nijhoff, 1963); and Ruth Pike, *Enterprise and Adventure: The Genoese in Seville and the Opening of the New World* (Ithaca, N.Y.: Cornell University Press, 1966).

of exchange and credit, and knew how to raise large amounts of capital needed to deal with the risks and delays of long-range oceanic commerce.

Between 1450 and 1500 the number of Genoese in Seville almost doubled. Great Italian merchant banking families originally from Genoa, such as the Spinoli, Grimaldi, and Centurioni, acted as contractors supplying naval stores or, often, as dealers in regional agricultural products and imported grain; they at once became involved in the new Atlantic Ocean trades. In Lisbon, a major port of call for Genoese and Venetian galleys en route for England and Flanders, Italian merchants such as Lomellini, Affaitati, Giraldi, and Marchione were bankers and moneylenders to the court and its envoys; they too invested in the new Atlantic island sugar production and in the slave trade. In association with the great south German bankers, the Welsers and Fuggers, these experienced Italian entrepreneurs supplied, through Antwerp, German silver and copper in return for olive oil, wine, fruit, Setúbal salt, and African spices and gold.

Thus when within a very few years of one another Bartoloméu Dias reached the Indian Ocean (1488), Christopher Columbus reached the Antilles (1492), and Vasco da Gama arrived on the coast of India (1498), they did so against the background of a preexisting and thriving system of Atlantic commerce. Based on sugar, slaves, and gold, it was firmly supported by a strong if largely informal partnership between the Spaniards and Portuguese who contributed their political and navigational skills and the foremost Italian and German bankers and merchants who were able to raise capital and sell the goods throughout Europe. Oceanic expansion at the end of the fifteenth century therefore succeeded largely because Spanish and Portuguese oceanic commerce could feed into a receptive network of European commerce; the two combined to stimulate and underwrite further expansion.

Once the Portuguese established trade with India after 1498, they also found it profitable to pay for Asian spices with silver, which was valued more highly in India than in Europe. In consequence, traders in south German silver found Lisbon an even more attractive market. The south German capitalists who controlled the production of Central European and Hungarian precious metals took advantage of the possibilities for commercial and financial expansion in the new overseas enterprises. The Imhoff merchant banking family of Nüremberg doubled their profits between 1503 and 1508 while taking part in the Asian spice trade. The Fuggers and Welsers from Augsburg invested heavily in the Portuguese Indian fleet of 1505 among other ventures. The vast fortunes of the participating merchant capitalists had other consequences, for example, loans to states; the dramatic expansion of commerce and the money market made Antwerp an important source for short-term loans used by both Spain and

Portugal to support their expensive courts and pay for their even more costly wars.

Christopher Columbus himself was a very typical product of this early Atlantic commercial system. Genoese by birth and an experienced seaman, he had worked as an agent for the Centurioni firm, which did business in Spain and Portugal. Linked to the sugar interests of Madeira by his first wife, he had also traded along the Guinea coast (ca. 1482–1485) and gained much practical knowledge of Portuguese navigation and especially the Atlantic wind system in the Portuguese-controlled Atlantic archipelagoes. The vessels for his transatlantic crossing (like those of Vasco da Gama for his Indian voyage) were filled with the cheap trinkets, beads, and brass utensils used by the Portuguese in their West African trade. Recent research shows that the approximately 1,300 Spanish ducats which Columbus contributed to the venture (the Catholic monarchs contributed about 3,000 ducats) were borrowed from Italian merchants, especially the Florentine Juanoto Berardi, a slave trader since 1486 who remained a close associate of Columbus until his death in 1495. The instinctive reaction of Columbus to the economic possibilities of the Caribbean was conditioned by his previous experience. His obsession with gold and slaves was not a personal foible; it was built into the system of which he had long been a part.

III

But if recent scholarship has helped to explain the setting within which Columbus made his voyages, the second great contribution of the past two decades has been to explain why Columbus's arrival in the Caribbean had effects throughout the world. The European intrusion into the fringe of the New World in 1492 had a devastating impact on the indigenous inhabitants quite unlike that arising from the simultaneous contacts between Europeans and the populations of Africa and Asia. The Caribbean experience, moreover, was to prefigure the widespread death that took place elsewhere in the Americas—most especially in the lowland tropical and subtropical regions, but also in the highlands. Why did this happen?

The early relations of Spaniards and native populations in the Caribbean were dominated by the Spanish desire to extract gold. Unlike the Portuguese in Africa, whose gold trade depended on African intermediaries, Columbus and his agents and successors found shallow gold deposits on several of the islands. To work the placer mines of Cibao and San Cristóbal in Hispaniola, and later the gold-rich streams of Puerto Rico (1508), the Isthmus of Panama (1509), and the arroyos of the central mountains of Cuba (1511), the Spaniards organized large gangs of

Amerindians. To secure European domination over the Caribbean populations and thus obtain the labor needed to exploit the gold deposits, they quickly asserted direct control over the Indians' lives.

By contrast, in Africa and Asia the European intruders rarely were able to establish direct administration over the local population beyond a few fortified enclaves. The methods used to draft labor in the Caribbean varied and passed from the loose per capita tribute system devised by Columbus himself and administered through the local Amerindian *caciques* (chieftains) to a period when Indian communities were given over to individual Spaniards by Adelantado Bartoloméu Columbus, and then to the more systematic mobilizing of labor imposed by Governor Nicolás de Ovando (1502–1509). Governor Ovando linked the use of *encomiendas* (grants of Indian labor) to the building of an economic base for the new villas (towns) he intended to settle with Europeans; he wanted to provide a source of income for their European *vecinos* (residents), who would either hire out the Indians for use in the gold mines or directly exploit the Indian labor themselves. The governor added an incentive to gold mining by lowering the share of the gold demanded by the Crown from one-half to one-fifth. Nicolás de Ovando also acted with great brutality. Soon after his arrival, the Higüey Indians rebelled to avenge the killing of one of their chiefs by a Spanish attack dog. Irving Rouse describes the consequences:

> Ovando rounded up six or seven hundred of them, put them in a chief's bohío, or house, and had them knifed to death. He then ordered the bodies to be dragged into the adjoining plaza and publicly counted. In the fall of 1503 he paid another formal visit to Xaraguá, where he was well received by Chief Anacaona, whose brother Behecchío had died. She convened a meeting of some eighty district chiefs in her bohío, whereupon Ovando ordered his soldiers to block the door and burn them alive. Anacaona herself was hanged in deference to her rank.

Carl Sauer's brilliant pioneering book on the early Spanish Main, originally published in 1966 and reissued for the quicentennial, as well as the work of the recent generation of demographic historians, showed that at the time of the arrival of Columbus in 1492, the island of Hispaniola supported a very substantial native population.[10] There is a very heated debate over the numbers, with low estimates in the 100,000-to-200,000 range (Angel Rosenblat) to figures as high as 8 million (Woodrow Borah and Sherburne F. Cook). The consensus seems to point to a figure of over a mil-

---

[10]Carl O. Sauer, *The Early Spanish Main* (Berkeley: University of California Press, 1992).

lion while Las Casas's estimate of three and one-half million is within the range of possibility. The various estimates are well summarized in the new edition of William Denevan's *The Native Population of the Americas in 1492*, which contains contributions by Woodrow Borah and William Sanders and others who have revolutionized demographic history.[11] The latest archaeological evidence is clearly described in the Smithsonian Institution's *Disease and Demography in the Americas.*[12]

The Caribbean islands, unlike Europe, enjoyed a continuous growing season. Indian agriculture, Sauer shows, was highly productive, depending on root crops, which were planted in forest clearings that had been previously burned over and dug up with pointed flattened sticks. The Indians constructed *montones* (earth mounds) that were knee-high and several feet wide. This planted area, called a *conuco*, provided well-aerated soils, was effective against erosion, and could be used on hill slopes; the root crops could be cultivated without greatly diminishing the fertility of the soil. In the *montones* the Indians planted bitter yuca, the roots of which were grated, drained of their poisonous juices, and baked into starchy unleavened bread (cassava) capable of being stored for long periods without deteriorating. Maize, beans, and squash, planted in the same *montones*, were grown from seed, and together with the abundant fish, salt, and turtles of the coastal waters provided the diet of the indigenous islanders. Bartolomé de las Casas, who arrived during 1502 with Ovando's expedition, estimated that twenty men working six hours a day for one month could plant sufficient yuca to provide enough bread for three hundred people for two years.

Irving Rouse's book *The Tainos: Rise and Decline of the People Who Greeted Columbus* is a model of clarity and lightly worn erudition, and it contains the best and most straightforward description of the four Columbus voyages and their implications for the Amerindians I have seen.[13] In it Rouse summarizes with great fairness the arguments for and against each position he takes. Columbus had found large, permanent villages of Taino Indians in Hispaniola and Puerto Rico, each governed by a chief, or *cacique*, and each containing an average of two thousand people. Rouse vividly describes their everyday life. The Spaniards were particularly amazed by their ball games, which they played in specially constructed courts using a bouncing ball made of rubber, whose elasticity the Spaniards had never seen before.

---

[11]William Denevan, *The Native Population of the Americas in 1492* (Madison: University of Wisconsin Press, 1976).

[12]John W. Verano and Douglas H. Ubelaker, eds., *Disease and Demography in the Americas* (Washington, D.C.: Smithsonian Institution Press, 1992).

[13]Irving Rouse, *The Tainos: Rise and Decline of the People Who Greeted Columbus* (New Haven: Yale University Press, 1992).

By 1530, however, only thirty-eight years after the arrival of Columbus, the original inhabitants of the islands had been reduced to a mere handful. The ecological base of their existence had been severely disrupted. By the third decade of the sixteenth century, the Indians of Jamaica and Puerto Rico were almost extinct, and the Bahamas had none at all. The European incursion into the Caribbean unquestionably had produced a holocaust with few parallels in world history.

The primary cause of the demographic catastrophe that befell the Amerindians of the Caribbean islands was certainly virulent epidemic disease. Isolated as they were, the people of the islands had little capacity for resisting imported diseases, even less so than the people of the Canary Islands when the Spanish had arrived. The introduction of temperate and tropical infections, including, probably, malaria, yellow fever, sleeping sickness, yaws, bilharzia, influenza, typhus, smallpox, and plague, brought havoc.

But many of the diseases were no less lethal to Europeans and Africans, and the catastrophe of the islands was compounded by other factors. The pre-Columbian population maintained a fragile equilibrium in an environment peculiarly rich in vegetable products, and without animals that would compete with human beings for food. The Europeans not only introduced disease, they also brought the first livestock, including cattle, horses, pigs, and dogs, all of which increased with phenomenal rapidity. The consequences for the Amerindians were disastrous. Feral hogs rooted up the *conucos* and disrupted the base of the Indian food supply. A lethal competition for food and land took place between the native population and the newly introduced animals. The European animals won. Indian plantings were replaced by pasture or reverted to forest land. The ecological transformation of the islands, which occurred within little more than half a century, contributed to the deep psychological shock that resulted from the arrival of Europeans. The Amerindians' physical environment was shattered.

Harsh labor in the gold fields also contributed to the decline of the island population. The crowded and unsanitary conditions of the mining camps encouraged the rapid spread of disease. According to Bartolomé de las Casas, during the labor draft (*demora*), which lasted from six to eight months, a quarter to one-third of the work gangs died. Many of the Indians in the camps suffered from malnutrition; although they were amply supplied with starch in the form of cassava bread, they were unable to acquire the necessary protein and fats, since hunting and fishing were prohibited by the Spaniards, who feared the Indians would flee. Sauer argues that the indiscriminate use of female workers in effect transformed the low fertility of Indian women into de facto sterility. Certainly the population had little chance of reproducing itself. By 1514, on the royal estates of Santo Domingo, where the working conditions of Indian workers were probably better than elsewhere, there was not even an average of one child to a couple. There was, however, a parallel process taking place: the census of 1514 found 40 percent of the officially recognized wives of the Europeans were Indian.

The equanimity with which most Spaniards accepted the huge loss of Indian lives did not result from mere callousness, though there was plenty of that. Monstrous death rates were commonplace in Europe. Recovery from the plague, which during the fourteenth century had killed at least 20 percent of the European population, had been painfully slow. Nor was the behavior of the early adventurers and its consequences in devastation and disease unprecedented. Many of the soldiers who went with Pedrarias Dávila to the Isthmus of Panama in 1514 were veterans of recent barbarous military campaigns in Italy, where they ravaged the countryside, causing even the insensitive King Ferdinand of Aragón to complain about their behavior.

The loss of life among the Europeans in the Antilles was staggering as well. Of the 2,500 colonists who arrived with Ovando in Hispaniola in 1502, 1,000 died within a short time. Without constant immigration, all the early European settlements in the Americas would have suffered the fate of the settlers who died after Columbus left them at La Navidad on the northern shore of Hispaniola. Continuous immigration to maintain the European population, let alone to achieve growth, was no less essential for the early transatlantic colonies than it was for the urban populations in Europe, where city death rates consistently surpassed birthrates and it was only the inflow of rural immigrants that kept numbers from declining.

Among the few voices raised to protest the extermination of the native population of the Caribbean and the Panamanian isthmus, the Dominican Antonio de Montesinos (1511), Bartolomé de las Casas (1515), and Licenciado Alonso Zuazo (1518) often proposed solutions no less destructive than the situation they sought to remedy. The reforming Hieronymite Fathers, governors of the Indies between 1518 and 1519, attempted to preserve the remaining population by establishing pueblos (villages) of four hundred to five hundred people, each with its own plantings and livestock, only to find the newly concentrated Indians were immediately infected with smallpox. It was fortunate for Europe that the New World did not export the virulent epidemic to Africa and Europe. The origin of syphilis, long claimed to be a New World importation into Europe, is still unclear. Grafton's book provides a lengthy description of the reaction to *morbus gallicus* in sixteenth-century Europe, but next to nothing about the demographic collapse of the populations Columbus called "Indians."

IV

The ravages of disease in the Americas, especially in the Caribbean islands and the lowland zones of the mainland, had a very direct, rapid, and permanent impact on the history of three continents. Catastrophe for some, as always, brought profit and opportunities for others. The elimination of the Caribbean island Indians left some of the best agricultural land in the tropics without workers to farm it. Columbus had envisioned a profitable slave trade in American Indians to supply "Castile, Portugal, Aragón, Italy, Sicily, the islands of Portugal, and the Canaries," and as early as 1495 a cargo of five hundred Indians had been sent to Seville. The extermination of the Indians in the Antilles put an end to this prospect. Local entrepreneurs seeking replacements for the diminishing supply of local laborers raided other Caribbean islands for Indian slaves and then captured the Indians who lived on the South American coast. But the supply of labor soon proved insufficient to meet the demands, even on the island of Hispaniola. By 1524 there were more slaves than Tainos, and by 1540 the former had almost completely replaced the latter.

The suggestion of a different source of labor came ironically from the "protectors" of the Indians. Both Licenciado Zuazo and Las Casas suggested that African slaves could be substituted for Indian labor, and, except for the temporary suspension of the African slave trade between 1516 and 1518 initiated by Cardinal Regent Cisneros, enslaved Africans were imported to help exploit the economic potentialities of the New World from the beginning of the sixteenth century onward.

The expanding demand for African slaves coincided with a significant shift of Portuguese interests in Africa. By the end of the first decade of the sixteenth century, the village of Mpinda at the mouth of the Congo River had developed into a major slave port, initially for the dispatch of slaves to Lisbon and the Algarve.[14] Mpinda also exported slaves to São Tomé. By the 1530s some four thousand to five thousand slaves per year were exported from the Congo, and as the decade progressed an increasing number of slaves were also obtained from the region near the mouth of the Kwanza in Angola.[15] By 1550, Lisbon had a slave population of almost ten thousand out of a total urban population of one hundred thousand.

Philip Curtin estimated that during the sixteenth century some 50,000 enslaved Africans were sent to Europe, some 25,000 to the Atlantic islands

---

[14]David Birmingham, *Trade and Conflict in Angola: The Mbundu and Their Neighbors under the Influence of the Portuguese, 1483–1790* (Oxford: Clarendon Press, 1966), 21–41.

[15]A. C. de C. M. Saunders, *A Social History of Black Slaves and Freedmen in Portugal, 1441–1551* (Cambridge: Cambridge University Press, 1982).

of Cape Verde, Madeira, and the Canaries, and 100,000 to São Tomé.[16] As in the Portuguese-controlled islands in the Gulf of Guinea, the African slaves were shipped in mainly to work in the sugarcane fields. (The gold of Cibao and San Cristóbal in Hispaniola had given out within twenty-five years and that of Cuba and Puerto Rico in half that time.) Island-based entrepreneurs, among them lawyers, military functionaries, and agents of the great Italian merchant families of Seville, turned quickly to sugar production. By 1528 there were some twenty water-powered mills (*ingenios*) on Hispaniola, mostly near the town of Santo Domingo, and in 1520 a Genoese-financed mill was producing commercial sugar in Puerto Rico.

It may seem illogical today that labor should have been transported across the Atlantic from Africa to the Americas rather than used locally, and that plantation economies did not arise in West Africa, which was apparently closer to European markets.[17] But linear distances in the sixteenth century bore little relation to distances as measured by time and difficulties of transport. The route from West Africa to Europe was, so far as the time and difficulty of travel were concerned, no shorter than from the Antilles. Ships from West Africa were obliged to sail near the equator, catch the southeast trade winds and westerly current and consequently join, at the Azores, the same route as ships inbound from North and South America. In fact for a sailing ship the coast of South America below the equator was often nearer to Europe in sailing time than the coast of Africa.

In addition, the diseases of West Africa caused intolerable losses of European lives, and made permanent settlement hazardous. Even in the early nineteenth century, the death rates for British troops on the Gold Coast ran as high as 668 per thousand each year. The tsetse fly prevented draft animals and livestock from surviving in the West African tropical forest zones. The West African coast, moreover, lacked safe anchorage except near the mouth of the Niger River, which was dominated by Benin, the most formidable of the West African states. Ships sailing on the West African grain and ivory coasts had to anchor in open roadsteads, with little protection against the wind. Hence in Africa, the threat of disease worked in favor of the native inhabitants and against the outsiders.

---

[16]Philip D. Curtin, *The Atlantic Slave Trade: A Census* (Madison: University of Wisconsin Press, 1969), 17–28, 268.

[17]See J. D. Fage, *A History of West Africa: An Introductory Survey* (Cambridge: Cambridge University Press, 1969), 52–68; M. A. Havinden, "The History of Crop Cultivation in West Africa, a Bibliographic Guide," *Economic History Review* 23, 2d series (1970): 532–553; Richard B. Sheridan, "Africa and the Caribbean in the Atlantic Slave Trade," *American Historical Review* 77, no. 1 (February 1972): 15–35; F. Guerra, "The Influence of Disease on Race, Logistics, and Colonization in the Antilles," *Journal of Tropical Medicine and Hygiene* 69 (1966): 23–35.

In the Caribbean islands as in the Canaries, the opposite was the case, and the demographic collapse of the local population of Taino Indians opened up land for the taking. Tainos ironically played a great role in the distribution of food to tropical zones in the Eastern Hemisphere. Slave traders carried the Tainos' principal crop, cassava, to sub-Saharan Africa. And they also contributed many products to what Professor Crosby has defined as the "Columbian exchange," including the sweet potato, bean, squash, and peanut, fruits such as guava, mamey, and pineapple, and rubber and tobacco.

The rise of sugar production and the slave trade in the islands of the greater Antilles (Hispaniola, Cuba, Puerto Rico) placed them, together with the Canary Islands, Madeira, Cape Verde, and São Tomé, firmly within a new commercial system stretching from the African coast to the Atlantic. Economic organization throughout these various archipelagoes, despite different chronologies of development, was remarkably similar. Almost always the distribution and marketing of sugar were in the hands of the Italians, who also predominated as slave traders, often working through Portuguese subcontractors. Production, on the other hand, was invariably controlled by Spanish and Portuguese settlers, sometimes on a small scale, as in Madeira. Often non-Iberian capital financed the sugar mills, which required substantial investment in machinery and tools. Transfer of expertise and skilled workers between sugar-producing regions was common, from Sicily to Madeira, for example, or from the Canaries to Hispaniola.

The sugar technician was, in fact, among the more mobile and successful artisans of this early Atlantic world, and was capable of accumulating capital on his own behalf, for he received in most cases a percentage (often one-tenth) of the sugar processed under his supervision. Sugar made an ideal freight. In the Canary Islands, in the period from 1508 to 1510, its value per pound was four to five times as much as the same quantity of wheat. Freight costs were relatively low, some 4 to 6 percent of market value as compared with 12 percent for wheat. It was therefore possible to transport sugar advantageously across the Atlantic to a profitable market in Europe.[18]

The connection between the sugar trade and the slave trade was a direct one, and it turned out to be a compact of death. Most of the slaves sent to

---

[18]José-Gentil da Silva, "Echanges et troc: l'exemple des Canaries au début du XVI-Ième siècle," *Annales ESC* 16e année (1961), 1004–1011; Rau and Macedo, *O açúcar da Madeira*, 20; Robert S. Lopez, "Market Expansion: The Case of Genoa," *Journal of Economic History* 24 (1954): 460–461; Chaunu, *Séville et l'Atlantique* 7, no. 1, 527; Pike, *Enterprise and Adventure*, 50.

Hispaniola between 1530 and 1540 by Vazques, Forne and Vivaldo, a Genoese company in Seville, were exchanged for sugar. Slaves, purchased in Africa with European barter goods of low intrinsic value, fetched high prices in the markets of the New World, where the price of African slaves in Hispaniola rose from forty-five ducats to one hundred between 1528 and 1556. Human beings shipped as a commodity provided the slave traders with a cargo of high value in relation to the space they took up. Slaves once landed were highly perishable, and required constant replacement, since they failed to reproduce themselves owing to the rigors of plantation labor, the low proportion of women imported, and the lack of incentive to procreate in conditions of forced labor and captivity. The more prosperous the sugar trade became, the higher were the death rates of slaves and the lower the proportion of women imported. Just as lands had been made available for sugar production in the first place by the extermination of the original inhabitants, the death rate of the imported labor force helped to guarantee the continuance of the slave trade, especially during the early years.

The planter did not have a strong incentive to encourage reproduction among slaves, for the return on investment of slaves was relatively rapid (between two years and thirty months, the period also required to recoup the purchase price of work animals such as oxen). The same capitalists who financed the slave trade would also sell the sugar produced on the islands, and insure the ships at staggering rates (under the terms of sea loans the merchant bankers accepted the risk of safe arrival of 80 to 90 percent of ships and 56 to 60 percent of the slaves on board); they would also sell to the new colonies most of the basic foodstuffs, clothing, and domestic animals they needed. The main profits of the early years in fact seem to have accrued more to the large foreign bankers than the Spanish or Portuguese shipowners and settlers.

The incorporation of Hispaniola into the Afro-Atlantic system was of great importance for the future development of the Caribbean and of many of the lowland coastal regions of the Americas. In their broad outlines the patterns established in the early years were to be repeated elsewhere. First, there was the headlong greed in the unscrupulous search for precious metals. Then there was the collapse of the indigenous population, followed by the exhaustion of the mineral wealth and the introduction of cash crops worked by slave labor imported from Africa. For three and one-half centuries the experience of the first thirty years was reproduced, and the resulting patterns of ethnic composition, economic possibilities, and social structure, and deeply rooted attitudes of resentment and resignation, made the Americas what they are today. Here indeed was the "shock of discovery," to use the title of Anthony Grafton's book, although the educated Europeans whose works he analyzed remained more concerned with classical and Renaissance literature and cosmology. But it should be kept in mind that they often did so while drinking their American-produced coffee, smoking American-produced tobacco, binding their texts between American leather hides, and enjoying the leisure that the dividends from overseas investments made possible.

V. S. Naipaul's comment in *The Mimic Men* almost a quarter of a century still holds:

> It was my hope to give expression to the restlessness, the deep disorder, which the great explorations, the overthrow in three continents of established social organizations, the unnatural bringing together of peoples who could achieve fulfillment only within the security of their own societies and the landscapes hymned by their ancestors, it was my hope to give partial expression to the restlessness which this great upheaval has brought about. The empires of our time were short-lived, but they have altered the world forever; their passing away is their least significant feature. It was my hope to sketch a subject which, fifty years hence, a great historian might pursue. For there is no such thing as history nowadays; there are only manifestoes and antiquarian research; and on the subject of empire there is only the pamphleteering of churls.[19]

The outpouring during the quincentennial year has only demonstrated once again how right Naipaul was, and how the task he sketched out remains to be done.

V

Strangely missing among the books provoked by the quincentenary of the first Columbian voyage is adequate recognition of the importance of Spain's main competitors, the Portuguese. In this respect their absence from Professor Grafton's book is striking and means he does not discuss the experience of the first Europeans, mainly Portuguese, to explore around the African coastline from Cape Verde in the West to the mouth of the Red Sea in the East; and he does not describe how the Portuguese linked the Atlantic to the Indian Ocean through a maritime route and mapped virtually the whole coastline of Asia, including Japan. No Portuguese book is discussed or even listed in Grafton's work—which is something like writing about the space age while ignoring the American space

---

[19]V. S. (Vidiadhar Surajprasad) Naipaul, *The Mimic Men* (New York: Macmillan, 1967).

program. Luís de Matos's encyclopedic discussion of the impact of the Portuguese on Renaissance literature at least deserved some notice here.[20]

Few historians in 1992 seemed to realize that while the Portuguese won the race to the East, Columbus lost it—even if he was never to admit to the fact; and the more bizarre and desperate his claims to have done so, the more recourse he had to the biblical and phantasmagorical allusions scholars like Professor Grafton take as confirming their arguments that surprisingly little had changed in the thinking of Europeans about the rest of the world.

Curiously, the only mention of Portugal in *New Worlds, Ancient Texts* concerns Prince Henry and the school for the study of geography and navigation that he allegedly established at Sagres in southwest Portugal during the early fifteenth century. The school's existence has long been dismissed as a nineteenth-century myth but is a very enduring myth nevertheless. In fact, Professor Charles Boxer, in his notes to the catalog of a 1990 exhibition at the New York Public Library, which is cited by Professor Grafton in his bibliography, succinctly demolished it.[21] Younger Portuguese scholars like Professor Alfredo Pinheiro Marques are especially irritated at the myth's persistence since it ignores a long and subtle process by which knowledge was in fact acquired. Despite the patient work of experts such as the late professor Luís de Albuquerque, doyen of the Portuguese cartographical historians, the myth was revived by Daniel Boorstin, just when they thought it was finally buried, in *The Discoverers*; and it is now here once more repeated, which only goes to prove Professor Grafton's point, I suppose, that "text" outlives "experience."

There is much to be said for detailed analysis of texts in their own right, certainly by an erudite scholar like Professor Grafton. Valerie Flint's book *The Imaginative Landscape of Christopher Columbus* is a good example of how revealing that type of careful exegesis can be.[22] Through a meticulous examination of Columbus's reading, annotations, and expressed religious beliefs, Professor Flint very skillfully shows us "not the New World Columbus found, but the Old World, which he carried with him in his head."

But not all scholars today have Flint's and Grafton's skills. In fact, most scholars today lack mastery of Greek and Latin and are less well prepared

---

[20]Luís de Matos, *L'expansion Portugaise dans la littérature latine de la renaissance* (Lisbon: Fundação Calouste Gulbenkian, Serviço de Educação, 1991).
[21]C. R. (Charles Ralph) Boxer, "The Politics of the Discoveries," in *Portugal-Brazil: The Age of Atlantic Discoveries* (Lisbon: Bertrand Editora, 1990), 264–267; Professor Luís de Albuquerque outlined his reasons for dismissing the idea of the "School of Sagres" in his "Portuguese Navigation: Its Historical Development," in *Circa 1492: Art in the Age of Exploration* (New Haven: Yale University Press, 1992), 35–39.
[22]Valerie I. J. Flint, *The Imaginative Landscape of Christopher Columbus* (Princeton: Princeton University Press, 1992).

for these tasks than they were a century ago. The curious consequence of the surge of interest in literary analysis in the quincentennial year has been to revive a great deal of Columbus's most outrageous claims, and by doing so give emphasis to a resilient medievalism that emphasizes the continuities rather than the innovations of this period. Columbus, of course, paid dearly for his misapprehension of the territories he reached. Las Casas later complained bitterly that Amerigo Vespucci had stolen Columbus's prize. But as Garry Wills points out in his preface to the Vespucci *Letters from a New World*, "Columbus *had* named what he had reached—the Indies. It was not a new name because he did not think he had found anything new. And his misnomer stuck."[23]

One also suspects that a closer examination of the Spanish background might have unraveled some of the enigmas in Columbus's professions of orthodoxy. As Peggy Liss shows in her readable and comprehensive *Isabel the Queen*, this was the period in which the Inquisition was converted into a terrifying organ of state power, the Muslim inhabitants of Malaga were conquered, enslaved, and sold, the concept of "purity of blood" was used to humiliate and destroy thousands, homosexuality was declared to be high treason, and the Jews were expelled.[24]

The books of the quincentennial year have also demonstrated how narrow and self-contained much contemporary scholarship has become. Few of these books appreciate how the Portuguese and the Spaniards acted on a great leap of global geographical perception at the turn of the fifteenth century. It was the translation of this new geographical perception of the world into European commercial and military domination and, in the Caribbean and elsewhere, racial hegemony, which set the pattern for the explosive "encounter of civilizations" that the quincentennial used as an incantation but rarely examined.

It is therefore worth recalling that precisely during the long hiatus while the Catholic monarchs sought to confirm Columbus's claims to have reached Asia, the Portuguese, in fact, reached India, and King Manuel of Portugal (1495–1521) wrote in 1499 to inform his Castilian colleagues of his claims to the "suzerainty and dominion of the navigation, and commerce, of Ethiopia, Arabia, Persia, and India."[25] This was of course hyperbole—but it demonstrated that the Portuguese had done in fact what Columbus claimed to have done—reach Asia by sea. And as Professor

---

[23]Luciano Formisano, ed., *Letters from a New World: Amerigo Vespucci's Discovery of America* (New York: Marsilio, 1992).

[24]Peggy K. Liss, *Isabel the Queen: Life and Times* (New York: Oxford University Press, 1992).

[25]C. R. (Charles Ralph) Boxer, *The Portuguese Seaborne Empire, 1415–1825* (London: Hutchinson, 1969), 37.

Alfredo Pinheiro Marques argues in *Portugal and the Discovery of America,*
it was no coincidence that Columbus was soon after recalled in chains from
his "Indies."[26]

While Columbus and his travels cannot be fully explained without reference to the evolution of the fifteenth-century Atlantic system, their significance is even less understandable if we do not also take account of the
global expansion by Europeans that took place early in the sixteenth century within an extraordinary period of no more than fifteen years, in
which the Portuguese reached the Seychelles, Socotra, and the coast of
Arabia (1503), Ceylon and the Bay of Bengal (1509). In the Pacific they explored the coast of Southeast Asia and reached China in 1513. Contact
with Japan came during the 1540s. And even in the Americas, Portugal
claimed Brazil in 1500.

Professor Marques provides an instructive comparison of the first images of the New World by juxtaposing two maps of the world as it was
known in the first years of the sixteenth century—the planisphere made by
the Spaniard Juan de la Cosa (ca. 1501–1506) from the Museu Naval in
Madrid, and the anonymous Portuguese planisphere of 1502 known as the
Cantino after the Italian agent who smuggled it out of Portugal, and which
comes from the Biblioteca Estense in Modena. Here the imprecise con-
tours of the Spanish map stand in striking contrast to the impressive accu-
racy of Portuguese cartography. And the Portuguese did not intend that
the point should be missed. With the famous embassy of Tristão da Cunha
to Pope Leo X in 1514, King Manuel planned to dazzle Rome with Portugal's Asian exploits. Here, Angela Delaforce describes the spectacle:

> a theatrical display of figures dressed in exotic Indian and African
> costumes, Persian horses and the first living elephant seen there
> since antiquity was paraded on the streets of the eternal city [and]
> captured the popular and artistic imagination of Rome.[27]

---

[26]Alfredo Pinheiro Marques, *Portugal and the Discovery of America: Christopher
Columbus and the Portuguese* (Lisbon: Portuguese State Mint, 1992).

[27]Angela Delaforce, "The Baixela da Victoria: Its Context and Iconography in the
Art of Portugal," in *Portugal's Silver Service: A Victory Gift to the Duke of Wellington,*
ed. Angela Delaforce and James Yorke (London: Victoria and Albert Museum,
1992), 75–79. Essential background to the rich cultural connections between Flanders, Italy, and Portugal during this period can be found in the two brilliant books
by Sylvie Deswarte: *Les enluminures de la Leitura Nova 1504–1552: Étude sur la culture artistique au Portugal au temps de l'humanisme,* preface by André Chastel
(Paris: Fundação Calouste Gulbenkian, 1977) and *Il Perfetto Cortegiano: D. Miguel
da Silva* (Rome: Bulzoni Editore, 1989). D. Miguel da Silva was Portuguese ambassador to the Holy See, and it was to him that Baldassare Castiglione dedicated his
Cortegiano (Venice, 1528).

The most dramatic result of Portugal's voyages and the explorations of Bartoloméu Dias, Diego Cão, Vasco da Gama, and Pedro Álvares Cabral was not the territorial empire they tried to claim in Asia and Africa and the Americas. By and large they lacked the resources for imperial dominance and power. What they did do, however, was establish connections: when we talk of relations among China, Japan, or India, or Europe for that matter, we are really talking about contacts established on their peripheries. The seventeenth-century Brazilian historian Father Vicente de Salvador tellingly compared the Portuguese to crabs crawling along a coastline. And if this was true of Brazil until well into the eighteenth century, it was even more true of China or of Japan.

With this first period of oceanic contact an entirely new way of viewing the world emerged and the Portuguese were in large part responsible for it. They established an oceanic dominion that linked strategically placed trading posts in a worldwide imperial system.

In this accomplishment, the rapid evolution of Portuguese cartography during this period was particularly important; a new graphic conception of global space gave the Portuguese, and later Europe, a decided advantage. It permitted, for instance, a very rapid conversion of navigational knowledge to strategic and commercial (one might say protoimperial) advantage. The political and economic aspects of the Portuguese intrusion into Asia and the subsequent vicissitudes of their presence there are well captured in Sanjay Subrahmanyam's fascinating *The Portuguese Empire in Asia*.[28] Synthesizing a generation of research, his book is an indispensable starting point for comprehending the Portuguese exploits both in Asia and Europe. He casts new light, for example, on the ways in which the Portuguese, by opening the oceanic routes, displaced the Venetians in importing spices, especially pepper, into Europe.

All the Portuguese outposts established while the Spaniards remained largely confined to the Caribbean were located at key strategic connections between seas and oceans, the key passageways for trade and naval control, for example, Hormuz at the mouth of the Persian Gulf, Mombasa and Mozambique at the Malagasy Strait, Malacca for the passage between the Bay of Bengal and the South China Sea, the Azores on the sea routes back from the North and South Atlantic to Europe, Macao at the mouth of the Pearl River in China, and Cape Verde, which could monitor movements across the Atlantic to the African coast. These places are still identified by naval strategists as "choke points." Their importance for control of navigation had been known, of course, to those who had used them for centuries

---

[28]Sanjay Subrahmanyam, *The Portuguese Empire in Asia 1500–1700: A Political and Economic History* (London: Longman, 1993).

before the Portuguese arrived, but they had never before been seen as affecting movements across the globe.

With extraordinary rapidity at the beginning of the sixteenth century the Portuguese turned their geographical knowledge into a global system. Only at the mouth of the Red Sea, when they attempted to seize and hold Aden, did they fail. What is surprising in view of this record is how long it took Spaniards to reach Mexico, almost thirty years after Columbus's landfall in 1492. It was after all not until 1513 that Vasco Núñez de Balboa crossed the Isthmus of Panama to see the Pacific Ocean. And the first circumnavigation of the globe (which achieved of course what Columbus had wanted to do—sail west to arrive in the East) was made possible when Fernão de Magalhães (Ferdinand Magellan), a Portuguese navigator in the service of the Castilian Crown, set sail in 1519 to discover the straits that now bear his name and crossed the Pacific to the Philippines, in the same year in fact that Hernán Cortés arrived in Tenochtitlán.

The capacity of the Portuguese to see the big picture is one of the more remarkable perceptual innovations of the early sixteenth century. This was a leap of imagination that Columbus, despite his great voyages, singularly failed to make—at least in part because he had deluded himself, as, it seems, he still deludes some historians.

CACAO.

CHAPTER **3**
Chocolate

"Give me chastity and continence, but not just now."
—Saint Augustine, *Confessions 8.7*

In 1544 Dominican friars took a delegation of Maya nobles to visit Prince Philip of Spain. Among the presents they brought to his courts, together with various kinds of chilies, beans, sarsparilla, maize, liquidambar (a plant of the witch hazel family), and two thousand quetzal feathers, their most precious offering, were receptacles of beaten chocolate. This was, according to Sophie Coe and Michael Coe, the first appearance of chocolate in Europe. The future Philip II, however, seemed more concerned about his visitors' nakedness than their gifts, and may not have been aware of the historic event.[1]

The Coes return to the Mayas at the end of their story. Inhabitants of the clouded, forested mountains and the fertile valleys bordering the Petén lowlands, called Verapaz ("True Peace") by the Spaniards, the Kekchí Maya people were for the Dominicans a striking example of how kindness and understanding could bring greater rewards than violence. It was here, in what is now Guatemala and southern Mexico, that Bartolomé de las Casas began his locally successful, but ultimately doomed, efforts to counter the rapacious destruction he saw all around him in the ancient worlds the Europeans had stumbled onto in 1492, with devastating consequences for the indigenous populations.

---

[1]Sophie D. Coe and Michael D. Coe, *The True History of Chocolate* (New York: Thames and Hudson, 1996).

I

The title of the Coes' book is an allusion to *The True History of the Conquest of Mexico*, completed in 1572 in Guatemala's capital by the old, poor, and partially blind conquistador Bernal Díaz del Castillo, a warrior who wished to get the facts straight, free from "lofty rhetoric," about the fate of the Aztecs. The Coes seek to do the same for chocolate and also to bring seriousness to the study of the history of food and drink. "Although food, sex, and mortality are the three great givens of human existence," they note, "earlier generations of academics generally avoided these topics as not quite respectable." This is not entirely true: Gilberto Freyre's trilogy on Brazil is full of sex and accounts of exotic and erotic sugary delicacies of one sort or another.[2] Nevertheless, what the Coes have achieved is to strip away, as Bernal Díaz del Castillo tried to do, the myths and misunderstandings, and to reconstruct from often very obscure sources, with some exciting archaeological fieldwork and hieroglyphic deciphering, the remarkable passage of chocolate from its origins in the lowland jungles of southern Mexico to "Hershey's Kisses" and Cadbury's "chocolate box," and to reestablish its genealogy over three millennia.

Chocolate for nine-tenths of its long history was drunk, not eaten, and only one-fifth of that history postdates the fall of the Aztec capital in 1521. The dark brown, pleasantly bitter, chemically complex substance bears little resemblance to the pulp-surrounded seeds of the cacao plants from which it is produced. The European invaders had to name many of the plants and plant derivatives, new to them, that they encountered in the Western Hemisphere, and to fit them into their own schemes of classification, as well as within the health theories of classical authors, who had been totally unaware of the existence of the New World but whose ideas dominated medicine until the eighteenth century.

Chocolate was first used in Europe as a curative. The scientific name given to the cacao tree in 1753 by Carl von Linné, more commonly known as Linnaeus, in Latinized form, was based on the binomial system he invented. As a chocolate lover, Linnaeus named the cacao tree *Theobroma cacao*; the first part, the name of the genus to which the cacao belongs, he took from the Greek meaning "food of the gods." The New World name *cacao* he found barbaric, and put in the second place as the specific name. Yet as the Coes demonstrate in fascinating detail, it is the word *cacao* that provides the clue to the unraveling of chocolate's earliest history.

---

[2]Gilberto Freyre, *The Masters and the Slaves (Casa-Grande & Senzala): A Study in the Development of Brazilian Civilization*, trans. Samuel Putnam (New York: Knopf, 1946); *New World in the Tropics; The Culture of Modern Brazil* (New York: Knopf, 1959); and *The Mansions and the Shanties: The Making of Modern Brazil*, trans. Harriet de Onís (New York: Knopf, 1963).

The cacao tree itself is a spindly shade tree. Exceedingly difficult to grow, it will not bear fruit outside the region from 20 degrees north to 20 degrees south of the equator. Even then it will not grow in the tropical highlands, where the temperature falls below 60 degrees Fahrenheit. It requires year-round moisture. There are two major varieties of cacao tree: the *criollo*, native to Central America, and the *forastero*, originally from South America. The flavor and the aroma of the seeds of *criollo* are superior to the more hardy and now more widely cultivated *forastero*. Like other tropical fruit trees, the cacao tree produces flowers from small nodes on the trunk and on the larger branches. Europeans could not at first believe this, and their illustrations moved the cacao pods out to the smaller branches, assuming the indigenous watercolorists whose work they were engraving had not accurately observed the plants.

In the damp, shaded depths of the tropical forest the five-petaled flowers are pollinated by midges and, once pollinated, each flower produces a large pod of thirty or so almond-shaped seeds, or "beans," surrounded by a sweet, juicy pulp. The cacao pods, which cannot open on their own, are cracked in the wild by monkeys seeking the pulp. It was the pulp, the Coes believe, that first attracted human beings as well. Once the pods are opened and the pulp extracted, four steps are necessary to produce cacao "nibs," or kernels, which are ground into chocolate. Whatever the technology employed, from that of the earliest forest dwellers to the modern factory, the steps are: first fermentation, then drying, roasting, and winnowing.

The cacao plant was first domesticated by the Olmecs, the complex culture of the Mexican Gulf Coast, around 1500 B.C. The Maya took the word "cacao" from these distant ancestors and, at some time between 400 B.C. and 100 A.D., began using the word to mean, as it still does, the domesticated *Theobroma cacao*. The Coes provide a brilliant excursion through the pre-Conquest Mesoamerican city-states in the forests of northern Guatemala and southern Yucatán, with their towering temple pyramids of stucco masonry, their palaces, stone relief carvings, and delicately painted and carved ceramic vases. Archaeological evidence and some remarkable hieroglyphic deciphering have brought to light the central role of the production and consumption of chocolate in Maya society, and this extraordinary detective work is beautifully described by the authors. From a tomb in a medium-sized Maya city at Río Azul in Guatemala, a trove of the paraphernalia of chocolate consumption was discovered in 1984, including a chocolate jar with a screw-on lid. Among the many fine illustrations the Coes include in their book is a scene from an eighth-century A.D. vase from the Nakbé area of north-central Petén, now in the Princeton University Art Museum, depicting a Maya woman carefully pouring a dark substance from a cylindrical jar into a larger one—the first known picture of a chocolate drink being made.

The Aztecs, too, were great chocolate drinkers. Chocolate was much favored by warriors as well as the nobility because the drink was, among its other attributes, nonalcoholic, and the Aztecs, whatever else they may have been, were notably abstemious. Cacao beans served as money as well as for making chocolate and became objects of long-distance trade. Huge storehouses of cacao beans were kept by the Aztec rulers.

Columbus during his disastrous fourth voyage met with a huge Maya dugout canoe in 1502 near the Bay Islands off the Honduran coast. With typical alacrity, Columbus had the canoe seized and stripped of its trading goods, including a cargo of "almonds" which, the Spaniards were very surprised to see, the Maya traders valued highly. Also typically, Columbus did not comprehend what he had seen. The inventor of the phrase "New World," the Milanese chronicler Peter Martyr, knew better. He called cacao beans "happie money . . . which I call happy, because . . . the bowelles of the earth are not rent a sunder . . . For this groweth upon trees."

For the Aztecs, chocolate, which they called *cacahuatl*,was apparently a cool drink prepared in much the same way the Maya did. The cacao beans were crushed, pulverized, soaked, and steeped. Water was added sparingly, followed by aeration, filtration, and straining. The liquid was then poured back and forth from one vessel to another to produce a head of foam. All pre-Conquest chocolate drinks were made by this method.

By the late sixteenth century the bitter, usually unsweetened cold liquid had become transformed in the early colonial kitchens where conquered and conqueror met. In the same period cacao also met, again in the colonial kitchen, a product of another domesticated crop. Sugar arrived by way of the long process of continental and transoceanic transplantation that brought sugarcane to the Americas—from Asia, through the Mediterranean and the Atlantic islands, to Santo Domingo, and finally to the estates established by the family of Hernán Cortés in colonial Mexico. The Coes make too little, perhaps, of this momentous encounter between cacao and sugar; but it was a mix that made chocolate sweet and hot.

The Spanish conquerors suspected, perhaps hoped, that chocolate had aphrodisiac properties. But this, according to the Coes, was a Spanish obsession, "as was the chronic constipation" caused by their diet of meat and lard and few fresh vegetables. "The conquistadors searched for native Mexican laxatives as avidly as they did for aphrodisiacs," the Coes observe.

The authors' ingenious explanation for the transformation of the word for the drink from *cacahuatl* to *chocolate* is not unrelated to these particular Spanish concerns. The Spaniards, the Coes suggest, were uncomfortable with a noun beginning with caca to describe the thick, dark-brown drain they were increasingly appreciating. In Latin and most Romance languages caca, as in cacahuatl, is a vulgar word for feces. *Chocolatl* and *choco-*

late, a neologism derived from a Maya and Aztec mix, had a more respectable sound. Philologists will doubtlessly argue over such derivations, but it is an explanation that would have been much appreciated by the Marquis de Sade, a chocoholic who became grotesquely obese during his long captivity, when, denied other outlets, he spent his time overindulging in all manner of chocolate delicacies, of which he was always demanding more from his loyal and long-suffering wife. "I asked . . . for a cake with icing, but I want it to be chocolate," he demanded in 1779, "and black inside from chocolate as the devil's ass is black from smoke. And the icing is to be the same."

Chocolate had become well established as an elite drink in Europe and Spanish America by the mid-seventeenth century. In all cases the dried chocolate mass in the form of cakes, rolls, or bricks was placed in hot water in a special jug or chocolate pot fitted with a lid pursed in the middle to hold the handle of the *molinillo* (swizzle stick) and beaten to produce a froth. Initially, the Spaniards sipped their foamy chocolate the Mesoamerican way, from gourds or small open clay bowls called *jícaras*; but the viceroy of Peru, the Marqués de Mancera, in the 1640s was concerned about the ladies-in-waiting at his reception spilling chocolate on their court dresses. He had Lima silversmiths make up a plate or saucer with a collarlike ring in the middle in which a small cup could sit without slipping. This *mancerina* soon became ubiquitous, and was the progenitor of the magnificent eighteenth-century Viennese porcelain cups and saucers called *trembleuses*. At the French court the silver *chocolatière* was introduced with the lid adapted to hold a *moussoir* directly borrowed from Spanish and Mesoamerican prototypes. The French added a straight angle to the spout; because it unscrewed clockwise, the handle remained tight while the liquid was poured in a counterclockwise motion.

The profligate Cosimo de' Medici became addicted to chocolate on a visit to Spain and on becoming Cosimo III, grand duke of Tuscany, was one of the great chocoholics of all time. Francesco Redi (1626–1697), the grand duke's renowned physician and apothecary, invented the novel perfume flavors introduced into chocolate for the Tuscan court, most famously a delicate jasmine aroma. The jealously guarded secret formula for this most baroque of chocolate drinks is printed by the Coes for those who would like to re-create it, along with many other recipes and methods of chocolate preparation scattered throughout their book.

The Italians, in fact, were lyrical about chocolate. For Geronimo Piperni: "Chocolate is a divine, celestial drink, the sweat of the stars, the vital seed, divine nectar, the drink of the gods, panacea and universal medicine." Another Florentine, Marcello Malaspina (1689–1757), composed a curious dithyramb called "Bacchus in Tuscany," set on the coast of

Guatemala, where shipwrecked Tuscans, finding themselves in a grove of cacao trees, sing out:

> Che il CIOCCOLATTA d'ogni Beva è il Re.
> [That chocolate is the king of drinks.]

Chocolate, it was soon learned, could also effectively disguise poisons. Horace Walpole's old friend, Sir Horace Mann, believed that Pope Clement XIV, who had suppressed the Jesuits in 1773, had been poisoned by them. The Jesuits were great drinkers and producers of chocolate. Their cacao trade from the Amazon was one of their most profitable enterprises until the Marquês de Pombal expelled them from the region. The pope, Mann told Walpole, persisted in drinking his chocolate despite fears of assassination and was slowly poisoned through his "dish of chocolate last Holy Thursday at the Vatican."

By the late eighteenth century, chocolate was indelibly associated with decadence, aristocracy, and the Catholic Church, especially with the Jesuits, all of which made it suspect to the philosophes, enlightened thinkers, enterprising Protestant businessmen, and aspiring radical politicians who preferred coffee. Nor had the technology employed in chocolate's preparation changed much since the time of the Olmecs, despite the invention of better pots, nonslip saucers, and exotic aromas. The plate dedicated to chocolate making in the *Encyclopédie* of Denis Diderot and Jean d'Alembert shows a worker toasting cacao in a cauldron, another breaking them in a heated mortar, and another grinding them on a heated surface—all steps familiar to the Maya and the Aztecs. In this as in so much else, the *Encyclopédie* was a compendium of things past rather than of things to come.

II

Yet the nineteenth century also saw chocolate go down-market. Chocolate became a product worked on by chemists and promoted by billboards. No longer a drink favored by gluttonous grand dukes, villainous Jesuits, and notorious marquises with specialized tastes, it became the respectable snack food of virtuous Quakers, of Royal Navy sailors weaned from grog, and of the unromantic Swiss. The leap into the modern era came in 1828 when the Dutch chemist Coenraad Van Houten took out a patent on a process for the manufacture of a new kind of powdered chocolate with a very low fat content. He had developed a very efficient filtering process which reduced the cocoa butter content, leaving a cake that could be pulverized into a fine powder. This powder he treated with alkaline salts so that it would mix well with water.

Van Houten's defatting and alkalizing process made possible large-scale manufacture of cheap chocolate in powdered or solid form. From then on, it was no longer necessary to stir and beat the heavy liquid to make a palatable drink, and the chocolate pot fell out of use. In Bristol, Joseph Fry & Sons developed a method for casting chocolate into a mold and in 1849 exhibited the first hard eating chocolate. Fry later became the sole supplier to the Royal Navy. The Cadburys of Birmingham, using Van Houten's method, introduced cocoa powder and the first "chocolate box." The Rowntrees of York developed similar lines of merchandise. The Frys, Cadburys, and Rowntrees were all Quakers with a social conscience. Cadbury and Rowntree developed model towns for their workers, whom they expected to be God-fearing and sober. The Frys refused to accept cacao from Portuguese plantations on the island of São Tomé, off the West African coast, whose working conditions they regarded as unacceptable.

In Switzerland, Henri Nestlé invented a process for making powdered milk by evaporation, and Daniel Peter used Nestlé's powder to make milk chocolate by drying out the moisture in the mix and replacing it with cacao butter. Another Swiss, Rudolph Lindt, devised a machine to make chocolate smoother, a process which became universal. And in Pennsylvania, a pious Mennonite, Milton Snavely Hershey, the "Henry Ford of Chocolate Makers," brought mass production to the chocolate business, constructing around his factory his own chocolate kingdom and an oversized imitation of George Washington's Mount Vernon to house himself. With Hershey, everything was mechanized. By the 1980s, 25 million Hershey's Kisses, little bite-sized, flat-bottomed drops of milk chocolate, dropped off Hershey's conveyor belts daily into their waiting boxes. Even the streetlights of Hershey's "Chocolate Town" are in the shape of Kisses.

Hard chocolate was an eminently respectable product—it was sold in corner shops, not drinking houses, and advertised in campaigns that invented the idea of "family values" by using wholesome little girls and neatly dressed Victorian schoolboys to promote it. But there was a darker side. Chocolate's profitability brought adulteration and, to counter it, the first consumer protection legislation.

Chocolate's popularity among the expanding middle classes in Europe and North America also made for expanded opportunities for colonial enterprise overseas. In 1824 the Portuguese had transplanted *forastero* cuttings from Brazil to São Tomé. By 1850, cacao cuttings were taken to Equatorial Guinea. By 1900 *Theobroma cacao* reached Ghana, Nigeria, and the Ivory Coast, and then went on to Sri Lanka, Java, Sumatra, and Oceania. By 1991, Africa was the source of 55 percent of the world's cacao; Mexico, where chocolate was born and cacao originated, accounted for only 1.5 percent.

Yet mass production and mass marketing have brought their own historical antidote. While the *criollo* beans are now the source of a mere 2 percent of the world cacao crop, the premier chocolatiers have returned to the variety of those beans once enjoyed by Maya nobles, Aztec warriors, and European aristocrats. With this remarkable full circle the Coes bring their book to conclusion. The Kekchi Maya of Belize, who first brought their precious beans to Europe as a gift to Prince Philip four hundred and fifty years ago, are today, through the good offices of the Fairtrade Foundation, an organization established by Oxfam, once again producing cacao beans in traditional three-acre forest plots where the *Theobroma cacao* is pollinated by midges safe from pesticides. From these cacao beans, Maya Gold, a new, expensive, ecologically friendly chocolate bar, is produced by the Green and Black's Company.

I was visiting the U.K. while writing this piece and was pleased to find that my brother-in-law stocked Maya Gold in his natural-foods store in Tiverton, Devonshire. The town has a street called Gold and many old schoolhouses, almshouses, and chantries built and endowed in the sixteenth century by local merchants, some of whom engaged in overseas trade and, on occasion, piracy (at least the Spanish considered it such). The parish church of St. Peter bears on its outer walls some of the finest stone carvings of the sixteenth-century armed merchant vessels in England, commissioned by one of the town's richest merchant adventurers. Devon privateers were the most notorious raiders along the Spanish Main. But they did not always know that cacao beans were "happie money" and to the Central Americans as good as gold. In 1579, after seizing a Spanish ship off the Isthmus of Panama, they burned the whole cargo in frustrated anger, thinking the cacao beans were sheep droppings placed there to deceive them. Now the descendants of these sixteenth-century mariners are buying Maya Gold, which seems to me as delicious as the Coes say it is.

Sophie Coe was a pioneer of culinary history, author of *America's First Cuisines*.[3] She was struck down suddenly by incurable cancer while she was working on her *True Story of Chocolate*. Michael Coe, her husband and a distinguished Yale anthropologist, completed her work. The book was conceived out of a fascination with chocolate, and completed out of the love for a partner lost. Sophie Coe has given us, and Michael Coe has delivered to us, a splendid treat.

---

[3]Sophie D. Coe, *America's First Cuisines* (Austin: University of Texas Press, 1994).

BUCCANEERS EMBARKING ON AN EXPEDITION.

CHAPTER 4

Pirate Democracy

"They change their climate, not their soul, who rush across the sea."
—Horace, *Epistles 1.11.27*

The first books about pirates appeared surprisingly soon after the piracy they described. The most successful of all the early pirates, Henry Morgan, who sacked the Spanish colonial city of Panama in 1671, was portrayed as a monster of depravity and cruelty in Alexander Exquemelin's best-selling *Buccaneers of America,* first published in Dutch in 1678, and in English in 1684.[1] Morgan brought suit for defamation of character. He strongly objected to a passage which said that he had first gone to the West Indies as an indentured servant and argued that because the governor of Jamaica, Sir Thomas Modyford, authorized his raids against the Spanish possessions, he was not a pirate. The matter was settled out of court, and Morgan received substantial damages.

Recalled to London in order to placate the Spaniards, Morgan was soon knighted by Charles II and later returned to Jamaica as lieutenant governor, where he acquired landed estates and over a hundred slaves. He died a rich man. It was his gargantuan drinking bouts that did him in. "Falling after into his old course of life and not taking any advice to the contrary, his belly swelled so as not to be contained in his coat," Hans Sloane, who attended him, reported. Whereupon Morgan turned to an African shaman who plastered him with mud and made him drink urine. "But he languished and, his cough augmenting, died soon after."

---

[1]For a recent and accessible edition see Alexander O. Exquemelin, *The Buccaneers of America,* trans. Alexis Brown (New York: Dover Publications, 2000).

The governor of Jamaica ordered a state funeral for Sir Harry. A solemn service took place at St. Peter's Church, of which Morgan was a benefactor. When the warships in the harbor honored the old villain with a twenty-one-gun salute, the cannons of the merchant vessels answered with their own disorderly but thunderous barrage. But in all this Henry Morgan was an exception. Most of his fellow pirates had short careers, met early and nasty ends, and died penniless, having lost their spoils in the taverns and brothels of Port Royal, Jamaica's capital, and one of the Caribbean's great buccaneer havens until it was destroyed by an earthquake in 1692, a suitable punishment for its past crimes and misdemeanors, some argued at the time.

I

One thing, however, seems certain: books about pirates tend to make more money than did most pirates. The London Maritime Museum's 1992 exhibition "Pirates: Fact and Fiction," a show planned to last four months, remained open for three years by popular demand. So it was not surprising that a New York literary agent encouraged David Cordingly, one of the curators, to take up the theme of the exhibition in a book contrasting the fictional image of pirates with historical reality.[2]

Cordingly concentrates principally on the great age of piracy between the last half of the seventeenth and the early eighteenth centuries, essentially the 1650s through 1725. For the "real world" of the pirates, he examined contemporary English language sources, principally the logbooks of the Royal Navy vessels sent out against the pirates, reports from colonial governors, and the depositions of captured pirates and their victims. He also has much to say about the popular image of pirates based on three centuries of ballads, melodramas, epic poems, films, and romantic novels, as well as the two classics of pirate lore, *Treasure Island* (1883) by Robert Louis Stevenson and *Peter Pan* (1904) by J. M. Barrie. He draws extensively, as he acknowledges, on the work of the historians Robert Ritchie, Marcus Rediker, Peter Earle, and Nicholas Rodger, each of whom, in different ways, has revolutionized the study of everyday life at sea during this period.[3]

---

[2]David Cordingly, *Under the Black Flag: The Romance and the Reality of Life among the Pirates* (New York: Random House, 1995).

[3]Robert C. Ritchie, *Captain Kidd and the War against the Pirates* (Cambridge: Harvard University Press, 1986); Marcus Rediker, *Between the Devil and the Deep Blue Sea: Merchant Seamen, Pirates and the Anglo-American Maritime World, 1700–1750* (Cambridge: Cambridge University Press, 1987); Peter Earle, *The Sack of Panama: Sir Henry Morgan's Adventures on the Spanish Main* (New York: Viking, 1982); N. A. M. Rodger, *The Wooden World: An Anatomy of the Georgian Navy* (London: Collins, 1986).

Cordingly concedes almost immediately that the popular conception of how pirates dressed turns out to be surprisingly accurate. As other mariners in this period did, they wore short blue jackets, a checkered shirt, a pair of long canvass trousers or baggy petticoat breeches, and often a red waistcoat and neckerchief. Pirates did indeed tie scarves or large handkerchiefs around their heads (a sensible and practical protection from the rays of the sun at sea or in the tropics); they slung several pistols on ribbons around their shoulders (also a wise precaution, since flintlock pistols were unreliable at sea and if one failed owing to a damp charge, a second or third backup came in handy); they wielded cutlasses and their elected chiefs were flamboyant and charismatic characters. The pirate captain Bartholomew Roberts, known as "Black Bart," said to have captured four hundred vessels, fought his last sea battle in 1722, clad "in a rich crimson damask waistcoat and breeches, a red feather in his hat, a gold chain round his neck, with a diamond cross hanging to it."

But dress is one thing, behavior is another. The pirates we meet in Cordingly's book are a bloodthirsty bunch, far from the grandees fallen on hard times depicted by W. S. Gilbert and Sir Arthur Sullivan in their *Pirates of Penzance*. The *Boston Gazette* in March 1726 gave a graphic description of Philip Lyne, the notorious pirate who, when he was tried in Barbados, confessed to killing thirty-seven masters of vessels and an unspecified number of seamen; the commander walked to the trial

> with about 20 other pirates, with their black silk flag before them. . . . As they were much wounded, and no care taken in dressing, they were very offensive, and stunk as they went along, particularly Line the commander; he had one eye shot out, which with part of his nose, hung down on his face.

"Pirate" was a very specific designation and the distinction between pirate and privateer was an important one, at least in law if not in practice. A "privateer" was an armed vessel, or the commander and crew of a vessel, that was licensed to attack and seize the vessels of a hostile nation. The license took the form of a "letter of marque and reprisal." By the sixteenth century, the licensing system provided all the European seafaring nations with a cheap way of attacking enemy shipping in time of war. The letter of marque was an impressive and ponderous legal document, and the privateer captain was expected to keep a journal and hand over the ship and goods he had seized to an admiralty court, where the sovereign took his share (or her share in the case of Queen Elizabeth, who always displayed a greedy interest in such divisions of spoils). The rest of the loot was divided among the ship owners, captain, and crew. A "pirate," on the other hand, was legally defined in England from the time of Henry VIII as someone who robs and plunders on the sea; and the laws against piracy provided for punishment for "felonies, robberies, and murders committed in any haven, river, creek, or place where the Lord High Admiral had jurisdiction."

Pirates had different regional names. "Buccaneer" was used in the Caribbean and along the Atlantic seaboard of the Americas. The term was first applied to hunters in the woods and valleys of western Hispaniola (today's Haiti) who lived off the herds of feral hogs and cattle, whose numbers rapidly increased after the first Spanish settlers introduced them into a land without natural predators. Mostly French frontiersmen, these hunters cooked and dried strips of meat over open barbecues, a method borrowed from the indigenous Arawak inhabitants. The word for this process, *boucaner* (meaning to smoke-dry or cure), gave the men their name. They dressed in leather and, with their knives and bloodstained appearance, "looked and smelled like a man from a slaughterhouse," according to Cordingly. By the 1630s, the buccaneers were established on Tortuga, off the north coast of what is now Haiti, and an ideal launching ground for attacks on the merchant vessels using the windward passage between Hispaniola and Cuba. Here the buccaneers formed a loose confederation calling itself the "Brethren of the Coast."

Much of what is known of the Caribbean pirates of Harry Morgan's time comes from Alexander Exquemelin's *Buccaneers of America*. He claimed in his book to "give no stories taken on hearsay, but only those to which I was eyewitness." Born in the French channel port of Honfleur, Exquemelin had arrived on Tortuga about 1666 as an indentured servant. He was sold to a barber-surgeon, learned his master's trade, and gained his freedom. Being "naked and destitute of all human necessities," he wrote, "I determined to enter into the wicked order of the pirates." For five years, he served with the buccaneers under both Henry Morgan and François l'Olonnais, joined them in their raids out of Tortuga and Port Royal, and was paid handsomely for his medical skills. He broke with Morgan after the attack on Panama, in which he participated. Like many of the buccaneers, he believed that Morgan had cheated him. After the raid, Exquemelin returned to Europe where, in Amsterdam, he published his best-seller. He later returned to the Caribbean and in 1697 joined in the combined French and buccaneer attack on Cartagena, again serving as a surgeon to the pirates.

Exquemelin's account of the activities of François l'Olonnais, born Jean-David Nau in western France at Les Sables d'Olonne (hence his nickname, "the man from Olonne"), fully justified l'Olonnais's other designation: "Fléau des Espagnols," or Flail of the Spaniards. A former indentured servant like Exquemelin, he had joined the cattle hunters on Hispaniola and then turned buccaneer. He was a psychopath whose torture and murder of prisoners became so feared throughout the Caribbean that he began to meet with far more determined opposition than most pirates. The merchant ships, Exquemelin said, "fought until they could fight no more."

As well they might, since the man from Olonne was merciless. It was common practice for pirates to torture their prisoners, as Morgan's men had done in Panama to obtain information. The favorite pirate torture was "woolding," after the word for the binding of cords around a mast. Exquemelin describes how slender cords were "twisted about [the] heads, till [the] eyes burst out of the skull." But l'Olonnais clearly enjoyed torturing men as much as he did taking their valuables: "When l'Olonnais had a victim on the rack, if the wretch did not instantly answer his questions he would hack the man to pieces with his cutlass and lick the blood from the blade with this tongue, wishing it might have been the last Spaniard in the world he had thus killed." Eventually l'Olonnais met with a suitably bizarre fate, if we can believe Exquemelin's story that he was captured on the Gulf of Darien, near Panama, by cannibals, hacked to pieces, and roasted limb by limb.

Together with Exquemelin's book, the other major source is Captain Charles Johnson's 1724 *General History of the Pirates*. Since the early 1930s, this book has been attributed to Daniel Defoe and is so listed in most library catalogs. This attribution is retained by Jan Rogozinski in his comprehensive encyclopedia *Pirates!*[4] But Cordingly, following the research of P. N. Furbank and L. R. Owens, claims that not a single piece of documentation links Defoe to the *General History*. Unfortunately nothing much is known about the mysterious Captain Johnson, although his history is the origin of most later accounts, film scripts, and myths about pirates; so even if Defoe is not the author, the problem of distinguishing fact from fiction remains. In one notorious case, however, that of Edward Teach, famous as Blackbeard, Cordingly demonstrates convincingly that Johnson's description was close to the truth. Lieutenant Maynard, who fought him to the death on the deck of his ship in Ocracoke Inlet of Pamlico Sound, North Carolina, in November 1718, wrote later of Captain Teach that he "went by the name of Blackbeard, because he let his beard grow, and tied it up in black ribbons." According to Johnson, Teach used these ribbons to twist his beard up into small tails about his ears, and stuck lighted matches under his hat when ready for action, so that "his eyes naturally looking fierce and wild, made him altogether such a figure, that imagination cannot form an idea of a fury, from Hell, to look more frightful."

---

[4]Jan Rogozinski, *Pirates! An A-Z Encyclopedia: Brigands, Buccaneers, and Privateers in Fact, Fiction, and Legend* (New York and Cambridge, Mass.: Da Capo, 1996). For a recent and accessible edition see Manuel Schonhorn, ed., *A General History of the Pyrates* [attributed to Daniel Defoe] (New York: Dover Publications, 1999).

The Mediterranean pirates of the Barbary Coast were called "corsairs" and operated from Algiers, Tunis, Salé, and other North African ports where the Muslim rulers issued them licenses to attack Christian shipping. Using swift galleys powered by oars and sail, they attacked heavily laden, slow-moving merchantmen; they looted the cargoes, captured the passengers and crew, and held them for ransom or sold them into slavery. Since he was licensed, the corsair was technically a privateer and the term was used without a particular geographic designation in French, Italian, and Portuguese, but in English it applied more restrictively to the Barbary raiders. Piracy was business for the Barbary rulers, and the corsairs formed a guild that tried to regulate it. Although the Barbary states justified their actions as a form of religious warfare, many Christian renegades were prominent in the corsair fleet.

The Barbary corsairs thrived in the shifting and ambiguous maritime zone between Ottoman and Spanish sea power in the Mediterranean. Their bases were strategically placed to prey on the merchant ships using the Strait of Gibraltar. They were most active between 1580 and the late seventeenth century, and returned with increased firepower during the long European wars between 1792 and 1815. "The depredations committed by the Algerine corsairs, on the commerce of the United States" provided the justification for a reluctant Congress in 1794 to approve the construction of the frigates that marked the beginning of the permanent navy. The United States fought a series of indecisive naval engagements with the corsairs between 1801 and 1815, when the Barbary fleet was led by the Glaswegian Peter Lisle, who had converted to Islam, taken the name of Murat Reis, and married the daughter of the pasha of Tripoli. The phrase in the U.S. Marine Corps anthem "to the shores of Tripoli" refers to the seven marines who took part in a harrowing march across the Libyan desert to capture Derna in 1805 on orders from President Thomas Jefferson. Despite this victory, the United States was still obliged to pay a humiliating $60,000 ransom for the crew of the frigate *Philadelphia*, captured by Peter Lisle when the vessel ran aground on a sandbar while trying to mount a blockade of Tripoli harbor.

The literary image of the Barbary pirates, like that of the buccaneers, emerged with their increasing notoriety. Lord Byron's *The Corsair* told the story in couplets of the proud and tyrannical pirate Conrad, who, Cordingly observes, had "the vices of a Gothic villain with the ideals of the noble outlaw." On its day of publication in 1814, *The Corsair*, which would later inspire works by Verdi and Berlioz, sold 10,000 copies and went through seven editions within a month. Ironically, in 1816, a mere two years later, a combined British and Dutch fleet bombarded Algiers, virtually destroying the real corsairs as a serious threat to merchant shipping. Cordingly uses the painting *The Bombardment of Algiers* by George Chambers from the National Maritime Museum in London as the cover illustration of his book, even though he has very little to say about the corsairs and criticizes the moviemakers of Hollywood for putting their pirates into precisely the sort of large, three-masted, heavily gunned vessels from a later phase of warfare that were far removed from the smaller, swifter vessels preferred by the buccaneers in the Caribbean.

Robert Louis Stevenson was more accurate in *Treasure Island* with Long John Silver's parrot, "Cap'n Flint," as when Silver told Jack Hawkins that the bird had been "at Madagascar, and at Malabar, and Surinam, and Providence, and Portobello. She was at the fishing up of the wrecked plate ships. It's there she learned 'Pieces of Eight,' and little wonder; three hundred and fifty thousand of 'em, Hawkins!"

"Pieces of eight" were the most famous coins associated with pirate lore. These coins were eight *reales*—silver coins. Pieces of eight minted in Peru and Mexico bore the Spanish coat of arms on one side and a design representing the pillars of Hercules on the other, symbolizing the limits of the ancient world at the Straits of Gibraltar. To this design, by the eighteenth century, two hemispheres were added in the space between the pillars, representing the New and Old Worlds. The pieces of eight became so familiar in oceanic commerce that the twin pillars eventually became the dollar sign. (Gold coins were *escudos* and the famous doubloon was an eight-*escudo* gold coin.)

II

The ubiquity of Spanish silver and gold coins in pirate narratives was not accidental and helps to explain the historical and geographical background of piracy, something largely missing from Cordingly's book. The early appearance of French, English, and Dutch privateers in Caribbean waters was a response by seafaring nations to Spanish claims of monopoly in the New World and their exploitation of the silver mines in northern Mexico and the High Andes. By the 1570s, Spanish-American silver fed the great demand in Europe and Asia for coinage, trade, and metal for the decorative arts; Spanish silver had a huge effect on Atlantic, and later Pacific, commerce and navigation.

Word of the riches of the New World had spread fast. Only two years after the fall of the Aztec capital in 1521, a French pirate, Jean Fleury, captured two Spanish caravels off Cape St. Vincent, Portugal, and stumbled upon an astounding Aztec treasure plundered by Hernán Cortés: three enormous chests of gold ingots, 500 pounds of gold dust, 680 pounds of pearls, emeralds, topazes, golden masks set with gems, helmets, and feathered cloaks. French privateers soon arrived in the Caribbean. Captain

François le Clerc, known as "Jambe de Bois" because of his wooden leg, sacked Santiago de Cuba in 1554, and the English, in the formidable persons of John Hawkins and Francis Drake, followed.

By the late sixteenth century, in order to protect their ships from raiders, the Spanish established a system of armed convoys between the Caribbean and Europe. Mexican treasure was embarked at Vera Cruz, while the silver from Peru was transported from Nombre de Dios, and later Portobello, on the Isthmus of Panama. At Havana the galleons would rendezvous and take on water and supplies for the voyage to Spain. The outbound fleets from Europe wintered in the well-fortified and sheltered harbor of Cartagena on the northern coast of South America.

The timing of pirate, privateer, and buccaneer attacks on these Spanish ports and treasure fleets thus followed a logical strategy, one governed by geography. French privateers seized and burned Cartagena and Havana in 1559. Sir Francis Drake attacked Nombre de Dios in 1572, and sacked Cartagena in 1585. Spain went to great pains to make the defenses of these harbors as near to being impregnable as was possible, as one can still see from the ramparts of the port of Havana; but by concentrating its forces so largely on protection of the treasure fleets, Spain virtually abandoned the rest of the Caribbean to the freebooters, and the Dutch, French, and English soon filled this void.

The cruising grounds of the buccaneers and the strategic location of their lairs were largely determined by the shipping lanes of the Atlantic, Caribbean, and Indian Oceans—the Bahamas were used to prey on Spanish ships that had left the treasure ports of the Isthmus of Panama and Mexico and were en route to Europe; Tortuga was the place from which to attack merchant ships inbound from Europe and Africa for Jamaica and the Caribbean; and Madagascar was perfectly placed on the path of ships trading in the Indian Ocean. There was also a seasonal pattern to the pirate voyages. The winter months were spent in the Caribbean. In April or May, the buccaneer might head north. Blackbeard was on the coast of Virginia in October 1717. In 1718 he raided Charleston, South Carolina, blockaded the harbor, and held the town to ransom. In the intervening winters, he plundered ships off St. Kitts and in the Bay of Honduras. Pirates also scavenged off the coast of West Africa in search of gold, ivory, and slaves or rounded the tip of South America as Drake had done to prey on Spanish treasure ships in the Pacific.

Cordingly provides some fresh insights into the rough democracy of pirate life. On a pirate ship the captain was elected, and occasionally deposed, by the votes of the majority of the crew. In most cases it was the crew, not the captain, who decided the destination of pirate voyages and when to attack. John Rackam, known also as Calico Jack because of his colorful clothes, took command of a pirate vessel in 1718 by challenging a captain who had declined to attack a French frigate in the windward passage. Henry Avery, also known as Long Ben, was a former Royal Navy midshipman who took over the privateer *Charles* in 1694 in Spanish waters when her captain was found wanting and was incapacitated by drink. Avery renamed the ship *Fancy* and set sail for Madagascar and the Red Sea where, lying in wait for pilgrim ships outbound from India to Mecca, he captured and looted the *Ganj-i-Sawai*, the largest ship belonging to the great mogul of India, a raid that earned each man a thousand pounds. Avery's feat was soon celebrated on the London stage at the Theatre Royal in Drury Lane in 1713 in a long-running melodrama titled *The Successful Pirate*, which, Cordingly observes, began a long line of pirate melodramas, later parodied in Gilbert and Sullivan's light opera. Avery himself died a pauper in the fishing port of Bideford, in Devon, having been cheated out of his riches by local traders and "not being worth as much as would buy a coffin."

The crews of the pirate vessels often signed written articles. These set the rules for behavior aboard the ship and for the distribution of plunder, and established rates of compensation for injuries (600 pieces of eight for the loss of the right arm, 500 for a left arm, 100 each for the loss of an eye or a finger). Cheating fellow pirates brought severe retribution. Under the articles drawn up by the men led by Bartholomew Roberts, defrauding the company was punished by marooning—that is, by setting the offending sailor ashore on some uninhabited cape or island. Where "robbery was only betwixt one another," after the "slitting of ears and nose of him that was guilty," the offending pirate was left off in a region known to be inhabited. The articles of Roberts's crew set the time for lights out at eight o'clock. After that hour those "still . . . inclined for drinking" had to go on the open deck.

Pirate flags were red and black, emblazoned with skulls, bleeding hearts, hourglasses, spears, cutlasses, and whole skeletons. By 1730, the skull and crossbones on a black cloth had edged out other symbols and was adopted by English, French, and Spanish pirates in the West Indies. Captain Richard Hawkins, captured by pirates in 1724, described how they "hoisted Jolly Roger (for so they call their black ensign, in the middle of which is a large white skeleton with a dart in one hand, striking a bleeding heart, and in the other an hourglass). When they fight under Jolly Roger, they give quarter, which they do not when they fight under the red or bloody flag."

During the early eighteenth century, pirates were young men whose average age was twenty-seven. Many pirate captains refused to take on married men. Edward Low of Boston was adamant that "he might have none with him under the influence of such powerful attractives as a wife and children, lest they should grow uneasy in his service. . . ." Article Six of one pirate code of conduct decreed "no boy or woman to be allowed amongst them. If any man were to be found seducing any of the latter sex, and carried her to sea, disguised, he was to suffer death." The historian B. R. Burg suggested some years ago that all-male pirate crews were often homosexual.[5] Cordingly is not convinced (nor was Christopher Hill),[6] though he is less sure about the proclivities of the naval ship captains and their young servants and cabin boys. He points to the case of Samuel Norman, which he discovered among the papers of the High Court of Admiralty. Captain Norman was being bathed by the fourteen-year-old Richard Mandervell while his ship was anchored in Oporto, and "had the carnal use of him & was then guilty of the crime commonly called buggery or sodomy & he twice afterwards used the Informant in the same way. . . ."

Captain Norman's behavior, however, does not really get at the broader question that Burg raised. Portuguese shopkeepers in Brazil, their sexual activity in no way constrained by the all-male companionship of a ship at sea, were regularly investigated by the Inquisition for their pursuit of shop-boys. Captain Norman, anchored off Oporto, could have gone ashore for female companionship had he so desired. Rogozinski is more to the point in *Pirates!* when he describes how buccaneers recognized a same-sex relationship called *matelotage*—comrades who were "mates," shared hardships, fought side-by-side, and pooled possessions.[7] The pirate captain Edmund Cook sailed for many years with an unnamed servant who was captured and forced to confess that "his Master had oft times Buggered him in England . . . in Jamaica . . . ; and once in these seas before Darien." The confession apparently did not offend the rest of the crew. Bartholomew Sharp returned to England in 1682 with a sixteen-year-old Spanish boy captured in South America, and Captain George Shelvocke infuriated his crew by promoting his cabin boy to first mate.

There were cross-dressing female pirates, the most famous being Mary Read and Anne Bonny, who sailed with Captain John "Calico Jack" Rackam, out of New Providence in the Bahamas. At their trial for piracy in 1720, in the town of St. Jago de la Vega, today Jamaica's Spanish Town, one of the witnesses against them, Dorothy Thomas, said: "Each of them had a machet and pistol in their hands, and cursed and swore at the men, to murder the deponent [i.e., Thomas]; and that they should kill her, to prevent her coming against them; and the deponent further said, that the reason of her knowing and believing them to be women then was by the largeness of their breasts." Read and Bonny, "largeness of their breasts" notwithstand-

---

[5]B. R. (Barry Richard) Burg, *Sodomy and the Perception of Evil: English Sea Rovers in the Seventeenth-Century Caribbean* (New York: New York University Press, 1982).
[6]Christopher Hill, "Jolly Rogers," *New York Review of Books*, May 12, 1983.
[7]Rogozinski, *Pirates!*, 217–218.

ing, had fallen in love, each thinking the other to be a man, or so they told Calico Jack. Convicted of piracy, they were sentenced to death by hanging, but were reprieved at the last moment when both were found to be pregnant. Calico Jack suffered the fate of many convicted of piracy. He was put in an iron cage, hanged from a gibbet on Deadman's Cay, a small island within sight of Port Royal now known as Rackam's Cay, and his corpse was coated in tar to preserve it as a warning to others.

The pirate crews were multinational and multiracial. Dutch smugglers and pirates appeared in the Caribbean after Dutch traders were expelled from the Iberian peninsula in 1598, and Dutch freelance marauders continued to attack ships in the West Indies into the early eighteenth century. French privateers were active in the Caribbean in the early eighteenth century, and Spanish coast guards often launched freelance attacks on the English colonies. Cordingly finds that the pirates based on the island of New Providence in the Bahamas between 1715 and 1725 were mostly English-speaking—35 percent of them were from England, 25 percent from the American colonies, 20 percent from the West Indies, 10 percent Scots. The rest were Swedes, Dutch, French, Spanish, and Portuguese. Among the English, most came from London and the West Country.

The crews of the pirate vessels often included black Africans. Cordingly assumes that they were slaves and believes that however contemptuous the white pirates might have been of the customs of their day, they were not likely to accept blacks as equal partners. But this seems a hasty judgment. African seamen had participated in the oceanic voyages of the Portuguese for over two centuries before the buccaneers roamed the same seas. The Japanese screen paintings depicting the arrival of the Portuguese carracks in Nagasaki Bay in the sixteenth century show African sailors on the riggings. That pirates stole and sold slaves as part of their booty in no way precluded the participation of black pirates in the looting and selling of human cargoes, any more than it prevented Africans from selling other Africans into slavery.

III

Yet as the power of Spain declined and that of France and Britain rose, the pirates began to be perceived in a very different manner; they were no longer seen as potential allies in times of adversity, as the old privateers had been, but as enemies of good commerce. How, Cordingly asks, was it that the pirates acquired a heroic and relatively benign image? The answer lies in early pirate literature in English, which often conflates the anti-Spanish privateers of Elizabethan England with the predators of a later epoch. Against the background of a powerful anti-Spanish and anti-Catholic tradition, it is not surprising that the people who read pirate stories in the late seventeenth and early eighteenth centuries displayed no great sympathy for the Spanish victims. In any case, "singeing King Philip's beard," and those of his successors, was seen as the patriotic duty of any good Englishman (or Welshman), pirate or privateer; and such was in essence Captain Morgan's justification for his atrocities in Panama.

Already by Morgan's later years, however, there was grumbling about his unsuitability to hold official positions in Jamaica and, in many ways, he was identified with the old Caribbean at a time when the prospects for freelance plunder were rapidly diminishing. Sugarcane cultivation was rapidly expanding in the West Indies as was sugar consumption in Britain, and so too was the importation of slaves from Africa. The merchants and the slave traders backed by powerful commercial and political interests in London, Bristol, and Liverpool had little time for the buccaneers; and following the Treaty of Utrecht in 1713 the English obtained the formal right (the *asiento*) to supply slaves to the Spanish American markets. By the eighteenth century, the British were learning, as were the French, that it was easier to subvert the Spanish Empire from within than to attack it on the high seas. It was better to use the credits of London merchants to take indirect control of Spanish American trade, and smuggle and barter along the coasts of South and Central America than to loot and destroy potential customers. And the pirates no longer confined their attacks to the Spanish. As wealth and power shifted in the Atlantic shipping lanes, it was the English who became the object of pirate assaults.

Around 1720, at the time of peak pirate activity in the Atlantic, the pirates were thought to number about two thousand in all. Within a decade they were reduced to fewer than two hundred. As soon as the British government decided to respond in force, the pirates stood little chance. The Royal Navy in 1718 had sixty-seven ships of the line. Even the smallest of these had fifty guns, equal in force to Blackbeard's *Queen Anne's Revenge*, the largest pirate vessel. Changes in the law in 1700 made it possible thereafter to try to impose the death sentence in Vice-Admiralty Courts overseas. One of the first cases took place in Boston in 1704, when John Quelch, after plundering along the coast of Brazil, made the mistake of returning to the port of Marblehead, where he had seized his vessel. Quelch and six of his crew were sentenced to death. After a barrage of sermons from the Reverend Cotton Mather, they were hanged on the shoreline by Hudson's Point.

To comply with the jurisdiction of the lord high admiral, all such hangings took place from gallows set up "within the flood marks," since his authority was held to extend up to the low-tide line. Between 1716 and 1726, four hundred men were hanged for piracy by such courts around the Atlantic seaboard, from Port Royal to Barbados, to New Providence, to London, and from Boston to the Cape coast of West Africa. Captain Woodes Rogers, a famous former privateer, was sent to New Providence as governor of the Bahamas in 1718 at the request of the merchants of Bristol and London, and proved to be one of the most effective scourges of the pirates. Woodes Rogers, accompanied by the buccaneer William Dampier, had captured a Manila galleon in 1709, one of only two English privateers to do so, and circumnavigating the world, returned to London in 1711 with gold bullion, precious stones, and silks valued at 800,000 English pounds. He had also rescued the castaway sailor Alexander Selkirk, said to be the model for Defoe's *Robinson Crusoe* (1719), from the Juan Fernandez Islands off the coast of Chile. A poacher turned gamekeeper, Woodes Rogers sent out the naval ships to capture Calico Jack, Anne Bonny, and Mary Read. The coat of arms granted to the colony of Bahamas in 1728 summed up the new situation. It portrayed a Royal Navy warship with three more in the background, and bears the motto *Expulsis Piratis, Restituta Commercia* (Pirates Expelled, Commerce Restored). Woodes Rogers commissioned a family portrait from the young William Hogarth in 1729. In it he sits comfortably in an armchair before the Fort at Nassau, a globe by his side represents his voyage around the world, his son holds open a map of New Providence Island, and in the harbor a warship fires a salute. After the 1730s, pirates were best left to novelists and playwrights. Commerce replaced plunder.

Yet out of the rich mixture of fact and fiction of the early eighteenth century, the pirate genre emerged in which the works of J. M. Barrie and Robert Louis Stevenson were sold along with adventures of earnest amateur sleuths and treasure hunters; where ancient sea chests were found to have secret compartments, and ambiguous ink blots on old charts were claimed to represent, at the same time, Pacific atolls, islets off the coast of Indochina, or Gardiner's Island off Montauk. The early-eighteenth-century pirate narratives, cleaned up a bit, of course, have been taken over by Disney World and dozens of Hollywood B movies.

I was delighted to find, the other day, my well-thumbed copy of *Treasure Island*, a present from my father when I was seven. It brought back memories of summer rambles along the coastlines and bays of Devon and Cornwall. Doubtless with the intention of keeping me quiet, he used to promise that around the corner of some profusely hedgerowed seaside lane, or beyond some bracken-clad headland, or at the edge of some rocky inlet or cove, we would find the Admiral Benbow Inn. For boys growing up in the west of England, Drake, Hawkins, Raleigh, and assorted sea dogs, freebooters, smugglers, and pirates, real or invented, were part of popular culture. Cordingly has, to some degree, set out to clarify and debunk this rich imagined heritage. So it was some relief to discover in his book, all these years later, that even if the Admiral Benbow Inn did not exist, Admiral John Benbow did. An opponent of pirates, Spaniards, and the French, he died heroically of his wounds off Cartagena in 1702, after his right leg was smashed by chain shot and he refused to leave the quarterdeck.

BAY OF PANAMA, FROM THE SOUTHEASTERN RAMPART.

CHAPTER 5

Hegemonies Old and New

"The universal monarchy of the Seas."
—Abbé Raynal, 1770

If we look at the Atlantic in the eighteenth century, it seems to me that we still lack a comprehensive view of what changed during this period, where we should set its boundaries, and how we might interpret the salient characteristics of the century. Perhaps, we have been both too general and too specific, simultaneously seeking with the synthesizers to explain too much and with the more specialized monographic literature to explain too little.

If we begin in the South, which is my own starting point, this is a frustrating situation. Because our historiography on the Ibero-American and Afro-American Atlantic is still in a state of development, not to say underdevelopment, we are often forced to establish context and frameworks out of thin air, to ask what must appear from the perspective of the more developed historiographers of the North Atlantic to be obvious, foolish, and even naive questions. We are obliged, I think, to look at the "big picture" if only to see if what happens in our sphere has any resonance elsewhere. I will try to tackle two themes. The first relates very broadly to economic chronologies within the Portuguese and Spanish Atlantic and whether what we see here allows us to speak sensibly of an Atlantic system in the eighteenth century, and what the dimension and limits of such a system might be. The second theme relates more to geopolitics and questions of empire or, if you will, of imperial hegemonies and the challenges that these hegemonies faced as the century ended.

I

We are of course confined to some degree, as we must be in any historical speculation, not only by our own research but by what our colleagues have chosen to write about. And inasmuch as history writing since the Second World War has tended to deemphasize the role of individuals, of institutions, and of events—instead plotting the longer-term trends in economic development and delineating social and economic structures—the recent decades have seen an accumulation of more information about the first theme, the economic aspects of the Portuguese and Spanish Atlantic systems, than about the second, the policies and politics of empire. While much has been achieved by the emphasis on conjunctural economic analysis and social history, it has unquestionably also led to the almost total exclusion of detailed examinations of elites, institutions, and above all intellectual life and politics and policy. Hence, today, if we look at the late colonial period of the Spanish and Portuguese empires in America, we tend to know more about slaves than their masters, more about the forced Indian labor drafts of the Andes than the attitudes of Peruvian merchants and bureaucrats in Lima, more about Mexican silver production than the political role of mining entrepreneurs. The best book on the Enlightenment in Latin America, for example, remains the collection of essays edited by the late Arthur Whitaker in the early 1940s, twice reissued in the early 1960s but long since out of print.[1]

The end of our period is also compromised by the consequences of colonial emancipation in the sense that a relatively cohesive imperial past is fragmented into a series of sometimes spurious national histories, and we can no longer rely on the well-organized archives of the Indies in Seville or of the overseas dominions in Lisbon to help reveal to us what happened—or at least what the record keepers thought happened. For the western shores of the Atlantic we thus have a division of historical output into two broad categories, one of which might be called the vertical dimension, the other the horizontal. By the vertical dimension I mean a form of history writing confined by the geographical limits of what became, after independence, national entities. National histories inevitably stress originality and uniqueness, rather than any common colonial background, and are sometimes hostile to a point of view that would place the new nations that emerged in the Americas within an international or comparative

---

[1]Arthur Preston Whitaker, ed., *Latin America and the Enlightenment* (Ithaca, N.Y.: Cornell University Press, 1961). I am drawing in this section on my chapter, "The Impact of the American Revolution on Spain and Portugal and Their Empires," in *The Blackwell Encyclopedia of the American Revolution*, ed. Jack P. Greene and J. R. Pole (Cambridge, Mass.: Blackwell Reference, 1991), 528–543.

framework, or even within a colonial or neocolonial context. The horizontal dimension is, of course, the comparative one—but this is also something we still largely lack even for North America (with the possible exceptions of Canada and the Caribbean). Despite the heroic efforts of Jack Greene and J. R. Pole, most U.S. historians still seem locked within the concept of the "singularity" of U.S. history. For Latin America the situation is no less extreme. The *Cambridge History of Latin America* (1984–), for example, is almost totally devoid of comparative analysis, especially in its colonial and early national volumes, a factor emphasized by the ease with which the original volumes are now being subdivided and reissued as what are essentially national histories. And a final caveat: According to a popular textbook, *Early Latin America*, by James Lockhart and Stuart B. Schwartz (Cambridge University Press, 1983), national independence is, in any case, a shadow thing at best. As they put it, "It has been said often and truly that the division between colonial and national periods is an artificial one, especially in the social, economic, and cultural domains where so much current scholarly interest lies." But if this is true, the eighteenth century becomes a mere blip on a very broad canvas. It is significant that Schwartz and Lockhart have long been leading rejectionists of what they call "institutional history," by which they appear to mean essentially Atlantic history and the history of European ("Eurocentric") colonialism, including the great works on Atlantic commerce and navigation written by their immediate predecessors, such as C. H. Haring, Richard Pares, and Vincent Harlow. Not all revisionists have taken this narrow view. Radical comparativists like Susan Deeds and Edward Countryman see the political emancipation from Europe as a critical transition, which at the very least requires an inquiry into the place of North and South America within the process of industrial, political, and social transformation that flowed from the circum-Atlantic upheavals of the late eighteenth century, of which the American Revolution was the most dramatic colonial manifestation.[2] The question they raise is one Stanley and Barbara Stein raised some time ago,[3] that is, why at independence did the histories of South and North America diverge so dramatically; or to put it in Immanual Wallerstein's terms, how was it that North America moved from the periphery to the core of the world system, while Latin America remained peripheral?[4]

---

[2]Susan Deeds and Edward Countryman, "Independence and Revolution in the Americas," *Radical History* 27 (May 1983).

[3]Stanley J. Stein and Barbara H. Stein, *The Colonial Heritage of Latin America; Essays on Economic Dependence in Perspective* (New York: Oxford University Press, 1970).

[4]Immanuel Wallerstein, *The Modern World System*, 2 vols. (New York: Academic Press, 1980).

Currently there are two major interpretive frameworks for examining the impact of the North Atlantic democratic revolution in Latin America. First, there is the Robert Palmer–Jacques Godechot vision of an Atlantic-based transformation, an essentially political and institutional view, which sees mutual influence in political theory, constitutional experimentation, and the politics of democratic incorporation. In this view, the Enlightenment is a positive, benign, and causative influence, essentially a progressive force.[5]

A second view is a more economic view—partly Marxian but also capable of incorporating much of classical liberalism; that is, it is a view that sees a general crisis of the old colonial system which affects the British Empire in the 1770s and the Spanish and Portuguese empires in the early nineteenth century, all of which flows from the shift from commercial to industrial capitalism. In this view, the intellectual contribution is minimal. The revolutions in America, both North and South, represent a shift from formal to informal domination, with the newly industrializing states of Europe—especially Great Britain—replacing the decaying bureaucratic and mercantilist empires of Spain and Portugal.

Brazilian historians such as Fernando Novais have also been concerned to place the late-eighteenth and early-nineteen-century experience of Brazil within the context of a crisis of the old regime of the old colonial system in the face of the Atlantic and Industrial revolutions.[6] Less work of this nature has been done on Spanish America, although Tulio Halperín has long focused on the economic and political complexities of the independence period in the La Plata region and more broadly in Spanish America.[7] And Nancy Farriss, in her brilliant book on the Maya, sees the impact of the reformist protoliberal policies of the Spanish Bourbons as marking the critical divide in the history of Meso-America.[8] Much of the new economic history of late colonial Mexico is seeking some explanation for the paradox of the coexisting boom and rising social tensions within

---

[5]R. R. (Robert Roswell) Palmer, *The Age of Democratic Revolutions,* 2 vols. (Princeton: Princeton University Press, 1959 and 1964); Jacques Godechot, *Les Révolutions, 1770–1799* (Paris: Presses Universitaires de France, 1970) and *L'Europe et l'Amérique à l'époque napoléonienne, 1800–1815* (Paris: Presses Universitaires de France, 1967).

[6]Fernando Novais, *Portugal e Brasil na crise do antigo sistema colonial, 1777–1808* (São Paulo: Editora HUCITEC, 1979). Also see Emília Viotti da Costa, "Introdução ao estudo da emancipação política do Brasil," in *Brasil em perspectiva,* ed. Carlos Guilherme Mota (São Paulo: Difusão Européia do Livro, 1969).

[7]Tulio Halperín Donghi, *Reforma y disolución de los imperios ibéricos, 1750–1850* (Madrid: Alianza Editorial, 1985).

[8]Nancy Farriss, *Maya Society under Colonial Rule: The Collective Enterprise of Survival* (Princeton: Princeton University Press, 1984).

the most important of Spain's colonial holdings in the Western Hemisphere. And we have the now substantial body of new writing on the Bourbon reforms in Spanish America with major contributions by John Lynch, John Fisher, and David Brading. Yet, it seems to me that mainstream economic historians remain skeptical about the significance of the Atlantic-based commercial system to the onset of industrialization. The important point about these disagreements is how "scatter shot" they are and to emphasize how very little explicit discussion we have had about the broader context of some of the most critical elements in eighteenth-century Atlantic history and their implications.

Perhaps we would be better off speaking of process, which involves, in part, a rethinking of the history of ideas within their social and economic context—again, looking from the South, which is my basic perspective here. For Latin America and the Iberian powers, this involves very much a new look at the impact of the ideas of the Enlightenment, which for Spain under Charles III (1759–1788) and Portugal during the predominance of the Marquês de Pombal (1750–1777) led to major reforms in the management of colonial affairs. This was motivated in both cases by a decision to fortify their colonial links, retake the benefits of Atlantic commerce from their northern competitors, and reestablish their power and prosperity by adapting the techniques they believed Britain and France, in particular, had used to surpass them. These measures by Portugal and Spain in some instances served also to preempt and in others to mitigate the impact of the North American revolution, although neither Spanish nor Portuguese America was able to avoid the consequences of the late-eighteenth-century European upheavals. Second, however, it is important to look not only from South to North but also from the North to South. The issue of revolution as example and as potentiality, involving the creative articulation of new institutional mechanisms of government was a central concern to would-be anticolonialists in the late eighteenth century. In both Brazil during the late 1780s and in Spanish America in the aftermath of the wars of independence, the North American constitutional model proved attractive. Yet, thirdly, we are also dealing with colonial opposition to metropolitan powers and it is this aspect, of course, the achievement of national independence, where the ambiguity of the Iberian and Ibero-American role in the Atlantic as a whole is most apparent. Spain was an important component of the European alliance that helped the thirteen colonies in North America escape from British rule. Many would-be Latin American nationalists on the other hand saw Britain, the erstwhile colonial power, as a potential ally against Spain for their own independence movements. Process, therefore, is a critical element in the period because we are dealing with a complex interaction between two aspects of the Enlightenment—its absolutist form which involved a reformulation of imperial policy along neomercantilist lines, as well as a reassertion of the rights of the state on the one hand, as opposed to its more liberal form on the other, where the Enlightenment provided a guide to experimentation with new forms of governance and constitution making, defining thereby the rights of the individual within the process of decolonization. Both imply a de-linking of previously set patterns and upsetting, changing, and resetting of the institutional context within which collectivities define themselves.

II

How do the Portuguese and Spanish Atlantic fit into this picture? The case of Portugal and Brazil is especially interesting, given the Atlantic focus of their trade, Brazil's large slave population and consequent links to Africa, and the interpenetration of the Luso-Atlantic system via Lisbon by the British-dominated commercial system of the North Atlantic. But first it is essential to establish the parameters of the system we are talking about— for, if the eighteenth-century Luso-Atlantic commercial system is characterized overwhelmingly by the rise of gold production in Brazil and its subsequent fall, both cycles took place within a broader framework which changed surprisingly little between the 1660s and 1807, the year of the Napoleonic invasion of Portugal. Hence, we are here talking about what I would call the long eighteenth century. Let me look briefly at the origins of this long eighteenth century and explain why I take these origins back to the 1660s.

The Dutch assault on the Portuguese overseas possession during the mid-seventeenth century had been transatlantic in scope. The Dutch were well aware that control of the sugar-producing northeast of Brazil was useless to them unless they also controlled the source of slaves in Africa. Hence, in 1641, the Dutch seized the slave supply port of Luanda, the capital of Portuguese Angola, the slave transshipment depot located on the offshore island of São Tomé, as well as the sugar-producing Brazilian captaincy of Pernambuco. These Dutch successes, however, were temporary. In 1648, an expeditionary force mounted by the Portuguese governor of Rio de Janeiro retook Angola, and after a long and bitter guerrilla campaign in Pernambuco the Dutch were expelled from Recife in 1654.[9]

The Portuguese victories in Africa and Brazil were not repeated in the Orient. The 1650s, in fact, saw Portuguese power virtually eliminated in Asia, or at least reduced to a shadow of what it had been in the sixteenth century. The oceanic dimension of Portuguese imperial interest, therefore,

---

[9]C. R. (Charles Ralph) Boxer, *Salvador de Sá and the Struggle for Brazil and Angola, 1602–1680* (London: Athlone Press, 1952).

from the 1660s until the early nineteenth century came to be preeminently focused on the South Atlantic. As early as 1644, moreover, direct trade between Bahia and the West African coast had been authorized, Bahia exporting tobacco and importing slaves. These trading and commercial links between South America and West Africa remained important well into the nineteenth century, making Bahian merchants involved in African trade wealthy and virtually independent of Lisbon.

On the mainland of South America, the northern and southern frontiers of the Portuguese dominions were also established, or, at least, the claims to these frontiers were staked out in the seventeenth century. In 1670, for instance, the bishopric of Rio de Janeiro was created, its jurisdiction reaching in theory to the northern banks of the Rio de la Plata. In 1680, the Portuguese established a "new colony" (*Nova Colonia do Sacramento*) opposite the Spanish port city of Buenos Aires. The reaction of the Spaniards was rapid and Nova Colonia was seized after only a few months. But, in 1681, the Portuguese reestablished and fortified the outpost. The issue of the Portuguese presence on the Rio de la Plata caused continuous friction with Spain. Despite several treaties, the problem was not resolved and remained after the independence of both Spanish and Portuguese America to complicate the relations between the successor states.

In the far north, the Amazon frontier also remained subject to dispute—in this case by France, which had in 1676 established a strategic presence on the coast of South America in Cayenne. French interest in Brazil, in fact, did not abate throughout the eighteenth century, despite the fact that in 1712, following the War of Spanish Succession, France formally renounced all claims to the left bank of the Amazon.

In the late seventeenth century, therefore, the focus of Portugal's imperial interest shifted decisively westward from the trading-post thassalocracy of the Indian Ocean first established in the early sixteenth century to the plantation-based colonies of the South Atlantic. The Afro-American Atlantic commercial complex which had predated the Asian empire and thrived even while overshadowed by the Asian spice trade now came fully into its own.[10] Within the South Atlantic system itself, integrated by the triangular interdependence of Lisbon, the slaving enclaves of the West and Central African coast, and the expanding colonies of European and African settlements in Portuguese America, imperial priorities were reordered to favor support of Portugal's territorial empire in Brazil.

Portuguese America in the 1650s was also very different from the collection of small coastal enclaves it had been sixty years before at the time of the union of the crowns of Spain and Portugal. The development of a fleet

---

[10]Kenneth Maxwell, "Portugal, Europe, and the Origins of the Atlantic Commercial System, 1415–1520," *Portuguese Studies* 8 (1992): 3–16.

system between Lisbon and Brazil in the immediate aftermath of Portugal's independence from Spain, and the imposition of heavier customs duties to support the construction of warships at midcentury as well as the newly imposed monopoly of the Brazil company, proved advantageous to the south of Brazil which had previously competed under serious disabilities in terms of access to European markets with Bahia and Pernambuco. The sugar ships from all the Brazilian regions now arrived at Lisbon together. The escort vessels left Rio de Janeiro toward the end of March and picked up the sugar ships of Bahia in April, the fleet arriving at Lisbon during early July or August.

Between the mid-1640s and 1650, sugar prices were high in Europe, but after that date the price of Brazilian sugar plummeted on the Amsterdam market, falling constantly until the 1680s. The major cause was competition from the Caribbean. The Dutch, and later the British, were developing their own sugar trade, and in the case of the British beginning to develop a system of preferential tariffs to protect British markets for British-grown Caribbean sugar. The response of the Brazilian sugar sector to this loss of markets is very imperfectly understood, and little research has been done on the second half of the seventeenth century. There are some indications of attempts by Brazil mill owners to lower costs by vertically integrating their enterprise. The Jesuit-managed Sergipe mill in Bahia, for instance, which had relied entirely on sharecropping arrangements in the early years of the century, was directly producing 60 percent of its own cane by the 1680s. Producers also managed to transfer some of their losses to salaried employees whose wages suffered a substantial real decline over the second half of the seventeenth century.[11]

The social and political consequences of the new economic situation were significant. Planters and mill owners tended to lose their dominant position in urban institutions. Certainly, merchants began to hold positions of importance in prestigious urban voluntary lay organizations, such as the *misericórdia* in the Brazilian port cities. And in the municipal government the old planter domination was challenged by the appointment of a university-trained lawyer as presiding officer (*juiz de fora*) and the appearance (at least in Bahia in 1641) of representatives of the urban artisan population, the "people's tribune" (*juiz do povo*).[12]

At the same time, the municipal councils in Brazil were acquiring added importance in the broader imperial context. This autonomy was undoubtedly enhanced by the fact that the recovery of Pernambuco from the Dutch

---

[11]Stuart B. Schwartz, *Sugar Plantations and the Formation of Brazilian Society: Bahia, 1550–1835* (Cambridge and New York: Cambridge University Press, 1985).
[12]A. J. R. Russell-Wood, *Fidalgos and Philanthropists: The Santa Casa da Misericórdia of Bahia, 1550–1755* (Berkeley: University of California Press, 1968).

had resulted as much from the actions of the inhabitants themselves and their allies from São Paulo and Bahia within Brazil as from the intervention by Lisbon. Indeed, the Pernambucans had been prepared at one point to seek the support of the Catholic monarch of France when the aid of Portugal for their cause had seemed problematical. The municipal councils had raised money for defense. They subsequently instigated a vigorous opposition to the monopoly of the Brazil company, and with the aid of the Inquisition (which opposed the privileges granted to New Christian bankers who had invested in the Brazil company) they succeeded in destroying the company's monopolies in 1659. The fleet system which had been imposed at the time of the company's establishment, however, was retained and continued to operate under the administrative direction of a new Lisbon-based board of commerce (*junta do comércio*). The Brazilian municipal councils, however, were represented in Lisbon by procurators; and the council of Bahia acquired the right in 1653 of sending two representatives to the Cortes, Portugal's ancient parliamentary institution. This was a privilege of some importance because the Cortes played a vital part in the years following the restoration of Portuguese independence, meeting eight times between 1641 and 1698. Peace with Spain in 1668 and the treaties with the Dutch in 1661 and 1688 and with the English in 1654 and 1662 had been bought at considerable cost in terms of special privileges granted to foreign merchants and indemnities paid, including the theoretical right of British merchants to reside in Brazil, something which in practice was rigorously opposed.[13]

The weakness of Portugal undoubtedly contributed to the relative autonomy of Brazilian institutions. Portugal was well aware of the need to treat Brazilians with care and respect since Portugal's power to coerce obedience was very limited. By the 1690s Brazilian sugar no longer dominated world markets. It did not, however, disappear from circulation. Brazilian white sugar was of high quality and remained an important export (and for Lisbon reexport) item. The major positive impact of sugar's relative decline in value was to stimulate diversification and give new incentive to exploration and expansion into the vast hinterland of South America. Tobacco, for instance, became a key Brazilian export to both Portugal and Africa; the quantity of tobacco sent to Portugal doubled between 1662 and 1672. Attempts were made to introduce cloves and cinnamon from Asia

---

[13]Carl Hanson, *Economy and Society in Baroque Portugal, 1668–1703* (Minneapolis: University of Minnesota Press, 1981); also the classic works by C. R. (Charles Ralph) Boxer, *The Portuguese Seaborne Empire, 1415–1825* (London: Hutchinson, 1969) and *The Golden Age of Brazil, 1695–1750: Growing Pains of a Colonial Society* (Berkeley: Published in cooperation with the Sociedade de Estudos Históricos Dom Pedro Segundo, Rio de Janeiro, by the University of California Press, 1962).

and to develop a trade in cacao. The cattle frontier was also pushing inland, opening up connections between the São Francisco river valley and the São Paulo plateau. With *paulista* aid the long-lasting complex of fugitive slave settlements known as *Palmares* in the backlands between Pernambuco and Alagoas was destroyed. Since 1670 the Crown had also used the *paulistas* extensively for systematic exploration of the interior, rewarding them with the titles of nobility and membership in the chivalric military orders.

The most dramatic and decisive consequence of Portuguese exploration of the interior, however, was the discovery of gold. The search for precious metals had of course brought many of the first Europeans to the Western Hemisphere, and also provoked the most audacious explorations of the vast interior of South and North America, and the Spanish had been well rewarded for their early explorations. In the Caribbean within months of Columbus's landfall, gold had been discovered. During the 1540s in the barren mountains of the Andes, the Spaniards came upon a vast mountain of silver at Potosí in present-day Bolivia, and in Mexico along the eastern slope of the Sierra Madre they were no less successful in exploiting silver ore. The Portuguese, on the other hand, were less fortunate. For almost two hundred years after Portugal laid claims to the territory which became known as Brazil, they had to make do with more prosaic products—first Brazil wood used to produce red dye, then sugar, hides, cacao, and to-bacco—worthy and valuable products all, but the precious metals the early settlers hoped for eluded them. At the end of the seventeenth century, however, half-Indian frontiersmen from the small inland settlement of São Paulo struck it rich. São Paulo was a resource-poor community which made its living by capturing and selling Indian slaves and raiding the prosperous Jesuit missions in Paraguay. The *paulistas* were ever on the lookout for booty. In the 1690s, after years of searching, they eventually came across rich deposits of alluvial gold in the streams along the flanks of the mountain range of Espinhaço, which runs north-south between the present-day cities of Ouro Preto and Diamantina in the state of Minas Gerais across the great interior plateau of Brazil. Three hundred and fifty miles inland from the port city of Rio de Janeiro, the Mantiquira range marked the watershed for the great north-flowing São Francisco River, as well as for the tributaries which flowed south into the vast La Plata river basin. As word spread, avid speculators used both river systems to reach the gold field and within a decade of the *paulistas'* discovery, the first great gold rush of modern history was in full swing. More than anything else, it was gold that pushed Portuguese settlements deep into the interior of Brazil—first to Minas Gerais, later to Goiás and Mato Grosso—well beyond the traditional sphere of Portuguese interest determined by the Treaty of Tordesillas. The issue of the interior frontier hence became a matter of acute concern to the courts of both Lisbon and Madrid.

As the negotiations for a treaty to establish boundaries between Portuguese and Spanish America progressed during the 1740s, it became generally accepted that clear topographical landmarks such as rivers and mountains should serve to delineate frontiers. The Portuguese had two major bargaining chips. First, they held Colonia do Sacramento on the east bank of the Plate Estuary. Second, the westernmost Portuguese mining region, in what is now Mato Grosso, had been integrated administratively and economically with the northern Brazilian coast by means of a fluvial transportation and communications route running along the Guaporé, Mamoré, and Madeira Rivers in the western Amazonia basin. When an agreement was finally reached, these rivers constituted the northwestern border of Portuguese lands, much to the satisfaction of authorities in Lisbon.[14]

It was within these broader geographical limits that the economic characteristics of the long eighteenth-century Portuguese-Atlantic system need to be seen. They were therefore, first and foremost, marked by the flow of specie (gold and silver, the latter obtained from the contraband trade with the Spanish) and the preeminence of colonial, mainly Brazilian, staples. Second, the growth, decline, and revival of the manufacturing industry in Portugal were inversely proportional to the rise and fall of gold production in the Brazilian interior. That is to say, Portuguese domestic manufacturing thrived prior to 1700 and again after 1777, but languished during the golden age. This had major implications for the Portuguese foreign and colonial policy. Portugal also remained throughout the eighteenth century a chronic grain importer—from Northern Europe at the beginning of the century and from North America, especially Virginia and the Carolinas, toward the end. This fact during the 1780s and 1790s had a major impact on the attitudes of the new North American republic, for example, marked especially in the person of Thomas Jefferson, toward protonationalist republican movements in Brazil. These attitudes were ambivalent at best when Virginia's trade with Portugal was placed in the balance against support for nationalist movements for independence from Portugal of uncertain origin in Portugal's vast South American territories.

The third important characteristic of the long eighteenth century was the British presence in Portugal and indirectly within its empire, protected by treaties and exercising de facto extraterritorial rights and privileges much on the pattern later imposed during the nineteenth century on China. For example, the whole period from the late 1660s through 1807

---

[14]David M. Davidson, "How the Brazilian West Was Won," in *Colonial Roots of Modern Brazil*, ed. Dauril Alden (Berkeley: University of California Press, 1973), 61–106; J. R. (José Roberto) do Amaral Lapa, *Economía colonial* (São Paulo: Editora Perspectiva, 1973).

was marked by the dominant—the Portuguese felt—domineering presence of influential British merchant communities established in Lisbon and Oporto. The British merchants in Lisbon and Oporto were organized within so-called factories, which were in effect legally recognized commercial corporations, their privileges guaranteed by the Cromwellian treaty of 1657, reinforced by the Methuen Treaty of 1703. Through their entrepreneurial skills and access to capital, British merchants penetrated the whole fabric of the metropolitan and colonial economy.[15]

The need for external political and military support was at the core of the commercial concessions Portugal had made to the British and others in the seventeenth century. This need remained a basic given throughout the eighteenth century, setting the parameters within which Portuguese foreign and colonial policy had to be conducted. Political and military dependency, however, did not mean there was no room for maneuver in the national interest or options open to a skillful Portuguese nationalist to extract whatever benefits he could from the Anglo-Portuguese relationship. In fact a central preoccupation of Portuguese economic thinkers and diplomats throughout the eighteenth century had been precisely how to achieve balance in what had become an unequal relationship but which intrinsically need not be so if a true reciprocity could be achieved. Nor did all British economic thinkers see pure benefit in the series of treaties and tariff privileges which governed Anglo-Portuguese commerce. The issue in fact became, as the eighteenth century wore on, a central topic of debate among the leading lights of the new science of political economy engaging Adam Smith and later David Ricardo.[16]

The eighteenth-century Luso-Atlantic world, finally, was caught up in the struggle between France and England, a struggle that increasingly compromised Portugal. Lisbon tried to accommodate both, but by its very Atlantic nature, and because of the central economic role of Brazil within the Luso-Atlantic commercial system, Portugal was tied inextricably to Britain and, although it always sought to remain neutral and thereby retain the prosperous entrepôt function of Lisbon for the reexport of colonial products, it was very rarely able to maintain neutrality for long.

The role of Brazil in Portuguese calculations and diplomacy, economic and institutional, thus held much higher priority than did the colonial weight of North America in British calculations. These preoccupations with the development of the Portuguese Atlantic Empire on the one hand,

---

[15]Kenneth R. Maxwell, *Conflicts and Conspiracies: Brazil and Portugal, 1750–1808* (Cambridge: Cambridge University Press, 1973).

[16]H. E. S. Fisher, *The Portugal Trade: A Study of Anglo-Portuguese Commerce, 1700–1770* (London: Methuen, 1971). Also, Virgílio Noya Pinto, *O ouro brasileiro e o comércio anglo-portugués* (São Paulo: Companhia Editora Nacional, 1979).

and with Portugal's diminished stature and apparent backwardness on the other, permeated the Portuguese intellectual milieu of the age.

The most dramatic reformulation of Portugal's policy toward Brazil occurred during the long period of rule by the Marquês de Pombal, between 1750 and 1777. Pombal himself took much from classic mercantilist theory and practice in his policymaking; both from its British and its French or Colbertian origins, but the use of the term *mercantilism* to describe Pombal's policy is not entirely appropriate. Mercantilism, when defined narrowly, as we know, describes a policy whereby trade is regulated, taxed, and subsidized by the state to promote an influx of gold and silver—the objective of such state intervention being aimed more broadly at achieving a favorable balance of trade.

Pombal's policy was at once limited and more focused than this. Its objective was to use mercantilist techniques—monopoly companies, regulation, taxation, and subsidies—to facilitate capital accumulation by individual Portuguese merchants. This aid to individual Portuguese capitals had wider objectives and consequences because it was part and parcel of a scheme to fortify the nation's bargaining power within the Atlantic commercial system.[17]

The problem for an enlightened Iberian economic nationalist, which is perhaps a more accurate way to describe Pombal, was not so much to encourage the influx of precious metals; this was rarely a problem for Iberian economic policymakers given the fact that Spain, Portugal, and their empires were the principal source of the world's bullion supply in this period, with gold from Brazil and silver from Peru and Mexico. The dilemma was precisely the opposite; that is, policymakers needed to devise measures to retain capital within their own economic system and at the same time to multiply the positive and diminish the negative economic impact of being producers of precious metals. The theory and practice of mercantilism were, after all, the creation of bullion-starved northwestern Europe. The application of the theory and practice of mercantilism in the bullion-rich Iberian Peninsula was bound to be partial because the end of the policy was fundamentally different from that sought by mercantilism's progenitors. The Iberians aimed to retain bullion, the northwest Europeans aimed to attract it.

Pombal's methods reflected, in fact, the peculiarities of Portugal's position within the Atlantic system, and the particular impact on Portuguese entrepreneurship of the Brazilian gold boom of 1700–1760. Essentially, the

---

[17]Kenneth Maxwell, *Pombal: A Paradox of the Enlightenment* (Cambridge and New York: Cambridge University Press, 1995); and Francisco José Calazans Falcón, *A época pombalina: política, económica e monarquia ilustrada* (São Paulo: Editora Ática, 1982).

all-powerful minister, Pombal, placed the power of the state decisively on one side of the conflict that had developed between Portuguese entrepreneurs as a consequence of the gold boom. He chose the large established Portuguese and Brazilian merchants over their smaller competitors because he saw the small merchants as mere creatures or commission agents of the foreigners. With support from the state he hoped the Portuguese merchants would in time be able to challenge the foreigners at their own game. His economic policy was a logical one in view of Portugal's position within the eighteenth-century international trading system. It protected mutually beneficial trade (such as the Portuguese wine trade), but it also sought to develop a powerful national class of businessmen with the capital resources and the business skills to compete in the international and Portuguese domestic markets with their foreign, especially British, competitors. It was not an easy policy to pursue, at least overtly, because it was essential to achieve this outcome without bringing into question the political and military support that the treaties with Britain guaranteed and that was essential if Spanish ambitions were to be kept at bay.

At the same time in Brazil, in striking contrast to the Bourbon reformers in Spanish America, Pombal sought to incorporate and co-opt the Brazilian oligarchy. Portugal was, after all, a small country with a large empire. It did not possess the resources of a Britain or France. It did not have the military capabilities or the economic resources to force Brazil into a subservient role. Indeed, as Pombal watched the British attempt to repress the rebellious colonists in English-speaking North America during the 1770s, he was fortified in his belief that conciliation was a more effective weapon against colonial uprising than military force.

Portugal's colonial policy under Pombal in effect served to diffuse tensions within the colonial nexus by preventing any polarization along colonial versus metropolitan lines. The intervention of the Pombaline state had almost always been sectoral; that is, it had swung state support behind one side in a series of preexisting conflicts which themselves bridged the metropolitan-colonial divide. Hence, Pombal supported the large entrepreneurs against their smaller competitors; he had aided the educational reformers within the church such as the Oratorians, while destroying the Jesuits and their colleagues; he had crushed powerful elements among the old aristocracy while encouraging the access of businessmen to noble status. The benefits and the displeasure of the Pombaline state, in other words, helped and hindered both Brazilian and Portuguese, forging a series of alliances across the Atlantic, as well as counteralliances that linked Portuguese and Brazilian interests at a variety of levels. Some of these results of policy were unintentional; but the conciliatory aspect of Pombal's policy toward powerful Brazilian interests was entirely explicit.

The fundamental problem for Portugal, however, arose from the logic of the Brazil-based Atlantic system within which Pombal had operated. In the final analysis, Brazil would inevitably become the dominant partner within the Portuguese-speaking empire. If the political constraints that had governed the whole period from the 1660s to the end of the eighteenth century also changed, that is, if for example Great Britain no longer saw it in its own interest to protect Portugal from her continental neighbors, then the British might opt for a direct relationship with the colony rather than with the mother country.[18] Since the whole basis of Portugal's prosperity had been built on the manipulation of colonial monopolies, cash-crop exports, colonial markets, and colonial gold, such a rupture would bring fundamental change and would close an epoch. Ironically it was the French seizure of Lisbon in 1807 that forced the effective political and economic emancipation of Brazil in 1808 by neutralizing the power of those in Portugal opposed to recognition of Brazil's central economic and political role within the Luso-Brazilian Atlantic system, collapsing thereby the

---

[18]There had long been a clandestine direct trade between British merchants and Brazil, especially involving the slave trade. The rolled tobacco of Bahia, most of it from the Cachoeira and Mantiba regions, was the basic commodity of exchange on the African coast, as necessary to other European slavers as to the Portuguese. [See José da Silva Lisboa to Domingos Vandelli, Bahia, October 19, 1781, *Anais da Biblioteca Nacional, Rio de Janeiro (ABNRJ)*, XXXII (1920), 505; José Honório Rodrigues, *Brazil and Africa*, trans. Richard A. Mazzara and Sam Hileman (Berkeley: University of California Press, 1965) and Pierre Verger, *Flux et reflux de la traite des nègres entre le Golfe de Bénin et Bahia de Todos os Santos, du XVIIe au XIXe siècle* (Paris: La Haye, Mouton, 1968).] Some fifty vessels a year, corvettes and smaller vessels, left Bahia for Africa, four-fifths of them for the Guiné Coast and the remainder for Angola. [See Luís dos Santos Vilhena, *Recopilação de noticias soteropolitanas e brasilicas . . .* (1802), 3 vols. (Bahia: Imprensa Official do Estado, 1922–1935).] European goods and gold dust came back to Bahia with the cargoes of slaves. This clandestine commerce had outraged the secretary of state for overseas dominions, Martinho de Melo e Castro, as had the degree of control that the merchants of Bahia exercised over the African commerce to the exclusion of metropolitan merchants. ["Instrucção para o Marquês de Valença, no qual informa a respeito da referida devassa . . . ," Bahia, February 4, 1783, ibid., 529.] The contraband manufactures, however, did underprice those imported from the metropolis, and restricted the market for metropolitan goods. [See José da Silva Lisboa to Domingos Vandelli, Bahia, October 19, 1781, ibid., p. 505.] The profitable subsidiary trade which accompanied the slave and tobacco commerce contributed to the favorable balance Bahia enjoyed with the metropolis. Most of the capital obtained was sunk into the purchase of more slaves. Melo e Castro held that the working of the Bahian-African trade was the same as "according to the English, French and Dutch a free trade by the ports of Africa between those nations and the Portuguese dominion in Brazil without the intervention of the merchants of the metropolis." ["Instrucção para o Marquês de Valença," Martinho de Melo e Castro, Queluz, September 10, 1779, *ABNRJ*, XXXII (1910), 444.]

structure of the Luso-Atlantic system as it had existed since the 1660s and replacing Lisbon as the required intermediary between South America and Europe by direct access between Europe and the ports of Brazil.[19]

III

But what of the Spanish American Atlantic world? Here the eighteenth century had seen three major processes at work. First, the old monopolistic trading connection of Atlantic convoys of protected ships sailing on a regular pattern between the Caribbean and the monopoly port of Seville (later Cádiz) had been superseded by a de facto diversification of trade. Some of this diversification was illegal—but like the trade through Jamaica, this had become a substantial contribution to overall Atlantic commerce. After 1715, in fact, the old fleet system was clearly limiting the growth of trade as economic and demographic expansion occurred throughout Spanish America. Spain had also eventually permitted other Spanish ports into Atlantic commerce, gradually ending the Cádiz monopoly between 1765 and 1789 and giving formal administrative recognition to the peripheral coastal regions in South America away from the old highland Indian-populated core areas, where Spain's major bases in the Western Hemisphere had been since the time of the Conquest. Thus, while Lima and Mexico City remained important (Mexico still accounted for half the population of Spanish America in this period), new regions also developed, such as the Rio de la Plata, Caracas, and Cuba, which had previously been backwaters—good for provisions but producing very little else. These regions all became major exporters in the late eighteenth century—Buenos Aires, an exporter of salt beef, silver, hides, and grains; Caracas for cacao and hides; Cuba, especially after the revolt in Haiti, a major center for sugar and slaves.

Second, starting at midcentury Spain had attempted to implement a series of major administrative, mercantile, and fiscal reforms aimed at the enhancement of the power of the metropolis through the more efficient exploitation of its colonies.[20] As in Portugal, there had been growing

---

[19]José Jobson de Andrade Arruda, *O Brasil no comércio colonial* (São Paulo: Ática, 1980); Joseph C. Miller, *Way of Death: Merchant Capitalism and the Angolan Slave Trade, 1730–1830* (Madison: University of Wisconsin Press, 1988).

[20]I am drawing here on the work of Stanley J. Stein and Barbara H. Stein in "Concept and Realities of Spanish Economic Growth, 1759–1789," *Historia Ibérica* I (1973): 103–119, and also see their more recent work, *Silver, Trade, and War: Spain and America in the Making of Early Modern Europe* (Baltimore and London: Johns Hopkins University Press, 2000). Also see Charles C. Noel, "Charles III of Spain," in *Enlightened Absolutism*, ed. H. M. Scott (Basingstoke, Hampshire: Macmillan, 1990), 119–143.

awareness in Spain that its role as a great power was severely undermined by the failure to adapt to modern conditions; which in eighteenth-century terms meant using the power of the state to increase revenues and impose a more centralized administrative system. This preoccupation with national regeneration during the first half of the eighteenth century was in the forefront of the minds of several high government officials who saw Spanish America as the means for Spain to recuperate its position in Europe if colonial resources could be more effectively utilized. The 1743 proposal of José de Campillo, minister of finance, in which he called for a "New system of economic administration for America" (*Nuevo sistema de Gobierno Económico para la América*) encapsulated the intention to develop the empire as a market for Spanish manufactures and as a source for raw materials. Campillo wished to see a system of general inspectors (*visitas generales*), the creation of intendancies on the French model, and the introduction of "free trade" into colonial administration, by which they meant the ending of the Andalusian monopoly and the opening of Spanish American trade to all ports of Spain, as well as the creation of a more economically integrated society within Spanish America by changing the way in which the Indian communities within the New World were governed. Campillo's proposals, however, were not published until 1789 under the Bourbon monarch Charles III (1759–1788), whose reign became associated with the implementation of a series of far-reaching new governmental measures for the administration of the vast Spanish territories in the New World. The urgency of these reforms became more than ever evident after the seizure of Havana by the British in 1762, during the Seven Years' War.[21]

Each major Spanish crisis in the eighteenth century had a colonial component. Commercial competition between England and France for the Spanish contract (*asiento*) to supply African slaves to Spain's colonies in America had been a prominent issue in the War of the Spanish Succession. At midcentury, the second crisis in 1759–1762 was precipitated by English commercial expansion in India, Canada, and the Caribbean, gateway to Spain's colonies in Middle America and northern South America. The third crisis at the century's end came with conflict between England and Napoleonic France in large measure over seapower and trade with Spain's colonies. What defined these crises was Spain's monopoly of American silver production, its inability to develop a manufacturing industry to supply

---

[21]John Robert Fisher, *Commercial Relations between Spain and Spanish America in the Era of Free Trade, 1778–1796* (Liverpool, U.K.: Centre for Latin-American Studies, University of Liverpool, 1985); and Antonio García-Baquero González, *Cádiz y el Atlántico (1717–1778): el comércio colonial español bajo el monopolio gaditano*, 2 vols. (Sevilla: Escuela de Estudios Hispano-Americanos, Consejo Superior de Investigaciones Científicas: Excelentísima Diputación Provincial de Cádiz, 1976).

its colonies, and the competition between two of the more developed European economies over exploiting the Spanish Empire in America.

To England and France, Spanish America represented, above all, a market for manufactured goods and a source of silver essential for expanding international trade and settling the imbalance of payments. At the end of the War of Succession, however, the forms of British and French commercial penetration in Spain diverged. Less developed commercially and industrially than the British, and linked to Spain as a wartime ally and tied by the Bourbon dynasty, French merchants and shippers had to expand inside the Spanish colonial trading system now centered on Cádiz. The Utrecht settlement confirmed the concessions yielded by Madrid over the last half of the seventeenth century to foreign resident merchants and shippers at Cádiz. Such concessions included extraterritorial rights, the exemption of firms and vessels from certain customs controls, and lower duties on imports such as French linens and other select items.[22]

Over the decades of 1724–1778 there were on average about sixty major French commercial houses established in Cádiz. Of the declared value of the Cádiz merchants, moreover, the French merchants accounted for 43 percent, the Spanish merchants only 18 percent. Until 1789, the French remained the largest foreign colony in Cádiz, always conspicuous and sensitive, like the British factory in Lisbon, to any infringement of their treaty rights. A significant percentage of the French textiles shipped to Cádiz were reexported; and the sales of French linens, woolens, and silks at Cádiz had important repercussions for employment and earnings in France's textile-producing centers.[23] French industry also absorbed appreciable quantities of Spanish primary exports—raw wool, soda ash, raw silk—along with products from Mexico and Guatemala like cochineal and indigo dyes. As little as 10 percent of colonial cargoes consisted of Spanish goods, with the balance made up by the production of Spain's French ally. Sales to the Spanish colonies generated a counterflow of silver that fed into the private banking system centered on Paris and Lyons, which was vital for trade with India and China and for the deficit-plagued finances of the

---

[22]Lutgardo Garcia Fuentes, *El comércio español con América, 1650–1700* (Sevilla: Escuela de Estudios Hispano-Americanos; Consejo Superior de Investigaciones Científicas, 1980); Miguel Artola, "América en el pensamiento español del siglo XVII," *Revista de indias XXIX* (1969); and N. M. Sutherland, "The Origins of the 30 Years War and the Structure of European Politics," *English Historical Review* CVII (July 1992): 586–625.

[23]Carlos D. Malamud, "España, Francia y el comércio directo con el espacio peruano, 1695–1730," "Cádiz y Saint Marlo," in *La economía española al final del antiquo regime: comércio y colonias, III* (Madrid: Alianza; Banco de España, 1982). Also, Albert Girard, *Le commerce français à Seville et à Cadix aux temps des Habsbourgs: contribution à l'étude du commerce étranger en Espagne aux XVIe et XVIIe siècles* (Paris and Bordeaux: Féret & fils, 1932).

French state. Silver, in fact, continued to dominate the Spanish American traffics: between 1717 and 1778 it composed 77.6 percent of the annual value; and 75.4 percent of the value of the trade of New Spain. And this was still a very substantial business comparatively speaking—the value of the commerce of Spanish America being double that of the British West Indies in the 1780s.[24]

English merchants were less important at Cádiz. They enjoyed other channels of trade with Spain's American colonies, especially along Spain's Caribbean coasts. Between Utrecht and the outbreak of war in 1739, the British managed the slave supply contract (the *asiento*) at Havana, Veracruz, Cartagena, and Buenos Aires, where along with African slaves they introduced smuggled goods; from Jamaica the British developed an extensive smugglers' network to Havana and Santiago on the island of Cuba, to the Campeche and Belize coasts, and to New Spain's sole major Caribbean port of Veracruz. Jamaica also served as both entrepôt and naval base; there British naval forces could threaten the French sugar islands and Spanish American ports. This threat materialized, of course, in the war beginning in 1757, when English forces took Canada and occupied first Guadeloupe and later Martinique.[25]

The accession of Charles III offered an opportunity for Spain to reform traditional attitudes. For France, which saw its colonial empire in India and Canada collapse, and for Spain, unprepared to withstand English assaults upon its Caribbean trading zone alone, the accession of Charles III was the opportunity at last to renew their dynastic alliance of mutual convenience. Charles III, and the key collaborator he brought from Naples, the Marqués de Esquilache, wished to diminish the pressure from French commercial and manufacturing interests who had long enjoyed direct and indirect participation in Spain's transatlantic trading system, much as Pombal sought to diminish British influence in Portugal. Yet, there was a paradox to the Franco-Spanish diplomatic and military collaboration not dissimilar to that within the Anglo-Portuguese alliance.

Charles revived projects of economic reform outlined earlier by men like Campillo. Charles and Esquilache's first actions were to terminate the seventeenth-century tariff concessions hampering the development of domestic industry; this was followed by standardizing tariffs and procedures at all peninsular ports. Given the importance of colonial trade in Spain's aggregate external exchanges, Madrid was, in effect, shifting much of the

---

[24]D. A. Brading, "Bourbon Spain and Its American Empire," in The *Cambridge History of Latin America*, ed. Leslie Bethell (Cambridge and New York: Cambridge University Press, 1984), I, 389–439.

[25]Dorothy Goebel, "British Trade to the Spanish Colonies, 1796–1823," *American Historical Review* XLIII (1938): 288–320.

burden of customs revenue to colonial consumers. Charles's government also attempted to reduce the illegal foreign share in Spain's colonial exchanges, in effect, attempting to increase Spain's participation and advantage in colonial trade. And, in light of Franco-Spanish diplomatic and defense collaboration symbolized in the family pact, Madrid expected French manufacturing interests to tolerate Spanish protectionism designed, as Madrid saw it, to make Spain's contribution in the joint containment of English commercial and naval power more effective.

The impact of the new governmental measures within Spanish America varied considerably from region to region. One immediate consequence was that tensions were aggravated between European Spaniards and the old Latin American white Creole oligarchies, which had for several centuries, it should be remembered, found a political niche within local administrations throughout the Americas. The Bourbon reforms, especially the intendant system, were therefore first introduced in the regions where the opposition of the old Creole oligarchies was less formidable; Cuba after 1764 and the Rio de la Plata after 1776. Only in 1784 was the system introduced in Peru, and in 1786 in Mexico. The articulation of the new system owed much to the reforming visitor general of New Spain (Mexico), José de Gálvez (1765–1771), who later became the long-term secretary for the Indies (1776–1787). His objective in Mexico had encompassed the establishment of a tobacco monopoly (to raise revenue), the reorganization and raising of the sales tax (the *Alcabala*), and the stimulation of silver production (by lowering the price of mercury).[26]

In practice, Spanish neomercantilism proved limited in its impact. State intervention did not create an industrial base in textile manufactures, except in Catalonia whose cotton mills were the product of private rather than state initiatives. In the mid-1780s, the colonial trade expanded, but the increase in colonial exchanges appears to have been based largely on the sustained surge in Mexican silver mining and colonial staple exports, more shipping in low-tonnage vessels, and Europe's insatiable appetite for silver and staples.[27]

---

[26]Allan Kuethe and Douglas Inglis, "Absolution and Enlightened Reform: Charles III, the Establishment of the Alcabala and Commercial Reorganization in Cuba," *Past and Present* CIX (1985): 118–143; and Jacques Barbier, "Indies Revenues and Naval Spending: The Cost of Colonialism for the Spanish Bourbons, 1763–1805," *Jahrbuch für Geschichte von Staat, Wirtschaft und Gessellschat Latinamerikas*, XXI (1984).

[27]Jacques Barbier, "Peninsula Finance and Colonial Trade: The Dilemma of Charles IV's Spain," *Journal of Latin American Studies* XII (1980): 21–37; John Fisher, "The Imperial Response to 'Free Trade': Spanish Imports from Spanish America, 1778–1796," *Journal of Latin American Studies* XVII (1985): 35–78; and Antonio García-Baquero González, "Comércio colonial y producción industrial en Cataloñia a fines del siglo XVIII," *Actas del I coloquio de história economica de España* (Barcelona: n.p., 1975), 268–294.

Spain, Europe, and the East were still linked to American (now largely Mexican) silver, and transforming a bullionist into a neomercantilist Spanish state was no easy process. The threat to the system from northwest Europe remained. The English manufacturers and merchants in preferring their Caribbean outposts from which they participated directly (and illegally) in Spanish colonial markets to the French method of participation via Cádiz were, in effect, pointing to one of the basic flaws in the Spanish neomercantilist project. The inability of the Spanish state to curb smuggling from English Caribbean ports, or from Dutch and French islands for that matter, demonstrated clearly what the merchants well understood: that multiple charges on goods within the formal Spanish trading system—repeated duties, commissions, and insurance fees—all raised the price of legal goods in Spanish America to levels that compensated for the risks of smuggling.

French textile manufacturers were also unable to provide the Spanish colonial system with merchandise whose quantity, quality, and pricing was competitive with other European goods. To protect their deteriorating competitive position, the French defended traditional commercial privileges in Spain's colonial trade. Yet it was precisely here that the French manufacturers faced the competition of Spain itself which was trying to reduce the privileged status of French merchants and goods in colonial trade. The fundamental premise of mercantilism was economic competition, not cooperation. Thus, ironically, both French commercial agents and their Spanish counterparts failed to observe that by the last third of the eighteenth century both Spanish and French economic policies were being bypassed by the rapid expansion of the international economy. English industrial development was generating products whose price and quality would permit them to penetrate most mercantilist barriers.

Neither Spaniards nor Frenchmen engaged in colonial trades with Spanish America wanted to recognize that the age of mercantilism was rapidly passing. Ironically, by the end of the eighteenth century, the British had made this leap, and in their relationship with Portugal, no less; and partly because of the comparative success of Pombal's policies, not because of their failure; and it was France, or more precisely Napoleon, who forced the issue to a denouement. Let me explain.

Between 1785 and 1790 the balance of trade between Portugal and Great Britain was brought almost to an equilibrium. From 1791 to 1795 for the first time during the whole eighteenth century, Portuguese exports to Britain showed a surplus over British exports to Portugal. From 1783, and especially from 1788, there was rapid growth in Brazilian raw cotton reexports from Portugal to Britain, and by the first decade of the nineteenth century, about a quarter of Lancashire's cotton wool export came from Brazil, especially Pernambuco and Maranhão. Robert Walpole, British envoy to Lisbon, looked on in astonishment as Britain remitted gold to Lisbon to pay for its now unfavorable balance of trade. "It may be looked upon as a kind of phenomenon," he told Lord Grenville in 1791.[28]

It was now the British who clamored for reciprocity, a reversal of circumstances which would have gratified the subtle old Marquês de Pombal had he lived long enough to see it. Between 1786 and 1788, extensive investigations were conducted in London into the changed Anglo-Portuguese commercial relationship. Both the old woolen and wine industries and the new cotton manufacturing interest pressured the government and the committee of the Privy Council for Trade. The cotton spinners and the calico and muslin manufacturers of Manchester and Neighbourhood were especially vocal as were the borough reeve and constable of Manchester.[29] In 1801 Lord Hawkesbury instructed the British minister in Lisbon to let it be known that "in the case of invasion, the British envoy was authorized to recommend that the court of Portugal embark for Brazil . . . and the [British] were ready for their part to guarantee the security of the expedition and to combine with [the Portuguese government] the most efficacious ways to extend and consolidate [their] dominions in South America."[30]

This was an astonishing change of policy. But its immediate implementation was not easy—the traditional commercial organizations and their lobbies remained powerful—not only in the form of the British factories in Portugal, but also among the new Portuguese merchant industrial bourgeoisie Pombal had created. But the British government was clear on the issue. As Robert Fitzgerald, Walpole's successor in Lisbon, wrote to Lord Hawkesbury, "the British property within these dominions forms no object of great national importance . . . especially where in the opposite balance are viewed the innumerable advantages to be derived from an open, unrestrained trade with the Brazils."[31] It took the French invasion of 1807 to neutralize the old interests. One cannot help thinking that it would have

---

[28]Michael M. Edwards, *The Growth of the British Cotton Trade, 1780–1815* (Manchester: Manchester University Press, 1967); Arthur Redford, *Manchester Merchants and Foreign Trade, 1794–1858* (Manchester: Manchester University Press, 1934); and [Robert Walpole] to [Lord Grenville], Lisbon, October 12, 1791, PRO, FO, 63/14.

[29]"Minute of Propositions Impeding the Treaty with Portugal," September 1786, Chatham Papers, PRO 30/8/342 (2) f. 59; Office of the Committee of Privy Council for Trade, June 25, 1787, PRO, BT 3/1. 102; [W. Fawkener] to [Borough Reeve] and [constable of Manchester], Office of Privy Council for Trade, August 23, 1788, PRO, BT, 3/1, 290.

[30]D. José de Almeida de Melo e Castro to Dom João, September 1, 1801, Arquivo Instituto Histórico e Geográfico Brasileiro, Rio de Janeiro, lata 58, doc. 17.

[31][Robert Fitzgerald] to [Lord Hawkesbury], Lisbon, October 21, 1803, PRO, FO, 63/42.

been better for the French if they had left Iberia alone when after the victories of Nelson they could not challenge British naval superiority in the Atlantic Ocean. A factor incidentally the citizens of Liverpool well noted at the time.

IV

If the policies of neomercantilism in both Spain and Portugal were thwarted, and thwarted be it noted where they succeeded as much as where they failed, and if Enlightened Absolution proved incapable in the long term of preventing the inexorable rise of the British commercial and naval hegemony within the Atlantic system as a whole, what of the forces of protonationalism on the other side of the ocean—can we speak here of an age of Democratic Revolution, as Robert Palmer proposed, or of an Atlantic Revolution in the sense Jacques Godechot used the term? Or are we indeed seeing a more economically based transformation from direct to indirect dominion, from the old formal to the new informal empire of trade and industrial power. The ferment of innovation and the difficulty of implementing reform in the Americas had certainly revealed just how complex Spanish American colonial society had become in the late eighteenth century. It also demonstrated how difficult it would be in Spanish America for a clear regional focus of protonationalistic sentiment to emerge, or for the creation of a cohesive social base to support any rebellion against Spain. Internal social, racial, and caste divisions permeated colonial society, and it was very difficult anywhere in Spanish America for European Spaniards living in the colonies, Creole magistrates, soldiers, and local businessmen to come together in even the embryonic independence movement that had briefly made the idea of an economically independent and Republican Minas Gerais on the North American model so pertinent in Brazil in 1788–1789.

The example of the American Revolution had been particularly important in Brazil for reasons that lay in the coincidence of its anticolonial message with the severe tension between Lisbon and major segments of the local elite in the one area in Portugal's American territories that had the capacity to articulate as well as make effective an independent state, possessing as it did in the 1780s adequate revenues, military forces, administrative experience, and a close attention to international developments. That it failed despite all these elements is an indication of how difficult the achievement of colonial independence would be in Ibero-America.[32]

---

[32]Maxwell, *Conflicts and Conspiracies*, especially 115–140.

Movements of social protest did, of course, emerge in Spanish America, and with much more violence, bloodshed, and disruption than ever occurred in Brazil, where protonationalist movements, however articulate, never got further than conspiracy in the eighteenth century. But the movements of social protest in Spanish America were limited in their ideological content; they did not make the leap from protest against bad government to an attack on the rule of Spain in America. The most significant of these movements of protest and rebellion, the Comunero rebellion in New Granada (present-day Colombia and Venezuela) in 1781 and the Túpac Amaru rebellion in upper Peru (present-day Bolivia) in 1780–1781, never projected themselves into an anticolonial struggle and both, especially the latter, served to terrify the Creole elites and make them acutely aware of the risk of race and ethnic violence implicit in the complexity of Spanish America's social makeup.

Given the heterogeneity of Spanish America in the late eighteenth century, the uneven impact of imperial reform, the diversification of the economic system, and its reorientation toward the Atlantic trading system in the new peripheral growth areas, such as Venezuela and the Rio de la Plata, as well as the limited anticolonial sentiment apparent in the rebellions of the 1780s, incipient nationalism was, when it emerged, more a characteristic of disgruntled individuals than of the masses. The latter were, on the whole, more preoccupied with immediate inequalities and exploitation than with intraimperial injustices, and they felt more the oppression of the local oligarchies than of the Crown in Madrid. The rebels in both Peru and Venezuela, in fact, had looked to the Crown for redress of grievance. The notion of independence from Spain, of a colonial emancipation from Europe, was hence confined to a very small number of the white Creole elite and developed after the putative popular revolts of the early 1780s had been repressed. These aspirations also were of a reformist rather than a revolutionary nature, and while the institutional model of the new North American nation was often an inspiration, in terms of overseas contacts and hope of assistance it was Britain to which they looked rather than to the United States.[33]

By the turn of the century, it is true that works by John Adams, George Washington, and Thomas Jefferson were circulating in both Mexico and South America, and key leaders of the Spanish American independence movement, most notably Francisco de Miranda, visited the United States, as did Simón Bolívar, who admired Washington. Miranda, however, summed up the complex reaction of whites to the events of 1776 in North

---

[33]John Leddy Phelan, *The People and the King: The Comunero Revolution in Colombia, 1781* (Madison: University of Wisconsin Press, 1978).

America and 1789 in France. "We have before our eyes two great examples," he wrote in 1799, "the American and the French Revolutions: let us prudently imitate the first and carefully shun the second." After the revolt in French Saint-Domingue (Haiti) in 1792, as in Brazil, property owners throughout Spanish America became even more cautious, especially if their property included African slaves. "I confess that as much as I desire the liberty and independence of the New World," Miranda observed, "I fear anarchy and revolution even more."[34]

The impact of the American Revolution would be confined mainly to the peripheries in Spanish America. Very little impact can be discerned in the two great core regions of Spanish dominion, Peru and Mexico. In many respects, the North Americans, in terms of trade, influence, and contacts, followed the sea-lanes, and their role was most significant with the Caribbean and along the coastlines where they had long been involved in the transatlantic commercial complex as purveyors of codfish, sugar, slaves, grain, tobacco, and most recently cotton. But here it was the North American commercial role within the Atlantic commercial system as a whole that was decisive. The grain trade, in particular, found ready customers in the Iberian Peninsula, among the colonial overlords of South and Central America. And trade more than republican ideology would be the watchword in the United States' dealings with both Spain and Portugal. These powers, Spain in particular, had aided in a very substantial way the attainment of American independence; it was a connection that made for some caution when it came to aiding and abetting revolutionaries to the south, at least until the Napoleonic period, when the United States gained direct access to Spanish American ports and Spain to all intents and purposes lost direct administrative control of its empire in America due to British control of the sea-lanes.[35]

In the case of Portugal and Brazil, it had become very evident that the impact of the American Revolution in Brazil, which was a powerful influence before 1789, was nonetheless diluted and eventually rejected by the

---

[34]Peggy K. Liss, *Atlantic Empires: The Networks of Trade and Revolution, 1713–1826* (Baltimore: Johns Hopkins University Press, 1983). Also see final chapter of Bernard Bailyn, *To Begin the World Anew: The Genius and Ambiguities of the American Founders* (New York: Knopf, 2003) as well as Karen Racine, *Francisco de Miranda: A Transatlantic Life in the Age of Revolution* (Wilmington, Del.: SR Books, 2003).

[35]John Lynch, *The Spanish American Revolution, 1808–1826* (New York: Norton, 1973); *The North American Role in the Spanish Imperial Economy, 1760–1819*, ed. Jacques Barbier and Allan Kuethe (Manchester [Greater Manchester] and Dover, N.H., U.S.A.: Manchester University Press, 1984); also *The Economics of Mexico and Peru during the Late Colonial Period, 1700–1810*, ed. Nils Jacobson and Hans-Jürgen Puhle (Berlin: Colloquium Verlag; Bibliotheca Ibero-Americana, 1986).

mid-1790s. This rejection was partly due to the failure of the Nationalist and Republican conspiracy in Minas Gerais during early 1789, but it was due also to the counterinfluence of the French Revolution and most particularly the manifestation of the French Revolution in the Americas, the great slave revolt in the French Antilles.

The white Brazilian elite, slave owners and those opposed to slavery alike, found by the 1790s that republicanism and democracy were concepts too dangerous for experimentation within a society half slave, and where blacks outnumbered whites two to one. The consequence was that those who avidly and approvingly followed the events in North America before 1790 turned away from the North American model and, encouraged by the Portuguese government, which had learned its own lessons from the revolt of the thirteen colonies, embraced monarchy in the interest of preserving the status quo against racial and social upheaval. A similar interaction between the chronology of revolutions and elite attitudes took place in all the American states and ex-colonies where slavery was entrenched.

In mainland Spanish America, independence followed from external more than internal events: the collapse of the Bourbon monarchy in Spain itself in the face of the Napoleon onslaught in 1808. Unlike Portugal, where the French invasion brought about a denouement to the dilemmas of the metropolitan-colonial relationship with the removal of the Portuguese Court to Brazil and the de facto (later de jure) establishment of Rio de Janeiro as the seat of a New World monarchy, in Spain the invasion in effect cut Spanish America loose from the old metropolis for a critical six years between 1808 and 1814, with major consequences for Spanish American unity and stability. The successor Spanish American republics often took shape within the new boundaries imposed by the eighteenth-century reformers, but they all faced massive problems of social cohesion and economic and administrative dislocations. The conflicting pressure arising from unequal economic growth within the Spanish Empire in America, the ambiguities of an administrative reform that was in part an attempt to respond to those changes, as well as the several social, ethnic, and racial tensions that permeated the social makeup of Spanish America had all served to limit the development of a broad-based anticolonial sentiment prior to 1808 and fragmented the social bases of support for a nationalistic project on the North American model, limiting thereby the potential impact of the North American example. Again, as in the lowland tropical areas of the Western Hemisphere, the example of the great slave revolt and consequent bloody conflicts in Haiti reinforced the fears arising from the uprising in Upper Peru in the early 1790s. Those who saw the North American model as relevant tended after 1800 to see it as the conservative option, a solution to the colonial dilemma that preserved the basic social organization, especially the system of slavery, but brought political emancipation from Europe. For an effective partnership they more often looked to Great Britain and to trade: espousing "liberalism" in the sense of access to world commerce rather than liberalism in the sense of democratic government.

For Latin America, especially for the areas where plantation economies and African slavery predominated, it is essential, therefore, if we are seeking to mark the end to the long eighteenth century, to look at the relationship between the three revolutions of the late eighteenth century, the American, the French, and the Haitian, and for Spanish America to look to the vicissitudes of the eighteenth-century experience with reform and rebellion. From the perspective of the Americas at the time, the great slave revolt of 1792 in French Saint-Domingue was a second "American" revolution that seemed no less important than the first. It brought to the forefront of elite consciousness fears and tensions inherent to plantation systems throughout the New World. Within the empires of Spain and Portugal, the Haitian revolt served both to stimulate a reapproximation between local oligarchs and the more progressive elements within the metropolitan governments, as in the Portuguese-speaking empire, and, as in Spanish America, to make it inevitable that the independence movements, when eventually they came, would always find questions of race, class, and social stability close to the surface. Whereas in the 1780s would-be Latin American revolutionaries had found inspiration in George Washington, by the 1790s, they would recoil in fear before the example of Toussaint L'Ouverture.

The Haitian revolt also had a major impact on the attitudes of the governments of Spain, France, and Britain toward independence movements in the Americas. For Britain, in particular, Haiti brought great caution to the encouragement of colonial rebellion if such revolts threatened to bring about so much instability and violence as to destroy the very wealth which had attracted British traders and merchants to the region in the first place. Here, the British soon began to see the advantages of the Luso-Brazilian solution to the dilemmas of the epoch of the Atlantic revolutions. As John Barrow summarized the issue in 1806:

> Revolutions in states where each individual has some interest in their welfare are not effected without the most serious calamities. What, then, must be the consequences in a country where the number of slaves exceeds the proprietors of the soil? In promoting revolutions, I trust England will never be concerned, being fully convinced that however much South America might gain by a quiet

change of masters, she will be soon thrown back into a state of barbarianism by revolutions.[36]

From the early-nineteenth-century British perspective, the reasons for this essentially conservative stance are not hard to discern. Hegemonic powers, then as now, never like to see their interest challenged or their commercial interests destroyed by radical and unpredictable change. The recently independent North Americans were the first to see through such stratagems and their implications for Spanish America and Brazil. The American secretary of state, John Quincy Adams, writing on June 28, 1818, ably summed up the British attitude toward the political emancipation of South America when he wrote:

> The Revolutions in South America had opened a new world to her commerce, which the restoration of Spanish colonial domination would again close against her. Her Cabinet, therefore, devised a middle term, a compromise between legitimacy and traffic . . . She admits all the pretension of legitimacy until they come in contact with her own interest, and then she becomes the patroness of liberal principle and colonial emancipation.[37]

Only two months later the British envoy in Rio de Janeiro, Henry Chamberlain, in fact was writing secretly to Viscount Castlereagh (August 22, 1818) in terms which reflected Adam's supposition exactly:

> The political state of this part of the South American continent has become so changed by the establishment of the seat of the Portuguese Monarchy in the Brazils that a change in the system under which Spain formerly governed her colonies in the Plata is become necessary and unavoidable, even if they had remained faithful; they

---

[36]John Barrow, *A Voyage to Cochinchina in the Years 1792 and 1793* (London: T. Cadell and W. Davies, 1806), 133–134; Also see John Lynch, "British Policies and Spanish America," *Journal of Latin American Studies* I (1969): 1–30; French Saint-Domingue had been producing about 40 percent of the world's sugar and over half of the world's coffee, according to David Geggus, when the 1791 slave revolt occurred. The government of William Pitt and Henry Dundas sent some 15,000 soldiers to their deaths in Saint Dominique and spent some £10 m trying to conquer it. Geggus calls this "among the greatest disasters in British Imperial History." D. Geggus, "The British Government and the Saint Dominique Slave Revolt 1791–1793," *EHR* XCVI (1981): 285–305. Also see Lester D. Langley, *The Americas in the Age of Revolution, 1750–1850* (New Haven: Yale University Press, 1996).

[37]John Quincy Adams, secretary of state to George W. Campbell, United States minister to Russia, Washington, June 28, 1818, in *Diplomatic Correspondence of the United States concerning the Independence of the Latin American Nations*, ed. William R. Manning, 3 vols. (New York: Oxford University Press, 1925), vol. I, 72.

have, however, thrown off their allegiance, and have maintained a struggle of several years for Independence ... For Brazil, having ceased to be a colony and being become an independent kingdom open to the commerce of the whole world, they cannot return to their former state. However, as I regard the re-establishment of Spanish authority as impossible, it appears to me that the real interest of His Catholic Majesty would be secured by his putting an end to the contest as soon as possible, ... such as to promise stability, revolution would cease and prosperity would be restored in these fine countries to the advantage of the whole world, and of none more than of Great Britain.[38]

John Quincy Adams and Henry Chamberlain were both right. The characteristics and options that had marked the long eighteenth century in the Spanish and Portuguese Atlantic had been permanently transformed. Yet this had occurred at least in part because the options for two very important participants in the eighteenth-century South Atlantic world, Spain and Portugal, had been largely superseded and destroyed. For them, the long eighteenth century had ended.

---

[38]Henry Chamberlain to Viscount Castlereagh (Secret), Rio de Janeiro, August 22, 1810, in *Britain and the Independence of Latin America, 1812–1830; Selected Documents from the Foreign Office Archives*, ed. Sir Charles Webster, 2 vols. (London: Oxford University Press, 1938), vol. I, 190–193.

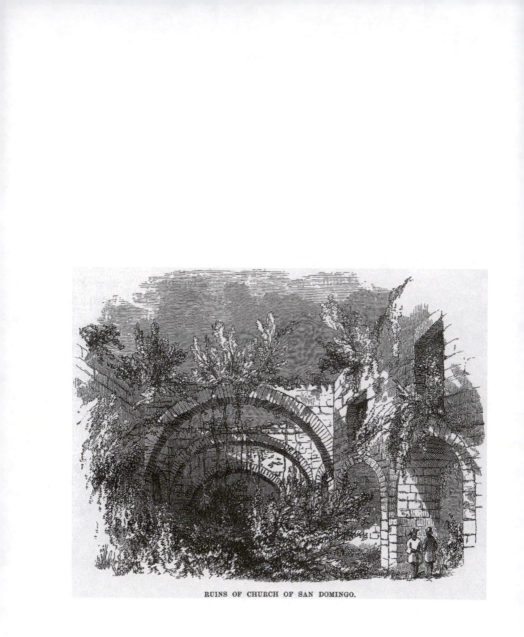

RUINS OF CHURCH OF SAN DOMINGO.

CHAPTER **6**

The Spark

The Amazon and the Suppression of the Jesuits

"The Kings of Portugal could come to have an Empire like China in Brazil."
—Duke Silva Tarouca, 1752

For the past two decades, historians—or many of them—have been downgrading the role of events and of personalities. There has also been a tendency to reject the history of ideas, or at least any easy cause-and-effect interaction between ideas and the implementation of policy. On the positive side, however, we have witnessed the growth of a more international, less Eurocentric, history. I say this at the outset, obvious as it may be, because we are dealing here very much with an event (the expulsion of the Jesuits from Portugal and its empire in 1759); with a very dominant—not to say domineering—personality (the Marquês de Pombal, who in effect governed Portugal from 1750 to 1777); with ideas (especially in the case of the Iberian monarchies, a reinvigorated and systematic thinking about the role of the state in promoting economic development and in securing for itself a monopoly over coercion, budgets, administration, and justice); and with international history (in that I will be focusing on a very remote periphery of the eighteenth-century world: the Amazon basin).

This event: the Portuguese expulsion, this personality: Pombal, and this periphery: the Amazon basin, however, provided the spark that set in motion a process throughout Catholic Europe that brought the Society of Jesus down. In the aftermath, in Portugal, it was the Enlightenment that provided a rationale, a justification, as well as the means to remedy some of the damage done by the Jesuits' forced departure.

It is important to stress perhaps that this is where and when the expulsion began. We still tend to look out from the center to the edges—yet it was at the very outer edges of the European world, where the Jesuits had always been most active, that the first decrees to suppress the Society of Jesus were enforced. Why an action in Brazil found such resonance elsewhere is a separate issue. Here I am interested in the spark. Why the Amazon? Why Pombal?

I

There were two distinct but interrelated aspects of the intellectual environment in eighteenth-century Portugal that influenced the way Pombal thought about the problems confronting him as he took office in 1750; each of them, in different ways, had an impact on the dispute with the Jesuits.[1] First, there was the intense debate over fundamental questions concerning philosophy and education. Second, a considerable body of thought existed about various aspects of Portugal's political economy. The stimulus for the former in Portugal, as elsewhere in Europe, was the intellectual achievement of Descartes, Newton, and Locke. The most important works to emerge from this intellectual school in Portugal included those of de Martinho de Mendonça Pina e Proença (b. 1693, d. 1743), who attempted to adapt to Portugal some of Locke's theories, especially on education; the writings of the New Christian[2] Dr. Jacob de Castro Sarmento (b. 1692, d. 1762), who introduced Newtonian ideas in Portugal; and the works of Dr. António Nunes Ribeiro Sanches (b. 1699, d. 1783), another New Christian who had left Portugal in 1726, working thereafter in England, Holland, Russia, and finally in France, where (from 1747 until his death in 1783) he was a collaborator of the Encyclopedists and wrote on medicine, pedagogy, and economics.[3] Most influential of them all was the Oratorian Luís António Verney (b. 1713, d. 1792), the author of *O verdadeiro método de estudar* (The true method of education), published in

---

[1] I use "Pombal" here as a shorthand, since this is usually how Sebastião José de Carvalho e Melo (b. 1699, d. 1782) is referred to by historians. But it is an anachronistic and perhaps misleading shorthand to the extent that it anticipates his elevation to marquês in 1769. He had become the count of Oeiras in 1759. For details on Pombal's family background see Kenneth Maxwell, *Pombal, Paradox of the Enlightenment* (Cambridge and New York: Cambridge University Press, 1995), especially 2–4.

[2] So-called New Christians were the descendants of Portuguese Jews compelled to embrace Christianity in 1497 rather than face expulsion.

[3] See António Alberto Banha de Andrade, *Vernei e a cultura do seu tempo* (Coimbra: Universidade de Coimbra, 1966); also *The Portuguese Jewish Community in London: 1656–1830* (London: Jewish Museum, 1992).

1746. Luís António Verney lived most of his adult life in Naples and Rome, where he studied with Antonio Genovesi (b. 1712, d. 1769) and was a friend of Ludovico Antonio Muratori (b. 1672, d. 1750). In Rome he became a member of the Arcadia, as well as for a time secretary to the Portuguese envoy to the Vatican, Francisco de Almada e Mendonça, who was Pombal's cousin.[4]

The congregation of the Oratória de S. Felipe de Nery, to which Verney belonged, had taken the lead in Portugal, as elsewhere in Catholic Europe, in the introduction of scientific experimentation and in the conflict with the Jesuits over pedagogical models. The Oratorians were strong promoters of the natural sciences, and they also stressed the importance of the Portuguese language, grammar, and orthography, which they believed should be studied directly and not via Latin. The reason the Jesuits were the butt of this criticism was obvious: they held a monopoly of higher education in Portugal and of secondary education in Brazil.[5]

In addition to this philosophical debate, part of a Europe-wide phenomenon, there existed a second important current of thinking more specific to Portugal. This was a body of ideas and discussion about governance, economy, and diplomacy, which had emerged in the first half of the eighteenth century among a small but influential group of Portugal's overseas representatives and government ministers, a group within which

---

[4]For Muratori see Derek Beales, *Joseph II: In the Shadow of Maria Theresa, 1741–1780* (Cambridge and New York: Cambridge University Press, 1987), 47; and Franco Venturi, *Da Muratori a Beccaria (1730–1764)*, vol. 1, *Settecento riformatore* (5 vols.) (Turin: Giulio Einaudi Editore, 1969). There is a vast literature on Verney. For a brief introduction see António Alberto Banha de Andrade, *Vernei e a projecção de sua obra* (Lisbon: Instituto da Cultura Portuguesa; Biblioteca Breve, 1980), which contains an appendix with extracts from Verney's correspondence with Muratori. Also by the same author, *Contributos para a história da mentalidade pedagógica portuguesa* (Lisbon: Imprensa Nacional, 1981). For a more complete account see Andrade, *Vernei e a cultura do seu tempo*. Also valuable is the broad overview by J. S. (José Sebastião) da Silva Dias, *Portugal e a cultura européia (séculos XVI a XVII)* (Coimbra: Universidade de Coimbra, 1953), and Samuel J. Miller, *Portugal and Rome, c. 1748–1830: An Aspect of the Catholic Enlightenment* (Rome: Università Gregoriana, 1978).

[5]João V had granted the convent of Nossa Senhora das Necessidades to the Oratorians in 1744 with the obligation to conduct classes in Christian doctrine, rhetoric and grammar, moral philosophy, and theology. See Manuel H. Côrte-Real, *O Palácio das Necessidades* (Lisbon: Ministério dos Negocios Estrangeiros, 1983). The convent is now the seat of the Portuguese Foreign Ministry. For a comprehensive overview of the Jesuit activity in Portugal and its empire, see Dauril Alden, *The Making of an Enterprise: The Society of Jesus in Portugal, Its Empire and Beyond, 1540–1750* (Stanford: Stanford University Press, 1996), especially 597–613. For Brazil in particular see Caio Boschi, "Jesuítas," vol. 3 in Francisco Bethencourt and Kiri Chaudhuri, eds., *História da expansão portuguesa*, 5 vols. (Lisbon: Círculo de Leitores, 1998–1999), 295–300.

Pombal was a key figure. D. Luís da Cunha, successively Portuguese ambassador to the Dutch Republic and France, was the most formidable of these thinkers and author of a comprehensive analysis of Portugal's weaknesses and the means to remedy them. D. Luís was in many respects Pombal's mentor.[6]

This debate focused on Portugal's location within the international system and confronted directly both the constraints and the options with which a small country like Portugal, part of Iberia but independent of Spain, had to live. Central to these discussions was the problem of retaining and exploiting the considerable overseas assets Portugal controlled in Asia, Africa, and, above all, Brazil; and developing at the same time a mechanism to challenge English economic domination of Portugal and its vast American colony without weakening the political and military alliance with Britain, which Portugal needed to contain Spain.

D. Luís da Cunha, in particular, had placed Portugal's problems in the context of its relation to Spain, its dependence on—and economic exploitation by—England, and what he believed were Portugal's self-inflicted weaknesses in terms of the lack of population and spirit of enterprise. This sad mental and economic condition he attributed to the excess number of priests, the activity of the Inquisition, and the expulsion and persecution of the Jews. He proposed the creation of monopolistic commercial companies on the Dutch and English model.[7]

Pombal also drew models from his interpretation of the experience of other European countries. From 1739 until 1744, he had represented the Portuguese king in London. For Pombal, the threat the British posed to Portugal's vast and rich dominions in Brazil became a major preoccupation. It was essential, he believed, to understand the origins of Britain's commercial and military superiority and of Portugal's economic and political weakness and military dependence.[8]

In London, Pombal, who had become a member of the Royal Society in 1740, set out to investigate the causes, techniques, and mechanisms of

---

[6]For Pombal's family connection see Joaquim Veríssimo Serrão, *O Marquês de Pombal: o homen, o diplomata e o estadista* (Lisbon: Edição Câmara Municipal de Lisboa, Oeiras e Pombal, 1982).

[7]See Pedro de Azevedo and António Baião, eds., *Instrucções inéditas de D. Luís da Cunha e Marco António de Azevedo Coutinho* (Coimbra: Universidade de Coimbra, 1930). For a detailed discussion of the intellectual sources of Pombal's ideas see Francisco José Calazans Falcón, *A época pombalina: política, economia e monarquia ilustrada* (São Paulo: Editora Ática, 1982).

[8]The contents of Pombal's London library are catalogued in several codices in Lisbon's National Library. In particular see Colecção Pombalina, Codices 165, 167, 342, 343, Biblioteca Nacional, Lisbon. Also see Sebastião José de Carvalho e Melo, *Escritos económicos de Londres, 1741–1746* (Lisbon: Biblioteca Nacional, 1986).

British commercial and naval power. But England was not his only foreign experience. From London, Pombal moved to Vienna. Here he was no less observant, and became involved in a long, arduous, and frustrating negotiation with the papacy on behalf of the Austrian government, in the course of which he became the very intimate friend of Manuel Teles da Silva, a Portuguese émigré of aristocratic lineage who had risen high within the Austrian state. Manuel Teles da Silva, who had been created Duke Silva Tarouca by the Holy Roman Emperor Charles VI in 1732, was president of the Council of the Netherlands and of Italy and was a confidant of Empress Maria Theresa. Pombal had married for a second time while in Vienna, a successful and highly advantageous match with Maria Leonor Ernestina Daun, by whom he eventually had five children. The Countess Daun was a niece of Marshal Heinrich Richard Graf von Daun, the commander in chief of the Austrian army. The Empress Maria Theresa took a special interest in the union. The Portuguese envoy in Rome observed sourly that it was this marriage which guaranteed Pombal the position of secretary of state in Lisbon. And it was in fact the Austrian wife of João V, Maria Ana of Austria, queen regent during João V's final illness, who recalled Pombal from Vienna in 1749 to join the ministry in Lisbon.[9]

There exists an extraordinarily frank and intimate private correspondence between Duke Silva Tarouca and Pombal, covering the first decade after Pombal's assumption of office in Lisbon, which provides a uniquely revealing discussion of Pombal's objectives and governmental measures. Silva Tarouca, excited by Pombal's rise to power in Lisbon, wrote in 1750 to congratulate his friend and to remind him of their conversations and hopes for the future. "We are not slaves of fashion and foreign practices," Silva Tarouca told Pombal, ". . . but still less are we slaves of ancient habits

---

[9]See Maxwell, *Pombal*, 3–4. The negotiations with the Vatican were extremely vexing for the future marquês, though they served to cement his close relationship with Silva Tarouca. His private correspondence with Lisbon was conducted via the Jesuits who were intermediaries in the most sensitive state business, given their key positions at the court of D. João V as confessors and de facto private secretaries to the royal family. The correspondence with the Jesuits also reveals the mutual antagonism between Pombal and the Portuguese minister in Rome and his continuing complaints about his lack of financial resources (also a theme of his correspondence in London), as well as his dependence on the English for credit lines (John Bristow of London and Lisbon). Later, when in power in Lisbon, Pombal removed the Jesuits from their positions as confessors and restored to Portuguese merchants the ability to sustain credit lines, both central planks of his policy agenda. See António Lopes, *Marquês de Pombal e a Companhia de Jesus, correspondência inédita ao longo de 115 cartas* (Cascais: Principa, 1999), and *Collecção dos negócios de Roma no Reino de El-Rei Dom José, Ministério do Marquez de Pombal e Pontificados de Benedicto XIV e Clemente XIII*, Parte I (1755–1760), Parte II (1759–1769), Parte III (1769–1774), and Additamento a Parte III (1774–1775), (Lisbon, 1874).

and preoccupations." He spoke of the "great new dispositions" they had discussed together.[10] The reign of D. João V had seen a considerable strengthening of royal prerogatives largely as a consequence of the vast riches which flowed in from Brazil after the discoveries of gold. The Bragança monarchy did not need to have recourse to Portugal's ancient representative institution, the Cortes, for taxes for the whole eighteenth century, and D. João V used his colonial wealth to enhance his prestige in Europe and persuade Rome to grant him the title of "Most Faithful." Well over half of all the revenues of the state came directly or indirectly from the overseas dominions of Portugal, especially Brazil.[11]

II

But how did this general climate of ideas and preoccupations affect policy? What were Pombal's "great new dispositions"? Why did they bring him so quickly into conflict with the Jesuits, particularly as there is no evidence to suggest hostility toward the Jesuits on Pombal's part prior to 1750, and Jesuits in fact may well have aided his rise to power?

In part, it resulted from the fact that it was the colonial situation that first forced itself on the attention of the new administration in Lisbon. The Treaty of Madrid between Spain and Portugal had been signed in January 1750.[12] The treaty was the first negotiated settlement between the Iberian powers to delineate the landward boundaries of their colonial territories in South America in their entirety. Portuguese claims to the Amazon were upheld, particularly the fluvial interior boundary formed by the Guaporé-Mamoré-Madeira Rivers.[13] When Pombal took office as secretary of state

---

[10][Manuel Teles da Silva] to [Sebastião José de Carvalho e Melo], Vienna, September 24, 1750, in Carlos da Silva Tarouca, S.J., ed., "A correspondência entre o Duque Manuel Teles da Silva e Sebastião José de Carvalho e Melo," *Anais da Academia Portuguesa de História*, VI, 2d series (Lisbon: Academia Portuguesa de História, 1955), 277–422; citation from 313–315; author's translation.

[11]Fernando Tomaz, "As Finanças do Estado Pombalino, 1762–1776," in *Estudos e ensaios em homenagem a Vitorino Magalhães Godinho* (Lisbon: Editora Don Quixote, 1990), 255–388. An important reevaluation of the reign of D. João V is contained in Angela Delaforce, *Art and Patronage in Eighteenth-Century Portugal* (Cambridge and New York: Cambridge University Press, 2002).

[12]The classic account is Jaime Cortesão, *Alexandre de Gusmão e o Tratado de Madrid (1750)*, 8 vols. (Rio de Janeiro: Ministério das Relações Exteriores, Instituto Rio Branco, 1955–1963). Also Luis Ferrand d'Almeida, "Problemas do Comércio Luso-Espanhol nos Meados do Século XVIII: um Parecer de Sebastião Carvalho e Melo," *Revista econômica e social* 8 (1981): 95–131.

[13]See especially the account by David M. Davidson, "How the Brazilian West Was Won," in *Colonial Roots of Modern Brazil*, ed. Dauril Alden (Berkeley and London: University of California Press, 1993), 61–106. Also "Consolidação do Roteiro Madeira-Guaporé," in José Roberto do Amaral Lapa, *Economia colonial* (São Paulo: Editora Perspectiva, 1973), 23–111.

for foreign affairs in July 1750, therefore, he was inheriting a fait accompli, some parts of which he did not approve.

These inland frontier demarcations were of great sensitivity for the missionary orders, since the Jesuit missions in particular were strategically placed deep in the continental interior between Spanish and Portuguese territories as well as along the key river systems. The Jesuits had cooperated with Spain in the 1740s, and the use of the Jesuits' Indian neophytes as troops and labor was an indispensable part of Spanish plans to counter Portuguese frontier expansion, Spanish strategy at this point merging with the traditional goal of the Jesuits for a united, well-defended chain of missions throughout the interior of the South American subcontinent.[14] Portugal's fears as to the loyalty of the Jesuits, therefore, were not unfounded.

With the Treaty of Madrid the Portuguese ceded Colonia do Sacramento and the land immediately to the north of the Rio de la Plata to Spain in return for Spanish recognition of the western fluvial frontiers of Brazil. This included the Uruguay River, which placed the seven Jesuit missions in the region, long under Spanish sovereignty, under that of Portugal. The Madrid agreements called for the evacuation of the Jesuits and their Indian neophytes from the Uruguayan missions, as well as over a million head of cattle, and envisioned a survey of the line of demarcation between Spanish and Portuguese America by two joint commissions. The governor general of Brazil, Gomes Freire de Andrade, was appointed Portuguese commissioner for the south. To the Amazon region in the north, Pombal sent his own brother, Francisco Xavier de Mendonça Furtado.[15]

---

[14]The principal source on the Jesuits in Brazil remains Serafim Leite, *História da Companhia de Jesus no Brasil*, 10 vols. (Lisbon and Rio de Janeiro: Livraria Portugalia, 1938–1950), supplemented now by Alden, *The Making of an Enterprise*. For the Amazon region still valuable is João Lúcio de Azevedo, *Os Jesuítas no Grão-Pará, suas missões e a colonização: bosquejo historico, com vários documentos inéditos* (Lisbon: T. Cardoso & irmão, 1901).

[15]Marcos Carneiro de Mendonça, ed., *A Amazônia na era pombalina: correspondência inédita do Governador e Capitão-General do Estado de Grão Pará e Maranhão, 1751–1759*, 3 vols. (Rio de Janeiro: Instituto Histórico e Geográfico Brasileiro, 1963). This comprehensive collection contains the official and private correspondence between Pombal and his brother, the governor of Grão Pará and Maranhão. Padre José Caeiro (b. 1712, d. 1791) provides a counterpoint to the account in the letters from Mendonça Furtado to his brother Pombal, covering many of the same events from a Jesuit perspective. For this intimate account of the expulsion from a Jesuit contemporary, see the remarkably detailed "Sobre o Exílio das Provincias Transmarinas da Assistência Portuguesa da Companhia de Jesus," published by the Academia Brasileira de Letras, *Primeira publicação após 160 anos do manuscrito inédito de José Caeiro sobre os Jesuitas do Brasil e da India na perseguição do Marquês de Pombal (século XVIII)* (Bahia: Escola Tipográfica Salesiana, 1936). For Portugal proper see Padre José Caeiro, *História da expulsão da Companhia de Jesus da Província de Portugal (séc. XVIII)*, 3 vols. (Lisbon: Editorial Verbo, 1991, 1995, 1999).

The "very secret" letter to the Gomes Freire supplementing his general instructions revealed the full extent of Pombal's aims and hopes for Portuguese America and demonstrated how powerful the Viennese experience and his discussions with Silva Tarouca were for Pombal. "As the power and wealth of all countries consists principally in the number and multiplication of people that inhabit it," he wrote, "this number and multiplication of the people is most indispensable now on the frontiers of the Brazil for their defense . . ." As it was not "humanly possible" to provide the necessary people from the metropolis and adjacent islands without converting them "entirely into deserts," it was essential to abolish "all differences between Indians and Portuguese," to attract the Indians from the Uruguay missions and to encourage their marriage to Europeans.[16] The instructions to Mendonça Furtado reflected similar objectives. In order to promote an increase in population and to deepen its commitment to Portugal, Pombal recommended that his brother emancipate the Indians from the control of the missionaries, stimulate the migration and settlement of married couples from the Azores, and greatly increase the commerce in African slaves to the region.[17]

In practice, the implementation of these ideas, as far as the Indians were concerned, meant the removal of the tutelage of the Jesuits and envisioned their assimilation into—rather than separation from—Portuguese society in Brazil. These ideas received warm commendation from Vienna: Duke Silva Tarouca wrote to Pombal in 1752, "The kings of Portugal could come to have an empire like China in Brazil [. . .] Great care," he said, must be taken to populate Brazil. "Moor, white, negro, mulatto, or mestizo, all will serve, all are men, and are good if they are well governed." Above all, the vast Amazon basin should be secured. "Population is everything, many thousands of leagues of deserts serve for nothing. . . ."[18] The interests of the state so defined, of course, collided with the most basic philosophical tenet of the protectionist Indian policy of the Jesuits, and in effect placed state policy on the side of the colonists with whom the Jesuits had always struggled in their efforts to protect the Indians from exploitation.

Drawing on Luís da Cunha's and Pombal's ideas about monopoly companies, Pombal's brother soon after his arrival in Belém, the capital of Pará

---

[16]"Carta Secretíssima de [Carvalho e Melo] para Gomes Freire de Andrade, Lisboa, September 21, 1751," in Marcos Carneiro de Mendonça, *O Marquês de Pombal e o Brasil* (São Paulo: Editora Nacional, 1950), 184; author's translation.
[17]"Instruções régias, públicas, e secretas para [Mendonça Furtado] . . . ," Lisbon, May 31, 1751, in Mendonça, *A Amazônia na era pombalina*, 1, 26–31.
[18][Teles da Silva] to [Carvalho de Melo], Vienna, August 12, 1752, in *Anais*, 323–329; author's translation.

at the mouth of the Amazon River, recommended that a commercial company be established to facilitate the supply of African slaves to the Amazon region; he believed African slave imports would relieve the pressure on the colonists to enslave and mistreat the native Indian population. He also wanted to see more investment in the Amazonian economy, which he believed a monopoly company would provide, to help develop its potential exports.[19]

In 1755, in response to this advice, Pombal established the Company for Grão Pará and Maranhão.[20] The company was given the exclusive right to all commerce and navigation between Portugal, Africa, and these Amazonian captaincies for a period of twenty years. Simultaneously, Pombal issued decrees on June 6 and 7, 1755, suppressing the Jesuits' secular authority over the Indians, declaring them to be "free men."[21] In addition, he ordered the expulsion from Brazil of those itinerant traders (*comissários volantes*), who acted as commission agents of foreign, mainly British, merchant houses established in Lisbon.[22]

These three decisive measures were linked. The hidden objective of the Company of Grão Pará and Maranhão was broader than its regional focus might indicate. In fact, Pombal began his efforts to "nationalize" sectors of the colonial trade where the foreign merchants were least active to camouflage his wider intentions. Pombal hoped by granting special privileges and

---

[19][Mendonça Furtado] to Diogo de Mendonça, Corte Real, Belém, January 18, 1754, and [Mendonça Furtado] to [Carvalho de Melo], Belém, January 26, 1754, in Mendonça, *A Amazônia na era pombalina* 2, 456–459, 465–470.

[20]Alvará, June 7, 1755, "Confirma os estatutos da Companhia Geral do Grão Pará e Maranhão." For a detailed account see Manuel Nunes Dias, *Fomento e mercantilismo; a Companhia Geral do Grão Pará e Maranhão (1755–1778)*, 2 vols. (Belém: Universidade Federal do Pará, 1970). Also see António Carreira, *As Companhias Pombalinas de Grão-Pará e Maranhão e Pernambuco e Paraíba*, 2d. ed. (Lisbon: Presença, 1982), which contains the statutes of incorporation of the two companies: "Instituição da Companhia Geral do Grão-Pará e Maranhão," 252–271; and "Instituição da Companhia de Pernambuco e Paraíba," 281–302.

[21]Lei, June 6, 1755, "Restitui aos índios do Grão-Pará e Maranhão a liberdade das suas pessoas, bens e comércio." Also see discussion by Colin M. MacLachlan, "The Indian Labor Structure in the Portuguese Amazon, 1700–1800," in *Colonial Roots of Modern Brazil*, ed. Dauril Alden (Berkeley and Los Angeles: University of California Press, 1973), 199–230; and Dauril Alden, *Royal Government in Colonial Brazil; With Special Reference to the Administration of the Marquis of Lavradio, Viceroy, 1763–1779* (Berkeley and Los Angeles: University of California Press, 1968).

[22]Alvará, December 11, 1755, "porque . . . he servido prohibir que passem do Brasil comissários volantes . . . ," in Colecção Pombalina, Codex 453, fls. 79–80. Also see Kenneth R. Maxwell in "Pombal and the Nationalization of the Luso-Brazilian Economy," in *Hispanic American Historical Review* XLVIII, no. 4 (November 1968): 608–631.

protection to stimulate the issuance of longer credits by Portuguese merchants so that via such a mechanism national merchant houses in Portugal would be able to accumulate sufficient capital to compete more effectively with British merchants in the colonial trade as a whole, and by extension in Portugal proper. In this way the Pombaline state would contain and limit the role of foreign participation in Luso-Atlantic commerce. And by striking at the itinerant traders he hoped to remove one key link between the foreign merchants in Portugal and the Brazilian producers, and, in the case of Amazonia, the Jesuits, whose trade in Amazon products he saw as competing unfairly with that of Brazilian and Portuguese entrepreneurs whom he wished to encourage. Pombal told Duke Silva Tarouca that his aim in establishing the Company of Grão Pará and Maranhão was "to restore [to] the merchant places of Portugal and Brazil the commissions of which they were deprived, and which are the principle substance of commerce, and the means by which there could be established the great merchant houses which had been lacking in Portugal. . . ."[23] Pombal also urged his brother, in private correspondence, to use "every possible pretext to separate the Jesuits from the frontier and to break all communications between them and the Jesuits of the Spanish dominions."[24]

Pombal's monopoly company thus met objectives on several levels—not all of them made explicit. The fundamental objective in the colonial trade was to try to diminish the influence of the British, but the methods employed to achieve this aim were subtle, pragmatic, and enveloped in subterfuge. The unavoidable problem with the British-Portuguese relationship was that it was circumscribed by treaties which, for political and security reasons, the Portuguese wanted to maintain. One way of taking action against British influence, however, while avoiding open confrontation over the terms of the treaties between the two countries, was to use a variety of techniques in Portugal and within the colonial setting to shift concessionary economic advantages from foreigners to Portuguese merchant groups. In this respect the choice of the Amazon to begin the process was a very clever subterfuge. The British did not perceive the threat to their interests until the end of the decade. In Vienna, Silva Tarouca, when informed of Pombal's actions, much appreciated the idea.[25] These were precisely the type of great new dispositions of which he approved, and surrounded by the camouflage he recommended should always disguise them.

---

[23][Carvalho e Melo] to [Teles da Silva], no date (internal evidence suggests early 1756), in *Anais*, 419–420; author's translation.
[24]"Instruções régias, públicas, e secretas para [Mendonça Furtado] . . . ," in Mendonça, *A Amazônia na era pombalina*, 1, 26–31.
[25][Teles da Silva] to [Carvalho e Melo], November 3, 1759, in *Anais*, 348.

III

This is not to say Pombal's intervention went unopposed. Far from it. The promulgation of the Company of Grão Pará and Maranhão's monopoly privileges and Indian emancipation from mission tutelage provoked an immediate response from the dispossessed traders and Jesuits. Both found an organ for agitation in the *mesa do bem comum*, a rudimentary Lisbon commercial association established in the late 1720s.[26] In the face of these provocations, Pombal acted swiftly. He dissolved the commercial fraternity of Espírito Santo as prejudicial to the royal service, common interest, and commerce, and the offending deputies were condemned to penal banishment. The confiscated papers of the *mesa* revealed the extent of Jesuit involvement, and Pombal interpreted and dealt with the protest as if it were a conspiratorial uprising against royal power.[27]

The creation of the Company of Grão Pará and Maranhão thus had several important and probably unintentional consequences. First, it linked the attempts to assert national control over sections of the colonial trade to wider geostrategic questions, arising from the implementation of the Treaty of Madrid. Second, it brought Pombal, and no less importantly his brother, into headlong conflict with the Jesuits because Grão Pará and Maranhão was a stronghold of Jesuit missionary activities and a region with a history of bitter disputes between the Jesuits and the colonists.

The Jesuit Indian missions on the southern frontier had in the meantime taken up arms do defend themselves and oppose the implementation of the Treaty of Madrid, provoking a joint Spanish-Portuguese military campaign against them.[28] The image of the militarized Indians under Jesuit control opposing unilaterally the mandates of the Iberian monarchs had a significant effect on the European mind. Voltaire, in *Candide*, portrays a sword-wielding Jesuit riding on horseback.[29] More significantly, the

---

[26]See J. (João) Lúcio d'Azevedo, *Novas eponáforas: estudos de história e literatura* (Lisbon: Livraria Clássica Editora, 1932), 54–56; and his *O Marquês de Pombal e a sua época*, 2d ed. (Lisbon: Seara Nova, 1922), 138–140.

[27]See [Carvalho e Melo] to [Mendonça Furtado], August 4, 1755, in Colecção Pombalina, Codex 626, fl. 90, and also in Mendonça, *A Amazônia na era pombalina*, 2, 784–788.

[28]There is a vast literature on the Guarani missions and their destruction: the best starting point remains Magnus Morner, ed., *The Expulsion of the Jesuits from Latin America* (New York: Knopf, 1965) and Magnus Morner, *The Political and Economic Activities in the La Plata Region: The Hapsburg Era* (Stockholm: Victor Pettersons; Institute of Ibero-American Studies, 1953). Also the discussion by John Hemming, *Amazon Frontier: The Defeat of the Brazilian Indians* (Cambridge: Harvard University Press, 1987), 1–80, and his *Red Gold: The Conquest of the Brazilian Indians* (Cambridge: Harvard University Press, 1978), 441–461.

[29]Voltaire, *Candide*, trans. and ed. Robert M. Adams (New York and London: W. W. Norton & Co., 1966), 30–31.

events surrounding the attempted implementation of the Treaty of Madrid fortified Pombal's conviction that the presence of the Jesuits in Portuguese lands, strategically placed as the missions were throughout the border region, was an impediment to the realization of his designs for reestablishing Portugal's power and prosperity and to protecting its frontiers by encouraging population growth through the incorporation of the Indians via miscegenation and secularization into Portuguese colonial society. From Vienna, Duke Silva Tarouca, reversing his earlier view on the desirability of Jesuit cooperation, observed in February 1758:

> It was not evangelical spirit that armed with muskets eighty or a hundred thousand Indians, and erected an intermediate power from the River Plate to the Amazon, which one day could be fatal to the dominant powers of South America.[30]

The 1750s, therefore, marking the first decade of Pombal's preeminence, had seen Portugal embark on an ambitious plan to reestablish some measure of national control over the riches flowing into Lisbon from Portugal's overseas dominions, Brazil most especially. To do this he adapted to the peculiarities of the Portuguese position many of the techniques of economic development he had seen deployed in London and Vienna, especially the use of state power to enhance national entrepreneurial skills and the imposition of state monopolies to protect nascent national industry and commerce. He had also been faced with implementing the Treaty of Madrid, involving a major effort to delineate and survey the vast frontiers of Brazil. In both cases the Jesuits provided major obstacles to his plans. On the southern border, a military campaign had been needed to defeat forces put into the field by the Jesuit missions. In the north of Brazil, the Amazonian missions ran into a headlong conflict with Pombal's brother.

In the midst of these accumulating struggles, the earthquake of 1755 struck Lisbon, propelling Pombal into virtual supreme power and opening the way for a radical reconstruction of the city. Yet the disenchantment of the old nobility with Pombal's policies was also growing. The Company of Grão Pará and Maranhão had used the allurement of ennoblement as an incentive to invest. The company's statutes offered to nonnoble investors certain exemptions and privileges that had previously been the exclusive prerogative of the nobility and the magistracy, and admitted them to membership in the military orders.[31] The exclusivist aristocracy was upset at the exclusion from office and by the favors Pombal bestowed on the

---

[30][Teles da Silva] to [Carvalho e Melo], Vienna, 10 February 1758, and Vienna, April 1, 1758, in *Anais*, 386–387, 395; author's translation.
[31]See Alvará of January 5, 1757, Colecção Pombalina, Codex 456, fl. 138.

merchants and businessmen. In addition, small merchants and tavern keepers were angry at being excluded by the new monopoly company Pombal set up to protect the wine producers of the upper Douro Valley, and these reactions combined to produce a series of violent riots and assassination attempts to which Pombal reacted ferociously, not only against the popular classes but also against the high nobility and the Jesuit order.[32]

The *mesa do bem comum* affair, the attack on contraband, and the regulation of colonial commerce thereby forged an identity of interest between the dispossessed itinerant interlopers, their English creditors, and the Jesuits, and the favors bestowed on Pombal's collaborators produced an identity of interests between those groups and the discontented nobles. For the old aristocracy Pombal's merchant collaborators represented a potent challenge to aristocratic privilege within the Portuguese social structure, and the reaction to this state sponsoring social engineering was not slow in developing.

The crisis came to a head with the attempted regicide in 1758. King D. José I was returning to the Palace of Belém after an evening visit to his mistress, the young wife of the marquis of Távora, when his carriage was fired upon. The king was wounded sufficiently seriously for his queen Dona Mariana Vitória (b. 1718, d. 1781) to assume the regency (September 7, 1758) during his recuperation. There was official silence on the incident until early December, when a substantial number of people were arrested in a large dragnet operation, including a group of leading aristocrats. The most prominent prisoners were leading members of the Távora family, the count of Atouguia, and the duke of Aveiro. The Duke D. José de Mascarenhas, who was the most powerful noble in Portugal, excluding the royal family, was president of the Supreme Court. The marquis of Távora was a former viceroy of India and commander of the cavalry. The count of Atouguia headed the Palace Guard.[33]

The king established a Supreme Junta de Inconfidência (December 9, 1758), presided over by the three secretaries of state and seven judges, but

---

[32]For a good discussion of the suppression of the uprising in Oporto against the Douro monopoly company, see Susan Schneider, *O Marquês de Pombal e o vinho do Porto: dependência e subdesenvolvimento em Portugal no século XVIII* (Lisbon: Regra do Jogo, 1980).

[33]See Guilherme G. de Oliveira Santos, *O caso dos Távoras* (Lisbon: Livraria Portugal, 1958), 15. For discussion of this episode also see Tarcisio Beal, "Os Jesuítas, a Universidade de Coimbra e a Igreja Brasileira: Subsídios para a História do Regalismo em Portugal, 1750–1850" (Ph.D. diss., Catholic University of America, 1969), 45. Pombal denunciation in Arquivo Nacional da Torre do Tombo, Lisbon, in Inquisition papers, No. 18, proceeding No. 8064, fos. 1–6, listed in "O Marquês de Pombal e o seu Tempo," *RHDI/MdP*, 2 vols. (Coimbra, 1982), vol. 1, 370–376.

in fact dominated by Pombal.[34] The tribunal, which was granted wide powers that denied to the defendants the usual protections in Portuguese law, acted with dispatch. On January 12, 1759, the prisoners were found guilty of attempted regicide and sentenced. The duke of Aveiro was to be broken alive, his limbs and arms crushed and exposed on a wheel for all to see, his ashes thrown into the sea. The marquis of Távora was to suffer the same fate. The limbs of the rest of the family were to be broken on the wheel, but they were to be strangled first. The grotesque sentence, the violence of which against aristocrats shocked much of Europe, was carried out the next day in Belém.

The day before, eight Jesuits were arrested where they had worked in Maranhão for alleged complicity, among them Gabriel Malagrida, a missionary and mystic of Italian origin who had gone to Brazil in 1721. After a brief sojourn in Lisbon between 1749 and 1751, he returned to Brazil where he quickly ran afoul of Pombal's brother. Malagrida had published a pamphlet on the Lisbon earthquake, attributing the disaster to Divine Wrath. Pombal had gone to great efforts to explain the earthquake as a natural phenomenon, and he personally denounced Malagrida to the Inquisition, at the head of which he had installed his other brother, Paulo de Carvalho.

A royal *alvará* on September 3, 1759, declared the Jesuits to be in rebellion against the Crown, reinforcing the royal decree of July 21 of the same year, which ordered the imprisonment and expulsion of the Jesuits in Brazil. By March and April of 1760, 119 Jesuits had been expelled from Rio de Janeiro, 117 from Bahia, and 119 from Recife. The order's vast properties in Brazil, Portugal, and throughout the remnants of the once vast Portuguese Empire in Asia were expropriated.

On September 21, 1761, after an auto-da-fé in Lisbon, Malagrida was garroted and burned, and his ashes were thrown to the wind. About the Malagrida case Voltaire wrote, "this was the excess of the ridiculous and the absurd joined to the excess of horror. (Ainsi l'excès du ridicule et de l'ab-

---

[34]*O processo dos Távoras, prefaciado e anotado por Pedro de Azevedo, inéditos* I (Lisbon: Biblioteca Nacional, 1921). Padre José Caeiro claimed that the order to liquidate the Jesuit properties in Brazil had been given in June 1758, three months before the assassination attempt. Also Francis A. Dutra, "The Wounding of King José I: Accident or Assassination Attempt?" *Mediterranean Studies* VII (1998): 221–229. On the important role played by young Brazilians and other artists, especially José Basílio da Gama, author of *O Uruguay*, in the promotion of anti-Jesuit measures and Pombaline reforms, as well as of those protected by the minister, see Ivan Teixeira, *Mecenato pombalino e poesia neoclássica* (São Paulo: EDUSP, 1999), and his *Obras poéticas de José Basílio da Gama, ensaio e edição crítica* (São Paulo: EDUSP, 1996). José Basílio da Gama became private secretary to Pombal. Ivan Teixeira's books also provide an invaluable depiction of Pombaline iconography.

surdité fut joint à l'excès d'horreur.)" The reaction elsewhere in Europe was strong enough to prompt Pombal to print the sentence against Malagrida with a justification in French.[35] That the last individual burned at the stake by the Portuguese authorities at the instigation of the Inquisition should have been a priest and a member of an order that had been at the very spearhead of the Counter-Reformation was heavy with symbolism and served as a launching pad for Pombal's formidable promotion of state propaganda in the anti-Jesuit cause. The Pombaline administration thereafter stimulated and subsidized throughout Europe a virulent campaign against the order. Pombal himself was intimately involved in the writing and formulation of the remarkable piece of propaganda known as the *Dedução chronológica e analítica*.[36] The "Chronological and analytical deduction" divided the history of Portugal between the useful and the disastrous, essentially linked to the influence of the Jesuits. It upheld a rigorous regalist view concerning the Catholic Church in Portugal. Professor Samuel Miller describes the work not unjustifiably as "a monotonous repetition of all the accusations ever leveled at the Jesuits by anyone at any time."[37] The history of the assault by the Portuguese and Spanish Crowns on the Jesuit missions along the Uruguay River in South America during the late 1750s was also encapsulated—and was for many years defined—by another piece of state-supported and financed propaganda, the *Relação abreviada*.[38] Published in Portuguese, Italian, French, German, and English in Amsterdam, the *Relação abreviada* was an account of the joint Portuguese and Spanish military campaign against the Jesuit missions in what is now the southern borderlands of Brazil. Some 20,000 copies are estimated to have been distributed. It was a major weapon in the Europe-wide battle that led to the suppression of the Jesuits by Pope Clement XIV in 1773.[39] As Franco

---

[35]Claude-Henri Frèches, *Voltaire, Malagrida et Pombal* (Paris: Fundação Calouste Gulbenkian, 1969). Also see the comments on Malagrida in C. R. (Charles Ralph) Boxer, *Some Contemporary Reactions to the Lisbon Earthquake of 1755* (Lisbon: Faculdade de Letras, Universidade de Lisboa, 1956) and *Liste des personnes qui ont été condamnées à l'act public de Foi, célèbré dans le cloître du convent des Dominiques de Lisbonne le 20 septembre 1761* (Lisbon: 1761).

[36]*Dedução chronológica e analítica . . . dada à luz pelo Doutor Joseph de Seabra da Silva . . . em Lisboa*, Anno de MDCCLXVII, 3 vols., original manuscript with annotations and additions in handwriting of Pombal. Colecção Pombalina, Codices 444–446. For discussion of the *Dedução chronológica* see d'Azevedo, *O Marquês de Pombal e a sua época*, 290–291.

[37]Miller, *Portugal and Rome*, 187.

[38]First published in late 1756 and probably written mainly by Pombal, the full title is: *Relação abreviada da República que os religiosos das Províncias de Portugal e Espanha estabeleceram nos Domínios Ultramarinos das duas Monarquias, e da guerra que neles tem movido e sustentado contra os exércitos espanhois e portugueses* (1758), Biblioteca Nacional, Lisbon, Reservados 4.394.

[39]See discussion by Miller, *Portugal and Rome*, 53.

Venturi has shown, Venice and Rome in particular specialized in printing vivid accounts of the goings-on in Lisbon.[40]

The expulsion of the Jesuits left Portugal virtually bereft of teachers at both secondary and university levels. Not surprisingly, the establishment of a state-sponsored school system of secondary education and the reform of the University of Coimbra drew directly on the recommendations of the old enemies of the Jesuits, the Oratorians and Luís António Verney, the latter by now a paid consultant to the Portuguese government.[41] Both of these reforms were later to provide Pombal with his claim to being a proponent of an Enlightenment government. Both reforms were financed in part by expropriated properties of Jesuits and aristocrats condemned for regicide.[42]

Finally, let us return to the question posed earlier: Why Pombal, and why the Amazon? The answer lies in five key points of conflict. First was Pombal's plan for economic regeneration through the rational exploitation of the colonies. Second, there was a geopolitical conflict over frontiers and the security of the empire, in which the Guarani missions in particular opposed Portugal's decisions by force of arms. Third, the attempted regicide. Fourth, there was an ongoing conflict within the church over education and regalism; this important schism enabled an attack on the Jesuits to proceed under the cover of Catholic tradition, in which the leading anti-Jesuit spokesmen were fellow churchmen. Fifth and finally, the situation constituted a direct conflict between the Jesuit Order and a powerful and ruthless minister who would not tolerate dissent, for whom *raison d'état* was supreme policy, and who did not hesitate to act when provoked.

That these five causes served as a catalyst for the expulsion of the Jesuits from Portugal owed much to the receptivity of European enlightened opinion, Church politics, and the diplomatic acquiescence of the other European Catholic monarchies. But European opinion alone would not necessarily have been sufficient to bring about an act of expulsion, much less lead to the momentous decision of Pope Clement XIV in 1773 to suppress

---

[40]Franco Venturi, *La Chiesa e la Repubblica dentro i loro limiti (1758–1774)*, vol. 2, *Settecento riformatore* (5 vols.) (Turin: Giulo Einaudi Editore, 1969), 21, 27–29.
[41]Miller, *Portugal and Rome*, 51, 54.
[42]See Rômulo de Carvalho, *História da fundação do Colégio Real dos Nobres de Lisboa, 1761–1772* (Coimbra: Atlântida; Universidade de Coimbra, 1959) and Francisco de Lemos, *Relação geral do estado da Universidade, 1777* (facsimile edition) (Coimbra: Universidade de Coimbra, 1980); Luís de Bivar de Sousa Leão, *Inventário e sequestro da Casa de Aveiro em 1759* (Lisbon: Tribunal de Contos, 1952) and Luís de Bivar de Sousa Leão, *Inventário e sequestro das Casas de Távora e Atouguia em 1759* (Lisbon: Tribunal de Contos, 1954). For a fuller discussion of the consequences of the expulsion of the Jesuits for the educational reforms of Pombal see Maxwell, *Pombal*, especially 87–109.

the Jesuit order entirely. The European Catholic monarchs in Spain, then France and Austria, were quick to follow Portugal's example in expelling the Jesuits, but it is not at all clear that any of them would have acted, had Portugal not acted first. It is here that the currents of Enlightenment thought I outlined earlier conveniently provided justification for actions that at the core, as we have seen, had more prosaic motivations.

VIEW OF RIO FROM BOA VISTA.

CHAPTER 7

The Idea of the Luso-Brazilian Empire

"However much South America might gain from a quiet change of masters, she will be thrown back into a state of barbarism by revolutions."
—Sir John Barrow, 1806

Between 1786 and 1808, critical changes occurred in the attitudes of Brazilians and Portuguese which were to have profound repercussions on the later development of Portuguese-speaking America. Internal and external influences combined and interacted to suggest a peculiarly Luso-Brazilian solution to the problems of nationalism and colonialism, republicanism and monarchy. This chapter attempts to delineate some of these changes, to seek causes, and to explain results.

I

During October 1786, Thomas Jefferson, the envoy of the United States in France, received a letter from the ancient University of Montpellier signed only with the pseudonym *Vendek*. The writer indicated that he had a matter of great consequence to communicate, but as he was a foreigner he wished Jefferson to recommend a safe channel for correspondence. Jefferson did so at once. In a second letter *Vendek* declared himself a Brazilian. The slavery in which his country lay was "rendered each day more insupportable since the epoch of your glorious independence," he wrote. Brazilians had decided to follow the example of the North Americans, he continued, to break the chains that bound them to Portugal and "relive their liberty." To solicit the aid of the United States was the purpose of his visit to France. "Nature made us inhabitants of the same continent," *Vendek* told Jefferson, "and in consequence in some degree compatriots."[1]

Vendek, José Joaquim Maia e Barbalho, who arranged a secret rendezvous and met Thomas Jefferson near Nîmes, was a native of Rio de Janeiro.[2] He had entered the faculty of medicine at Montpellier in 1786, having previously matriculated at the University of Coimbra in Portugal where he studied mathematics.[3] Maia may have been commissioned by merchants in Rio de Janeiro to enter into contact with the American envoy.[4] Probably he was one of a group of students who during the early 1780s had joined hands at Coimbra and vowed to work for the independence of their homeland.[5] An accurate account of Jefferson's encouraging but noncommittal response to *Vendek* reached Brazil via Domingos Vidal Barbosa, another Brazilian student at Montpellier.[6]

Maia and Vidal Barbosa were not alone in their educational accomplishments or their political enthusiasms. Between the Marquês de Pombal's reform of the University of Coimbra in 1772 and 1785, three hundred Brazilian-born students had matriculated there.[7] Others continued their studies or went directly to the faculty of medicine at Montpellier, where fifteen Brazilian-born students matriculated between 1767 and 1793.[8] Vidal Barbosa, a landowner from the captaincy of Minas Gerais, was an enthusi-

---

[1] *Vendek* to Jefferson, Montpellier, October 9, 1786; *Vendek* to Jefferson, Montpellier, November 21, 1786; Jefferson to *Vendek*, Paris, December 26, 1786; *Vendek* to Jefferson, Montpellier, January 5, 1787, *Anuário do Museu da Inconfidência* (hereafter cited as *AMI*), II (Ouro Preto, 1953), 11–13.

[2] Thomas Jefferson to Mr. Jay, Marseille, May 4, 1787, ibid., 13–19. Also see Julian P. Boyd, ed., *The Papers of Thomas Jefferson* (Princeton: Princeton University Press, 1950–), vol. 10 (1954), 427, 546–547; vol. 11 (1955), 338–343; vol. 17 (1965), 258–259.

[3] "Estudantes Brasileiros em Coimbra 1772–1872," *ABNRJ*, LXII (1940), 174; Manoel Xavier de Vasconcelos Pedrosa, "Estudantes Brasileiros na Faculdade de Medicina de Montpellier no fim do século XVIII," *RIHGB*, CCXLIII (April–June 1959), 35–71.

[4] Such was the view expressed in *Autos de devassa da inconfidência mineira* (hereafter cited as *ADIM*), 7 vols. (Rio de Janeiro, 1936–1938) II, 81–95. It is difficult to identify with any certainty the merchants in Rio de Janeiro who might have been implicated in this enterprise. Possibly the idea had something to do with Francisco de Araujo Pereira, for he is cited at a later date as being openly critical of the colonial administration (*ADIM*, I, 280), and he was, according to Viceroy Lavradio, the only merchant in the city worthy of the name; the rest Lavradio dismissed as being simple commissaries (Lavradio, *Relatório*, *RIHGB*, IV [2d edition, 1863], 453.)

[5] Visconde de Barbacena to Martinho de Melo e Castro, Vila Rica, July 11, 1789, *AMI*, II, 68.

[6] Jefferson made a detailed report on his conversation with *Vendek* and his response to the request for aid, Jefferson to Mr. Jay, Marseille, May 4, 1787, ibid., 17.

[7] "Estudantes Brasileiros em Coimbra," 141–181.

[8] "Estudantes Brasileiros . . . Montpellier," 40.

astic propagandist for the writings of the Abbé Raynal, passages of which he was in the habit of reciting by heart.[9] Raynal was a dominating influence in the thinking of many educated Brazilians during the 1780s. His *Histoire philosophique et politique des établissements et du commerce des Européens dans les deux Indes* was invariably part of the greatest private libraries in the colony, and a much-quoted textbook for many of those inspired by the example of the United States.[10]

Raynal's *Histoire* contained an extensive account of Brazil, presented a contemptuous picture of Portugal, condemned British political and economic influence, and recommended that the ports of Brazil be opened to the trade of all nations.[11] During 1785, José Bonifácio de Andrada e Silva, a *paulista*, who matriculated at Coimbra in the same year as Maia, was writing poems, heavy with a bewildering profusion of heroes, including Rousseau, Locke, Voltaire, Pope, Virgil, and Camões, which attacked "the horrid monster of despotism."[12] José Alvares Maciel, son of a wealthy merchant, landowner, and tax farmer in Vila Rica (today Ouro Preto), and a contemporary of Maia at Coimbra, traveled to England.[13] Maciel spent a year in Britain studying manufacturing techniques and whenever possible obtaining accounts of the American Revolution. He discussed the possibility of Brazilian independence with sympathetic English merchants.[14] Even

---

[9]Ibid., 41, 48–50; for comments on Vidal Barbosa's habit of citing Raynal, *ADIM*, II, 59.

[10]Abbé (Guillaume-Thomas-François) Raynal, *Histoire philosophique et politique des établissements et du commerce des Européens dans les deux Indes* (Amsterdam: n.p., 1770), 8 vols. For the influence of Raynal on the thinking of Luís Vieira da Silva and the members of the Literary Society of Rio, see *ADIM*, I, 445–465; II, 95; IV, 207, and *ABNRJ*, LXI, 384, 409–412, 435. Also "Relação completa dos livros pelos autores," Rio de Janeiro, April 10, 1791 [the books of Dr. António Teixeira da Costa] cited by Herculano Gomes Mathias, *A coleção da casa dos contos de Ouro Preto* (Rio de Janeiro: Arquivo Nacional, 1966), 145; and "Sequestro feito em 1794 nos bens que forão achados do bacharel Mariano José Pereira da Fonseca extrahido do respectivo processo," *RIHGB*, LXIII (1901), 14–18.

[11]For wider-ranging discussions of intellectual currents in late colonial Brazil, see Alexander Marchant, "Aspects of the Enlightenment in Brazil," in *Latin America and the Enlightenment*, 2d ed., ed. Arthur Preston Whitaker (Ithaca, N.Y.: Cornell University Press, 1961), 95–118; E. Bradford Burns, "The Enlightenment in Two Colonial Libraries," *Journal of the History of Ideas* XXV (1964): 430–438; E. Bradford Burns, *Nationalism in Brazil: A Historical Survey* (New York: Praeger, 1968), especially 23–26. And for a fascinating and broadly based discussion of Portuguese intellectual development see "The 'Kaffirs of Europe,' the Renaissance, and the Enlightenment," in C. R. (Charles Ralph) Boxer, *The Portuguese Seaborne Empire, 1415–1825* (London: Hutchinson, 1969), 340–366.

[12]Octávio Tarquínio de Sousa, *História dos fundadores do império do Brasil: 1, José Bonifácio* (Rio de Janeiro: J. Olympio, 1960), 63. All translations by author.

[13]Maciel matriculated in 1782 and graduated in 1785. Maia matriculated in 1783. See "Estudantes Brasileiros em Coimbra," 172, 174.

[14]*ADIM*, II, 11, 40, 251; IV, 400.

on the far-off frontiers of Portuguese America, ideas and opinions subversive to the colonial system were aired. During 1786, Antônio Pires da Silva Ponte was denounced to Martinho de Melo e Castro, secretary of state for the overseas dominions, for his rebellious discourses in Mato Grosso. Ponte had claimed that his homeland, Minas Gerais, would become "the head of a great kingdom."[15]

The designation of Minas Gerais as the potential leader of an emancipated colony was not surprising. The captaincy had become the cultural center of late colonial Brazil.[16] Among the native-born whites, there existed a highly literate elite. For forty years rich *mineiros* had been sending their sons to the University of Coimbra. In 1786, twelve of the twenty-seven Brazilians matriculated at Coimbra were from Minas, and in 1787, ten of nineteen.[17] Doyen of the older generation of Brazilian-born graduates was the gracious poet Cláudio Manuel da Costa, a wealthy Vila Rica lawyer who had entered Coimbra in 1749. In 1759 he had been elected a member of the Academia Brasílica dos Renascidos of Bahia, a short-lived literary and historical association, one of the few enterprises which had genuinely sought to embrace the whole of Portuguese America as its parish. Accumulating landed estates and slaves, the successful young Brazilian had been appointed secretary to the government of Minas, a post he held between 1762 and 1765 and again from 1769 to 1773. In 1771 he was appointed attorney to the Third Order of Saint Francis of Vila Rica, one of the most prestigious sodalities in Minas's capital.[18]

The poet's elegant town house was a gathering place for the intellectuals of the captaincy. Among his regular visitors during the 1780s was the superior crown magistrate (*ouvidor*) of Vila Rica, Tomás Antônio Gonzaga, an ambitious and fastidious legalist, son of one of Pombal's confidants. Gonzaga's father was a Brazilian-born magistrate who had served as ouvidor of Pernambuco, as a judge of the Bahian High Court, intendant-general of gold, first minister of the Inspection House of Bahia, and as a judge of the High Court of Oporto. He had personally presented his son's dissertation on the natural law to Pombal. The treatise was dedicated to the marquês, described in the preface as "that hero and lover of true science." Tomás An-

---

[15]José de Lacerda e Almeida to Martinho de Melo e Castro, September 24, 1786, Mato Grosso, maço 12.

[16]See comments by C. R. (Charles Ralph) Boxer, *Some Literary Sources for the History of Brazil in the Eighteenth Century* (Oxford: Clarendon Press, 1967).

[17]"Estudantes Brasileiros em Coimbra," 181–187.

[18]Cláudio Manuel da Costa, "Sequestro," *ADIM*, I, 356–364; "Traslado dos sequestros;" *ADIM*, V, 263–276; Manuel Rodrigues Lapa, *As "Cartas chilenas": um problema histórico e filológico* (Rio de Janeiro: Ministério da Educação e Cultura, Instituto do Livro, 1958), 28, 37; Lúcio José dos Santos, *A Inconfidência Mineira: papel de Tiradentes* (São Paulo: Escolas Profissionaes do Lyceu Coração de Jesus, 1927), 234–239.

tônio Gonzaga was born in Oporto but brought up almost entirely in Brazil. He had attended the Jesuit college at Bahia, witnessing the expulsion of the Black Robes in 1759. He was nominated ouvidor of Vila Rica in 1782. Long an admirer of the works of Cláudio Manuel da Costa, he himself was a poet of merit and originality. The two men formed the center of a group which embraced Ignácio José de Alvarenga Peixoto, ouvidor of São João d'El Rei, and Luís Vieira da Silva, canon of the cathedral of Mariana, the episcopal seat of Minas Gerais.[19]

Ignácio José de Alvarenga Peixoto, a Brazilian graduate of Coimbra, had composed some fulsome verses in honor of the Marquês de Pombal and his family. His appointment as ouvidor of the *comarca* of Rio das Mortes in Minas Gerais was a consequence of these poetic endeavors. He himself selected the post because of his vast landed estates, slave holdings, and mining interests in the area, though the Portuguese government did not ordinarily sanction such initiative.[20] Luís Vieira was a well-known and persuasive preacher, much in demand on solemn and festive occasions, of which there were many in the ecclesiastical calendar of Minas Gerais. An erudite and thoughtful cleric in his early fifties, he had studied at the Jesuit college in São Paulo during the 1750s, and was appointed to the chair of philosophy in the seminary at Mariana in 1757. He was elected commissary of the Third Order of Saint Francis of Vila Rica in 1770. Luís Vieira was outspoken in his enthusiasm for the events in North America. He held that the European powers had no right to dominion in America. The Portuguese monarchy had spent nothing on the conquest of Brazil, and the Brazilians themselves had restored Bahia to the Crown from the Dutch and ransomed Rio de Janeiro from the French. Luís Vieira, a man who had never left Brazil, was close in opinion to those conspiratorial students who had attempted to negotiate with Thomas Jefferson in France.[21]

---

[19]*Obras completas de Tomás Antônio Gonzaga: I, poesias, Cartas chilenas*, ed. Manuel Rodrigues Lapa (Rio de Janeiro: Instituto Nacional do Livro, Ministério da Educação e Cultura, 1957), ix–xv; "Auto de inquirição summario de testemunhas," Vila Rica, May 26, 1798, *ADIM*, II, 441–452; "Direito Natural accommodado ao estado civil catolico, offerecido ao Ill° e Ex° Sn^r Sebastião José de Carvalho e Mello, Marquês de Pombal, por Thomás Antônio Gonzaga," BNLCP, códice 29.

[20]Manuel Rodrigues Lapa, *Vida e obra de Alvarenga Peixoto* (Rio de Janeiro: Instituto Nacional do Livro, Ministério da Educação e Cultura, 1960), x, xxvii, xxviii.

[21]"Avaliação dos livros sequestrados, conego Luís Vieira da Silva," *ADIM*, I, 445–465; "Auto de perguntas," Rio de Janeiro, November 20, 1789, *ADIM*, IV, 292–293; "Auto de continuação de perguntas," Rio de Janeiro, July 21, 1790 (*sic*; this must be 1791, for the interrogating judge in this instance, Chancellor Vasconcellos Coutinho, did not arrive in Rio de Janeiro until late December 1790), ibid., 304; Vicente Vieira da Mota, witness, Vila Rica, June 23, 1789, *ADIM*, I, 110–111; Vicente Vieira da Mota, Witness, Vila Rica, August 3, 1789, *ADIM*, III, 336; "Auto de perguntas," Rio de Janeiro, July 19, 1791, *ADIM*, V, 19–20; *AMI*, II, 68.

The Vila Rica circle was not the only group of like-minded and intelligent men who met informally to discuss poetry, philosophy, and the events in Europe and America. Similar groups of lawyers and writers met in São João d'El Rei and elsewhere in the captaincy for conversation and cards.[22] The members of the Vila Rica circle, however, by the quality of their writing, and by their position, influence, and wealth, stood at the apex of Minas society. Books and information often reached them more rapidly than official dispatches which had to pass through the cumbersome bureaucracy from Lisbon to the secretariat of the captaincy. The canon Vieira's cosmopolitan collection of books, some 600 volumes all told, contained William Robertson's *Histoire de l'Amérique*, and the *Encyclopédie*, as well as the works of Bielfeld, Voltaire, and Condillac.[23] Cláudio Manuel da Costa was reputed to have translated Adam Smith's *Wealth of Nations*.[24]

Literate and open-minded, the intellectual elite of Minas Gerais proved creative and original.[25] The history of the captaincy became the theme of Cláudio Manuel da Costa's epic poem *Vila Rica* and the subject of a lengthy prose dissertation by him replete with statistical tables.[26] During 1781 Alvarenga Peixoto reflected this powerful self-awareness in his *canto*

---

[22]Lapa, *Alvarenga Peixoto*, xxxii.

[23]"Avaliação dos livros sequestrados," *ADIM*, I, p. 458; Also see José Ferreira Carrato, *Igreja, iluminismo, e escolas mineiras colonias: notas sôbre a cultura da decadencia mineira setecentista* (São Paulo: Cia. Ed. Nacional, 1968), 113–114; and Eduardo Frieiro, *O diabo na livraria do cônego: como era Gonzaga? E outros temas mineiros* (Belo Horizonte: Editôra Itatiaia, [1957]).

[24]Joaquim Noberto de Sousa Silva, "Commemoração do centenário de Cláudio Manuel da Costa," *RIHGB*, LIII, I (1890), 150.

[25]There is a very large bibliography on the cultural flowering of Minas Gerais during the late eighteenth century; especially useful studies are, Augusto de Lima Júnior, *A capitania de Minas Gerais, origens e formação* (3d edition) (Belo Horizonte: Instituto de História, Letras e Arte, 1965), 123, 791–793; José Ferreira Carrato, *As Minas Gerais e os primórdios do caraça* (São Paulo: Companhia Editora Nacional, 1963), 57–62; Fritz Teixeira de Salles, *Associações religiosas no ciclo do ouro* (Belo Horizonte: Universidade de Minas Gerais, 1963), 27, 36, 65, 71; Sílvio de Carvalho Vasconcellos, "Architectura colonial Mineira," *I° Seminário de estudos mineiros* (Belo Horizonte: Universidade de Minas Gerais, 1956), 67; Curt Lange, "Música Religiosa de Minas Gerais," *MEC* (Ministério da Educação e Cultura, Rio de Janeiro, May–June, 1958), 19–25; Francisco Antônio Lopes, *História da construção da igreja do Carmo de Ouro Preto* (Rio de Janeiro: Ministério da Educação e Saúde, 1942); for the extensive bibliography on the Minas Baroque, an excellent introduction is provided by Germain Bazin, *L'Architecture religieuse baroque au Brésil*, 2 vols. (Paris: Plon; São Paulo: Museu de Arte, 1956), I, 173–213; and by Robert C. Smith Jr., "The Arts in Brazil: Baroque Architecture," in *Portugal and Brazil*, ed. Harold Livermore (Oxford: Clarendon Press, 1963), 349; and his "Colonial Architecture of Minas Gerais," *The Art Bulletin* XXI (1939): 110–142.

[26]"Noticia da capitania de Minas Gerais por Cláudio Manuel da Costa," IHGP, lata 22, doc. 13.

genetlíaco, an enthusiastic apology for the riches, men, and promise of the Brazilian land. He compared the deeds of the *Mineiros* to those of Hercules, Ulysses, and Alexander the Great. And he did not fail to include "strong and valiant" slaves in his panegyric. In a portentous phrase which could well have applied to the rest of his countrymen, the poet asserted: "They are worthy of attention."[27]

Gonzaga, Cláudio Manuel da Costa, and the canon Luís Vieira were men "who have ascendancy over the spirits of the people," the commandant of the Minas Dragoons told Alvarenga Peixoto in 1789.[28] All three were involved in the plot to foment an armed uprising against the Portuguese Crown during late 1788 and early 1789.[29] Much later an inquiry into the implication of one of the conspirators described the intention of the Minas movement as being "to change the government of Minas from monarchical to democratic."[30] At the time, however, as far as the evidence shows, the word democratic was never used. The American Revolution was thought especially pertinent because the Minas conspirators saw the course of events in North America as remarkably similar to their own situation. "Nothing caused the break [between Britain and her colonies] but the great duties that were imposed," one of the conspirators claimed.[31] The demands of the Portuguese government that the colossal arrears due on the royal fifth of the gold production of the captaincy be made up by the imposition of a per capita tax (*derrama*) on the Minas population seemed

---

[27]Lapa, *Alvarenga Peixoto*, xli, 33–38.

[28]"Continuação de perguntas feitas ao . . . Alvarenga Peixoto," Rio de Janeiro, January 14, 1790, *ADIM* IV, 138.

[29]For a summary of the evidence against the conspirators, see Desembargador José Pedro Machado Coelho Torres to Luís de Vasconcellos e Sousa, Rio de Janeiro, December 11, 1789, with "a lista das pessoas . . . dando hum idea das prezumsoens, ou prova que rezulta contra cada hum deles," AHU, Minas Gerais, caixa 92, folder no. 47. Some discussion in English of the Minas Conspiracy can be found in Manoel Cardoso, "Another document on the Inconfidência Mineira," *Hispanic American Historical Review* XXXII (1952): 540–551; and Alexander Marchant, "Tiradentes and the Conspiracy of Minas," *Hispanic American Historical Review* XXI (1941): 239–257; the standard account in Portuguese remains Lúcio José dos Santos, *A Inconfidência Mineira*, supplemented by two articles by Herculano Gomes Mathias, "O Tiradentes e a cidade do Rio de Janeiro," *Anais do Museu Histórico Nacional*, XVI (1966), 102, and "Inconfidência e Inconfidentes," *Anais do congresso comemorativo do bicentenário da transferência da sede do governo do Brasil da cidade do Salvador para o Rio de Janeiro*, 3 vols. (Rio de Janeiro, 1967) III, 250; and by Célia Nunes Galvão Quirino dos Santos, *A Inconfidência Mineira* (Separata do Tomo XX dos *Anais do Museu Paulista*, São Paulo, 1966).

[30]The reference came concerning a petition by Padre Oliveira Rolim, one of the priests implicated in the plot, August 1822, *RAPM*, IX (1904), 624.

[31]"Continuação de perguntas feitas a Francisco de Paula Freire de Andrade," Rio de Janeiro, July 29, 1791, *ADIM*, IV, 230.

all too reminiscent of the duties levied on the American colonists. The conspirators concluded that "the Abbé Raynal had been a writer of great vision, because he had prognosticated the uprising in North America, and the captaincy of Minas Gerais because of the imposition of the derrama was now in the same circumstances.[32] Their intention was to establish a republican and constitutional state in Minas Gerais. Parliaments were to be set up in each town.[33] These would be subordinate to a supreme parliament (*um parlamento principal*). A university was to be founded in Vila Rica.[34] The plotters contemplated the total abrogation of past laws and statutes.[35]

How far the institutions to be established imitated those in North America is not clear. There is some evidence of opposition to a slavish imitation of the North American example at least as far as the arms of the state were concerned, and perhaps on more fundamental matters.[36] However, circulating among the conspirators was the *Recueil de Loix Constitutives des États-Unis de l'Amérique*, published in Paris in 1778, which contained the Articles of Confederation and drafts of the state constitutions of Pennsylvania, New Jersey, Delaware, Maryland, the Carolinas, and Massachusetts.[37] The conspirators also possessed constitutional commentaries by Raynal and Mably.[38] Gonzaga, despite his disparagement of democracy in

---

[32]"Auto de perguntas feitas ao Freire de Andrade," Rio de Janeiro, November 16, 1789, *ADIM*, IV, 207.
[33]"Continuação de perguntas feitas ao vigário . . . Carlos Corrêa;" Rio de Janeiro, November 27, 1789, *ADIM*, IV, 171.
[34]Sentença de Alçada (1792), Santos, *Inconfidência Mineira*, 591.
[35]"Joaquim Silverio dos Reis and Carlos Corrêa, auto de acareação," Rio de Janeiro, July 13, 1791, *ADIM*, IV, 193.
[36]"Continuação de perguntas feitas ao . . . Alvarenga Peixoto," Rio de Janeiro, January 14, 1790, *ADIM*, IV, 147.
[37]"Translado e Appensos, No. 26; neste lugar e debaixo do No. 26 vai apo aos dos Autos originais o livro em Frances intitulado, Recueil des Loix Constitutives des États-Unis de L'Amérique," AHU, Minas Gerais, caixa 92. The full reference for this collection is: *Recueil des loix constitutives des colonies angloises, confédérées sous la dénomination d'États-Unis de l'Amérique-Septentrionale. Auquel on a joint les Actes d'Indépendance de Confédération, et autres actes du Congrès général, traduit de l'anglois. Dédié à M. le Docteur Franklin.* (En Suisse: Chez les Libraires Associés [i.e. Paris: Cellot], 1778). In fact two editions of this work were published in Paris; the first with the place of publication noted as Philadelphia and the second pirated edition claiming to have been published in Switzerland. The copy in the possession of the Minas conspirators was the pirated edition noted above. For a history of these works see Durand Echeverria, "French Publications of the Declaration of Independence and the American Constitutions, 1776–1783," *The Papers of the Bibliographical Society of America* 47, no. 4, (1953), 313–338.
[38]"Item, le droit public de l'Europe de Mably," tres volumes em oitavo," avaliação dos livros, *ADIM*, I, 461; and for other books by Mably, "Termo de encerramento, Marianna," *ADIM*, I, 466.

his treatise on the natural law, was even at that time a firm supporter of the contractual nature of government. The king, the young Gonzaga had written, was a mandatory of the people, a minister of God, the end of whose rule was the utility of the people. Gonzaga's acrimonious dispute with the government of Luís da Cunha Menezes of Minas, immortalized in his *Cartas Chilenas,* had centered on the dangers of arbitrary rule. His memorials to court during the 1780s strongly emphasized the legal and moral restraints on the actions and power of the executive.[39]

The Minas plot was betrayed. With others, Gonzaga, Cláudio Manuel da Costa, Alvarenga Peixoto, and the canon Luís Vieira were arrested. The ideology of the Minas Conspiracy, however, influenced by the success of the American Revolution and the impact in Brazil of the ideas of Raynal and others had projected the movement into a much greater context. There had been uprisings far more damaging in lives and property before. The Vila Rica uprising of 1720, for example, was more dramatic in action and more bloody than the nonevents of 1788–1789. But no previous plot had possessed motivations so fundamentally anticolonial and so consciously nationalistic. Members of an important segment of that group in society on whom the metropolitan government most relied for the exercise of power at the local level, in one of Brazil's most important, populous, and strategically placed captaincies, had dared to think that they might live without Portugal. Inspired by the example of North America and by current political theory, they had questioned what had been unquestioned. The new mental climate was not something that could be concretely defined, but it was obvious to all, and most especially to the agents of the metropolitan government in Brazil.[40] Men in Minas had thought they could be free, independent, and republican.

II

The conspiracy in Minas Gerais had occurred at a special moment in time. The plot was concerted before the French Revolution. But the arrests, the trial, and the sentencing of those involved coincided with growing revolutionary turmoil in Europe. Rumors of possible French invasion had been bandied around among the conspirators, but they meant the France of the

---

[39]There is a vast bibliography on the *Cartas Chilenas,* their attribution, identification of the characters, and so on. Hardly a literary scholar or historian in Portugal or Brazil has not at some time discussed the work. I have relied heavily on Manuel Rodrigues Lapa's masterly *As "Cartas Chilenas,"* though it is unlikely that even this profound and careful study will prove to be the definitive work.
[40]See, for example, the comments by Chancellor Vasconcellos Coutinho in his letter to Martinho de Melo e Castro, Rio de Janeiro, July 30, 1791, AHU, Minas Gerais, caixa 94.

Old Regime. The chronological relationship of the Minas Conspiracy to the French Revolution is important. The Minas oligarchs had believed they could control and manipulate the popular will. They had taken as their example the American Revolution, where political readjustments had taken place without social upheaval. But the example of the American patriots had not prepared them for the events of the French Revolution, particularly not for the spectacular repercussions of the French Revolution in the Americas. The revolt of the slaves in the French sugar island of Saint-Domingue during 1792 brought an awful awakening to those slaveowners who had talked naively of republics and revolt while ignoring the social and racial consequences of their words. The British scientist, traveler, and writer John Barrow, who was in Rio de Janeiro during 1792, noted the change "black power" had brought. "The secret spell that caused the Negro to tremble in the presence of the white man is in a great degree dissolved," he wrote. "The supposed superiority by which a hundred of the former were kept in awe and submission by one of the latter is no longer acknowledged."[41] Martinho de Melo e Castro recognized at once the threat the Saint-Domingue revolt posed for Brazil. He warned the governors against "the pernicious and perverse intent of the [Jacobin] clubs established in France to propagate the abominable and destructive principles of liberty, in order to effect by these means the fatal revolution." And he warned that it was these abominable principles that caused "the fire of revolt and insurrection that made the slaves rise against their masters . . . in Santo Domingo."[42]

The innocuous Literary Society of Rio de Janeiro, with its dedication to Raynal and Mably, and its alleged sympathy for the Minas conspirators, was an obvious target for the nervous colonial administration. In 1794, its members were arrested and subjected to prolonged interrogations. The society, founded in 1785 by Luís de Vasconcellos e Sousa, the former viceroy, had attempted to form a secret inner conclave where "good faith and secrecy might be maintained among the members." Democratically constituted, it was to discuss "philosophy in all its aspects." Among the papers confiscated from Jacinto José da Silva, a graduate in medicine from Montpellier, were two remarkable letters from a colleague, Manuel José de Novais de Almeida, which dramatically underlined the impact of the revolt in Saint-Domingue on his contemporaries. In February 1791, Dr. Novais de

---

[41]John Barrow, *A Voyage to Cochinchina in the Years 1792 and 1793* (London: T. Cadell and W. Davies, 1806), 117–118.
[42]Martinho de Melo e Castro to Bernardo José de Lorena, Lisbon, February 21, 1792, *DISP*, XLV (1924), 449–452.

Almeida had written enthusiastically of the "equality of men." But by May 25, 1792, his comments had a different tone. "I am very worried with respect to the Americas,'" he told da Silva. "What happened in French [America] demonstrates what might one day happen in ours, which god permitting I shall never see, for I am a friend of humanity. . . . Sell the slaves that you possess, have the generosity to grant them their freedom, you will have fewer enemies."[43]

The example of the Antillean revolt was especially pertinent for white Brazilians. In Minas Gerais the population in 1776, excluding Indians, was over 300,000, or 20 percent of the total population of Portuguese America. Over 50 percent of the population of Minas was black, and the remainder equally divided between browns (*pardos*) and whites. In 1786, the number of freemen to slaves was placed at 188,712 to 174,135.[44] In Bahia, the capital city of Salvador had a population of 40,000 during the 1790s, and the total for the captaincy was near 280,000, or 18 percent of the total population of Portuguese America. José da Silva Lisboa, a Brazilian graduate of Coimbra and professor of philosophy in Bahia, estimated that a mere quarter of the population was white.[45]

The only racial overtones during the Minas Conspiracy had come in the form of vague comments attributed to Manoel da Costa Capanema, and the evidence which linked him to the conspirators was so slight that he was

---

[43]"Autto do exame que fizerao o Dez[embargador] Ouvidor G[eneral] do Crime Francisco Alvarez de Andrade, e o Dr. Intendente General do Ouro, Caetano Pinto de Vasconcellos MonteNegro, em todos os Papeis do Dr. Jacinto José da Silva," Rio de Janeiro, January 8, 1795, which together with the rest of the documents concerning the Literary Society is published in *ABNRJ*, LXI (1939): 241–523, especially 364–370. The nervousness of the Rio administration had been very obvious the year before (1794), when the Brazilian justice of the peace in Rio turned over an anonymous letter he had received recommending an uprising and the methods by which it should be carried out, "Autos de Exame e Averiguação sobre o a autor de uma carta anonima escrita ao juiz de fora do Rio de Janeiro, Dr. Baltazar da Silva Lisboa (1793)," *ABNRJ*, LX, 261–313.

[44]"Taboa das habitantes da capitania de Minas Gerais, 1776, noticia da capitania de Minas Gerais," IHGB, lata 22, doc., 13; Dauril Alden, "The Population of Brazil in the late Eighteenth Century: A Preliminary Survey," *Hispanic American Historical Review* XLIII (1963): 173–205; "População da provincia de Minas Gerais, 1776–1823;" *RAPM* IV (1899), 249–276.

[45]"Mappa da enumeração da gente e povo desta capitania da Bahia, December, 1780;" *ABNRJ*, XXXII (1910): 480; Thales de Azevedo, *Povoamento da cidade do Salvador* (São Paulo: Companhia Editora Nacional, 1955), 201; José da Silva Lisboa to Domingos Vandelli, Bahia, October 18, 1781, *ABNRJ*, XXXII (1910): 505; Vilhena put the proportion of whites at nearer a third, Luiz dos Santos Vilhena, *Recopilação de noticias soteropolitanas e Brasilicas, contidas em XX cartas (1802)*, ed. Braz do Amaral, 3 vols. (Bahia: Imprensa official do estado, 1922, 1935), I, 49.

absolved by the court of inquiry (*Alçada*).[46] José Alvares Maciel had regarded the presence of so large a percentage of blacks in the population as a possible threat to the new republic, should the promise of their liberation by the Portuguese induce them to oppose the native whites. Alvarenga Peixoto recommended that the slaves be granted freedom, which would make them the passionate defenders of the new state, committed to its survival. Maciel, however, pointed out that such a solution might be self-defeating, for proprietors would be left with no one to work the mines. The conspirators appear to have reached a compromise solution whereby only the native-born black and mulatto slaves would be freed in the interests of the defense of the state.[47] The proposition was itself a startling one for 1789, but the conspirators seem to have underestimated the potential consequences of their plans. They assumed the situation could be controlled with ease, just as they assumed the uprising could be instigated, manipulated, and controlled in their own interests.

III

In the climate of opinion that followed the Saint-Domingue revolt, the discovery of plans for an armed uprising by the mulatto artisans of Bahia during 1798 had a very special impact by demonstrating what whites had already begun to realize: that ideas of social equality propagated within a society where a mere third of the population was white risked being interpreted in racial terms. The Bahian affair revealed the politicization of levels of society barely concerned with the Minas conspiracy. The middle-aged lawyers, magistrates, and clerics in Minas Gerais (most of them opulent, members of racially exclusive sodalities, and slaveowners) contrasted markedly with the young mulatto artisans, soldiers, sharecroppers, and salaried schoolteachers implicated in the Bahian plot. Embittered and anticlerical, the Bahian mulattoes were as opposed to rich Brazilians as to Portuguese dominion. They welcomed social turmoil, proposed the overthrow of existing structures, and sought an egalitarian and democratic society where differences of race would be no impediment to employment and social mobility. The *pardo* tailor João de Deus, who at the time of his arrest possessed no more than eighty reis and eight children, proclaimed that "All [Brazilians] would become Frenchmen, in order to live in equality

---

[46]The statement attributed to him was: "Estes branquinhos do Reino que nos quirem tomar a terra cedo os havemos de deitar fora," Sentença da Alçada, Santos, *Inconfidência Mineira*, 607–617.

[47]"Perguntas feitas a José Alvares Maciel," Rio de Janeiro, November 26, 1789, *ADIM*, IV, 398.

and abundance. They would destroy the public officials, attack the monasteries, open the port . . . and reduce all to an entire revolution, so that all might be rich and taken out of poverty, and that the differences between white, black and brown would be extinguished, and that all without discrimination would be admitted to positions and occupations."[48]

It was not the North American patriots who provided the example for João de Deus and his colleagues. It was the sans-culottes. It was not the constitutional niceties of the United States that inspired them. It was the slogans of the Paris mob. Handwritten manifestoes appeared throughout the city on August 12, 1798.[49] Addressed to the "Republican Bahian people" in the name of the "supreme tribunal of Bahian democracy," the manifestoes called for the extermination of the "detestable metropolitan yoke of Portugal."[50] Clergy who preached against popular liberty were threatened. All citizens, especially mulattoes and blacks, were told that "all are equal, there will be no differences, there will be freedom, equality and fraternity."[51] There was no equivocation over slavery. "All black and brown slaves are to be free so that there will be no slavery whatsoever."[52] The government would be "Democratic, free and independent."[53] "The happy time of our liberty is about to arrive, the time when all will be brothers, the time when all will be equal."[54]

---

[48]"Denuncia publica, jurada . . . que da Joaquim José da Veiga, homen pardo forro . . . ," August 27, 1798, *ADIB*, I, 8; Cel. Ignácio Accioli de Cerqueira e Silva, *Memorias históricas e políticas da Bahia* (hereafter cited as *MHPB*), ed. Braz do Amaral, 6 vols. (Bahia: Imprensa Official do Estado, 1919–1925), III, 93.

[49]F. Borges de Barros, "Copia de varios papeis sediciosos que em alguns lugares públicos deste cidade se fixarão na manha do dia 12 de agosto de 1798," *Anais do Arquivo Público da Bahia*, II (1917): 143–146; Carlos Guilherme Mota, *Idéia de revolução no Brasil (1789–1801): estudo das formas de pensamento* (Petrópolis: Editora Vozes, 1979). For a brief account in English of the Bahian plot see R. R. Palmer, *The Age of Democratic Revolution*, II, 513. Two documentary collections are available. *A Inconfidência da Bahia, devassas e sequestros* (hereafter cited as *ADIB*), 2 vols. (Rio de Janeiro, 1931); "Autos de devassas do levantamento a sedição intentados na Bahia em 1798," *Anais do Arquivo Público da Bahia*, XXXV, XXXVI (1959–1961). Also see the article by Kátia M. de Queirós Mattoso, "Conjoncture et Société au Brésil à la fin du XVIIIe Siècle: Prix et Salaires à la veille de la révolution des Alfaiates, Bahia 1798," *Cahiers des Amériques Latines* V (January–June, 1970): 33–53.

[50]"Aviso ao clero e ao povo Bahinense indouto," *MHPB*, III, 110.

[51]"Prelo," *MHPB*, III, 109.

[52]"Denuncia pública . . . que da o capitão do regimento auxiliar dos homens pretos Joaquim José de Santa Anna," *ADIB*, I, 13.

[53]"Auto . . . para proceder a devassa pela rebelião a levantamento projectada nesta cidade, para se estabelecer no continente do Brasil, hum governo democratico . . . ," August 28, 1798, *ADIB*, 1, 7.

[54]"Aviso," *MHPB*, III, 106. Also see Kátia M. de Queirós Mattoso, *Presença francesa no movimento democrático baiano, 1798* (Salvador: Itapuá, 1969).

Long before they had concerted even the most rudimentary plan, the Bahian artisans were caught red-handed.[55] The causes of the plot had been an amalgam of social resentments, high food prices, and the impact of the revolutionary slogans of France. The appointment of a white *sargento-mor* as commandant of the auxiliary regiment of free *pardos* crossed racial lines and placed the mulatto regiment in an unfavorable relationship with the regiment of free blacks, the famous *Henriques*, with its black commandant colonel.[56] The price of manioc flour, the basic subsistence food, had risen during the previous four years from 640 reis per *alqueire* to between 1,280 and 1,600 reis.[57] "The most vile meat imaginable was selling for prices twice what it was worth," according to the professor of Greek in Salvador, Luís dos Santos Vilhena.[58] The mulatto artisans and soldiers, many of them literate, had been receptive to revolutionary ideology. But the appearance of the manifestos in Bahia, the demand for "liberty, equality and fraternity," and the racial composition of the conspiratorial conclave provoked a reaction out of all proportion to the incidents themselves. Since 1792, slaveowners throughout the Americas had barely hidden their concern that the revolution in the Caribbean might prove contagious. For slaveowners in Brazil at least, the actions of Bahian mulattoes made the contagion a concrete reality. After 1798 all white men in Portuguese America faced the question posed by Admiral Campbell, commandant of the Brazilian squadron of the Portuguese navy during the early nineteenth century: Was it indeed true that "the transactions at St. Domingo had plainly evinced that there was no stability in the sovereignty of whites in a country necessarily worked by blacks?"[59]

The government in Lisbon suspected that more important and influential men might be behind the Bahian conspiracy, a concern understandable in light of events in Minas Gerais. In addition there had been rumors in Portugal "that the principal people [of Bahia] were infested . . . with the abominable French principles . . . with great affection for the absurd and intended French constitution. . . ." If French troops landed, it was said, the city would unite with them. Specifically, the wealthy priest and entrepre-

---

[55]"Os conspiradores que foram presos," *MHPB*, III, 99–102; also see account by Braz do Amaral, ibid., 96–97, and Affonso Ruy de Souza, *A primeira revolução social brasileira (1798)* (São Paulo: Companhia Editora Nacional, 1942). Also see the more recent study by István Jancsó, *Na Bahia, contra o Império: historia do ensaio de sedição de 1798* (São Paulo: HUCITEC-EDUFBA, 1996).

[56]"Denuncia . . . que da . . . Santa Anna," *ADIB*, I, 12.

[57]Vilhena, *Cartas*, I, 159; Carlos Guilherme Mota, "Mentalidade Ilustrada na colonizacão Portuguesa: Luís dos Santos Vilherna," *RHSP*, no. 72 (1967): 405–416.

[58]Vilhena, *Cartas*, I, 128–129.

[59]Donald Campbell, London, August 14, 1804, Chatham Papers, Public Record Office, London (hereafter cited as PRO) 30/8/345 part 2, f. 223.

neur Francisco Agostinho Gomes was denounced to the authorities in Lisbon. The governor of Bahia, D. Fernando José de Portugal, was instructed to investigate these charges.[60]

Gomes was an erudite and enlightened man with as fine a private library as that which canon Luís Vieira had built up in Minas Gerais. Thomas Lindley, who met him at the turn of the century, was singularly impressed. "In the French I noticed Alembert's *Encyclopedia*, Buffon, and Lavoisier, among our own authors he had chiefly selected natural history, political economy, travels and philosophical works . . . Robertson's *America* he particularly commended and Smith's *Wealth of Nations* . . ." Lindley also noted how Father Gomes praised the works of Thomas Paine.[61] D. Fernando, however, found nothing to incriminate Gomes. The ideas and organization of the Bahian conspiracy were such, he wrote, "that no persons of consideration, or understanding, or who had knowledge or enlightenment had entered. . . ."[62] With respect to the priest, he pointed out to Lisbon that "the reading of English papers did not make a man a Jacobin." Moreover, he found it highly improbable that any of the principal people of the captaincy were implicated in the Bahian conspiracy. He had no indication of this implication among either the businessmen or the men in public office, or the people of property, all of whom reacted strongly when the seditious papers appeared. Those involved in the plot were all of the lower class (*classe ordinária*). "That which is always most dreaded in colonies are the slaves, on account of their condition and because they comprise the greater number of the inhabitants," he told Lisbon. "It is therefore not natural for men employed and established in goods and property to join a conspiracy which would result in awful consequences to themselves, being exposed to assassination by their own slaves." He did not seek "to apologize for the inhabitants of Bahia"; he wished "only to express his sentiments."[63]

D. Fernando had made a vital distinction, and his comments stressed the change which had occurred since 1792. The sugar planters and their apologists desired "liberty," to be sure, and the more literate of them were avid disciples of European thinkers; but the theories that appealed to them articulated and provided justification for their own self-interest, and this

---

[60]D. Rodrigo de Sousa Coutinho to D. Fernando José de Portugal, Queluz, October 4, 1798, *MHPB*, 111, 95. The suspicion that more important members of society were implicated has been put forward by both Souza, *A primeira revolução*, and Antônio de Araujo de Aragão Bulcão Sobrinho, "O patriarcha da liberdade Bahiana, Joaquim Inácio de Sequeira Bulcão;" *RIHGB*, 217 (1952), 167–185, though neither has presented any evidence.
[61]Thomas Lindley, *Authentic Narrative of a Voyage from the Cape of Good Hope to the Brazils . . . in 1802 and 1803 . . .* (London: J. Johnson, 1805), 66–68.
[62]D. Fernando José de Portugal to D. Rodrigo de Sousa Coutinho, Bahia, October 20, 1798, *MHPB*, III, 123.
[63]D. Fernando José de Portugal to D. Rodrigo de Sousa Coutinho, Bahia, February 13, 1799, *MHPB*, III, 132–134.

self-interest, D. Fernando discerned, was not in conflict with the colonial relationship. The liberty the planters most desired was the freedom Bishop Azeredo Coutinho proposed in his memorial on the price of sugar, presented to the Lisbon Academy of Sciences in 1792. It was the liberty "for each to make the greatest profit from his work."[64] Freedom for capitalist enterprise was not the freedom João de Deos had in mind. As D. Fernando saw, the firmest opponents of the demands of the Bahian mulattoes would be the Bahian planters, for it was they, not Lisbon, who had the most to lose if those demands were met.

Paradoxically the slave revolt in the West Indies had added acuteness to the sugar planters' demands for freedom from government interference and control, just as the events in Saint-Domingue had stimulated apprehensions about the racial balance of the population, and produced the socioeconomic situation out of which the Bahian conspiracy emerged. Collapse of French sugar production in the West Indies during the 1790s gave Bahia the opportunity for economic renaissance.[65] So profitable had sugar become and so high the prices fetched on European markets that, according to Luís dos Santos Vilhena, "there is no one who does not wish to be a sugar planter."[66] Azeredo Coutinho, who before becoming an ecclesi-

---

[64]José Joaquim da Cunha de Azeredo Coutinho, "Memória sobre o preço do açucar (1791)," in *Memórias económicas da Academia Real das Ciências de Lisboa para o adiantamento da agricultura, das artes, e da indústria em Portugal e suas conquistas (1789–1815), Colecção de obras clássicas do pensamento económico português* (I in 5 vols.) (Lisbon: Banco de Portugal, 1990–1991), vol. 3, 273–280. The Academy of Sciences had been founded in 1779. Some indication of its importance to the intellectual life of the period can be obtained from António Baião, *A Infância da Academia (1788–1794): visita aos arquivos do Reino; corrêspondencia a tal respeito de João Pedro Ribeira, Santa Rosa de Viterbo* . . . (Coimbra: Imprensa da Universidade, 1934); António Ferrão, "O segundo duque de Lafões, e o marquês de Pombal (subsídios para a biografia do fundador da Academia das Ciências)," *Boletim da segunda classe, Academia das Ciências de Lisboa*, XIX (1924–1925), 407–588. For listing of the Academy's publications, see Moses Bensabat Amzalak, *Do estudo e da evolução das doutrinas económicas em Portugal* (Lisbon: n.p., 1928). For Azeredo Coutinho, Manoel Cardozo, "Azeredo Coutinho and the Intellectual Ferment of His Times," in *Conflict and Continuity in Brazilian Society*, ed. Henry H. Keith and S. F. Edwards (Columbia, S.C.: University of South Carolina, 1969), 72–103, and E. Bradford Burns, "The Role of Azeredo Coutinho in the Enlightenment of Brazil," *Hispanic American Historical Review* XLIV (May 1964): 145–160.

[65]Caio Prado Junior, *A formação do Brasil contemporâneo, colónia*, 7th ed. (São Paulo: Editora Brasiliense, 1963), 126, 159.

[66]Vilhena, *Cartas*, I, 158; "Exportação da Bahia para Portugal (1798)," ibid, I, 53. Comment on the high price of South American products was made by Robert Walpole to Lord Grenville, Lisbon, October 12, 1791, PRO, Foreign Office, 63/14. For price of Brazilian sugar on the Amsterdam market see N. W. (Nicolaas Wilhelmus) Posthumus, *Inquiry into the History of Prices in Holland*, 2 vols. (Leiden: E. J. Brill, 1946, 1964), 1, 122, 124.

astic had administered a sugar mill in Brazil, urged that full advantage be taken of the favorable market conditions provided by the "providential revolution of the French colonies." As the price of sugar rises, he wrote, "the greater becomes our production and our commerce."[67]

The sugar boom was partly responsible for the favorable balance of trade with the metropolis enjoyed by Bahia during the 1790s, as a result of which it became necessary to send bullion from Portugal to Brazil.[68] It was a spectacular reversal of circumstances. A mere forty years before, Brazilian gold had provided the mainstay of colonial exports to Lisbon. Azeredo Coutinho's essay on the commerce of Portugal and her dominions attempted to rationalize the new situation. "The mother country and the colonies taken together ought to be regarded as the farm of a single farmer," he wrote. "The owner of many estates does not care whether such and such a one procures him more revenue, but he only rates the collective revenues of the whole. If the mother country could not consume all the produce of the colonies or provide sufficient manufactures so that instead money had to be sent, what prejudice could arise to the mother country? The more colonial products it possesses, the more it has to dispose to foreigners. Though the mother country be in this case made the debtor to the colonies, yet it becomes, at the same time, a creditor doubly considerable in its claims upon the foreigner."[69]

The high price of sugar led planters to exploit all available land. They strongly resented the obligation imposed by law to plant subsistence crops.

---

[67] Azeredo Coutinho, "Memória sobre o preço do açucar (1791)," in *Memórias económicas* in *Colecção de obras clássicas* I, vol. 3, 273–280. For a discussion of prices of a variety of colonial commodity exports in the late eighteenth-century, see Dauril Alden, "Late Colonial Brazil, 1750–1808," in *The Cambridge History of Latin America*, ed. Leslie Bethell (Cambridge and New York: Cambridge University Press, 1984), II, 601–662.

[68] In 1796 the value of goods exported to Portugal from Bahia was assessed at 3,702,181,721 reis, and the value of goods sent from Portugal to Bahia at 2,069,637,404 reis, "Tableau général de la valeur des marchandises importées dans le royaume de Portugal." Adrien Balbi, *Essai statistique sur le royaume de Portugal et d'Algarve* (2 vols.) (Paris: n.p., 1822) I, 431. For detailed analyses of the trade balances of this period see Jorge Miguel Viana Pedreira, *Estructura industrial e mercado colonial, Portugal e Brasil (1780–1820)* (Lisbon: Difal, 1994) and José Jobson de A. Arruda, *O Brasil no comércio colonial* (São Paulo: Ática, 1980).

[69] Azeredo Coutinho, *Ensaio económico sôbre o comércio de Portugal a suas colónias . . . D. José Joaquim da Cunha de Azeredo Coutinho, Bispo em outro tempo de, Pernambuco . . . e actualmente Bispo d'Elvas . . .* in *Colecção de obras clássicas* III (Lisbon: Banco de Portugal, 1992). There is an English translation published in 1807, *An Essay on the Commerce and Products of the Portuguese Colonies in South America, Especially the Brazils* (London: G. G. & J. Robinson, 1801). The quotations are taken from this edition, 154–155.

Professor Luís dos Santos Vilhena condemned the great sugar producers for their failure to plant sufficient manioc and warned that such an unthinking pursuit of their self-interest threatened famine. He firmly believed that plantation owners should be obliged to plant manioc, for there was no other source of supply available. Vilhena held that "European ideas" which had led to the removal of price controls on meat and manioc were responsible for the shortage of subsistence food and for high prices. Such ideas should only be applied in a place like Brazil after the most careful attention had been paid to local factors. In Europe, one nation in time of dearth might have recourse to its neighbors for added supplies, but mutual dependence was impossible in South America, where food supplies were inelastic. Vilhena saw a direct relationship between the removal of price controls and "the ineffectual uprising and cruel massacre" projected by the Bahian mulattoes in 1798.[70]

The "European ideas" Vilhena especially condemned were those of Adam Smith and J. B. Say. Both economists were used by João Rodrigues de Brito and Manuel Ferreira da Câmara to document and justify their rejection of state interference to regulate production or control the prices of commodities. Rodrigues de Brito and Ferreira da Câmara had been consulted over the state of agriculture in Bahia, and their responses were a clear defense of the interests of the great sugar planters. Manuel Ferreira da Câmara, speaking as proprietor of the great sugar mill of Ponte, categorically rejected all laws and regulations that restricted the liberty of the proprietors. He was violently opposed to the Inspection House which regulated the prices of sugar and tobacco, and also to the public granary established by Governor D. Rodrigo José de Menezes in the city of Salvador during 1785 in an attempt to provide regular food supplies at reasonable prices to the population. These institutions, Ferreira da Câmara claimed, "had been set up out of the fantasy of those in government as obstacles to the freedom of commerce." He attributed the granary "to a zeal more religious than practical. . . ." He could conceive of nothing worse than that commodities "should be sold for less than they cost to produce or transport." He boasted that he had not "planted a single foot of manioc in order not to fall into the absurdity of renouncing the best cultivation of the country for the worst." Each "must be master to do what most benefits him, and what benefits him is that which most benefits the state."[71]

---

[70]Vilhena, *Cartas*, I, 128–129; I, 159; II, 445–448.
[71]Carta II, M[anuel] F[erreira] da C[âmara], *Cartas economica-politicas, sobre a agricultura a commercio da Bahia . . . pelo Desembargador João Rodrigues de Brito a outros* (Lisbon: Imprensa Nacional, 1821), 80–85.

For Rodrigues de Brito, admissible direction in agricultural matters by the government could be reduced to three points: "the granting of liberties, facilities, and instruction." The proprietor should not be forced to plant manioc. De Brito opposed "restrictions that prevented our farmers from taking their goods to the places where they could obtain most value." He argued in favor of the removal of the prohibitions against the *commissarios volantes*, the itinerant free traders outlawed by the Marquês de Pombal during the 1750s. He was strongly opposed to price fixing. Capitalist enterprise should be liberated in order to encourage entrepreneurs to participate in agricultural improvement, and the institutional and judicial obstacles to investment should be removed. "Intolerable inconveniences placed on the capitalist in the matters of debt collection and foreclosure should be abolished," he contended, and in particular "foreign investment should be welcomed."[72]

The apologists for the sugar planters were making a frontal attack on the whole concept of state regulation and government interference in economic matters. Yet the planters' demands were so closely related to their own self-interest that they were also limited by them. Planters desiring emancipation from government interference did not necessarily desire emancipation from the colonial relationship with Portugal. To Ferreira da Câmara, Rodrigues de Brito, and Azeredo Coutinho, laissez faire was not synonymous with free international commercial exchange. It was this basic distinction that another disciple of Adam Smith, D. Fernando José de Portugal, whose elimination of price controls in Bahia provoked Vilhena's criticism, had evidently perceived in 1798. The sugar interests did not lead the demand for free international commerce for one simple reason. Brazilian sugar was sold in the continental European market, for which Lisbon was a logical and necessary entrepôt. Britain, the most likely candidate for any free trade relationship outside the Luso-Brazilian commercial system, placed prohibitive duties on the importation of Brazilian sugar, in the interests of its own sugar colonies in the West Indies.

The marriage in the writing of Azeredo Coutinho between his attack on state interference and his restatement of the basic tenets of mercantilist colonial policy was a perfect rationalization of the situation. He held up the English Navigation Acts as "a pattern of imitation to all seafaring nations." It was "in the true interests of both [metropolis and colony] that the colony be permitted to carry on a direct trade with the mother country

---

[72]Carta, I, João Rodrigues de Brito, ibid. For a discussion of the commissarios volantes and Pombal's policy toward them see Kenneth R. Maxwell, "Pombal and the Nationalization of the Luso-Brazilian Economy," *Hispanic American Historical Review* XLVIII, no. 4 (November 1968): 608–631.

only, and that they [the colonists] should not have fabrics and manufactories of their own especially of cotton, linen, wool and silk." In fact, the interests of Brazil, defined as the interests of the great sugar planters, were compatible with those of Portugal.[73]

The point of view of the planters of the littoral, so accurately stated by Azeredo Coutinho, gained added weight during the 1790s as a result of the sugar boom, and of the temporary removal of any political influence from Minas Gerais, a region not dominated by an export-oriented plantation economy. The strongly regionalist emphasis of the Minas conspirators had verged at times on economic nationalism. Joaquim José da Silva Xavier (known as Tiradentes) claimed that once free and a republic like English America, Brazil might become even greater than English America, owing to better resources. With the establishment of manufactories, he said, there would be no need to import commodities from abroad.[74] Proposals for trade and commercial arrangements were noticeably absent from the discussions of the Minas plotters, and many believed that there was no necessity whatsoever to invite the support of foreign powers, for they would rush to establish relations with the new state on account of its natural riches.[75] But the influence of such views was suppressed in the aftermath of the failure of the uprising.

There were Brazilians, however, less closely linked to the interests of the sugar planters, who came to the same conclusion as Dr. Novais de Almeida in his letter to Jacinto José da Silva. The basic issue, as they perceived it, was slavery itself. D. Fernando had found it necessary to expel a Capuchin friar from Bahia during 1794 for his antislavery statements.[76] Professor Luís dos Santos Vilhena observed soberly that he was "not persuaded that the commerce in slaves is so useful as it seems." He believed that "Negroes were prejudicial to Brazil."[77] A similar attitude had been expressed some years before by his colleague, Professor José da Silva Lisboa, secretary of the Bahian Inspection House. Although he recognized the importance of slavery and sugar to the Bahian economy, Silva Lisboa did not believe that the number of slaves imported brought a commensurate increase in popula-

---

[73]*An Essay on the Commerce*, 155–157.

[74]Witness, Vicente Vieira da Mota, Vila Rica, June 22, 1789, *ADIM*, I, 108; Witness, Vicente Vieira da Mota, Vila Rica, August 3, 1789, *ADIM*, III, 334; Witness, José Aires Gomes, Vila Rica, July 28, 1789, *ADIM*, I, 207; Witness, José Aires Gomes, Vila Rica July 30, 1789, *ADIM*, III, 319–320; "Continuação de perguntas feitas ao coronel Alvarenga," Rio de Janeiro, January 14, 1790, *ADIM*, IV, 141.

[75]"Continuação de perguntas feitas ao Padre José da Silva de Oliveira Rolim Vila Rica," November 13, 1789, *ADIM*, II, 288.

[76]Dom Fernando José de Portugal to Martinho de Melo e Castro, Bahia, June 18, 1794, *RIHGB*, LX (1897), 155–157.

[77]Vilhena, *Cartas*, I, 136, 139–140.

tion or agricultural production. And, like Vilhena, he believed slavery was responsible for many of the ills of Brazilian society.[78]

The suggestion of slave emancipation was anathema to the planters. Azeredo Coutinho thought abolitionist sentiment sufficiently threatening to warrant a blistering attack on "the insidious principles of the philosophic sect." He asked what would happen to the agriculture of Brazil and in consequence the commerce and prosperity of Portugal if slavery was abolished. To Azeredo Coutinho "necessity has no law, because she is the origin of all law," and necessity clearly demanded the continuance of the slave trade. "To those that accuse me of occupying myself with a study more proper to a farmer or business man than to a Bishop, it is necessary to remember that before I was a Bishop I was, as I continue to be, a citizen linked to the interest of the state." He attacked those who "in the depths of their studies presume to give laws to the world without having dealt at first hand with the people of whom they speak." The bishop's concern at the growth of emancipationist sentiment was evidently justified, for his defense of the slave trade was refused by the Lisbon Academy of Sciences, and he was forced to publish a French edition in London. When he sought again in 1806 to have his polemic published in Portugal, the Royal Board of Censorship denied permission, on the ground that although slavery might be tolerated in present circumstances, nothing should be said to make its elimination even more difficult.[79]

No one was advocating immediate abolition, but a small group of men was beginning to regard slavery as the source of social ills in Brazil, and was starting to think in terms of an alternative model for Brazilian development, in which European immigration and free laborers would replace slavery. Vilhena's objections to slavery were not so much the result of "humanitarian" sentiment as they were a practical response to the problem of a society where the racial balance appeared to be dangerously unstable. The question of slavery raised fundamental questions about the most desirable course for Brazilian development. And during the 1790s that

---

[78]José da Silva Lisboa to Domingos Vandelli, Bahia, October 18, 1781, *ABNRJ*, XXXII(1910), 502, 505.

[79]Azeredo Coutinho, "Análise sôbre a justiça do comércio do resgate dos escravos da costa d'Africa (1798)," in *Obras econômicas, 1794–1804*, ed. Sérgio Buarque de Holanda (São Paulo: Companhia Editora Nacional, 1966), 175–185; Sonia Aparecida Siqueira, "A escravidão negra no pensamento do bispo Azeredo Coutinho, contribuição ao estudo da mentalidade do último inquisidor geral," I, *RHSP*, XXVII (1963), 349–365; II, *RHSP*, XXVIII (1964), 141–198. D. Fernando José de Portugal significantly also supported the views of the sugar planters with respect to slavery; see D. Fernando to Martinho de Melo e Castro, Bahia, June 18, 1794, *RIHGB*, LX (1897), 155–157.

question was beginning to divide enlightened men. Discussion about development resulted in a striking paradox. Those who were the strongest supporters of laissez faire when it meant removal of the regulatory functions of the state were also most committed to the slave trade and slavery. Those who supported government interference, particularly in the control of prices and in the guarantee of sufficient supplies of subsistence food to the population, were also most opposed to the slave trade and slavery. Novais de Almeida and Vilhena saw the slave population as enemies within, and José da Silva Lisboa believed Brazil would not develop without the creation of a free labor force and the Europeanization or whitening of the population.[80] Bishop Azeredo Coutinho saw slavery as essential to Brazilian prosperity. Those who attacked laissez faire where it demanded the removal of what they considered judicious government controls would be most in favor of free international commerce, because free trade promised to stimulate European immigration and offered the possibility of an alliance with Great Britain against the slave trade. Yet at the same time, because the solution to Brazil's problems by opponents of laissez faire was based on fear of the racial composition of the Brazilian population, they would be the least likely to take any initiative that might provoke the disaster they foresaw and sought to avoid. The division was profound. Vilhena attacked those "European ideas" he held responsible for creating the conditions that led to the Bahian plot. Azeredo Coutinho attacked the "humanitarians" and "philosophers" whose utopian concepts threatened, in his opinion, to destroy Brazilian prosperity.

IV

Republicanism had been discredited by its abortive uprising in Minas Gerais and later association with social and racial turmoil, and Brazilians were in very basic disagreement over fundamental issues; thus there was room for metropolitan initiatives. And for the white minority in Portuguese America, the failure of the oligarchic movement in Minas Gerais during 1789, and the threat from below revealed by the Bahian artisans in 1798, provided two powerful incentives for compromise with the metropolis. Psychologically, the situation was propitious for accommodation. The recognition of this fact by influential members of the Portuguese government during the 1790s had profound impact on the future development of Brazil. During 1788 Luís Pinto de Sousa Coutinho became Portugal's for-

---

[80]José da Silva Lisboa, *Memória dos benefícios políticos do governo de El-Rei Nosso Senhor D. João VI* (Rio de Janeiro: Na Impressão Regia, 1818), 2d ed. (Rio de Janeiro: Impressa nas Oficinas do Arquivo Nacional, 1940), 160, 169–175.

eign minister.[81] He was a man with firsthand knowledge of Brazilian conditions, having distinguished himself as governor of Mato Grosso (1769–1772) before succeeding Martinho de Melo e Castro as minister plenipotentiary to the Court of St. James.[82] In Britain he had provided William Robertson with information on South America for Robertson's famous history, a service he had also provided for the Abbé Raynal some years earlier.[83] Once back in Lisbon, Luís Pinto made contact with Brazilian intellectuals, many of them students of Domingos Vandelli, an Italian scholar brought to Portugal by Pombal as part of his program of educational reform. On May 31, 1790, Luís Pinto sent two young Brazilians and a Portuguese colleague on a grand European tour of instruction at the expense of the Portuguese government. The Brazilians were Manuel Ferreira da Câmara and José Bonifácio de Andrada e Silva. The group was instructed to proceed to Paris and take courses there in physics and mineralogy. Two years at Freiburg would be spent gaining "all practical knowledge." Afterward the scholars were to visit the mines of Saxony, Bohemia, and Hungary, and to return to Portugal by way of Scandinavia and Great Britain.[84]

Manuel Ferreira da Câmara, the leader of the expedition, had close links with those caught up in the events of Minas Gerais. His elder brother, José de Sá Betencourt, who graduated from Coimbra in 1787, was implicated on several occasions during the judicial inquiry into the conspiracy, and had fled from Minas by way of the backlands to Bahia. His uncle had been

---

[81]Caetano Beirão, *D. Maria I, 1777–1792; subsídios para revisão de história do seu reinado*, 2d. ed. (Lisbon: Emprensa Nacional de Publicidade, 1934); Simão José da Luz Soriano, *História da Guerra Civil* (Lisbon: Impr. Nacional, 1866) I, 349–350.

[82]Ibid., 355–356.

[83]William Robertson, *History of America*, 3 vols. (London: Printed for W. Strahan; T. Cadell, in the Strand; and J. Balfour, at Edinburgh, 1783), vol. 1, preface, xiv; J.-M. (Joseph-Marie) Quérard, *La France littéraire, ou dictionnaire bibliographique des savants*, 10 vols. (Paris: Firmin Didot père et fils, 1827–1839), VII (1835), 473. For an excellent synopsis of Robertson's *History of America* as well as of Raynal's influential books see D. A. Brading, *The First America: The Spanish Monarchy, Creole Patriots, and the Liberal State 1492–1867* (Cambridge and New York: Cambridge University Press, 1991), 422–446. Brading's notes to this chapter (703–704) provide a succinct listing of key bibliographic sources on these as well as other French and Spanish Enlightenment figures who wrote about the European overseas colonies.

[84]Instrução, Ajuda, May 31, 1790, in Marcos Carneiro de Mendonça, *O Intendente Câmara, Manuel Ferreira da Câmara Bethencourt e Sá, Intendente Geral das Minas e Diamantes 1764–1835* (São Paulo: Companhia Editora Nacional, 1958), 26–27. Among the Brazilians' distinguished colleagues at Freiburg were Alexandre de Humboldt and Andrés Manuel del Rio; see Charles Minguet, *Alexandre de Humboldt, Historien et Géographe de l'Amérique espagnole, 1799–1804* (Paris: F. Maspero, 1969), 44–45.

a member of the Bahian High Court, and his wealthy relatives were proprietors of the sugar mill of Ponte. (Manuel Ferreira administered this estate from 1801 to 1807; from it he wrote his observations about the agriculture of Bahia.)[85] At the time that Manuel Ferreira received his instructions for the study tour of Europe, the Portuguese government had known for three months of his brother's suspected implication in the projected uprising in Minas Gerais.[86]

Luís Pinto's extension of the powerful protection of his office during the critical year 1790 to these young Brazilian scholars, and his remarkable act of faith in sponsoring the visit of Manuel Ferreira and José Bonifácio to the center of European social and political upheaval, coincided with a series of public criticisms of the attitudes and assumptions which had dominated policymaking since the fall of Pombal in 1777. In 1790, D. Rodrigo de Sousa Coutinho, Luís Pinto's successor, published under the auspices of the Lisbon Academy of Sciences his "discourse on the true influence of mines of precious metals on the industry of the nations that possess them, and especially the Portuguese." D. Rodrigo was Pombal's godson. He was related by marriage to Mathias Barbosa, one of the famous Minas pioneers, and as a result possessed extensive properties in the captaincy. In his discourse, D. Rodrigo took issue with the view that mines were responsible for Portugal's decadence, as the *Encyclopédie* had stated. He attributed the stagnation of Portugal to the effects of the Methuen Treaty of 1703.[87] D. Rodrigo was preparing the way for Manuel Ferreira da Câmara's paper on "physical and economic observations about the extraction of gold in Brazil," in which the young Brazilian made an eloquent plea for improved methods and techniques. Manuel Ferreira recommended that mining companies be promoted and encouraged by royal privileges. These compa-

---

[85]Carneiro de Mendonça, *Intendente Câmara*, 9–10.

[86]Martinho de Melo e Castro acknowledged receipt of the first notice of the conspiracy in a letter to the Minas governor, the Visconde de Barbacena, dated March 9, 1790. A much-corrected minute of this dispatch in Melo e Castro's own hand survives at the AHU, Minas Gerais, caixa 92. Ignácio Ferreira da Câmara, a cousin of Manuel Ferreira and José de Sá, had been a student at Montpellier, *MHPB*, VI (1940), 283.

[87]D. Rodrigo de Sousa Coutinho, "Discurso sobre a verdadeira influência das minas dos metaes preciosos na indústria das nações que as possuem e especialmente da portuguesa," in *Memórias económicas* in *Colecção de obras clássicas*, I, vol. 1, 179–183; Marquês do Funchal, "Certidão do baptismo de Dom Rodrigo de Sousa Coutinho," *O Conde de Linhares, Dom Domingos António de Sousa Coutinho* (Lisbon: Typ. Bayard, 1908), 186. For information on D. Rodrigo's Minas connections, see Miguel Costa Filho, *A cana de açúcar em Minas Gerais* (Rio de Janeiro: Instituto do Açúcar e do Alcóol, 1963), 92, 97, and John Mawe, *Travels in the Interior of Brazil* (London: Printed for Longman, Hurst, Rees, Orme, and Brown, 1812), 181–182.

nies should not be monopolies but organizations which could mobilize capital for rational exploitation. He suggested that mining colleges be set up in Brazil to provide skilled mining engineers.[88] The papers of both D. Rodrigo and Manuel Ferreira implied that the imposition of fiscal demands on Minas Gerais had been wrong, and that what Minas Gerais needed was not increased tax burdens but rational reform and modern technology.

V

When Melo e Castro died in March 1795, Luís Pinto took over as interim secretary of state for the overseas dominions.[89] On May 27, 1795, he forwarded to the Brazilian governors a circular which contained a startling admission of past mistakes. "Defects in policy and fiscal restrictions had until now held back the progress of Brazil," he wrote. "Her Majesty, desiring to calm her subjects as much as possible," had made important decisions. First, the salt gabelle would be abolished in Brazil. Second, the mining and manufacture of iron would be encouraged, especially in Minas and São Paulo.[90] Both measures promised to ameliorate two principal irritants to the white minority in Brazil. And one of the few areas of agreement between Luís dos Santos Vilhena and Bishop Azeredo Coutinho was opposition to the salt monopoly, due to its restrictive effect on the development of salt meat production.

To formulate programs and implement the reforms, Luís Pinto relinquished his temporary portfolio to D. Rodrigo de Sousa Coutinho in 1796.[91] D. Rodrigo had impressive credentials. He had been a student at the College of Nobles, established by Pombal to create a "virtuous" nobility in Portugal.[92] In 1779 he had visited France and observed what he described as its "parasitic and useless court" and its "chaotic financial situation."[93] In

---

[88]Carneiro de Mendonça, "Memória de observações físico-econômicas acêrca da extração do ouro do Brasil, por Manuel Ferreira da Câmara," *Intendente Câmara*, 499–523.

[89]Luís Pinto's first dispatch as secretary of state for the overseas dominions was dated March 26, 1795, AHU, códice 610, f. 194v–195; the death of Melo e Castro was announced to the governors in Brazil on March 30, 1795.

[90]Luís Pinto de Sousa Coutinho to Bernardo José de Lorena, Queluz, May 27, 1795, Arquivo do Estado de São Paulo, caixa 63, N. orden 421, livro171, f. 159–161. For the complete transcription see Carneiro de Mendonça, *Intendente Câmara*, 174–175, and *DISP*, XLV (1924), 466–468.

[91]Luís Pinto announced the appointment of D. Rodrigo, September 9, 1796, *DISP*, XLV (1924), 486.

[92]Rómulo de Carvalho, *História da fundação do colégio real dos nobres de Lisboa, 1761–1772* (Coimbra: Atlântida, 1959), 182–186.

[93]D. Rodrigo to Dona Marianna de Sousa Coutinho, Fontainebleau, August 4, 1779, in Funchal, *O Conde de Linhares*, 191–194.

Paris he met Abbé Raynal. He told Raynal that the "population and resources of France would have made her insupportable to the rest of Europe were it not for the disorder of her financial administration." Raynal replied that "Providence had given France the forces but refused her good sense. France would indeed be terrible if her natural power was matched by a just and wise administration." Writing to his sister, D. Rodrigo later wondered: "What would be better for Europe, to be a factory of the English or a slave of France? The only thing that can console us is the almost total impossibility of France reforming her system of government."

D. Rodrigo was right in his analysis but wrong in his prediction. Reform in France had come through revolution, and as he had seen, the geopolitical consequences for Portugal threatened to be an intolerable choice between the Great Powers. Moreover, he attributed the collapse of the French monarchy to its fiscal situation. His opposition to monopolies and the contracting of revenues, and his fervent support of an efficient and solvent financial administration, grew from his belief that intelligent reform was essential if Portugal were to avoid a similar collapse. The financial problem was especially relevant because one of the prime issues in Minas Gerais was the tax farms. The "good administration of the royal exchequer would contribute most to the opulence and conservation of the vast overseas dominions," the new secretary of state observed."[94] To achieve sound fiscal policies, D. Rodrigo planned wise and enlightened reforms, executed by intelligent men, capable of forming well-organized systems, the utility of which would be recognized by all."[95] His optimism epitomized that of the Enlightenment itself.

The immediate problem was the status of mining in Minas Gerais. Theoretical debate and practical suggestion centered on this. D. Rodrigo would base his measures "on the most liberal principles, if it is legitimate to adopt to our language the sense which the English attribute to that word."[96] Domingos Vandelli, in a memorial on the gold of Brazil, complained that policy had previously been "left only in the hands of people ignorant of mineralogy to the grave prejudice of the state." Decisions about whether gold mines were advantageous or prejudicial to Portugal he left to "those who know how to calculate the true interest of nations." He recommended that practical experience be taken into account, especially that of scholars who might have been to Germany.[97] D. Rodrigo consulted Antônio Pires

---

[94]"Plano sôbre o meio de restabelecer o crédito público e segurar recursos para as grandes despesas, October 29, 1799," ibid., 172–179; "Plano de fazenda," March 14, 1799, ibid., 155–168.
[95]"Discurso, IV," ibid., 135
[96]"Discurso, II, ibid., 120.
[97]"Memória . . . sôbre as Minas de Ouro do Brasil por Domingos Vandelli," *ABNRJ*, XX (1898), 266–278.

da Silva Ponte, who embodied his thoughts in an essay on the mines. He emphasized the necessity for more training in the mathematical and physical sciences and metallurgy because "of the present great difficulties in extracting gold." He criticized the fact that in Minas Gerais the value of gold was kept artificially below its value outside the captaincy. He went so far as to suggest that the royal fifth be abolished and replaced by a tax on luxury goods proportional to their price. He noted that Minas abounded in agricultural and pastoral riches whose development should be encouraged. "The royal revenues do not depend so much on the fifth of the gold . . . as in the number of consumers (consumidores) and inhabitants in the region."[98] José Eloi Ottoni, in a memorial on the state of the captaincy, agreed that the extraction of gold was now beyond the capacities of the miners. He pointed to the absurd expense of the importation of iron and steel into Brazil. It was important to promote agriculture and commerce with the interior by removing import taxes. Communications should be opened, especially along the Rio Doce and the Rio São Francisco. He did not mean to suggest that all manufactures be permitted in Brazil, but he did think it wise to allow those which provided substitutes for items which "from negligence we buy from foreigners, iron, steel, saltpetre."[99] Azeredo Coutinho, like Ottoni, pointed to the absurd price of iron in Minas Gerais. A quintal of iron which in Portugal cost about 3,800 reis, he said, would in Minas Gerais be worth 19,000 reis, and in Goias and Mato Grosso 28,000 reis. It was "absolutely necessary that schools of mining be immediately established in São Paulo, Minas Gerais, Goias, Cuiabá and Mato Grosso."[100]

D. Rodrigo mobilized a task force of erudite Brazilians to provide practical information. José Vieira Couto and José Teixeira da Fonseca Vasconcelos were instructed to collect information on salt deposits, especially in the São Francisco River valley.[101] João Manso Pereira, subsidized by local tax money, was to conduct mineralogical and metallurgical investigations

---

[98]"Memória sôbre a utilidade pública em se estrahir o ouro das minas e os motivos dos poucos interêsses que fazem os particulares que minerão actualmente no Brasil, por Antônio Pires da Silva Pontes Leme [sic]," with a letter to D. Rodrigo, *RAPM*, I (1896), 417–426.

[99]"Memória sobre o estado actual da capitania de Minas Gerais por José Eloi Ottoni, estando em Lisboa no anno de 1798," *ABNRJ*, XXX (1908), 303–318.

[100]Azeredo Coutinho, "Discurso sôbre o estado actual das minas do Brasil," *Obras económicas*, 190–229.

[101]Rodrigo de Sousa Coutinho to Bernardo José de Lorena, Queluz, March 18, 1797, AHU, códice 610, f. 202v. Also "Memória sôbre as Minas da capitania de Minas Gerais, suas descripções, ensaios, e domicílio próprio, a maneira de itinerário com hum appêndice sôbre a nova lorena diamantina, sua descripção a utilidades, que d'êste país possa resultar ao estado, por ordem de sua alteza real, 1801, por José Vieira Couto," IHGB, lata 18, doc. 17.

and experiments in São Paulo, Minas Gerais, and Rio de Janeiro.[102] Joaquim Veloso Miranda, a student of Vandelli, whose information had been used by the Italian scholar in his memorial, was appointed secretary to the new governor of Minas, José de Lorena, a close personal friend of D. Rodrigo and a disciple of the Abbé Raynal.[103] Veloso Miranda was instructed to continue his studies of the natural resources of the region and most especially of the deposits of saltpeter. José de Sá Betencourt received a commission to investigate the copper and saltpeter deposits at Jacobina.[104] The secretary of state outlined explicitly the objective of these various investigations. He told Veloso Miranda that "orders might perhaps be issued to the governor to establish the manufacture of gunpowder on the account of the royal exchequer . . . as soon as sufficient saltpeter was found."[105] Governor Lorena was informed that the proposed iron works would be set up on the account of the exchequer and iron sold at "a price discrete and wise, equally beneficial to the royal exchequer and the inhabitants. . . ."[106] When Manuel Ferreira returned to Portugal during 1798, D. Rodrigo at once called for his views on the proposed legislation.[107]

VI

After three years of study and planning, the outlines of a general policy for the empire as well as specific legislative drafts had been composed.[108] Dur-

---

[102]D. Rodrigo de Sousa Coutinho to Bernardo José de Lorena, Queluz, March 18, 1797, AHU, códice 610, f. 202.

[103]D. Rodrigo de Sousa Coutinho to Bernardo José de Lorena, Queluz, February 21, 1797, AHU, códice 610, f. 201v, and D. Rodrigo to Joaquim Veloso de Miranda, Queluz, March 18, 1797, AHU, códice 610, f. 202v; Carvalho, *Fundação do Colégio dos Nobres*, 182–186; D. Rodrigo to Lorena, Queluz, October 11, 1798, AHU, códice 610, f. 215v–216; Lorena's comments on Raynal in D1, XLV, 10–11.

[104]D. Rodrigo de Sousa Coutinho to D. Fernando José de Portugal, March 2, 1798, and letter from José de Sá, Bahia, October 7, 1797, *MHPB*, VI, 278. Some observations on cotton by José de Sá had been favorably received in Lisbon and published as *Memória sôbre a plantação dos algodões e sua exportação; sôbre a decadência da lavoura de mandiocas no têrmo da villa de Camamu, comarca dos Ilheos, governo da Bahia . . . por José de Sá Bitencourt* (Lisbon: Academia das Ciências, 1798).

[105]D. Rodrigo de Sousa Coutinho to Joaquim Veloso de Miranda, Queluz, September 17, 1799, AHU, códice 611, f. 7.

[106]D. Rodrigo de Sousa Coutinho to Bernardo José de Lorena, Queluz, September 20, 1798, AHU, códice 610, f. 212v–213v.

[107]Carneiro de Mendonça, *Intendente Câmara*, 33–66.

[108]Numerous drafts for the future legislation were made: for some of these see AHU, Minas Gerais, caixa 57, document 221. (This is mistakenly dated 1780 on the folder. These projects were written between 1798 and 1800, the first drafts in the name of Queen Maria I, and the later ones in that of Dom João, the prince regent. Dom João formally became prince regent of Portugal in 1799 though he had been exercising the function of head of state since 1792.)

ing 1798, D. Rodrigo formally presented his ideas to the Council of State of Portugal.[109] He intended, he told the councillors, to "touch rapidly on the political system that it is most convenient for the crown to embrace in order to conserve its vast dominions, particularly those of America, that are properly the base of the greatness of the throne. . . ." D. Rodrigo asserted that "Portugal reduced to herself would within a very brief period become a province of Spain." He advised that the empire be regarded as being composed "of provinces of the monarchy, all possessing the same honors and privileges, all reunited with the same administration and all contributing to the mutual and reciprocal defense of the monarchy." Brazil should be divided into two centers of power, Rio de Janeiro in the south and Pará in the north. It was essential, he said, to "occupy our true natural limits," and in particular the northern bank of the Rio de la Plata. The choice of governors was important for the maintenance of justice and the efficient administration of the royal exchequer; with higher salaries, he believed, governors would have less incentive to become embroiled in business. Associations should be formed to exploit the mines more efficiently. The number of high courts in Brazil should be increased, and the need for appeal to Lisbon abolished. He proposed that taxation be reformed so that it would "be productive but not fall heavily on the contributors." The tax contract system would be abolished because it fell unequally and because most of the money remained in the hands of the tax farmers. Duties on slaves, iron, steel, copper, lead, gunpowder, and metropolitan manufactures sent to the interior of Brazil would be removed. The royal fifth would be reduced to a tenth, and the value of gold in Minas Gerais revalued to its market price.

The ideas of his Luso-Brazilian braintrust were very evident in the plan for empire proposed by the secretary of state. And the urgency of implementation of the plan was increased by the Bahian episode. D. Rodrigo

---

[109]Discurso de D. Rodrigo de Sousa Coutinho, document no. 4 (I) Carneiro de Mendonça, *Intendente Câmara*, 277–299. This is from the Coleção Linhares, Biblioteca Nacional do Rio de Janeiro, I, 29-13–16. Also in D. Rodrigo de Souza Coutinho, *Textos políticos, económicos e financeiros (1783–1811)* in *Colecção de obras clássicas do pensamento económico português* (XII in 2 vols.) (Lisbon: Banco de Portugal, 1993) II, 47–66. The Portuguese historian Valentim Alexandre rejects the view that the inconfidências represented any generalized challenge to Portuguese rule, nor does he accept that D. Rodrigo's plans in any way changed the basic colonial regime. See in particular chapter two ("Política colonial e 'inconfidências'") in his *Os Sentidos do Império: questão colonial na crise do antigo regime português* (Lisbon: Edições Afrontamento, 1993), 77–89. On the sharp debate among Portuguese and Brazilian historians over the economic relations between Brazil and Portugal in the late eighteenth century and early nineteenth century, within which Alexandre is a participant, see bibliographic essay in Kenneth Maxwell, *O Marquês de Pombal* (Lisbon: Editorial Presença, 2001), 207–208.

sensed more acutely than most the opportunities the situation presented, and he distinguished more clearly than most between the necessity of enlightened reforms and the dangers posed by the revolutionary slogans of the French Revolution. The severity with which he treated the Bahian mulattoes and the favors he continued to bestow on the Brazilian graduates of the University of Coimbra were indicative of his point of view.[110] His fear of revolution made it essential that "the federative system, the most analogous to Portugal's position in the world, be conserved with the greatest firmness and pure good faith."[111] He attacked "the banal declamations" of those who claimed "that in the . . . difficult circumstances of the moment great reforms should not be attempted and only palliatives employed; experience had shown the opposite."[112]

D. Rodrigo had employed many erudite Brazilians in the process of decision making. He had encouraged others to undertake state-sponsored scientific expeditions in Brazil. He had been especially responsive to those who were connected with the Minas conspiracy. The exiled José Alvares Maciel, for example, forwarded a memorial on the iron mines in Angola. It was favorably received and Maciel was given an official mission to investigate the situation more closely.[113] The members of the Literary Society of Rio de Janeiro, languishing in jail since 1794, were released.[114]

In 1800 D. Rodrigo was appointed president of the Royal Treasury.[115] The position had been created by Pombal as the linchpin of the government, and its occupant was principal minister of the Crown. At the treasury, Pombal's godson had the opportunity to implement the reforms he had long regarded as most important, for which draft legislation was prepared. The royal decree of April 24, 1801, "in favor of the inhabitants of Brazil," promulgated the reforms outlined by Luís Pinto in 1795. The salt

---

[110]Three of the leaders of the Bahian plot were hanged, beheaded, and quartered in the center of the city of Salvador. The rest of the plotters were taken to Africa and abandoned along the African coast. Charles R. Boxer has attributed the clemency displayed by the Crown toward the Minas conspirators, of whom only Tiradentes was hanged, in comparison with the severity of the repression of a similar movement in Goa during 1787, to "colour prejudice." The same could be argued in the Bahian episode. Boxer, *Portuguese Seaborne Empire*, 199–200.

[111]"Discurso 1," December 22, 1798, in Funchal, *O Conde de Linhares*, 108–109.

[112]"Plano de Fazenda," March 14, 1799, ibid., 168.

[113]José Alvares Maciel to D. Rodrigo de Sousa Coutinho, November 7, 1799, AHU, Minas Gerais, caixa 94.

[114]Devassa of Literary Society, introductory notes, *ABNRJ*, LXI (1939), 241–245. Also see *Autos da devassa: prisão dos letrados do Rio de Janeiro, 1794* (Rio de Janeiro: UERJ; Arquivo Público do Estado do Rio de Janeiro, Secretaria de Estado de Justiça; FAPERJ, 1994) and Afonso Carlos Marques dos Santos, *No rascunho da nação: Inconfidência no Rio de Janeiro* (Rio de Janeiro: Biblioteca Carioca; Prefeitura da Cidade do Rio de Janeiro, 1992).

[115]Soriano, *História da guerra civil*, II, 296–297.

monopoly was abolished and the mining and manufacture of iron permit-ted.[116] Manuel Ferreira da Câmara was nominated general intendant of mines and the Serro do Frio (the Diamond District),[117] Antônio Pires da Silva Ponte was appointed governor of the captaincy of Espírito Santo.[118] José Bonifácio de Andrada e Silva became intendant of mines and metals in Portugal.[119] There was precedent for the appointment of Brazilians to such high positions in the metropolitan and colonial administrations. But the nomination to a new and important post second only to the governor of Minas of a man whose brother had been seriously implicated in the pro-posed uprising of 1789, and the appointment as a governor in Brazil of a Brazilian whose loyalty had been gravely questioned in 1786, were little short of revolutionary.

In the meantime, however, the war in Europe had forced Portugal to face the choice D. Rodrigo had foreseen while in France during 1779. His views on the importance of Brazil made it logical that when he was con-sulted in 1803 on the European situation, he should recommend that the prince regent of Portugal, D. João, establish the seat of the monarchy in America. The idea was not original.[120] The proposal that the monarch leave for Brazil was a recurrent suggestion in times of difficulties. But to D. Rodrigo the factors in favor of the move were not merely those imposed by the deteriorating international situation. D. Rodrigo told the prince regent that "Portugal is not the best and most essential part of the monarchy." In his opinion a mighty empire might be established in South America. There the offensive might be taken against the Spaniards, and natural frontiers be established at the Rio de la Plata. In the event of a showdown over Portu-gal, the French would take Lisbon and the British would take Brazil. There-fore it was better for the prince regent to anticipate these moves by the Great Powers and take the initiative in moving the government to Brazil.

---

[116][José da Silva Lisboa], *Synopse da legislaçao principal do Senhor Dom João VI pela ordem dos ramos da economia do estado* (Rio de Janeiro: Na Impresão Regia, 1818), 28.

[117]Carta régia, November 7, 1800, and instrução, in Carneiro de Mendonça, *Inten-dente Câmara*, 86–91.

[118]RAPM, (1896) 417 note; also *ABNRJ*, LXII (1940), 145.

[119]"Carta de merce, concedendo a José Bonifácio de Andrada a Silva o cargo de in-tendente geral das minas a metais do Reino, 25, VIII, 1801," *Obras científicas, políti-cas, e sociais de José Bonifácio de Andrada e Silva*, (3 vols.) (Santos: Grupo de Trabalho Executivo das Homenagens ao Patriarca, 1964), III, 29. For a detailed dis-cussion of the activities and publications of many Brazilian scholars encouraged by D. Rodrigo during the late eighteenth century see Maria Odila da Silva Dias, "Aspectos da Ilustração no Brasil," *RIHGB*, 278 (January–March, 1968), 105–170.

[120]"Quadro da situação política da Europa, apresentado ao Principe por D. Ro-drigo de Sousa Coutinho," August 16, 1803, Angelo Pereira, *D. João VI, Principe e Rei I* (Lisbon: Empresa Nacional de Publicidade, 1953), 127–136.

The plan to transfer the court to Brazil, espoused by D. Rodrigo in 1803, was eminently acceptable to white Brazilians. Canon Luís Vieira da Silva had considered the establishment of Rio de Janeiro as the seat of the Portuguese monarchy the best possible solution to Brazil's problems in 1789.[121] Alvarenga Peixoto, in an ode to the queen in 1792, pleaded for her to visit her American subjects.[122] One of the few points to emerge from the investigation arising out of the seemingly trumped-up charges against Captain Francisco de Paula Cavalcante and others in Pernambuco during 1801 was the evident concern in Brazil about what would happen if the prince regent did not establish himself in America in the event of the loss of Portugal.[123]

In 1789, important members of the Minas oligarchy had been prepared to move in armed rebellion against the Portuguese Crown and to establish an independent and republican government. After 1792 "men established in goods and property," to use the words of D. Fernando José de Portugal, were wary of republicanism. The slave revolt in the Caribbean frightened slave owners throughout the Americas. The sugar boom in Brazil, in part a result of the collapse of production in Saint-Domingue, brought with it social and economic problems which in turn were partly responsible for the proposed uprising of the mulatto artisans of Bahia. The Bahian manifestos of 1798 confirmed that the slogans of the French Revolution propagated within a society like that of Portuguese America brought with them the risks of racial upheaval, risks that the American Revolution, the inspiration of the Minas conspirators, had not brought. After 1792 both the great slave owners of the coastal plantations and the chastened Mineiros were prepared for an accommodation with the metropolis. Even more than the reforms and reorganization proposed by D. Rodrigo, the establishment of the monarchy in Brazil was a welcome and hopeful compromise which offered political change without social disintegration.

The Brazil plan was anathema to many in Portugal. Admiral Campbell attributed the opposition to "the French, but also the Spanish influence, and finally to a greater part of the nobility, who dread the idea of seeking their fortunes in a new country while they can grasp at the shadow in their own."[124] The plan was unthinkable to Portuguese merchants and industrialists who, unlike D. Rodrigo with his extensive properties in Minas Gerais,

---

[121]Witness, Vicente Vieira da Mota, Vila Rica, June 22, 1789, *ADIM*, I, 111.

[122]Lapa, *Alvarenga Peixoto*, lii–liii.

[123]"Devassa de 1801 em Pernambuco," ed. J. H. Rodrigues, *DH*, CX, 151. For some comments on this so-called conspiracy see Cardozo, "Azeredo Coutinho," in *Conflict and Continuity*, ed. Keith and Edwards, 84.

[124]Donald Campbell, London, August 14, 1804, Chatham Papers, PRO, 30/8/345 (2) f. 224.

had much to lose and nothing to gain by such a move. Nor was D. Ro-drigo's distinction between reform and revolution appreciated by those who saw subversion in all Enlightenment philosophy. Combating nation-alism overseas, he had underestimated nationalism at home. His relega-tions of Portugal to a secondary status in his federative scheme provoked ferocious opposition.[125] The limitations of D. Rodrigo's influence were made apparent by his failure to protect his protégé, Hypólito da Costa, from arrest and imprisonment for masonic activities on his return from the United States, a visit D. Rodrigo himself had sponsored.[126] José Joaquim Vieira Couto, brother of the scientist José Vieira Couto, who came to Lisbon on behalf of the residents of the Diamond District, was also ar-rested and imprisoned on the orders of the intendant of police, Pina Manique.[127] Manuel Ferreira da Câmara remained intendant of mines in name only, and was forced to remain at his estate in Bahia waiting in vain for instructions to proceed to Minas Gerais.[128] When, in late 1803, the prince regent submitted the new mining legislation to ministers in the gov-ernment regarded by D. Rodrigo as incompetent to judge the issue and op-posed to his objectives, he found his position no longer tenable, and resigned.[129] The setback was temporary. D. Rodrigo had accurately fore-seen the course of events. In November 1807, the showdown between Britain and France over Portugal took place. With a British fleet off Lisbon and a French army marching across the frontier, the move to Brazil became essential if the monarchy was to survive at all.[130] But when the Portuguese

---

[125]For an account of the violence of the merchants' opinions see Robert Walpole to Lord Grenville, Lisbon, September 9, 1795, Foreign Office 63/21.

[126]Mecenas Dourado, *Hypólito da Costa, e o Correio Brasiliense*, 2 vols. (Rio de Janeiro: Ministério da Guerra, 1957), 1, 47–67; Carlos Rizzini, *Hypólito da Costa e o Correio Brasiliense* (São Paulo: Companhia Editora Nacional, 1957), 9, 13. Also see Hipólito José da Costa, *Correio Braziliense ou Armazém Literário* (Edição Fac-sim-ilar) (31 vols.) (São Paulo: Correio Braziliense; Imprensa Oficial do Estado, 2001–). The first volume contains essays by Barbosa Lima Sobrinho, José Mindlin, Paulo Cabral de Araujo, Sérgio Kobayashi, Alberto Dines, and Isabel Lustosa.

[127]Ibid., 12–13; also, "carta de Diogo Ignacio de Pina Manique em que trata sucin-tamente dos serviços prestados a tranquilidade publica combatendo os Jacobinos e maçons," September 4, 1798, IHGB, lata177, doc., 8.

[128]D. Rodrigo told Manuel Ferreira, "I hope that you have that quality of obstinacy necessary to overcome the obstacles of ignorance and those who oppose the public wellbeing." Carneiro de Mendonça, *Intendente Câmara*, 103.

[129]Ibid., 113–118, 491.

[130]Alan K. Manchester, "The Transfer of the Portuguese Court to Rio de Janeiro;" in *Conflict and Continuity*, ed. Keith and Edwards, 148–183, trans. as "A transferên-cia da corte portuguesa para o Rio de Janeiro;" *RIHGB*, CCLXXVII (October–De-cember, 1967), 3–44. Also see the recent book by Kirsten Schultz, *Tropical Versailles: Empire, Monarchy, and the Portuguese Royal Court in Rio de Janeiro, 1808–1821* (New York and London: Routledge, 2001).

fleet sailed from the Tagus with the Court of Portugal aboard, plans were ready for the new situation. A vindicated D. Rodrigo was reappointed to the government to implement the blueprint he and his associates had drawn up during the 1790s.

The fact that Dom João arrived in Brazil so well prepared was important to the success of the establishment of monarchy in Portuguese America. And the warm reception accorded the European Court in Brazil was also important. Part of the reason for both the preparation and the cordial reception lay in the course of events between 1789 and 1808. The timing of the Minas Conspiracy and the Bahian plot, and the relationship between the chronology of events in Brazil, the French Revolution, and the slave revolt in Saint-Domingue, caused a shift among white Brazilians from a flirtation with republicanism to an optimistic acceptance of monarchy. Sympathetic ministers in the Portuguese government, especially during the period of D. Rodrigo de Sousa Coutinho's control of the Department of Overseas Dominions between 1796 and 1800, encouraged many Brazilians who might have been nationalists—indeed many who had been sympathetic with the republican movement in Minas Gerais—to join in the highest levels of policymaking. This collaboration between Brazilian intellectuals and enlightened ministers produced an imperial idea, Luso-Brazilian in inspiration, which moved beyond nationalism to a broader imperial solution, and sought to defuse metropolitan-colonial tensions.

The idea of Luso-Brazilian Empire possessed weaknesses. The circumstances which compelled influential Brazilians to seek an accommodation during the 1790s were not permanent phenomena. Basic differences of opinion existed on vital matters such as slavery. In addition, the opposition in Portugal to the Luso-Brazilian concept was seriously underestimated, and had been neutralized only by the French invasion. In 1808, moreover, the viability and acceptability of the blueprints had yet to be tested. How fundamental these weaknesses might be only the future would reveal. But whatever the impact of the imperial idea itself, the Luso-Brazilian generation of the 1790s, which gave it shape, was to be extremely influential. D. Rodrigo became the principal minister of the first new world monarchy. José da Silva Lisboa was the ideologue of free trade. Manuel Ferreira da Câmara became intendant of mines and his family was instrumental in securing Minas Gerais and Bahia for Dom Pedro I. José Bonifácio de Andrada e Silva became the patriarch of Brazilian independence. And it is also noteworthy that following 1789, in the Lisbon Academy of Sciences and in the writing of private individuals, debates were opened on topics such as laissez faire, slavery, and the slave trade, which were to dominate discussion of Brazilian development for much of the nineteenth century.

Pierre Chaunu entitled a discussion of the transition of Portuguese America from colony to independent nation "Heureux Brésil."[131] If Brazil was indeed fortunate in its monarchical solution, in being spared the agonies of nineteenth-century Spanish America, part of the cause must be sought not in the Brazilians' lack of imagination, instruction, and enlightenment, or even in vague attributes of their national character, but in the perspicacity of the generation of the 1790s, who brought reason to the analysis of colonial problems and with optimistic faith projected a grandiose concept of Luso-Brazilian Empire.

---

[131]Pierre Chaunu, *L'Amérique et les Amériques* (Paris: A. Colin, 1964), 216. For a succinct overview of this period also see Luiz Carlos Villalta, *1789–1808: o império luso-brasileiro e os brasis* (*Virando Séculos*, coord. Laura de Mello e Souza and Lilia Moritz Schwarcz) (São Paulo: Companhia das Letras, 2000).

STATUE OF PEDRO I.

CHAPTER **8**

Why Was Brazil Different?

The Contexts of Independence

"The conservation of monarchy in one part of America is an object of vital importance to the Old World."
—George Canning, 1824

Over recent decades surprisingly little scholarly work has been done on the achievement of Brazilian independence. Even less attention has been devoted to the impact of the decolonization of Portugal's vast South American empire during the 1820s on Portugal itself. Portuguese historians still sometimes write as if Brazil never existed—the most recent and most prestigious history of Portugal in the eighteenth century, for example, barely mentions Brazil, even though for most of that century 60 percent of the state's revenues derived from Brazil—and Brazilian historians often ignore the important transatlantic dimensions of Brazil's domestic political conflicts and economic constraints.[1] The period that runs from late 1807, when the invasion of Portugal by General Jean-Andoche Junot forced the Portuguese Court to take refuge in Brazil, up to 1825, when Portugal and the major European powers recognized Brazil's independence, lacks even the most rudimentary interpretative outline. Yet events on each side of the Atlantic were intimately linked, and cannot be explained without an understanding of their connectedness. Indeed, between 1815 and 1821 Portugal and Brazil were formally and institutionally part of a "United

---

[1]See António Manuel Hespanha, ed., *O Antigo Regime*, vol. 4, *História de Portugal* (8 vols.), ed. José Mattoso (Lisboa: Editorial Estampa, 1997).

145

Kingdom." The interpenetration of Brazilian and Portuguese politics and economy was extensive, and remained so well into the mid-nineteenth century.

My objective is in a very preliminary way to take a fresh look at what happened during these critical years in a comparative Atlantic context; to suggest some of the theoretical and practical problems concerning the study of the independence of Brazil; and to delineate some key aspects of the international context of Brazilian independence. Finally, I will touch on the social and economic history of this period where the greatest continuities between the colonial and national periods are claimed in the current literature for Brazil, and the greatest discontinuities seen for Portugal.

I

We come to the study of the establishment of new nations out of old empires with certain expectations and preconceptions. Primarily we are thinking of political emancipation from colonial status; involved also are assumptions about the democratization of internal politics, or at least their liberalization; thus we expect a defeat of despotism and the emergence of some sort of institutional formula to express the popular will, essential for the legitimacy of any new state. Legitimacy, however, does not depend on internal or domestic factors alone: foreign recognition of the new national status is essential; as is, eventually, reconciliation with the former colonial master (or at least a formal acceptance of separation), usually by means of an international treaty. Geopolitical questions are, therefore, inevitably involved as well as great power politics. The constellation of external forces, their willingness to intervene or not intervene as the case may be, is perhaps more important than at any other time in a nation's history. The new nation must also satisfy obligations internationally: contract loans; engage in and finance trade; organize its economic and financial life; sometimes pay indemnities or assume obligations to pay off colonial debts.

Thus, as at few other times in a nation's history, at the moment of independence fundamental decisions of a *founding* nature are needed. These can involve profound questions about the organization of the social and economic sphere; continuity of property rights and claims; perhaps decisions over the relationship between church and state; as well as institutional decisions over constitutional structures, law courts, and public administration; organizational questions over how to set up banks and credit institutions; questions as to how to impose tariffs or negotiate commercial treaties, and how to create a credible currency.

It is the *explicit* nature of these challenges which makes such moments a fascinating topic for historical investigations; for once we are not speculating about the connections between perceptions, ideas, and actions, but watching the translation of ideas into institutional or social arrangements, and constitutional frameworks. And in all this, as we look back from the vantage point of a century and three quarters, we need to penetrate also the thicket of "invented" national tradition which is an inevitable component of any national consciousness.

We tend to assume that all these changes are for the better. I mention this only to indicate how subjective our view of national independence and decolonization can be. Rarely, for example, do we see independence as a "bad thing," as a regression, a triumph of "despotism" over "liberty," of "slavery" over "freedom," of an "imposed" regime over a "representative" one, of oligarchy over democracy, of reaction over liberalism. Yet the truth is, that in the case of Brazil's independence, almost all these charges against the new regime can be made; and indeed they were made at the time.

Brazil was not alone in confronting such dilemmas. As independent nations emerged in Latin America after three centuries of Iberian domination, the persistence of their colonial heritage was a preeminent issue. Brazil, for example, was at the time of its independence from Portugal already 322 years old; and today its experience as a nation free from formal European domination is still far shorter than its colonial life. Yet in Latin America this "colonial persistence" was unlike that inherited by many of the postcolonial states that emerged out of the European empires in Asia and Africa during the mid-twentieth century. The impact of Spain and Portugal within the Americas had been more disruptive, and hence more permanent, than was the impact of the Europeans who imposed themselves, temporarily as it turned out to be, over other ancient societies from the Middle East to China, where populations, religions, social structures, and behavior patterns were never uprooted and destroyed as catastrophically as were those of the ancient civilizations of pre-Columbian America. After the Second World War, particularly where there were no large-scale white-settler populations to complicate the transition, Africans and Asians achieved independence by negotiating the removal of, or by forcibly expelling, a handful of white soldiers, overseers, and administrators. In Latin America, it was *precisely* the white soldiers, overseers, and administrators who expelled the representatives of the Spanish or Portuguese Crown, while continuing or usurping the overlordship of large nonwhite, or indigenous populations, or African slaves.

Latin America is thus not fully comprehensible it seems to me if seen only within the "Third World" context of the new nations which came into existence as the French, British, and Dutch empires collapsed between 1945 and 1965. In this sense Brazil was indeed a "New World in the tropics," as Gilberto Freyre once put it, a settler society that had become rooted in the New World and where the population—whether of European,

African, or indigenous origin—was sufficiently intertwined to be not easily resegregated. The extraordinary depth of the impact of Spanish and Portuguese colonization in the Western Hemisphere was such that postcolonial nation building became intrinsically an incestuous affair.

II

In effect Brazil in the 1820s was negotiating its relationship to the outside world within the heavy constraints imposed on it by history, geography, and its colonial experience. Until recently, the interpretation of this critical period has been strongly influenced by dependency theory. But dependency theory tended to homogenize the Latin American experience into a worldwide explanatory model. Strongly influenced by the African and Asian decolonization movements of the twentieth century, this approach often denied autonomy to the social, political, and economic forces at play in the so-called peripheral regions. Above all, it discouraged an investigation of the process, causes, and dynamics of change, and it gave short shrift to institutional innovations or ideas. This created an enormous impediment in understanding the case of colonial Latin America, the control of which had been an essential component of the building of European world domination in the first place, something John Parry, in his marvelous book *The Establishment of the European Hegemony, 1415–1715*, demonstrated so skillfully and succinctly.[2] Dependency theory, on the other hand, tended to sublimate any investigation of how European preeminence was achieved, and confined explanations of major systemic changes (the ending of feudalism, the rise of capitalism, and so on) to the *internal* dynamics of European societies, an unconscious Eurocentrism which I must say in my view still seems to dominate much economic history writing to this day.

Brazilian scholars were much enamored of this theoretical construct, and played an important role in its evolution. Emília Viotti da Costa and Fernando Novais, for example, both placed the emergence of Brazil as an independent nation within the context of the shift from mercantile to industrial capitalism in Europe, and the consequent changes this provoked in the international economic system. Historians who were not part of a Marxist tradition also took a similar view: Robinson and Gallagher, for instance, saw the independence of the Latin American nations as the classic example of the shift from formal to informal imperialism.[3]

---

[2]John H. Parry, *The Establishment of the European Hegemony, 1415–1715; Trade and Exploration in the Age of the Renaissance* (New York: Harper & Row, 1961).
[3]R. H. Robinson and J. Gallagher, "The Imperialism of Free Trade," *Economic History Review* 1, 2d series (1953): 1–15.

Yet British interests in Portugal and Brazil were not monolithic; two distinct lobbies in Britain had been engaged in the economic relations with Portugal in the century prior to Brazilian independence: the wine import merchants and the woolen textile exporters, both of which had a very strong interest in *sustaining* the old favorable tariff regimes and privileged extraterritorial rights in Portugal which aided their enterprises and which dated back to the mid-seventeenth century. On the other hand, the new and aggressively expansionist Lancashire cotton textile manufacturers were interested in free trade and until 1818 drew a large percentage of their raw material from northeast Brazil, Pernambuco in particular. They had no interest whatsoever in perpetuating Portugal's political and economic dominion over Brazil, especially since Portugal had developed its own cotton textile mills and retained Brazil as a privileged and closed market.

It is important, therefore, not to overemphasize the power of purely economic forces, or to assume the inevitability of these broader shifts. The cotton textile interest in Britain and their lobbyists in Parliament certainly believed that their comparative advantage would allow their products to break through the old mercantilist tariff barriers of the Iberian powers, but they were also keen to see these barriers removed by government intervention. In this respect the continuity is notable in the mutually supporting strands of commercial, military, and diplomatic pressure the British exercised over Portugal and its overseas possessions. In the mid-seventeenth century, the new Bragança monarch had been extremely reluctant to agree to the Cromwellian treaty in the 1640s which provided British recognition for a country recently emancipated from Spanish domination in return for major commercial concessions. It was the threat of Admiral Blake's guns in the Tagus estuary that finally persuaded the king of Portugal to ratify the accord on May 1, 1656. The British fleet which escorted the Prince Regent Dom João, his mad mother, Queen Maria, and the court to Brazil in 1807 was also riding at anchor off the Lisbon waterfront to intimidate as well as to offer assistance. Had the Portuguese Court *not* left for Brazil as planned, and instead succumbed to French demands that the royal family remain in Lisbon, there was no doubt that the British would have bombarded Lisbon as they had only recently bombarded Copenhagen and destroyed or seized the Portuguese ships in the harbor. Admiral Sir Sidney Smith had clear instructions from London that on *no* account was the Portuguese fleet to be allowed to fall to the French.

The precociousness of these unequal treaties between Britain and Portugal recalled for C. R. Boxer, that rare historian who knew both Portugal and China intimately, the later unequal treaties of Nanking of the late 1840s, the heyday, it should be remembered, of the so-called age of free trade imperialism and informal empire. Portugal had in this respect been a forerunner of a relationship which imposed severe conditionalities over another nation's sovereignty without the direct exercise of sovereign power. As with China at midcentury, the British did not always produce what overseas customers wanted, and in these circumstances the British rarely hesitated to impose trade by military and political power, or to seek special concessions, even if this made them, as in the China trade, purveyors of narcotics.

The opening of the ports of Brazil in 1808 to the trade of "all friendly nations" was the first action taken by the newly arrived Portuguese Court after its escape from Lisbon. It was an action that ended over three centuries of mercantilistic practice where Lisbon had been the obligatory entrepôt for Brazilian colonial products. While this action had ideological motivations to be sure, that is, it was justified in terms of the superiority of free trade over protectionism, it was also an entirely pragmatic measure, made inevitable by the French determination to incorporate Portugal's ports within the continental blockade against Britain. And as far as the British traders in Brazil were concerned, many potential European competitors, not the least of which, the French, were temporarily out of the picture. In these favorable circumstances, the British merchants quickly saturated the consumer market in Brazil, where the majority of the population was composed of slaves, not a free population of middle-class consumers.

Only two years later, not surprisingly, the British were agitating again for special privileges. The Anglo-Brazilian Treaty of 1810 imposed on the Portuguese higher tariffs in Brazil than it did on the British, an imposition that dealt a severe blow to the already fragile chances of reconciling Portugal to Brazil's new status as center of the monarchy. It is ironic to note that the first and second partial editions of Adam Smith's *The Wealth of Nations* published in Brazil appeared in 1811 and 1812 in Rio de Janeiro and Bahia, respectively, as if to remind the British (and certainly to remind the Brazilians) that hegemonic powers do not always practice what they preach. In effect, as in the mid-seventeenth century, Portugal and later Brazil were obliged to balance the need for autonomy against the need for political and military support, especially in their relations with Great Britain, the dominant naval and economic power.

But how far did these circumstances lead Brazil to sacrifice its own economic prospects, and fall into a neocolonial relationship as the *dependentists* argue? Or were those who had promoted the transfer of the seat of the Portuguese government to Brazil in 1807 on the grounds that it would make the Bragança regime less susceptible to European pressure right or wrong in the light of subsequent experience?

Commercial pressure from the British was certainly counterproductive at times as far as Britain's broader political interests were concerned, especially if these ran headlong into powerful vested interests combined with strong nationalist sentiments. The British found this out the hard way in Buenos Aires in 1806 when their intervention force had been ignominiously defeated. This *should* also have been the lesson of the American Revolution. And it was a lesson Napoleonic France discovered with catastrophic consequences as a result of intervention in Haiti. In Brazil this was especially the case in the matter of the slave trade. Despite treaty commitments between Brazil and Britain to abolish the slave trade dating from the 1810 treaty, the influence of landed and slave trading interests in Brazil was strong enough to counteract over forty years of British gunboat diplomacy during the first half of the nineteenth century.[4]

Here again the economic influence of Britain was often at cross-purposes with Britain's political, diplomatic, and philanthropic initiatives. As Sidney Mintz has argued, the Industrial Revolution in Britain (and in the northern states of North America, for that matter) helped revive slavery throughout the Americas by creating a vast new urban consumer market for products such as coffee and sugar, as well as by creating the enormous demand for raw cotton to supply the textile mills of both old and new England. And it was not only merchants in Rio de Janeiro or Bahia who were financing the illegal slave trade or the legal commerce in cotton, coffee, and sugar that depended on slave labor. It was also the merchants of New York and Baltimore, and London and Liverpool. And it was ships of the North Americans that carried a large percentage of the slaves that were imported illegally into the Brazilian Empire as late as the 1850s.[5] Henry Wise, U.S. minister to Brazil, told Secretary John C. Calhoun in 1843: "without the aid of our citizens and our flag, the African slave trade could not be carried out [in Brazil] with success at all."[6]

Ironically, the resistance to antislavery and abolitionist arguments in Brazil was probably weaker in the independence period than at any time before or after. In the south of the country, especially in São Paulo, a critical region in terms of organized political opposition to Lisbon in the 1820s, large-scale coffee production only developed after national independence was achieved. In the decade 1821–1830 coffee accounted for a

---

[4]"Treaty of amity, commerce, and navigation, between His Britannic Majesty and His Royal Highness the Prince Regent of Portugal; signed at Rio de Janeiro, the 19th of February, 1810," in A. R. Walford, *The British Factory in Lisbon & Its Closing Stages Ensuing upon the Treaty of 1810* (Lisbon: Instituto Británico em Portugal, 1940), 163–184.
[5]See Sidney W. Mintz, *Sweetness and Power: The Place of Sugar in Modern History* (New York: Penguin Books, 1985).
[6]Robert H. Holden and Eric Zolov, ed., *Latin America and the United States: A Documentary History* (New York: Oxford University Press, 2000), 30.

mere 19 percent of total exports for Brazil, but over the next two decades this share rose to well over 60 percent. The expansion of the coffee market in Europe, and most especially in North America, led to a massive renewal of slave imports into Rio de Janeiro and the expansion of slavery into the Paraíba Valley and beyond into São Paulo. Economic historians have argued that the main reason for Brazil's slow overall economic development in the nineteenth century lay precisely in the country's agricultural sector, where low income and inelastic supply, intrinsic to slavery, constrained the pace of development in the rest of the economy.[7]

This was precisely what José Bonifácio de Andrada e Silva, who more than any individual helped shape the newly independent Brazilian state in the 1820s, had foreseen when warning his contemporaries about the long-term negative effects, for Brazil's future well-being, of the failure to deal with the question of slavery or to promote agrarian reform or to integrate the Indian population at the onset of national independence. This led to his courageous but in the end hopeless appeals to his fellow Brazilians in his manifesto in favor of abolition of slavery, his proposals for agrarian reform, and his plan for the "civilization of the wild Indians of Brazil," as he put it, all written during 1822: "Experience and reason demonstrate that richness rules where there is liberty and justice, and not where lives captivity and corruption." José Bonifácio argued that "If this evil persists we will not grow. Gentlemen, continually our domestic enemies grow; and they have nothing to lose; except above all to hope for a revolution such as that of Santo Domingo." In other words, to hope for a new Haitian revolution in Brazil.[8]

III

The ambiguity of Brazil's passage from colony to imperial center to independent nation is best exemplified on the one hand by the aborted plans

---

[7]Nathaniel H. Leff, *Underdevelopment and Development in Brazil* (2 vols.) (London and Boston: Allen and Unwin, 1982), and Stephen Haber and Herbert S. Klein, "The Economic Consequences of Brazilian Independence," in *How Latin America Fell Behind: Essays in the Economic Histories of Brazil and Mexico, 1800–1914,* ed. Stephen Haber (Stanford: Stanford University Press, 1997), 243–259.

[8]"Apontamentos sôbre as sesmarias do Brasil," in *Obras científicas, políticas, e sociais de José Bonifácio de Andrada e Silva* (3 vols.) (Santos: Grupo de Trabalho Executivo das Homenagens ao Patriarca, 1964), II, 20–21; "Representação à Assembléia Geral Constituinte e Legislativa do Império do Brasil sobre a Escravatura," por José Bonifácio de Andrada e Silva. Typographie de Firmin Didot, 1825, in ibid., II, 115–158; "Apontamentos para a Civilização do Indios Bravos do Império do Brasil," ibid., III, 103–114. See also *Projetos para o Brasil,* org. Miriam Dolhnikoff (São Paulo: Companhia das Letras, 1998) and the commentary by Carlos Guilherme Mota in *Introdução ao Brasil,* ed. Lourenço Dantas Mota (São Paulo: SENAC, 1999), 77–95.

for reform put forward by José Bonifácio, and on other in the enigmatic Dom Pedro, first emperor of Brazil after the break from Portugal. Bonifácio was one of the most remarkable figures in any of the independence movements in the Americas—a man in scientific achievement who matched and in some cases surpassed the remarkable generation of leaders who had made the American Revolution. Closer in personality and fame to a Franklin than to a provincial landlord like Thomas Jefferson, Bonifácio was born and raised in Santos. He had been a brilliant student at the reformed University of Coimbra in Portugal and arrived in Paris in 1790 as a postgraduate student supported by a grant from the Portuguese government brokered by the secretary of the new Lisbon Academy of Sciences, the Abbé Corrêa da Serra. He had witnessed the most turbulent stages of the French Revolution in person and then continued his studies in Germany and Scandinavia. During the French invasion of Portugal he had led the students of Coimbra in guerrilla warfare behind the enemy's lines. He had been a high government functionary, intendant of mines and metals; his scientific papers had appeared in the most prestigious journals; he was a corresponding member of Europe's great scientific bodies; and he went on to succeed Corrêa da Serra as secretary of the Lisbon Academy of Sciences. He was very much part of the remarkable late-eighteenth- and early-nineteenth-century circum-Atlantic community of scholars and political reformers. But his experience made him a firm believer in the role of the state in the tradition of enlightened reformers in Southern and Eastern Europe; he saw order as the handmaiden of progress. He was a constitutionalist, but not a democrat; more Burkian than Jeffersonian.

Dom Pedro was a populist, a classic man on horseback, the handsome son of grotesquely ugly and dysfunctional parents, and heir to a dynasty so inbred as to verge at times on lunacy. He was a temporary ruler who within a decade had abdicated in order to return to Europe to fight a civil war in Portugal against his brother to ensure that his daughter became queen of Portugal. Loyal father and chronic philanderer, savant and ignoramus, courageous soldier and clumsy politician, Brazilian and Portuguese, heir and usurper, he was a monarch too "liberal" for the Holy Alliance in Europe but too "despotic" for many Brazilians, not least the would-be republicans of Pernambuco who rose up twice in a decade to repudiate him. His role as portrayed in Portuguese history is that of the upholder of "constitutionalism," an image totally incompatible with his image in Brazilian history, where he was the ruler who rejected Brazil's first constitution as too liberal and exiled José Bonifácio and his brothers, the leaders of the small minority of Brazilians who wanted fundamental reform and who had provided the direction during the most critical moments of the transition to independence.

It is vital to recognize, therefore, that on September 7, 1822, when Dom Pedro stopped at the banks of the Ipiranga River near São Paulo, suffering from a bout of diarrhea, and cried out it was to be "Independence or Death", the young prince and heir apparent to the Portuguese throne was exaggerating. The problem in September 1822 was certainly not "death," and only indirectly "independence." His pithy declaration was, and soon became, very much part of a spurious myth of the origins of Brazilian nationality. Yet the reality was that Brazil had been independent for all intents and purposes since 1808; since December 16, 1815, Brazil had been a kingdom coequal with Portugal. But John Quincy Adams, the U.S. secretary of state, was not alone in quite misunderstanding the occasion and its significance when he told Ceasar Rodney on his appointment as U.S. minister to Buenos Aires that "in Brazil . . . an empire probably as ephemeral as that of Mexico at our door has taken the place of Portugal." What was really at stake in 1822 was a question of monarchy, stability, continuity, and territorial integrity. It was in *these* interests that Dom Pedro was preempting revolution in 1822 at Ipiranga, not promoting it.

The avoidance of revolution in Brazil in fact was also a paramount concern in Europe. Henry Chamberlain, British minister in Rio de Janeiro in 1824, was ever concerned that the social turmoil under the surface in Brazil and evident on the streets and in the constituent assembly in Rio would, as he put it:

> excite . . . such a flame . . . as it might not be possible to control, and would perhaps end in the destruction of the imperial government and the division of the country into a variety of small independent republican states, wretched in themselves and the cause of wretchedness amongst their neighbours, such as we have witnessed in the Spanish American colonies in our neighbourhood.[9]

Portugal's major European allies—both Britain and the members of the Holy Alliance—were quite clear on this point, as George Canning, the British foreign secretary who had previously served as British envoy in Lisbon, wrote very succinctly in 1824:

> The only question is whether Brazil, independent of Portugal, shall be a monarchy or a Republic. . . . The conservation of monarchy in one part of America is an object of vital importance to the Old World.[10]

---

[9]Henry Chamberlain to George Canning (secret), Rio de Janeiro, May 15, 1824, in Charles K. Webster, ed., *Britain and the Independence of Latin America, 1812–1830: Select Documents from the Foreign Office Archives* (2 vols.) (London and New York: Oxford University Press, 1938), I, 240–241.
[10]George Canning to Henry Chamberlain (secret and confidential), London, January 9, 1824, in Webster, I, 236.

The government in London, since the establishment of the Portuguese Court in Rio in 1808, in fact had always made a clear distinction between the circumstances of Brazil and Spanish America. Canning emphasized the contrast between the Brazilian situation and that of Spanish America writing to Sir Charles Stuart in 1825:

> Let it be recollected that the difference between the relation of Portugal to Brazil and that of Spain to her Americas is in nothing more than this—that all the Spanish colonies have gained in despite of the mother country, but that Brazil has been raised to the state of a sister kingdom, instead of colonial dependency, by the repeated and advised acts of policy of the common sovereign of Portugal and Brazil. Up to the period of the emigration of the Royal Family to Brazil, Brazil was as strictly a colony as Mexico or Peru or Buenos Aires. From that period began a series of relaxations first, and afterwards of concessions of privileges, which gradually exalted the condition of Brazil and almost inverted its relations with Portugal so as to make, during the residence of His Most Faithful Majesty in Brazil, the mother country in fact a Dependency.[11]

Dom João, the prince regent, soon to be Dom João VI on the death of his demented mother in 1816, had said as much to Thomas Sumter Jr., the U.S. envoy in Rio de Janeiro in 1815, "The times have been difficult but now the independence of Brazil is fixed."[12]

The important point about Brazil, therefore, is that it became economically and politically emancipated between 1808 and 1820 while acting as the center of the Luso-Brazilian Empire. It became "independent" in 1822 only *after* the experience as an "imperial center," to which subjects of the Portuguese monarchy in Europe, Africa, and Asia looked for leadership, had failed. This unusual circumstance explains why in 1820 it was Portugal that declared "independence" *from* Brazil, and only afterward, in 1822, that Brazil declared its "independence" from Portugal. The "Manifesto of the Portuguese Nation to the sovereigns and peoples of Europe," which was issued by the rebels in Oporto in 1820, reads very much like other such declarations of independence from colonial status and contained the same complaints; the only difference was this manifesto came from rebels in a European city, not rebels across the Atlantic in a colonial port city. It declared:

---

[11]George Canning to Sir Charles Stuart, London, March 14, 1825, in Webster, I, 262–272, citation from 265–266.

[12]Thomas Sumter Jr., U.S. Minister to the Portuguese Court in Brazil, to James Monroe, Secretary of State, Rio de Janeiro, December 29, 1815, in William R. Manning, ed., *Diplomatic Correspondence of the United States concerning the Independence of the Latin American Nations*, (3 vols.) (New York: Oxford University Press; 1925–[1926]), II, 696–700.

The Portuguese are beginning to lose the hope of the unique resource and the only means of salvation that remains to them in
midst of ruin which has almost consumed their dear homeland.
The idea of *the status of a colony to which Portugal in effect is reduced*, afflicts deeply all those citizens who still conserve a sentiment of national dignity. Justice is administered from Brazil to the
loyal people in Europe, that is to say at a vast distance . . . with ex-
cessive expense and delay . . . [italics added][13]

IV

But if the "anticolonial" revolution occurred in Oporto not in Rio de
Janeiro, the interesting questions from the Brazilian perspective are:
Would the independence of Brazil have occurred at this time had not the
1820 liberal revolution in Oporto taken place and had not the Portuguese
parliamentary assembly, the Cortes, forced the king to return to Europe?
Was the antimonarchist sentiment within Brazil on its own strong enough
to have sustained a republican movement, such as those in North America
and in much of Spanish America which rejected both monarchy and European rule?

These questions were not only theoretical—republicanism after all had
been the central ideological strand in the thinking of the Minas conspirators in 1788–1789; the Bahian plotters in 1798, and in 1817 in Pernambuco
as well as again in the 1820s. The problem for Brazil was that all these republican movements were, or at least could be interpreted as, regionalist
revolts against centralized authority and as a threat to the territorial integrity of Portuguese-speaking America. The centralized monarchical system had established a very strong institutional presence in Brazil since
1808. In fact, it had instituted in Rio de Janeiro almost all of the founding
institutions, usually the task of a postcolonial government: a centralized
administration and bureaucracy; superior law courts; a public library and
an academy of fine arts; a school of medicine and law; a national press and
national bank; and a military academy. This government had negotiated
international treaties, sent envoys abroad and received envoys in return,
had married the heir presumptive of the head of state to an Austrian
princess, and had defeated a regionalist revolt and conducted an expansionist war on the northern and southern frontiers. There was never a
question therefore of legitimacy. As George Canning told the British cabinet in November 1822:

---

[13]*Manisfeste de la Nation Portugaise aux Souverains e aux Peuples de l'Europe*
(Oporto: 1820); author's personal collection.

to refuse to recognize Brazil would not be, as it has hitherto been in the case of the Spanish colonies, an act merely negative. For we *have* with Brazil established relations, regulated commercial intercourse, and agencies if not actually political, affording channels of political correspondence. We cannot withdraw our consuls from Brazil. It is obvious that we *must* continue to cultivate the commercial relations of that country. [emphasis in original][14]

This would all be a critical heritage for the regime Dom Pedro was to head as first emperor of Brazil, as well as contributing to his ability to protect his new empire from republican challenge. So the answer to these questions is probably "no." In other words, the social base for radical change was stronger and opposition to it weaker in Portugal in 1820 than was the case in Brazil, and the reason for this is that in all ways continuity was greater in Brazil than it was in Portugal during the first two decades of the nineteenth century. Since 1808 Portugal had not only lost its role as the seat of the monarchy, but it had been subject to invasion and devastating warfare; it had mobilized a population against a common enemy; it had seen its commerce and industry destroyed and its profitable colonial markets lost; and the British, forgetting the cardinal rule of "informal" empire, had subjected a proud and nationalist population to the direct and insensitive rule by a British general.

In Brazil, moreover, threats to social order since the 1790s had been strongly associated with republicanism and this, in moments of crisis, tended to produce greater coalescence within the elite, especially among property owners whose ownership of human property, moreover, was far more widespread than was the ownership of land. Here the fear of contagion from the Haitian slave revolt was ever present in their minds, and "liberty," if it also implied "equality," was bound to raise fundamental questions about a society ordered by racial as much as by social hierarchy. We are, needless to say, talking in this context of "perceptions." I am not implying that social conflicts can or should only be seen in terms of slavery—obviously social structure and the interaction of class and race were much more complex and multifaceted in Brazil than this. And it should also be emphasized that the slave revolt in Haiti had dramatic impact not only because the balance of social and racial tensions within Brazil and elsewhere in the Americas made its example frightening to whites, but because of its *intrinsic* importance. The Haitian example was *qualitatively* of much greater significance than previous slave rebellions. First, because it

[14]Canning's memorandum for the cabinet, November 15, 1822, in Webster, II, 393–398.

was successful, the only successful slave uprising in modern history. Second, because Haiti sustained its independence—at vast cost to be sure—but a fact which made Haiti the Western Hemisphere's second independent nation after the United States.[15]

V

Yet again, Brazil presents ambiguities. One possible response to the perceived threat from below was to eliminate slavery, encourage European immigration, and substitute free for slave labor. This is what José Bonifácio wanted. But in Brazil the fear of slave revolt was not a sufficient argument of itself to force the Brazilian power brokers to defy their immediate material interests and embrace the reform of the system of production based on slave labor. In fact, slavery had the opposite effect: it cemented a unity around the defense of the institution. The *paulista* Diogo Antônio Feijó, priest, *fazendeiro*, deputy to the Portuguese Cortes in Lisbon, member of the General Assembly in Rio de Janeiro after Independence, minister of justice and regent in the 1830s, put the case quite succinctly:

> Slavery which certainly brings many ills to civilization, also creates within Brazilians a sense of independence, of sovereignty, that the observer can also see in free men whatever their status, profession or fortune.[16]

In this, the parallels with the attitudes toward slavery of the Virginian patriots who had played so large a role in the making of the United States are striking, even if the Brazilians in the 1820s were constructing a new national state, in an international environment where reaction had triumphed in Europe, and the consequences of slave revolution in the Caribbean were more stark and menacing than anything North Americans had to worry about in 1776. Jefferson in particular found much to admire in the Brazilian experience. In 1821 Prince Metternich, much like Dr. Henry Kissinger in the 1970s, believed strongly in the principle of counterrevolutionary interventionism. Kissinger's predecessors as secretary of state in the early nineteenth century thought just the opposite, shocked as they had been by the experiences of the War of 1812 and the vulnerability of the young republic to European attack it had revealed. Fearful that Metternich's Holy Alliance intended to bring Spain's rebellious colonies in the

---

[15]See the important observations on this point by Eugene D. Genovese in his *From Rebellion to Revolution: Afro-American Slave Revolts in the Making of the New World* (New York: Vintage Books, 1981), 92–98.

[16]Cited by Miriam Dolhnikoff, "A Civilização Contra a Sociedade," *Rumos* 1, no. 3 (May–June 1999): 11–19.

New World back into the European fold after the Austrian army had suppressed republican revolutions in Naples and the Piedmont, and France had restored the execrable Bourbon Ferdinand VII to the throne in Madrid, President Monroe in late 1823 announced his famous doctrine in a message to the Congress and it would be the guiding principle of U.S. policy in the Western Hemisphere for the rest of the century.

But the Monroe Doctrine had been foreshadowed some years before in conversations between Jefferson and the envoy of the court of Rio de Janeiro in Washington, the Abbé Corrêa da Serra, and as originally conceived it joined Brazil and the United States together in an "American system," where the two nations would act collaboratively to keep Europe at bay. Jefferson had sustained a long interest in Brazil since the time he was U.S. envoy in Paris. In 1786 he had held a secret meeting in Nîmes with a young Brazilian revolutionary who went by the pseudonym *Vendek*, a student from Rio de Janeiro who was then studying at the University of Montpellier. Later, he had met the Abbé Corrêa while presiding officer of the American Philosophical Society of Philadelphia. Corrêa da Serra, a brilliant Portuguese naturalist and founding secretary of the Lisbon Academy of Sciences, had come to the United States in 1812 and was perceived as a man of great learning and was avidly sought after by the leaders of the new republic.[17]

The Abbé became a regular visitor to Monticello. In their discussions there Jefferson and the Abbé Corrêa first traced their "American system." Jefferson wrote of the Abbé in 1820:

> From many conversations with him, I hope he sees and will promote in his new situation [the Abbé had been recalled to Rio de Janeiro and Jefferson assumed he would become the minister of external affairs] the advantages of a cordial fraternization among all the American nations, and the importance of their coalescing in an American system of policy, totally independent of and unconnected with that of Europe. The day is not distant, when we may formally require a meridian partition through the ocean which separates the two Hemispheres, on the hither side of which no European gun shall ever be heard, nor an American on the other; and when during the rage of the eternal wars of Europe, the lion and the lamb within our regions, shall lie down together in peace. The excess of the population of Europe and want of room, render war, in

---

[17]Richard Beale Davis, *The Abbé Corrêa in America 1812–1820: The Contribution of the Diplomat and the Natural Philosopher to the Foundations of Our National Life*, in *Transactions of the American Philosophical Society*, New Series, vol. 45, part 2 (1955). Reprinted with introduction by Gordon S. Wood and afterword by León Bourdon (Providence, R.I.: Gávea Brown, 1993).

their opinion necessary to keep down that excess of numbers. Here room is abundant, population scanty, and peace the necessary means for producing men, to whom the redundant soil is offering the means of life and happiness. The principals of society there and here are radically different, and I hope no American patriot will ever lose sight of the essential policy of interdicting in the seas and territories of both Americas, the ferocious and sanguinary contests of Europe. I wish to see this coalition begun. I am earnest for an agreement with the maritime powers of Europe, assigning them the task of keeping down the piracies of their seas and the cannibalisms of the African coasts, and to us, the suppression of the same enormities within our own seas, and for this purpose I should rejoice to see the fleets of Brazil and the United States riding together as brethren of the same family and pursuing the same object.[18]

Secretary of State John Quincy Adams was less sympathetic. And it was he, not Monroe or Jefferson, who was to have the most influence over U.S. foreign policy toward the newly independent nations of South America both as secretary of state between 1817 and 1825 and as president from 1825 to 1829. John Quincy Adams saw the merits of separation from Europe, but did not think this implied any mutual identity between the United States and the new nations to its south. He saw South Americans as irredeemably corrupted by the Roman Catholic religion, Iberian tradition, and the tropical climate. The U.S. commercial agent in Rio de Janeiro was reporting to him that the Portuguese monarchy in Brazil had "degenerated into complete effeminacy and voluptuousness. Hardly a worse state of society can be supposed to exist anywhere, than this country. Where the climate also excites to every sort of depravation and delinquency." John Quincy Adams, the dour New Englander from Massachusetts who described himself as a man of "cold and austere" temperament, was not amused by such an untidy and unpromising neighbor. (Such views I notice are still popular in some quarters around Harvard Yard.)[19]

Adams reluctantly acquiesced in President Monroe's desire in mid-1822 to proceed with U.S. recognition of Mexico, Chile, the United Provinces of

---

[18]Thomas Jefferson to William Short, August 4, 1820, in Andrew A. Lipscomb and Albert E. Bergh, eds., *The Writings of Thomas Jefferson*, (20 vols.) (Washington, D.C.: Thomas Jefferson Memorial Association, 1903–1904), XIV, 262–264.
[19]See Lars Schoultz, *Beneath the United States: A History of U.S. Policy toward Latin America* (Cambridge: Harvard University Press, 1998), 4–9, and *Memoirs of John Quincy Adams, Comprising Portions from His Diary from 1795 to 1848*, ed. Charles Francis Adams (12 vols.) (Philadelphia: J. B. Lippincott & Co., 1874–1877).

Rio de la Plata, and the Brazilian Empire. But he wanted as little to do with them as possible. He, like Jefferson, knew the Abbé Corrêa well, and thought him a man of "extensive general literature, of profound science, of brilliant wit, and of inexhaustible powers of conversation." But Adams also found Corrêa "quick, sensitive, fractious, hasty and when excited obstinate." He ridiculed the Abbé Corrêa's (and Thomas Jefferson's) suggestion that Brazil and the United States create an "American system." With the disdain and arrogance that was also to characterize U.S. attitudes toward Latin America for the next century, John Quincy Adams wrote: "As to an American system we have it; we constitute the whole of it."[20]

VI

In Brazil, however, the internal threat to stability and territorial integrity was not only a question of unfounded or unrealized fears; such a threat had come to fruition prior to 1822 in one very important test case, Pernambuco. The prices of sugar and cotton especially had reached an all-time high during the Napoleonic wars, but with peace in 1815 both suffered collapse. Pernambucan cotton especially faced massive competition in Europe from the United States. In 1817 the regionalist antagonisms in Pernambuco toward the central government resurfaced, and this time conspiracy broke into open revolt. Early in the year a republic was proclaimed in Recife and agents sent abroad to gain international recognition.

The seventy-four-day Republic of Pernambuco revealed ambiguities and divisions among the would-be opponents of the status quo no less acute than among its adherents. The enthusiastic support from the great proprietors and slaveholders and their hatred for the Portuguese merchants were a predominant and unifying factor among the separatists. But they could agree on little else. Fears and antagonisms were immediately brought into the open by the "Organic Law" promulgated by the provisional government as a draft constitution. The municipal councils of the hinterland balked at two sections in the Organic Law in particular, one promising religious toleration and the other "equality of rights." Inevitably the latter raised the issue of slavery. The provisional government explained that property, even that "most repugnant to the ideal of justice is sacred." No less offensive to the great landowners was the mobilization of the *povo*, small sharecroppers and squatters, the marginally employed free population, and artisans, whose ideas, fraternization and occasional interracial

---

[20]Cited by Schoultz, *Beneath the United States*, 10–11.

solidarity offended their sense of status and challenged their local authority. Rent by internal factionalism, blockaded by sea, and with a land army approaching from Bahia, Recife capitulated.[21]

There had been no response to Pernambuco's requests for international recognition. The provisional government had expected support from the United States and France—Jefferson's friend, the Abbé Corrêa, had worked mightily in Washington to thwart Pernambuco's representatives and frustrate the merchants of Baltimore who were helping them—but it was Britain that really mattered.[22] British influence over the central government in Rio de Janeiro, however, offered much greater opportunities than did the encouragement of separatist revolts. London had no strong material interests at stake in Pernambuco by 1817, for raw cotton could be obtained in great quantities from the United States and sugar from British islands in the Caribbean. The provisional government of Recife had little to offer that Britain had not gained in 1810. British policy too was strongly influenced by the slave trade. Strong pressure by the British government in 1810 had forced Dom João to promise the gradual abolition of trade "throughout the whole of his dominions." In 1815, the government in Rio agreed to abandon the trade north of the equator. Neither commitment was entirely satisfactory to Britain as the slave trade continued legally below the equator between Portuguese territories in Africa and those in South America. The separation Britain was less reluctant to support was that between Brazil and the Portuguese enclaves in Africa. Until 1820 this intraimperial trade was a question of internal Luso-Brazilian concern; after 1825, however, this major obstacle to outright interference was removed by the separation of Brazil and Portugal, and British insistence that the African territories remain linked to Lisbon, not to Rio de Janeiro. Now that they were independent and sovereign nations, the slave trade between them and South America became internationalized and open to suppression by the British navy on the high seas.

Yet even the British, who after all did not abolish slavery in their own colonies until the mid-1830s, privately recognized the strength of slave-owning interests in Brazil. Henry Chamberlain told George Canning:

---

[21]José Honório Rodrigues, ed., *Revolução de 1817; Documentos Históricos* (9 vols.) (Rio de Janeiro: Biblioteca Nacional, 1953–1955); Evaldo Cabral de Mello, *Frei Joaquim do Amor Divino Caneca (Coleção Formadores do Brasil)* (São Paulo: Editora 34, 2001); Carlos Guilherme Mota, *Nordeste* (São Paulo: Editora Perspectiva, 1972); and José Honório Rodrigues, *Independência, revolução e contrarevolução* (5 vols.) (Rio de Janeiro: Livraria F. Alves Editora, [1975–1976]).
[22]León Bourdon, *José Corrêa de Serra: Ambassadeur du Royaume-unide Portugal et Brésil à Washington 1816–1820* (Paris: Centro Cultural Português, Fundação Calouste Gulbenkian, 1975).

There are not ten persons in the whole Empire who consider the trade a crime, or who look at it in any other point of view than one of profit or loss, a mere mercantile speculation to be continued as long as it may be advantageous.[23]

José Bonifácio himself saw the Brazilian dilemma with great realism. He told the British envoy Henry Chamberlain in April 1823:

We are fully convinced of the impolicy of the slave trade . . . but I must candidly state to you that the abolition cannot be immediate, and I will explain the two principal considerations by which we have been led to this determination. One is economical, the other political.

The former is founded upon the absolute necessity for taking measures to secure an increase of *white* population previous to the abolition, that the ordinary cultivation of the country may go on, for otherwise upon the supply of Negroes ceasing, that cultivation would go backwards and be followed by great distress. . . . we shall lose no time in adopting measures for drawing European emigrants hither. As soon as these begin to produce this effect, the necessity for the African supply will gradually diminish, and I hope in a few years a stop will be put to it for ever. . . .

The latter consideration is founded upon political expediency as affecting the popularity, and perhaps even the stability, of the government. The crisis and representations in the trade we might perhaps venture to encounter, but we cannot, without such a degree of risk as no man in their senses think of incurring, attempt at such a moment as the present to propose a measure that would indispose the whole of the population of the interior. . . . Almost the whole of our agriculture is performed by Negroes and slaves. The whites unfortunately do very little work, and if the landed proprietors were to find their supply of laborers suddenly and wholly cut off, I leave you to judge the effect it would have upon these uninformed and unenlightened class of people. Were the abolition to come upon them before they were prepared for it, the whole country would be convulsed from one end to the other, and there is no calculating the consequences to the Government or to the country itself.

We know that as long as it is carried on and a state of slavery continued in the country, that real sound industry cannot take root,

---

[23]Henry Chamberlain to George Canning, Rio de Janeiro, December 31, 1823, in Webster, I, 232–234, citation from 233.

that a vigorous prosperity cannot exist, that our population is un-
sound, and so fully are we persuaded of these truths that were it
possible, we would at once abolish both.[24]

These objections to slavery were not, it must be emphasized, so much
the result of "humanitarian" or "philanthropic" sentiment, as they were in
Europe, but were more similar to the objections to slavery in the United
States in the same period, and were a response to the perception that the
racial balance of the population was potentially and dangerously unstable,
or would impede the growth of a nation on a European model. Those few
who urged eventual emancipation of the slaves, such as José Bonifácio, did
so not because of the humanity of slaves, but because they wished to see
Brazil Europeanized, not only in terms of aspirations, institutions, and national purpose, but also in terms of the composition of its population.

But Bonifácio was in one important respect far more radical than were
his North American counterparts, and his attitude reflected a strong current of thinking that had emerged in the eighteenth century, especially
during the long rule of the Marquês de Pombal of which Bonifácio was
very much an heir. He was skeptical, and explicitly so, about the ability of a
society so heterogeneous as that of Brazil, where, as he put it, white proprietors, black slaves, and poor mestizos did not possess a sense of identity
that united them. On the contrary, as enemies among themselves, they
were more predisposed to conflict than to unity. It was therefore, he believed, necessary to homogenize the population, which signified eliminat-
ing slavery, integrating the Indians, encouraging miscegenation between
Indians and whites and between whites and blacks. He intended thereby
to create a Brazilian "race" composed of mestizos united by a common
national identity. As a metallurgist of some fame in Europe, he used a metallurgical analogy for what he envisioned: he sought, he wrote, to "amalgamate so many diverse metals, so that a homogeneous and compact whole
might emerge." Only in this manner would the "sloth and vices" of the
whites be eliminated, "we tyrannize the slaves and reduce them to brute
animals, and they inoculate us with their immortality and all their vices"
was the way he described it.

We now know, of course, that Jefferson engaged in his own form of
clandestine amalgamation, but this was, as he might have said had he chosen to acknowledge his relationship with Sally Hemings as he did with
the Englishwoman Maria Cosway in Paris, an affair of the "heart" not of
the "head." Bonifácio's was very much a policy of the head. But Bonifácio,
the protégée of Jefferson's friend, the Abbé Corrêa da Serra, was after all,

---

[24]Henry Chamberlain to George Canning (secret), Rio de Janeiro, April 2, 1823, in
Webster, I, 222–223.

with his distinguished reputation and achievements as a natural scientist, the sort of natural philosopher Jefferson aspired to be. And over the question of slavery it was the patriarch of American independence, Thomas Jefferson, who equivocated, not the patriarch of Brazil's independence, José Bonifácio.[25]

The ideologues of "free trade" in Brazil also took an essentially racist view. José da Silva Lisboa, the Brazilian political economist who had urged the opening of the Brazilian ports to the prince regent in 1808, argued in 1818 that the progress of São Paulo was due "to extraordinary preponderance [there] of the white race." Rio Grande do Sul, the granary of Brazil as he called it, likewise had been colonized by "the Portuguese race, and not the Ethiopian population." Taking the example of Madeira, he asserted that "experience had shown that once the supply of Africans has been cut off, the race does not decrease and decline but becomes better and whiter . . ." He went on to ask: "Was the best area in America to be populated by the offspring of Africa or of Europe?" To avoid "the horrid spectacle of the catastrophe that reduced the Queen of the Antilles [Haiti, that is] to a Madagascar," Brazil should be prevented from becoming a "Negroland." He wished to see the cancer of slavery eliminated from the Rio de la Plata to the Amazon.[26]

The question of slavery thus raised fundamental questions about the most desirable course for Brazilian development, questions as to the type of society, state, legal system, and government Brazil as an independent state would adopt. But what to do about slavery divided "enlightened" men, and it consolidated the determination of those major commercial and landed interests whose welfare depended on slavery to make sure that the new structures of state power, as well as the new constitutional monarchy, remained firmly wedded to their interests.

In sum, Brazilian intellectuals, traders, and patriots might espouse "liberalism," but their zeal was strictly limited to a desire for access to markets, protection of property, and guarantees that debts would be paid. And in this centralism, monarchy and continuity were paramount. Brazil's "patriots" were realists and they could move no further than their base of social support. Those who did so, such as José Bonifácio, were soon jettisoned.

[25]William Howard Adams, *Thomas Jefferson: The Paris Years* (New Haven and London: Yale University Press: 1997), 207–250; also John Chester Miller, *The Wolf by the Ears: Thomas Jefferson and Slavery* (Charlottesville and London: University Press of Virginia, 1991).

[26]José da Silva Lisboa, *Memória dos benefícios políticos do governo de El-Rei Nosso Senhor D. João VI* (Rio de Janeiro: Na Impressão Régia, 1818), 2d. ed. (Rio de Janeiro: Impressa nas Oficinas do Arquivo Nacional, 1940) 160–164. Also see José da Silva Lisboa, *Escritos económicos escolhidos (1804–1820)* in *Colecção de obras clássicas do pensamento económico português* (V in 2 vols.) (Lisbon: Banco de Portugal, 1993).

Slavery and industrial capitalism in fact proved highly compatible within the nineteenth-century Atlantic system—industrial capitalism thriving on slave-produced cotton and coffee no less than commercial capitalism had thrived on slave-produced sugar. In this context, reformers like José Bonifácio were double victims. Not only did this economic system itself, both domestically and in its Atlantic dimensions, create conditions hostile to his proposal for fundamental reform; he was also a victim of the British policy, the overbearing pressure of which helped to undermine the one administration with any real commitment to the ending of slavery and slave trade. In secret conversations with Henry Chamberlain in April 1823, José Bonifácio warned the British not to push too hard or too soon:

> You know how sincerely I detest the Slave Trade, how prejudicial I think it to the country, how very desirous I am for its total cessation, but it cannot be done immediately. The people are not prepared for it and until this has been brought about, it would endanger the existence of the Government if attempted suddenly. This very abolition is one of the principle measures I wish to bring before the Assembly without delay, but it requires management, and cannot be hastened . . .
>
> With regards to Colonies or the Coast of Africa, we want none, nor anywhere else. Brazil is quite large enough and productive enough for us, and we are content with what Providence has given us.
>
> I wish your cruisers would take every slave ship they fall in with at sea. I want to see no more of them, they are the gangrene of our prosperity. The population we want is a white one, and I soon hope to see arrive here from Europe in shoals the poor, the wretched, the industrious; here they will find plenty, with a fine climate; here they will be happy; such are the colonists we want.[27]

VII

To feed this Atlantic system and to sustain its economic organization of production, however, one thing was clear: Brazil did not need Portugal. The resentments and the financial and economic difficulties which led to the Oporto revolution, the convocation of the Cortes in Lisbon in 1820, and to the formulation of a liberal constitution arose in large part from the loss of Portuguese privileges and monopolies in colonial trade; and once assembled, the measures of the Cortes quickly reflected these imperatives. Not only was Dom João VI forced to return to Lisbon, but the Cortes soon

---

[27]Henry Chamberlain to George Canning (secret), Rio de Janeiro, April 2, 1823, in Webster, I, 222–223.

legislated the end to many of the powers that he had granted to his eldest son, Dom Pedro, who had been left in Rio as regent. Brazilians increasingly saw the measures of the Cortes, strongly supported by the hated Portuguese merchants and immigrants in Brazil, as an attempt at "recolonization" which would turn back the clock on the thirteen years during which Rio had been the center of government. It was against this background that Dom Pedro defied the instructions of the Cortes to return to Europe, accepted the title "Perpetual Defender of Brazil" from the Municipal Council of Rio de Janeiro in early 1822, and then, on September 7, 1822, made his declaration of "independence" on the outskirts of São Paulo.

The political emancipation of Brazil is thus a long and cumulative process with much continuity retained along the way; 1808, 1816, 1822, even 1831 are all important moments in this gradual assertion of separation and definition of nationhood. The path was not without its arduous moments to be sure. International recognition only came after long negotiation in 1825 and the promise by Brazil to pay a large indemnity to Portugal. War in the south broke out with renewed vigor along the frontier in the Banda Oriental, and was not resolved until the end of the decade with the establishment, under British auspices, of the independent buffer state of Uruguay, establishing a southern boundary less ambitious than that of either colony or united kingdom. Much internal military activity both on land and by sea was necessary to bring about the adherence of Bahia, as well as the far north. Pernambuco again tried to break away in 1824. Administratively, the country was not "Brazilianized" until the end of Dom Pedro's short reign in 1831. And it was only in the 1840s that the actions of the duke of Caxias (a man who was, ironically, the nephew by marriage of the rich entrepreneur who had denounced the republican Minas Conspiracy in 1789 to the royal authorities) brought to an end regional separatist revolts. Yet by 1858, well into the long reign of Brazil's second emperor, Dom Pedro II, the satisfaction with this outcome was well summarized by Domingos Antônio Raiol in his *O Brasil político*: "How different [we Brazilians are] from other people who inhabit the same South American continent. When we rest, they fight. When we fraternize, they quarrel. A government monarchic, hereditary, is without doubt a true choice, which tames ambitions and because of stability forms a powerful element of order and prosperity." [28]

In these circumstances, it is not surprising that every attempt to alter the economic organization of labor failed. The alternative model for Brazilian development, in which European immigration and free laborers

---

[28]Domingos Antônio Raiol, *O Brasil político, dedicado ao Excelentíssimo Senhor Bernardo de Souza Franco, Ministro e Secretário dos Negócios da Fazenda, por Domingos Antônio Raiol* (Pará: Typographia do Diario do Commercio, 1858).

would replace slavery, was not to be, at least as long as emperors ruled in Rio de Janeiro, and as a consequence, the slave trade continued until midcentury, slavery until the 1880s. Nor is it surprising that when slavery fell, the monarchy fell with it; in part, at least, because with the emancipation of the slaves the republican alternative to the monarchy had at long last also been emancipated from the stigma of separatism and social upheaval.[29]

So I hope that by highlighting some of the multiple contexts within which Brazil became an independent nation, I also may have gone some way toward demonstrating why Brazil was different, and why it is high time historians took a fresh look in a comparative framework at this fascinating and complex transition.

---

[29]For a discussion of the interplay between centralism and regionalism, and between monarchy and republicanism from the perspective of Pernambuco, see Evaldo Cabral de Mello, *A ferida de Narciso. Ensaio de História Regional* (São Paulo: Editora SENAC, 2001), especially 69–90.

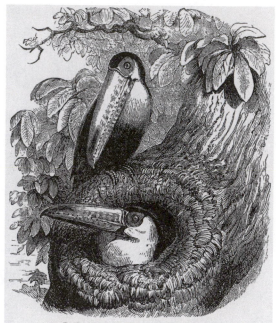

PAIR OF TOUCANS AND THEIR NEST.

CHAPTER 9

The Odd Couple

Jefferson and the Abbé

"The most learned man I have met in any country."
—Thomas Jefferson on the Abbé Corrêa da Serra

The friendship between Thomas Jefferson and the Abbé Corrêa da Serra involves an enigma, a mystery, and a remarkable historical coincidence. If you visit Monticello, Jefferson's mountaintop mansion in Virginia, you will see the grave of Jefferson, surmounted by the obelisk he designed. It is inscribed with the epitaph he wrote for himself. Jefferson did not want to be remembered for being president of the United States, or for being secretary of state, or the U.S. ambassador in Paris on the eve of the French Revolution. The three things he wished to see recorded on his obelisk are: first, that he was the author of the Declaration of Independence; second, that he wrote the Virginia Statute for Religious Freedom; and, third, that he was the father of the University of Virginia. These achievements of Jefferson's career of which he was most proud help unravel the enigma, the mystery, and the coincidence that is involved in the relationship between these two men.

I

But who was the Abbé Corrêa da Serra? José Corrêa da Serra was born in Portugal in 1750. His father was a physician who was forced to flee with his family in the face of a pending action by the Inquisition. Young Corrêa da Serra was six years old when the family moved to Naples where he later studied with two very important figures of the Italian Enlightenment, the Portuguese-born Luís António Verney, who was the author of a widely read treatise on educational reform, *O verdadeiro método de estudar* (Naples, 1746) and the Abbé Antonio Genovesi, an Italian philosophe who was interested in political economy and the reform of the church. Both were disciples of the three towering figures Jefferson considered his own intellectual progenitors—Locke, Newton, and Bacon—and whose portraits Jefferson displayed prominently at Monticello. Naples was a center of the Southern European Enlightenment in this period, ruled by Charles of Bourbon, the future Charles III of Spain, and the great reform minister Bernard Tanucci.

In the 1770s Corrêa da Serra moved to Rome to complete his education, became a presbyter, and took holy orders. In Rome, he became acquainted with the widely traveled Dom João Carlos de Bragança, the second duke of Lafões, grandson of King Pedro II of Portugal and his French mistress, Madame Laverger. This relationship to the Portuguese royal family, legitimized by the king, placed the duke of Lafões too close to the legitimate Bragança line for comfort, which was the principal reason it made it prudent for him to travel. But Lafões, who had known Corrêa da Serra's father at the University of Coimbra, was a well-educated and scientifically minded aristocrat and a member of the Royal Society of London.

The period the young Corrêa da Serra spent in Rome was a critical one. In 1773 the pope suppressed the Society of Jesus; a watershed event in the eighteenth century for the European Catholic monarchies. The suppression of the Jesuits had been made possible by the aggressive campaign against the Society of Jesus instigated in the first instance by the de facto ruler of Portugal between 1750 and 1777, the Marquês de Pombal. Luís António Verney, Corrêa da Serra's old mentor from Naples, became secretary to the Portuguese Embassy at the Vatican, the nerve center of the European-wide campaign against the Jesuits. The Abbé Corrêa da Serra returned to Portugal in 1778, and under the duke of Lafões's patronage a year later he became one of the founding members of the class of natural sciences of the new Academy of Sciences of Lisbon, established by Queen Maria I in 1779 and inaugurated in July 1780.

Lisbon remained, at this time, one of Europe's greatest ports; enriched by the flow of wealth from Brazil, Portugal's most important eighteenth-century colony. In the immediate aftermath of the rule of the Marquês de Pombal, following the death of Dom José I in 1777, however, an intense struggle between the reformers and traditionalists persisted in Portugal, and the rise and fall of anti- and pro-Pombaline factions at court had immediate impact on individuals like the Abbé Corrêa da Serra who were enlightenened reformers. Thus, in 1786 unfavorable conditions in Lisbon again forced him to leave Portugal. But in 1790 Corrêa da Serra was back in Lisbon and served as the secretary of the Academy of Sciences for six years.

During this period he published a series of critical works on bibliography and historiography, developed a wide correspondence with leading European scientists and philosophers, and pursued his passion for scientific experimentation and botany.

In 1790 the Abbé Corrêa da Serra, as the secretary of the Lisbon Academy of Sciences, drew up the itinerary for three promising young scholars, two young Brazilians and a Portuguese colleague, for a government-sponsored scientific tour of Europe, beginning in Paris. It was a remarkable initiative—if one thinks of Portugal in this period as being reactionary, backward, and the bastion of obscurantism—for the Portuguese government to send two young Brazilians to France at the very height of the French Revolution. One of them, Dr. Manuel Ferreira da Câmara, was related to a young natural scientist involved in a republican plot to throw off Portuguese control in Brazil a year before in Minas Gerais, and another, Dr. José Bonifácio de Andrada e Silva, would succeed Corrêa da Serra as secretary of the Lisbon Academy of Sciences and later become famous in history as the "patriarch" of Brazilian independence.

But in 1795, in the face of the reaction against the French Revolution, the situation again deteriorated in Portugal to the detriment of reformers such as Corrêa da Serra. This time he fled to England via Gibraltar and remained in London for a number of years. In 1796 he became a member of the Royal Society, as well as a member of the Linnaeus Society. By this time he was an internationally known botanist and was already well acquainted with the leading scientists in England, most notably Sir Joseph Banks, president of the Royal Society, with whom Corrêa da Serra conducted an important botanical expedition to the Lincolnshire coast in England. Sir Joseph Banks had visited Lisbon as a young man in the mid-1760s, as well as Rio de Janeiro in 1768 when he accompanied James Cook on his circumnavigation of the world. It was at Banks's request that the Abbé helped smuggle a French natural scientist, Peter Marie Auguste Broussonet, a Girodin who was escaping from the terror of the French Revolution through Portugal. This temporarily seems to have lost him the patronage of his old protector, the duke of Lafões, who had been appointed to the unlikely position of commander-in-chief of the Portuguese army, though his interests lay more in the minutiae of soldiers' uniforms and the organization of their campsites than in the fighting battles.

Lafões liked to style himself the "duke of Bragança" while traveling outside Portugal, but William Beckford, the caustic English esthete then in Lisbon, said that the "duchess of Bragança" would have been a more appropriate title. Beckford wrote in his diary:

> He is like an old lady of the bed chamber, as fiddle faddle and coquettish and gossiping. He has got on rouge and patches, and

though he is seventy years old, contrived to turn on his heel and to glide away with youthful agility. After lisping French with a most refined accent and complaining of the wind and the roads and the state of the architecture, he departed to mark the site for the encampment of the cavalry.[1]

In 1801, however, the situation in Portugal changed again in favor of the more liberal elements and Corrêa da Serra's close friend, Dom Rodrigo de Sousa Coutinho, the godson of Pombal, became the foreign minister and gave Corrêa da Serra a consular position in London intended to help him financially since the Abbé Corrêa was always in chronic need of emoluments.

While in London, Corrêa da Serra procured micrometers, theodolites, achromatic telescopes, threshing machines, and "engines" for watering gardens for the famous shops of James Ramsden. Thomas Jefferson, another scientific experimenter, was buying his scientific instruments from Ramsden in this same period. Many of the instruments Corrêa da Serra bought make up part of the unique collection of eighteenth-century scientific instruments owned by the University of Coimbra. Some of the instruments Jefferson purchased in this same period are displayed today at Monticello.

Unfortunately, the Portuguese ambassador in London came from a family of the aristocracy, the Ponte de Lima, that was most opposed to the reform faction in Portugal, and he made Corrêa da Serra's life miserable, despite the support of Dom Rodrigo. Finding his position in London intolerable, Corrêa da Serra left for Paris where he lived from 1801 to 1811.

In Paris, the Abbé Corrêa da Serra was very closely associated with the Encyclopedists. Among his close friends and colleagues in Paris were Antoine Laurent de Jussieu, professor of botany at the Museum of Natural History; Baron Alexander von Humboldt; and Baron Cuvier (Georges Léopole Chrétien Frédéric Dagobert), professor of natural history at the College de France and titular professor at the Jardin des Plantes. Like Thomas Jefferson before him, who while American ambassador had been smitten by the beautiful Maria Cosway, the Abbé fell in love. The object of

---

[1]William Beckford, *The Journal of William Beckford in Portugal and Spain, 1787–1788*, ed. Boyd Alexander (London: Hart-Davis, 1954), 172. The most comprehensive Portuguese account of the Abbé Corrêa da Serra's career remains Augusto da Silva Carvalho, *O Abade Correia da Serra* (Lisbon: Academia das Ciências de Lisboa, 1948). For a brief introduction and catalogue of documents from Corrêa da Serra's archive see Michael Teague, ed., *Abade José Correia da Serra, documentos do seu arquivo (1751–1795)* (Lisbon: Fundação Luso-Americana para o Desenvolvimento, 1997).

his amorous attention was a young French woman, Esther Delavigne, by whom he had a son, Eduardo José, in 1803.[2]

But Corrêa da Serra again ran into trouble. During the second French invasion of Portugal in 1811, Napoleon requested that Corrêa da Serra write a justification of the French action. Corrêa da Serra refused, and unsurprisingly found himself once more on the road. This time he left Europe altogether, taking passage on an American frigate, the famous USS *Constitution* (which still exists to this day docked at the Boston harbor). He arrived at Norfolk, Virginia, in the fatal year of 1812 when hostilities broke out between the young North American republic and Great Britain, one consequence of which was the humiliating capture by the British of the new federal capital, Washington, and the burning of the presidential mansion.

The Abbé Corrêa da Serra arrived in the United States well furnished with letters of introduction to President James Madison and to former President Thomas Jefferson, as well as to leading members of the American Philosophical Society in Philadelphia. These letters were from some of the leading figures of the European Enlightenment including André Thouin, the conservator of the Jardin des Plantes in Paris, his friend Sir Joseph Banks, the Marquis de Lafayette, Pierre Samuel du Pont, Alexander von Humboldt, and Joel Barlow, American envoy in Paris.

Corrêa da Serra's arrival in Washington, soon after the British had burnt the fledgling federal capital, was inauspicious. During his first week his coach turned over in a mud patch. He had little good to say about Washington thereafter. But in Philadelphia he found an extremely congenial environment and immediately became a favorite of the American Philosophical Society and its erudite members. Benjamin Franklin had presided over the American Philosophical Society from 1769 until his death in 1790, being eulogized by Corrêa da Serra before the Lisbon Academy of Sciences in 1791. The society was "dedicated to the improvement of useful knowledge more particularly what relates to this new world. It comprises the whole circle of arts, sciences, and discoveries, especially in the natural world." These were, of course, no less the objectives of Corrêa da Serra's

---

[2]Like Jefferson and his relationship with Sally Hemings, the Abbé apparently also had secrets. Professor David Higgs came across a denunciation among the papers of the Lisbon Inquisition (*Cadernos do Nefando*, no. 145, Arquivo Nacional Torre do Tombo, Lisbon). These involved accusations of sodomy; according to the documents, the Abbé had four times made a "sin against nature" with Faustina, a woman from the Praça das Flores. His most recent acts of sodomy, in 1792 and 1793, had been with "unknown persons in the darkness of night outdoors," and in particular five or six times with a boy (*moço*). See David Higgs, "Lisbon," in *Queer Sites: Gay Urban Histories since 1600*, ed. David Higgs (London and New York: Routledge, 1999), 127.

Lisbon Academy of Sciences, whose activities focused equally on natural history, with a strong interest in Brazil. Thomas Jefferson had been elected one of the three vice presidents of the American Philosophical Society in 1791 and had been installed in Philadelphia as its president in 1797, on the evening before his inauguration as vice president of the United States.

The Abbé Corrêa da Serra's first visit with Jefferson was so mutually satisfying to both men that he became a welcomed annual guest at Monticello between 1813 and 1816. On the first floor at Monticello, across the hallway from Jefferson's own suite, there are two bedrooms: one is the Madison room and the other the Abbé Corrêa da Serra room. This room was set aside for Corrêa da Serra and half a century later Jefferson's granddaughter still called it the Abbé Corrêa room. This was where Abbé Corrêa da Serra stayed when he visited Jefferson.

Some of Jefferson's friends have left records of their reactions to the Abbé at this time. One of the most interesting was from Francis Gilmore, Corrêa's companion on an extensive expedition collecting botanical specimens as well as social and natural historical information along the western frontier. Gilmore traveled with the Abbé Corrêa da Serra back to Philadelphia from Monticello in 1813 and said of Corrêa,

> He is the most extraordinary man now living or who perhaps ever lived . . . He has read, seen, understands, and remembers everything obtained in books, or to be learned from travel, observation, and the conversation of learned men. He is a member of every philosophical society in the world, and he knows every distinguished man living.[3]

Jefferson, himself had a very similar reaction to him, and his own description was equally flattering:

> Mr. Corrêa was a gentleman from Portugal of the first order of science, being without exception the most learned man I have met in any country. Modest, good humored, familiar, plain as a country farmer, he became the favorite of everyone with whom he becomes acquainted. He speaks English with ease.[4]

---

[3]Francis Gilmer to P. R. Gilmer, November 3, 1814, in Richard Beale Davis, *The Abbé Corrêa in America 1812–1820: The Contribution of the Diplomat and the Natural Philosopher to the Foundations of Our National Life*, in *Transactions of the American Philosophical Society*, New Series, vol. 45, part 2 (1955). Reprinted with introduction by Gordon S. Wood and afterword by León Bourdon (Providence, R.I.: Gávea Brown, 1993), 43.

[4]Thomas Jefferson to John Milledge, September 22, 1815, cited in ibid., 46.

II

But how is it that a Catholic priest in the late eighteenth century should become one of the closest friends of the sage of Monticello, a deist and Uni-
tarian who had little good to say about organized religion. This, of course,
is the enigma.

So let me try to unravel this enigma to some degree. First, one has to realize that there was an important strain in Portuguese intellectual life, government policy, and action in the eighteenth century that made it very
much a part of the fervor of change in Southern Europe exemplified by
Genovese and Verney. Three people stand out in this intellectual current:
Jacob de Castro Sarmento, António Nunes Ribeiro Sanches, and, of course,
the great Luís António Verney himself. These people were highly cosmopolitan; two of them were "New Christians"—"New Christians" in the
Portuguese context were the descendants of Jews who had been converted
forcibly or had claimed to be converted in the immediate aftermath of the
expulsions of the Jewish population from Spain in the late fifteenth century. By the eighteenth century they were a community who existed in a
very conflictive world between their Judaic past, their Christian accep-
tances, and, in not a few cases, their Judaic future. They remained always
threatened by the Inquisition, and subjected in law to many disabilities because of their so-called impurity of blood.

The "New Christians" were, therefore, a people who had a mixture of religious backgrounds, suffered persecution, and were often forced to leave their
own country if they had good family contacts or the luck to escape the Inquisition's torture chambers and the fires of the auto-da-Fé. Yet they remained
throughout the centuries in Portugal important in two key areas—business
and medicine—and they were extremely internationally minded in their
thinking and family connections. Jacob de Castro Sarmento and António
Nunes Ribeiro Sanches both became leading philosophes of the eighteenth
century. Yet, as with the Abbé Corrêa da Serra, you rarely see their names
mentioned when the Diderot encyclopedia is discussed, even though Ribeiro
Sanches was one of the contributors to the encyclopedia on medicine, particularly on issues of hygiene, and the Abbé Corrêa da Serra was commissioned to write a report on the Lisbon earthquake and the reconstruction of
the city which arrived too late for inclusion.

Ribeiro Sanches, like the Abbé Corrêa da Serra family later on, had been
forced by the Inquisition in the 1730s to leave Portugal. Fleeing to London,
during the 1740s he served as the personal physician of José Sebastião Carvalho e Melo, who later became the Marquês de Pombal. Ribeiro Sanches
studied in Holland at Leiden University under one of the greatest medical
innovators and natural scientists of the eighteenth century, Hermann

Boerhaave. Castro Sarmento and Gerhard Van Swieten were also Boer-haave students, as were several faculty members of the new College of Medicine in Philadelphia. Van Swieten, a Roman Catholic Dutchman, was to become reformer of the Austrian monarchy's educational and medical systems. Van Swieten was the personal physician to the future Marquês de Pombal when he served as Portuguese envoy in Vienna and was also the Empress Maria Teresa's personal physician.

Ribeiro Sanches had left London for Vienna at Van Swieten's suggestion. From Austria he traveled to Moscow where he was made responsible for the health of the Russian armies fighting the Turks and the Tartars. He wrote a series of important treatises at this time, one on venereal disease, where he claimed that venereal disease did not come from America but was of Asiatic origin. (Corrêa de Serra's French-born son, Eduardo José, also became a doctor and wrote his thesis for the Faculty of Medicine in Paris on venereal disease.) But Ribeiro Sanches's most important work was on saunas and hygiene. He believed soldiers should bathe and he was impressed by the Russian sauna and wanted to see the sauna introduced into Western Europe. His book on the sauna or on the use of vapors to cleanse the body was one of the best-sellers of the eighteenth century. In the late 1770s Ribeiro Sanches moved to Paris, and he collaborated with the philosophes and many of his ideas entered into the great encyclopedia. So we are not talking here about somebody who was marginal to the eighteenth-century Enlightenment; Ribeiro Sanches was central to it and was central to it as an exiled Portuguese "New Christian," with a fractured background of persecution and of religion and cultural experience.[5]

What came out of this experience was an emphasis on educational reform and religious toleration, the desire to do away with forced categorization of people. When Pombal, his former patient in London, took power in Lisbon, Ribeiro Sanches was able to exercise considerable influence over educational reform. In fact, both Castro Sarmento and Ribeiro Sanches served as consultants to the Portuguese government during the late 1760s through the 1770s and were involved in all the educational reforms that took place in this period, particularly the founding of the College of Nobles and the reform of the University of Coimbra.

For the College of Nobles in Portugal, Ribeiro Sanches provided concrete position papers on how the curriculum should be developed, based on his experience in Russia with the Russian Imperial Corps of Cadets. The college was to have lectures on hygiene. It also had a physics laboratory.

---

[5]See David Williamse, "António Nunes Ribeiro Sanches, élève de Boerhaave et son importance pour la Russie," *Janus: Revue internationale de l'histoire des sciences de la médecine, de la pharmacie et de la technique, Suppléments,* VI (Leiden, 1966).

Ribeiro Sanches in his *Cartas sobre a educação da mocidade* (Paris, 1759) had recommended the value of physics in the educational curriculum as well as the use of scientific apparatus so that the teachers could demonstrate "by means of the use of these instruments that results were caused not by miracles but through the effects of nature . . . [and] . . . the pupils would see the proofs of what they were taught."

The professor of experimental physics at the College of Nobles, Giovanni António dalla Bella, had arrived in 1766 from Italy and was responsible for the purchase of instruments, in part from England and in part by commissioning instruments constructed in Portugal. The young prince Dom José, heir apparent, had his own physics laboratory at the Royal Palace of Ajuda in Lisbon. William Beckford, who met the prince a year before he tragically succumbed to smallpox, observed that the very first thing the prince had spoken of was his physics laboratory. The writings of Corrêa da Serra's mentor, Antonio Genovesi, were cited in the statutes of the college. The college included among its first pupils the sons of recently ennobled merchants, some of them said to be "New Christians."

Later on in 1772, when the reform of the University of Coimbra took place, the principal elements of that reform included the setting up of a curriculum in natural sciences, anatomy, and hygiene and the formation of chemistry and physics laboratories and an observatory. The reform aimed to modernize the faculties of theology and canon law, to incorporate the study of Portuguese sources into the curriculum of the faculty of law, to thoroughly update the faculty of medicine by the return of the study of anatomy through the dissection of corpses (previously prohibited in Portugal for religious reasons), the study of hygiene "because it is easier to conserve health than to recuperate it once lost," as well as to adopt William Harvey's discoveries concerning the circulation of blood, Bernard Siegfried Albinus's theories in anatomy, Hermann Boerhaave's in pathology, and Gerhard Van Swieten's in pharmacology.[6]

Pombal also attempted to do away with the invidious distinctions between "old" and "new" Christian and to bring, in effect, a more tolerant attitude within the country. Ribeiro Sanches, then in Paris, was consulted by Pombal on this legislation. Ribeiro Sanches kept a day-by-day diary which contains his personal reactions to the reforms under way in Portugal. He was privately skeptical that legislation could counteract the prejudices of centuries. Are the prejudices, he wrote, that people hold in their hearts learned from their priests as children, learned in their confessionals; can

---

[6]For more details on educational reforms in eighteenth-century Portugal see Kenneth Maxwell, *Pombal, Paradox of the Enlightenment* (Cambridge and New York: Cambridge University Press, 1995), 13–15, 92–109.

this be changed by the legislation of the state? He was doubtful as to the results. Nevertheless the attempt was made to remove the legal impediments; the invidious distinction between "new" and "old" Christians was formally abolished by Pombal in the 1770s.[7]

It should be noted that throughout this whole reform processes Brazilians played a very important role. Of the Brazilians who came to the reformed University of Coimbra 65 percent worked in the new natural sciences faculties, taking degrees and doctorates for the first time in natural sciences, and many of them went on to be very important figures in the independence movement in Brazil—men such as José Bonifácio de Andrada e Silva, one of the students whose scientific education in Europe was sponsored by the Abbé Corrêa da Serra in 1790. Francisco de Lemos, a Brazilian, was the reforming rector of the university placed in this position by Pombal.

The role of Brazilians in these developments is interesting because reform in imperial relationships seemed important to all these thinkers and they tended—Ribeiro Sanches, Corrêa da Serra, and his great sponsor in Portugal, Dom Rodrigo da Sousa Coutinho—to argue that Brazil would eventually be the center of the Portuguese Empire. So it is no mere coincidence that in 1816, when in Rio de Janeiro the United Kingdom of Portugal, Brazil, and the Algarves was proclaimed, the Abbé Corrêa da Serra, by then in Philadelphia, should be chosen to be the first ambassador to the United States to represent the new South American–based monarchy.

Out of this background we can begin, I think, to unravel our enigma and begin to see some of the intellectual experiences that Jefferson would find so interesting in Corrêa da Serra. Jefferson regarded broadly diffused educational opportunity as the most important function of the state, and while in Paris he wrote to George Wythe, under whom he had studied law at the College of William and Mary in Virginia:

> I think by far the most important bill in our whole code, is that for the diffusion of knowledge among the people. No other sure foundation can be devised for the preservation of freedom and happiness.[8]

As we see from Jefferson's obelisk at Monticello and the correspondence between Jefferson and Corrêa da Serra, one major interest that joined

---

[7]See António Nunes Ribeiro Sanches, June 23, 1773, in "Journal," Bibliothèque de la Faculté de Médecine, Paris, ms. 2015, folio 117–118. Also see Maria Helena Carvalho dos Santos, "Ribeiro Sanches e a questão dos judeus" in *RHDI/MdeP* I, 117–142.

[8]Thomas Jefferson to George Wythe, Paris, August 13, 1786, in Andrew A. Lipscomb and Albert E. Bergh, eds., *The Writings of Thomas Jefferson*, (20 vols.) (Washington, D.C.: Thomas Jefferson Memorial Association, 1903–1904), V, 396.

them was the foundation of the University of Virginia, its curriculum, how the faculty should be recruited, and how the botanical garden should be organized. In 1820 Jefferson wrote:

> Mr. Corrêa's approbation of the plan of principles of our university flatters me more than that of all its other eulogists because no other could be put in a line with him in science and comprehensive scope of mind.[9]

This passionate interest in educational reform clearly provides part of an explanation of our enigma: the mutual interests of Corrêa da Serra and Jefferson which focused on the establishment of the University of Virginia, one of the three elements that Jefferson himself was most proud of in his life's work, and the third of his achievements he instructed should be carved on the obelisk over his tomb at Monticello.

III

But what is the mystery? The mystery is why we do not know about this remarkable story. Why is it that this very important friendship, and the mutual interests that joined Corrêa da Serra and Jefferson in discussions about subjects that were vital to Jefferson's sense of himself and what he had achieved in life, are so little known. I think there are several possible explanations; let me just give some of them. The first grows from our notions of the Enlightenment, particularly in the North American and northwest European context. We tend to think, and recent interpretations have led us to believe, that the Enlightenment was an exclusively northwestern European phenomenon, or if there was a Southern European influence in eighteenth-century North America, it was derived from a much earlier period. Yet curiously this misses the importance of contemporary influences, contemporary to Jefferson that is, and which came directly from personal engagement with men like the Abbé Corrêa da Serra. Thus, we know in the historical literature much about the role of the Scottish Enlightenment, or we tend to see the scientific revolution as a development confined to Protestant Europe, at least in its scientific and experimental aspects; but we lack any discussion or any awareness at all that the Enlightenment was a much broader movement that was shaking up Catholic Europe as much as it was Protestant Europe. I think that the first blockage therefore is the fog of lingering prejudice about what was happening in Southern Europe in general in the late eighteenth century.

---

[9]Thomas Jefferson to Corrêa da Serra, Monticello, October 24, [1820], in Davis, *The Abbé Corrêa in America*, 181.

But why is it Catholic historians have not dealt with this? I think there is a very interesting reason here. The Abbé Corrêa da Serra was anticlerical and he was anti-Jesuit; and he opposed the pretentions of the papal curia; here was an elderly Portuguese Abbé who strongly advised Jefferson that it was absolutely essential to preserve the separation of church and state in Virginia and especially within his new state university. To understand this position one has to go back and read what Antonio Genovesi and António Nunes Ribeiro Sanches were writing. Both were adamantly opposed to the monarchical conception of the papacy, and they favored an episcopal as opposed to papal domination of the Catholic Church. And they were fervently opposed to the Jesuits. As we know the Jesuits, following their suppression by the pope in 1773, were reestablished in the early nineteenth century, and they regained a dominant role in Catholic education. This is part of the explanation, I suspect, as to why we have very few Catholic historians dealing with the Enlightenment fervor within the Catholic Church in the eighteenth century with its very strong anti-Roman cast.

A further reason lies in the course of U.S. history, especially the history of the South following the Civil War. The state university was a southern invention; the northern universities were still in the eighteenth century and long dominated by religious denominations, exclusively in some cases, and were, as the Abbé Corrêa da Serra told Jefferson, no more than "seminaries" in his view. Later of course it was these northern private universities which became most prestigious in the American system of higher education, not the state universities. The University of Virginia itself did not, in the nineteenth century, fulfill the high objectives Jefferson set for it, though it did succeed in doing so in many ways in the twentieth century. So the originality of Jefferson's educational reform was not much recognized or appreciated until comparatively recently since most post–Civil War northern historians could not conceive of an advanced educational establishment embedded with Enlightenment thinking existing in the South.

The important role of the "New Christians" has also not been dealt with adequately by Jewish historians, and here again the story is complicated. Ribeiro Sanches, for example, went through a very complicated personal engagement with his own religious persona. He was baptized and brought up a Christian. It was only when he went to Lisbon at age thirteen or fourteen that he was made aware that he came from a "New Christian" family; and it was only then very slowly that he learned of what that meant in terms of Jewish heritage. Being a brilliant young person, he then read everything about Judaism that he could get his hands on, and he decided, in fact, that he wanted to be a Jew. When in London, he was circumcised and joined the Jewish community; but in only three years he grew to so dislike the Jewish community there that he left and went to Paris in order to become a Christian again. There are extensive observations in his personal diary as to the merits and demerits of the two religions, none too flattering to either. In this, Ribeiro Sanches was very much a child of the Enlightenment, of course, but as a consequence he does not fit easily in Portuguese historiography which sees him as a Jew, or Jewish historiography which is uncomfortable with his religious ambiguity. The story of Castro Sarmento is not dissimilar; he left the Jewish community to marry an Episcopalian.[10]

IV

What finally of the coincidence? It related to the second epitaph on Jefferson's tomb, his pride in the Virginia statute for religious tolerance. One of the more important Sephardic families in the United States was the Levy family of Philadelphia and New York who, for the better part of a century, owned Jefferson's Monticello estate. In 1834 Commodore Uriah Phillips Levy USN bought Monticello, then in an advanced state of disrepair, and in effect saved Monticello from disintegration and collapse. Jefferson had died bankrupt in 1826. Monticello was at first bought by a private individual, but the house was vandalized. Commodore Levy, one of the more controversial and flamboyant members of the United States Navy, was the first Jew to hold a high rank in the service. Born in 1792, as a boy he fought in the War of 1812 against the British and was later captured and imprisoned for eight months in England. Despite six court martials, he rose to command the U.S. Mediterranean fleet. Levy was a reformer who argued for the abolition of flogging in the U.S. Navy. He bequeathed Monticello to the U.S. government in 1862, but during the Civil War the Confederacy seized and sold the property. After the Civil War, years of litigation took place until Uriah Levy's nephew retook possession in 1879. His family owned Monticello until the Thomas Jefferson Memorial Foundation purchased the property in 1923.

Looking back over the genealogical origins of the Levy family, one finds listed the name of Dr. António Nunes Ribeiro Sanches. Ribeiro Sanches's uncle, a well-known doctor, had emigrated to Savannah, Georgia, in 1733, leaving Portugal as a baptized Christian but fleeing the Inquisition. Once in North America he remarried as a Jew and helped the then colony of Georgia overcome a yellow fever epidemic. His son-in-law, David Mendez

---

[10]On the activities of Castro Sarmento in London see Edgar Samuel, *The Jewish Community in London (1656–1830)* (London: The Jewish Museum, 1992), 10–11.

Machado, moved from Savannah to New York and became hazan [minister] of the Congregation Shearih Israel, the famous Spanish and Portuguese synagogue which had been founded in 1654 by Portuguese Jews fleeing from Recife after the fall of Dutch Brazil. His granddaughter, Rebecca, married Michael Levy, whose son was Commodore Uriah Phillips Levy, who bought and preserved Monticello. Rachel Phillips Levy, granddaughter of Ribeiro Sanches's uncle, is buried at Monticello and was thus related by marriage to Ribeiro Sanches, the educational reformer and mentor of the Abbé Corrêa da Serra, Thomas Jefferson's friend.

So we have here a remarkable historical coincidence. Ribeiro Sanches, one of the great scholars of the European Enlightenment, a Portuguese "New Christian" whose ideas were used to reform the University of Coimbra, and one of the people who had promoted the notion of religious toleration by the abolition of legal discrimination against people of Jewish origin, was a mentor of Corrêa da Serra, who in turn was linked with Jefferson at Monticello in discussions over the creation of the University of Virginia. And in this circular historical way, this same remarkable Portuguese "New Christian" was also linked to the very family that later saved and preserved Jefferson's home for future generations.

The Virginia statute for religious freedom is the second achievement Thomas Jefferson wished to be remembered by and have inscribed on his obelisk at Monticello. It is one of the great expressions of the Enlightenment in America. The statute reads:

> No man shall be compelled to frequent or support any religious worship or ministry or shall otherwise suffer on account of his religious opinions or beliefs, but all men shall be free to profess and by argument maintain their opinions in the matter of religion.[11]

Commodore Uriah Phillips Levy admired Jefferson precisely for what he had done "to mold our republic in a form in which a man's religion does not make him ineligible for political or governmental life." It was for this reason above all others that he wished to see Jefferson remembered, and his hilltop mansion Monticello preserved for the American nation.[12]

I have called this connection between Corrêa da Serra and Levy a coincidence. But there is one final question to ask: Why was the Abbé Corrêa da

---

[11]See Merrill D. Peterson and Robert C. Vaughan, *The Virginia Statute for Religious Freedom: Its Evolution and Consequences in American History* (Cambridge and New York: Cambridge University Press, 1988).

[12]See Melvin I. Urofsky, *The Levy Family and Monticello, 1834–1923: Saving Thomas Jefferson's House* ([Charlottesville, Virg.]: Thomas Jefferson Foundation, 2001), and Marc Leepson, *Saving Monticello: The Levy Family's Epic Quest to Rescue the House that Jefferson Built* (New York and London: Free Press, 2001).

Serra so hated by the old aristocracy, the so-called Puritans of the old nobility in Portugal who defined their "puritanism" as the absence of Jewish,
Moorish, or heretic blood? There is an odd note in Corrêa da Serra's biography which needs to be mentioned here; Corrêa da Serra took his
mother's, not his father's, name. Process number 1911 of the Inquisition,
held in the Torre do Tombo in the Lisbon National Archives, is an investigation to determine if Corrêa da Serra's family were "New Christians" and
the probable cause of this father's flight to Naples. It is, therefore, not impossible that the old Abbé was more part of this complex clandestine history than we yet know. But this is a mystery awaiting to be unraveled.

IN THE FIELDS.

CHAPTER 10

A Story of Slavery, Sex, and Mammon

"In all pride of supposed equality."
—*Middletown Gazette*, Connecticut, 1831

Timing is everything in the news business, and the timing of three post-graduate students at Yale University was perfect. Yale, the third-oldest U.S. university, celebrated its tercentenary in the year 2001. On May 21 the current occupant of the White House, George W. Bush, Yale Class of 1968, was invited back to New Haven, Connecticut, for the commencement ceremonies, where he extolled the merits of his fellow "C" students. And from August 31 until September 7, 2001, the predictably contentious United Nations World Conference against Racism, Racial Discrimination, Xenophobia, and Related Intolerance was to take place in South Africa.

I

Against this background in mid-August 2001, Anthony Dugdale, J. J. Fueser, and José Celso de Castro Alves released a remarkable polemic titled "Yale, Slavery and Abolition." They also launched a website.[1] Here their work was made accessible to a wider audience. In lean prose and with solid documentation they draw attention to some very inconvenient facts about their university: How can the buildings of Yale's residential colleges, the core of undergraduate life at the university, carry the names of Yale alumni

---

[1]http://www.yaleslavery.org

who were not only slaveholders, but who beyond that were also ardent advocates of slavery. And how could Yale have chosen to honor them not during the time of slavery but as late as the 1960s at the height of the struggle for civil rights in the United States? Within a few days of the report's release, Dugdale, Fueser, and Castro Alves had received a full article, an editorial comment, and an approving op-ed piece in the *New York Times*, an extended note on the AP wires and CNN, and a chiding editorial in the "Review and Outlook" section of the weekend *Wall Street Journal* which complained they had "presented Yale with something that is less a scholarly inquiry than a legal brief."

The brochure Yale University put out for its tercentenary year summarized Yale's official view on its relationship to slavery. Yale graduates, it says, "have a long history of activism in the face of slavery and a modern history of scholarship about it. Today the Gilder Lehrman Center for the Study of Slavery, Resistance and Abolition, located at Yale, is the first of its kind in the world." True as far as it goes, but as Dugdale, Fueser, and Castro Alves point out, Yale also helped in 1831 to stop the effort to expand higher education to African Americans in New Haven, and in the twentieth century chose to name most of its colleges after slave owners and proslavery leaders.

The three authors are active members of Yale's GESO, the Graduate Employees and Students Organization (Dugdale was the recent chair of the group), which is an affiliate of the federation of hospital and university employees union (HERE local 34). The GESO has been locked in a bitter dispute with Yale over recognition of the right of graduate student instructors to unionize. Their report is published under the auspices of the New Haven Amistad Committee, successor to the original Amistad Committee based in New Haven. In February 1839, Portuguese slave traders had taken a large group of Africans from Sierra Leone to Havana, violating the treaties then in effect against the slave trade. Fifty-three Africans had been purchased and put aboard the Cuban schooner *Amistad* for shipment. On July 1, 1839, they seized the ship, killed the captain, and attempted to sail back to Africa, arriving instead off Long Island where the schooner was seized by a U.S. warship. The Africans were imprisoned in New Haven and charged with murder. The cause was taken up by abolitionists, and the case eventually went to the U.S. Supreme Court. In 1841 former President John Quincy Adams argued the defendants' case, and the Court ruled in the Africans' favor. Thirty-five eventually returned to Africa. The Amistad Committee, formed in 1839 and supported by Yale students and faculty, led the campaign to free the *Amistad* captives. The story was the subject of a recent Steven Spielberg movie.

The challenge laid down to Yale is not only one to historical memory. The authors of "Yale, Slavery and Abolition," in addition to choosing their timing with care, have been equally selective in the institutions with which they wish to associate their findings. In the process they have picked at scabs over some of the most sensitive evasions that lie at the core of America's—not just Yale University's—benign historical view of itself.

There is also something heroic about what these three postgraduate students have done at such a critical moment in their careers. Because of the incestuous structure of U.S. graduate education, they are indentured now more than at any time to the good or ill will of their principal faculty advisers. They are thereby vulnerable to the multiple and subtle retribution that can be exacted in the future by the very cosseted professors whose hypocrisy they have exposed by their research and whose comfortable privileges their union challenges. Like all good scholars they have succeeded in turning over a long buried rock; yet even they underestimate all the slimy creatures that may sally forth from sundry dark places when exposed to the sunlight.

What is it precisely that Dugdale, Fueser, and Castro Alves uncovered? First they undermine conventional wisdom by showing that slavery was not only a southern phenomenon. In fact, slavery underpinned many facets of the economy in the North and in colonial New England, "from household to the field, from the legal system to religious education." Prominent New Englanders owned slaves, and many financial transactions at some point depended on slavery. Emancipation in the North took place gradually. The Connecticut emancipation law passed in 1784 envisioned a gradual phase-out of slavery which would allow it to slowly disappear. No slaves were immediately freed in 1784. The law provided for children born to slaves to remain bonded while children, but to attain freedom on reaching twenty-one years of age (at first the age was set at twenty-five). In 1774 there were 6,562 slaves in Connecticut, but by 1790 the number had fallen to 2,759 and to 97 by 1820. There were none by 1850. Yet even as slavery withered away in New England, many at Yale remained apologists for the institution of slavery. Yale in fact graduated twice as many proslavery clergy as its peer institutions.

Second, they reveal that some of the critical financial endowments which helped establish Yale University as a preeminent national institution of higher education were slavery-based. Yale's first endowed professorship, the Livingstonian Professorship of Divinity, was named for its benefactor, Colonel Philip Livingston of New York, one of the most prominent slave traders of the mid-eighteenth century. The first scholarship fund was named after Bishop George Berkeley and funded by the income from his slave-worked plantation in Newport, Rhode Island. Yale's first endowed library fund was named after Reverend Jared Eliot of Killingworth, a reforming agriculturist for whom slave labor was key.

Moreover, when Yale did have a choice between graduates who held high places within the political establishment of the country and who took opposing views over slavery, it chose to honor a slave owner and apologist of slavery. James Hillhouse, for instance, who served for fifty years as Yale's treasurer, was an outspoken antislavery leader as a U.S. senator. Hillhouse, as others in the North, hoped that slavery in the South would wither away as it had in Connecticut. It did not, of course, spurred in large part by the expansion of cotton plantations based on the invention of the cotton gin by another Yale graduate, Eli Whitney (Class of 1792). But Yale nowhere honors the abolitionist Hillhouse as it does John C. Calhoun, Yale Class of 1804, a South Carolinian who benefited greatly from the expansion of the world cotton market. Elected to Congress in 1811, Calhoun became secretary of war from 1817 to 1825; was elected vice president of the United States serving under two presidents until 1832; became a senator and then secretary of state; and later was elected a senator again. Calhoun was one of the most vociferous and successful defenders of American slavery over his long and turbulent political career. In the Senate Calhoun engineered passage of the gag rule that precluded discussion of slavery and arranged the annexation of Texas as a slave state. His defense of slavery led him to reject democracy itself. In a famous speech in the U.S. Senate chamber in 1837, Calhoun argued "concession or compromise" over slavery "to be fatal." And he continued: " . . . let me not be understood as admitting, even by implication, that the existing relations between the two races in the slaveholding states is an evil—far otherwise; I hold it to be good." In 1930 Yale named one of its residential colleges after him.

As late as 1961 Yale also chose to honor another alumnus with a residential college: Samuel F. B. Morse, the inventor of the telegraph, but a man who was the North's most virulent defender of slavery. Slavery, he wrote, was divinely ordained: "the greater declared object of the Savior's mission to earth." Morse also regarded the Declaration of Independence as a "mixture of truths, qualified truths and fallacious maxims." The special tercentennial edition of the Yale alumni magazine lists Morse as among the top graduates from its entire 300-year history. The invention of the telegraph was no mean feat, and he doubtlessly deserves on this count to be there; but as Dugdale, Fueser, and Castro Alves point out, the alumni magazine nowhere mentions Morse's proslavery views, or his leadership of proslavery societies during the Civil War, much less Morse's attack on President Abraham Lincoln as "the Fanatic on the Throne." Ten of Yale's twelve residential colleges are named after prominent men in Yale's history; eight owned slaves or preached in favor of slavery.

The third story Dugdale, Fueser, and Castro Alves bring to light is the fate of the attempt to establish a "negro college" in New Haven in 1831. The project for a multiracial educational institution was promoted by two local white men: Simeon Jocelyn, founding pastor of the African American Congregation in New Haven, and Arthur Tappan, who purchased land for the building and committed one thousand dollars to the fund-raising drive. They were supported by the famous abolitionist William L. Garrison. The proposal met a stone wall of resistance from the town and Yale College, led by the mayor of New Haven and prominent members of the Yale faculty, including Yale's then one professor of law, four of the five practicing lawyers in New Haven, three judges, and the U.S. representative in Congress.

As one of the resolutions passed at the town meeting to protest the idea stated bluntly:

> Yale College, the institutions for the education of females, and the other schools, already existing in this city, are important to the community and the general interests of science, and as such have been deservedly patronized by the public, and the establishment of a College in the same place to educate the colored population is incompatible with the prosperity, if not the existence of the present institutions of learning, and will be destructive to the best interests of the city. . . .

In New Haven, where town and gown rarely agreed on anything over the centuries, on the question of the establishment of a black college there was near unanimous sentiment. The vote at the town meeting opposing the "negro college" was 700 to 4.

The second resolution passed that day was no less revealing. It reads:

> [T]he propagation of sentiments favorable to the immediate emancipation of slaves in disregard of the civil institutions of the States in which they belong, and as an auxiliary thereto the contemporaneous founding of Colleges for educating colored people, is unwarrantable and dangerous interference with the internal concerns of other States, and ought to be discouraged.

The day after the resolution was passed a mob attacked Arthur Tappan's house. Simeon Jocelyn's home was also ransacked by a mob, and he was forced to end his leadership of the African American church. But a few years later both men were founders of the New Haven Amistad Committee and prominent advocates of justice in the *Amistad* affair. Undoubtedly Yale was concerned with the negative impact of the proposed "Black College" on their university's fund-raising prospects, a concern clearly present in the twentieth century as well. As the *Boston Courier* put it in 1831: "The real objection to the [Black] College appears to have been the apprehension of giving offense to the Southern patrons of Yale." But mammon was not all that was at stake here.

The editorials and comments in the Connecticut newspapers in 1831 make it evident that the citizens of New Haven and the professors at Yale were as much concerned about sex as they were with race; or more explosively to their way of thinking, they were worried specifically about interracial sex. The New Haven *Connecticut Journal* in an editorial argued that:

> The location of a college of blacks here would be totally ruinous to the city. . . . whose certain effect will be to lower the town's public morals—to drive from our city its female schools—its throngs of summer visitors—and stop the vital stream to the city, the influx of young men to Yale College.

The Connecticut *Middletown Gazette* agreed:

> [T]he support of Yale College and the numerous female seminaries, depends in no inconsiderable degree, on the character of the inhabitants. Hitherto, New Haven has been distinguished. . . . But now, if the young ladies are to be elbowed at every corner by black collegians, and the students of Yale are to be met by them in all pride of supposed equality, the interest of the city, identified as it is with the prosperity of the institutions, will suffer material injury.

Dugdale, Fueser, and Castro Alves cite these reports, but they do not follow them up, which is a pity because therein lies a fascinating and revealing adjunct to their story. The New Haven paper on the day of the town meeting had made a recommendation:

> If it is necessary to have an African college in Connecticut, may the projectors of it, on mature consideration, conclude to locate it in the town of Cornwall. . . . Cornwall possesses many advantages for such an institution, over other places; and it is not among the least of them, that the ladies of that town readily give themselves, better for worse, to the colored gentlemen.

II

I was struck by the reference to Cornwall, Connecticut. It is a remote place, and must have been even more so during the early nineteenth century. The township of Cornwall spreads over the higher elevations of the Litchfield hills and the steep valley where the Housatonic River cuts sharply through northwestern Connecticut. It is an upland landscape consisting of three parallel valleys with wooded ridges between them. The ridges, not the valleys, were settled first. It is a rough broken country with clear streams and little peaks. Today its small resident population is augmented by weekend residents from New York City, including several celebrities—most recently Whoopi Goldberg, the NBC news anchor Tom Brokaw, and the tennis great Ivan Lendl among others. I have in my library a *History of Cornwall*, a leather-bound volume published for private subscribers in 1926 by the Reverend Edward Comfort Starr, who had for twenty-four years served as pastor of the Cornwall congregational church and was a graduate of Yale College and its theological seminary. I remembered reading something of the story of the Cornwall missionary school and its misadventures, the evident origin of the aspersions about the proclivities of the girls of Cornwall, to which the New Haven press and Yale worthies referred disparagingly in 1831.

The Reverend Starr's account provides the bare bones of the history of the Foreign Mission School which opened in Cornwall in 1817 and closed its doors in 1827. The school's origins were said to go back to 1810 when Edwin Dwight, son of Yale's President Timothy Dwight, found a "dark skinned youth on the college steps at Yale crying because he had no means of getting an education." Edwin took the young man, a Hawaiian who New England sailors had brought to America and called Henry Obookiah, to his father. Partly inspired by Henry Obookiah, the clergy of Connecticut turned to the American Board of Commissioners of Foreign Missions to establish a school to train Obookiah and other Hawaiians as missionaries for the Pacific Islands. Cornwall was chosen because it was "apart from the temptations and distractions of the larger towns."

Obookiah had a remarkable story. Born in 1792 in Ka'u at Ninole near Punalu'u on the big island, he had survived the deaths of his parents, victims of warfare on the island. He was then schooled in the rituals of priesthood by his uncle at Hiki'au Heiau, where Captain Cook had been killed two decades earlier in 1779. Taken aboard a New England ship in Kealakakukua Bay, he and a young friend, Hopo'o, voyaged to the North Pacific, later on to Macao and around the Cape of Good Hope to New York. The two young Hawaiian boys then moved to New Haven to live with the captain of the vessel that had taken them from Hawaii, where they met Edwin Dwight.

By 1814 Henry Obookiah was speaking publicly, translating the Bible, and beginning a grammar dictionary on the Hawaiian language. Henry Obookiah (or Opukaha'ia as he is now known in Hawaii) became famous after his early death in 1818 from typhus fever at the age of twenty-six, when Edwin Dwight published a small book titled *Memoir of Henry Obookiah, A Native of the Sandwich Islands, Who Died at Cornwall, Connecticut.* This memoir comprising Obookiah's account of his life, feelings, and philosophies inspired fourteen American missionaries to volunteer to evangelize the Hawaiian Islands (or Sandwich Islands as they were then known). Obookiah was buried at Cornwall where his tombstone but not his body remains. He was, the inscription reads, "a worthy member [of the Mission School] he was once an Idolater, and was designed for a Pagan Priest; but by the grace of God and by the prayers of pious friends, he became a Christian." In 1993 a group of his descendants claimed the body which was returned to the big island of Hawaii and reinterred.

Beginning with twelve pupils, the number of students at the Cornwall Mission School tripled over the nine and a half years of its existence. Students were of several races, including many Native Americans, so that the school, the Reverend Starr said, was sometimes spoken of as "the Indian School." But Starr also reports that "two marriages of Indians who had been at the school, with white girls of the village, had produced great excitement and are popularly said to be the cause of the breaking up of the school . . . it also aroused much unpleasant gossip about the people of Cornwall." In fact, Starr tells us in a footnote, the editor of the *Litchfield Eagle* had declared that the Cornwall girls were left alone at unreasonable hours with the mission boys and were seen walking arm in arm with them.

The real history is more complicated and tragic. Among the "Indian" students at the Cornwall Mission School were two Cherokees: John Ridge and "Buck" Oowatie (later known as Elias Boudinot). John was the son of Major Ridge and Buck's father was Ridge's half-brother. Major Ridge led a body of Cherokee Indians in alliance with the United States under the command of General Andrew Jackson fighting against other Native Americans during the Creek War and first Seminole War, where he earned his military title. Ridge's Cherokee name was "kah-nung-da-tle-ghe," the man who walks on the mountaintop. He was a leader of the Cherokee nation settled at Pine Log, in present-day Bartow County, Georgia, under the orders of President George Washington. Here the Cherokees evolved an experiment in acculturation merging U.S. and Cherokee traditions and greatly prospering as settled farmers. John, Major Ridge's son, was educated by Moravian missionaries before being sent by the major to the Cornwall Mission School as a paying pupil. Major Ridge was a man of substantial property; his estates contained 240 acres under cultivation, 1,142 peach trees, 418 apple trees, a ferry, and a store. He also owned thirty black slaves.

At the mission school, both John Ridge and Buck Oowatie fell in love with local girls. John met Sarah Bird Northrupt, the daughter of the steward of the Mission School, John P. Northrupt. In the face of strong opposition from Major Ridge as well as Sarah's parents, they eventually married in 1824. Major Ridge had consulted the Moravian missionaries if "there was anything in your Bible to prevent such a marriage." They assured him there was not.

John Ridge's cousin, Buck Oowatie, on his way from the Cherokee nation in Georgia to the Cornwall Mission School had visited the former President Thomas Jefferson at his residence Monticello in Virginia as well as James Madison at his country house Montpelier. In Washington, D.C., Buck Oowatie had also met Dr. Elias Boudinot, briefly president of the United States under the Articles of Confederation and an early abolitionist and philanthropist who believed the American Indians were descended from one of the lost tribes of Israel. In appreciation of his support of the Cherokee nation, Buck took Boudinot's name as his own from then on. At Cornwall, the newly named Elias Boudinot fell in love with Harriet Gold, daughter of Colonel Benjamin Gold, a scion of one of Cornwall's most eminent families. Elias and Harriet were married in 1826 despite the fact that the pastor, Reverend Timothy Stone (honorary Yale M.A. 1804), refused to officiate at the ceremony at the Cornwall congregational church, fearing his congregation would eject him. Elias was burnt in effigy in the town. These two interracial marriages led to the closing of the Mission School in 1827.

Both John Ridge and Elias Boudinot were to play a key role in one of the most somber chapters in American history. In 1830 the Indian Removal Act, vigorously promoted by President Andrew Jackson, forced the expulsion of the Cherokee from their fertile lands in Georgia.[2] Under military escort tens of thousands of tribesmen were marched west to barren territory in the present state of Oklahoma. Over a third died en route. This shameful resettlement of 1838–1839 coincided ironically with the *Amistad* affair. The state of Georgia distributed the lands of the Cherokees by mean of a lottery. The disastrous trek of the Cherokees to Oklahoma from Geor-

---

[2]The Indian removals have not been a topic treated in much detail by American historians, even Jacksonian scholars. In fact in Arthur Schlesinger's classic account of Jacksonian democracy, *The Age of Jackson* (Boston: Little, Brown, 1945), the removals received no mention whatsoever. For a discussion of these events by the leading scholar in the field see Robert V. Remini, *Andrew Jackson and His Indian Wars* (New York: Viking, 2001). For a more critical approach to Jackson see Andrew Burnstein, *The Passions of Andrew Jackson* (New York: Knopf, 2003).

gia became known in history as "the trail of tears." Major Ridge, his son John, as well as Elias Boudinot, had all signed the Treaty of New Echota in 1835 which accepted the removal against the majority opinion of the Cherokee.

President Andrew Jackson was more responsible than most for the betrayal of the experiment of peaceful coexistence, alliance, and mutual respect between the United States of America and the Cherokee Nation, which Major Ridge had espoused and lived by. Pathetically, he called on his former commander at his home in Tennessee on the way to Oklahoma. But Ridge already knew that by signing the Treaty of New Echota he had also signed his own death warrant. Within days he was assassinated by Cherokees who saw his continued trust in the white man as base treachery. Within six months after the arrival of the Cherokee in Oklahoma, both John Ridge and Elias Boudinot had also been brutally murdered by Cherokee braves. John Ridge's wife, Harriet, had died in 1836 on the eve of the removal to Oklahoma and is buried in Calhoun, Georgia. Elias Boudinot's wife, Sarah, survived his assassination, moving with her children to Fayetteville, Arkansas. Their eldest son went to California where he became a newspaper editor and politician.

III

How sadly revealing it is that in opposing the "negro college" in 1831 the good citizens of New Haven, with the support of the worthy faculty of Yale, should have transformed the story of what was by all accounts two happy marriages into gossip about "the ladies of town [Cornwall, who] readily give themselves, better for worse, to the colored gentlemen." And how banal is the reduction of the tragedy that befell the brightest students of the Cornwall Mission School to a racist evocation of the danger of blacks on the street in New Haven "elbowing" the young ladies of the seminaries and discomforting the students at Yale College who would be confronted with this assertion of "supposed equality."

Yet this painful excursion into the underside of American history would undoubtedly have appealed to Antônio de Castro Alves, the namesake of one of the coauthors of the report on "Yale, Slavery and Abolition." Castro Alves, the nineteenth-century Brazilian romantic poet from Bahia, heart of Brazil's vibrant Afro-Brazilian culture, also lived a tragic life, was thwarted in love, and died at the age of twenty-four from tuberculosis with only one volume of his poetry published. Posthumously he became, and remains, one of Brazil's most powerful antislavery voices, author of *The Slaves* (*Os Escravos*, 1883), an oration from Africa imploring God's justice called

Voices of Africa (*Vozes d'África*, 1880), and, above all, *The Slave Ship* (*O Navio Negreiro*, 1880), a powerful portrayal of the horrors of the middle passage. A disciple of Victor Hugo, he was a model for the late Brazilian novelist Jorge Amado, who praised Castro Alves as a poet who saw Brazil naked in all its contradictions and full of social and racial prejudices. Dugdale, Fueser, and Castro Alves have seen Yale naked, and we are all the wiser for it.

A BRAZILIAN FOREST, WITH CHARACTERISTIC MAMMALIA.

CHAPTER 11

The Tragedy of the Amazon

"Order and Progress."
—Positivist inscription on
Brazil's national flag

Nineteen eighty-eight was the year of drought and fire in the Americas. It was a year of growing public concern about global warming, with dire projections of melting ice caps and ozone depletion. It was a year of dramatic images of the charred remnants of once majestic forests from the Rockies to the Amazon basin. For the first time the destruction of the tropical rain forest of Brazil became a major issue for North Americans and for people concerned about the danger to the environment throughout the world. But how did this vast ecological disaster occur? What can be done to deal with its effects? Some answers to these questions are provided by the books discussed in this chapter, each of which deals with some aspect of the tragedy of the Amazon.

I

The Amazon is a vast region; not all of it is rain forest, nor is all of it Brazilian. As it was legally defined in 1953, the Amazon region within Brazil incorporates about 60 percent of Brazil and includes savannah grasslands, wetlands, and shrublands, as well as humid rain forests, all connected with the Amazon River system, which contains one-fifth of the earth's freshwater supply. The river rises 17,000 feet in the Andes and flows some 4,000 miles until it reaches the Atlantic, yet as one follows it 3,000 miles inland from the sea it rises only to 300 feet. The river's mouth is 200 miles wide, and for 1,000 miles upstream it remains seven miles wide; oceangoing liners can travel 2,000 miles up the river from the sea. The river and the rain forest cover the heart of the subcontinent and encompass nine South American countries. Seventeen of the Amazon's tributaries are more than 1,000 miles long, each longer than the Rhine.

Brazil's Amazonian forest is the largest remaining tropical forest on earth, and its natural life is the richest and most diverse in the world, containing 20 percent of all higher plant life, the same proportion of bird species, and 10 percent of the world's mammals. The tall trees produce a dense overhead canopy, which keeps out all but a fraction of the sunlight. Within the semidarkness thousands of species thrive, only a tiny number of which are known or recorded by scientists. Each tree can support as many as four hundred insect species. The rainy season's floods deposit alluvium along the river banks to form flood plains (*várzeas*), rich in palms, fruits, turtles, fish, and aquatic birds. Naturalists have found five hundred different plant species in one forest patch of the flooded plains. To the south and east are forests filled with mahogany, tropical cypress, and cherry wood trees. The westernmost tributary, the Araguaia, flows through swampy grasslands and forests of mahogany, Brazil nut, and rubber forests.

A marvelously comprehensive introduction to the rain forest can be found in the thoughtful and readable *The Last Rain Forests: A World Conservation Atlas*, edited by Mark Collins.[1] It provides maps of the present distribution of forest worldwide and helps to place the Amazon in a global context, while one can study some of the extraordinary fauna of the region in the beautifully produced and illustrated *Neotropical Rainforest Mammals: A Field Guide*, the first such broad regional guide ever produced.[2]

The paradox of this "rich realm of nature," as the early Portuguese adventurers called it, is that while the soils of much of the Amazon region are extremely impoverished, they can still sustain more than 250 metric tons of living material per acre. For many years no one could explain how they did so. As Susanna Hecht and Alexander Cockburn point out in *The Fate of the Forest*, a survey of the region and its crisis, the beginning of an answer came in 1960, thanks to the cold war, when the U.S. Atomic Energy Commission sought to find out what would happen to forests in the event of a nuclear war, stimulating the first interdisciplinary study of the tropical forest.[3]

---

[1]Mark Collins, ed., *The Last Rain Forests: A World Conservation Atlas* (New York and Oxford: Oxford University Press, 1990).

[2]Louise H. Emmons, *Neotropical Rainforest Mammals: A Field Guide* (Chicago: University of Chicago Press, 1990).

[3]Suzanna Hecht and Alexander Cockburn, *The Fate of the Forest: Developers, Destroyers, and Defenders of the Amazon* (London and New York: Verso, 1989).

Students discovered that whereas forests in the temperate zone draw nutrients up from the soil, in tropical forests the nutrients derive from an exchange within the living forest and are held in the tissues of living organisms. The leathery leaves characteristic of the Amazon plant life conserve nutrients as well as high levels of secondary chemicals, which make tropical leaves tough or poisonous to eat, deterring predators and also making them a rich source of drugs. Latex, a substance that acts as a defensive membrane for the Brazilian rubber tree, *Hevea brasiliensis*, is just such an adaptation. The wild germ plasm of the forest includes cacao, palm hearts, *guaraná*, Brazil nuts, rubber, chicle, babassu oil, fish, manioc, cashews, and coca. As Hecht and Cockburn observe, the global annual value of Amazonian natural products may exceed one hundred billion dollars a year.[4]

II

The assault on the tropical forests has a long history, and so does the history of human habitation in the forest. The year 2000 marked the fifth century since the landfall on the Brazilian coast by the India-bound fleet of the Portuguese explorer Pedro Álvares Cabral. It was a land "with great groves of trees," according to the fleet's notary, Pero Vaz de Caminha, who described it in a letter to the king of Portugal on May 1, 1500.[5] Of the lush Atlantic coastal forest that so impressed the Europeans in 1500—a narrow belt of rain forest some one hundred miles deep, which then ran along virtually the whole coast of Brazil—no more than 4 percent remains today. From among its flora, ironically, Brazil took its name from the pau-brasil tree, which yielded a purple dye much in demand among sixteenth-century European textile manufacturers, and which can scarcely be found in the wild today. The Portuguese had called their new territory in South America the "Land of the True Cross," but this was soon forgotten and the more prosaic name stuck—resonant as it was of the forest and of business.

---

[4]These figures were disputed by Roger Stone in a review of the Hecht and Cockburn book, "The Politics of Deforestation," *Issues in Science and Technology* (spring 1990): 77–78. He says, "The total value of Brazilian exports, including manufactured goods, amounted to less than $34 billion in 1988." Hecht and Cockburn's figure, however, included coca, the main product exported (albeit clandestinely) from the western Amazon basin. See exchange in "Fate of the Amazon," *New York Review of Books*, June 13, 1991, which includes comments by Professor José Goldemberg, then Brazilian secretary of science and technology.

[5]Full text in W. B. Greenlee, ed., *The Voyage of Pedro Álvares Cabral to Brazil and India from Contemporary Narratives*, Hakluyt Series, No. 81 (1838), 3–33. Caminha's letter is reproduced in facsimile in the New York Public Library exhibition catalog, *Brazil-Portugal: The Age of Atlantic Discovery* (Milan and Lisbon: Editora Bertrand and Franco Maria Ricci, 1990).

Like the coastal forest, the Amazon rain forest before the arrival of the Europeans sustained a large population—it is virtually impossible to estimate how large.[6] In two brilliant books, John Hemming, then director and secretary of the Royal Geographical Society of London, has heroically tried to reconstruct from thousands of pages of travel accounts, official reports, diaries, and archeological and anthropological research the lost history of the annihilated peoples of South America. He calculates that the native population of the Amazon basin alone could have been about 3.5 million in 1500.[7] It was at most 200,000 by the late 1980s. The lost population of Indians did not live in an untroubled paradise, but they lived in harmony with the forest, and they did not destroy it.

Hecht and Cockburn tell us that the degree of human intervention in the forest ecosystem is much greater than we have realized. Scholars have learned from demographic reconstruction of the catastrophic and precipitate population decline in the Caribbean and in Mexico after the Spanish Conquest that we should be very cautious before we dismiss the early account of large indigenous populations as hyperbole.[8] As with the first reactions in our century to the Holocaust in Europe, it has been difficult for many people to accept the vast scale of extermination.

Both greed and good intentions caused the destruction of the native population. By the 1570s, the rich forests of the coastal region, especially those of the flood plains around the great natural harbors of Rio de Janeiro and Bahia, as well as further north at Recife in Pernambuco, had been cleared and the land converted to sugarcane production. The sugar mills

---

[6]All the early accounts spoke of large populations. See Sir C. R. Markham, ed., *Expeditions into the Valley of the Amazon: 1539, 1540, 1639*, Hakluyt Series, No. 24 (1859), 61, 79, passim.

[7]John Hemming, *Red Gold: The Conquest of the Brazilian Indians* (Cambridge: Harvard University Press, 1987), and *Amazon Frontier: The Defeat of the Brazilian Indians* (Cambridge: Harvard University Press, 1987). Hemming is also author of "How Brazil Acquired Roraima," *Hispanic American Historical Review* 70, no. 2 (May 1990): 295–325. Unfortunately, Hemming and other scholars rarely use the extraordinary riches of the Portuguese archives to study these questions. They are particularly valuable for any work on the Amazon, including scientific work. For an introduction to the extensive scientific mission of Alexander Rodrigues Ferreira in the late eighteenth century, for example, there is a good book by William Joel Simon, *Scientific Expeditions in the Portuguese Overseas Territories (1783–1808) and the Role of Lisbon in the Intellectual-Scientific Community of the Late Eighteenth Century* (Lisbon: Instituto de Investigação Científica Tropical, 1983). Also see Russell Mittermeier et al, *Viagem philosophica—uma redescoberta da Amazônia, 1792–1992/Philosophical Journey—A Rediscovery of the Amazon, 1792–1992* (Rio de Janeiro: Comissão Nacional para as Comemorações dos Descobrimentos Portugueses; Editora Index, 1992).

[8]Sherborne F. Cook and Woodrow Borah, *Essays in Population History*, 3 vols. (Berkeley: University of California Press, 1971, 1974, 1979).

required huge quantities of firewood to heat the cauldrons that processed sugar, and the coastal forests were increasingly depleted. Forced into slave labor, and lacking immunity to European and African diseases, the Indian population died by the tens of thousands. Enslaved Africans were imported to replace them, permanently transforming the ethnic composition of the Portuguese coastal enclaves on the edge of the continent.[9]

As the Indian populations of the coastlines died out, Portuguese missionaries who had arrived to proselytize the native population moved inland to gain new converts. The Franciscans established Belém (Bethlehem) at the mouth of the Amazon River in 1616, and after 1649, Jesuits, Carmelites, and Mercedarians divided up the main tributaries of the river between them. Throughout the colonial period royal governors, merchants, and Portuguese colonists regularly sent upriver heavily armed flotillas of canoes in search of slaves.

The religious orders, especially the Jesuits, sought to protect the Indian population from enslavement by organizing new communities of would-be peasant farmers. Although these concentrations initially led to an even more rapid spread of disease, the Jesuits in time were able to establish a network of protected villages throughout the lower Amazon to complement the great missions they organized on the plains along the Uruguay and Paraguay Rivers to the south. The struggle between the Jesuits and others who sought to protect the Indians and the colonists who argued that they should be integrated with the European communities, albeit as lowly workers, is a long one in Amazonian history, and the arguments on both sides were often well intentioned. The writings in defense of the Indians by the Jesuit polymath António Vieira are among the most eloquent works in the Portuguese language.[10] The Marquês de Pombal, King José's chief minister between 1750 and 1777, who expelled the Jesuits from Brazil, justified his actions in the language of the Enlightenment. (He ended African slavery in Portugal itself.)

As Hemming shows, the missions were eventually suppressed by jealous officials of the monarchy abetted by the colonists' avarice. In the late seventeenth century, gold was discovered and prospectors flooded into the interior. The colonial government, suspicious of the loyalty of the Jesuit missions that were strategically placed along the river systems, sent teams

---

[9]The African component in the formation of Brazilian society of course parallels the story of the destruction of the Indians and is essential to any understanding of Brazil. There is an excellent book by Joseph C. Miller, *Way of Death: Merchant Capitalism and the Angolan Slave Trade, 1730–1830* (Madison: University of Wisconsin Press, 1988), which provides a good introduction to this story.

[10]For Vieira, one of the most remarkable figures of the seventeenth century, see Thomas M. Cohen, *The Fire of Tongues: António Vieira and the Missionary Church in Brazil and Portugal* (Stanford: Stanford University Press, 1998).

of surveyors, soldiers, and administrators to establish Portugal's authority over the land and establish frontiers. By the mid-eighteenth century they thus had laid claims to tens of thousands of square miles of unexplored territory. When Brazil gained its independence from Portugal in the 1820s, the new nation inherited this "hollow frontier," containing within it many unknown Indian communities.

During the nineteenth and twentieth centuries these hidden peoples would slowly be "discovered." Natural scientists arrived to study the teeming life of the forest. European anthropologists were sent to study living societies but, more often than not, and certainly unintentionally, their contacts with unknown groups of Indians helped to bring about their rapid disintegration. The Indians were proselytized by Protestant fundamentalist missionaries who brought with them values regarded as simplistic and ignorant by many in the societies they themselves came from. The Indians were victimized by freelance miners, adventurers, and trappers, who were seeking gold, booty, or natural forest products, such as Brazil nuts and rubber. These pioneers were both fearful of the native forest dwellers and all too willing to exploit or kill them.

John Hemming has very little use for either the Christian missionaries or the slavers, or for their modern counterparts. Amid the relentless destruction of the indigenous population, his heroes are those Indians who were uncompromising in their opposition to the white man. In fact, he sometimes implies that the only good white man is a dead white man. There is a special poignancy and irony to this view. During an expedition out of Cachimbo near the geographical center of Brazil in 1961, then a crude airstrip in the forest, members of Kreen-Akrore tribe had ambushed and killed Richard Mason, a young Englishman, among whose companions was John Hemming.

But the killing of whites, when it occurred, never did the Indians any good. The whites always had more guns and more resources—an inexhaustible supply. They also brought the invisible influenza and other viruses that could cause mass destruction of the Indians. The fatal power of such infection was something that the closed Indian societies never comprehended when they came into contact with Europeans. Along the river banks throughout Amazônia the Indian population was in large part decimated, and often replaced by what Hemming calls "a growing proletariat of semi-acculturated and discontented free Indians and mixed races (*caboclos*)."

In 1835, this population exploded in the most violent and revolutionary of all nineteenth-century Brazilian rebellions, the Cabanagem revolt, named after the migrants' cabana huts on the flood plains near Belém. Led by priests, rubber workers, and mutinous soldiers, the revolt was a mass popular uprising of the *caboclos* and large numbers of Indians against property owners and government officials. The rebellion was put down with great ferocity. Some thirty thousand lives were lost, a fifth of the population of the region. The rise in world demand for rubber brought new settlers and new international attention at the end of the century. The rubber tappers pushed far up into the tributaries of the Amazon and toward the border territory of Acre, which was also claimed by Bolivia and Peru. In 1903, after a series of revolts and plots, and much international intrigue, Acre became part of Brazil.

Brazilian rubber could not compete with the new plantations in Asia, and the region once more sank back into relative obscurity, though not before more wild schemes and ambitions had been consumed by the jungle, including the infamous and corruption-ridden construction of the Madeira-Mamoré railroad in the early part of the century and the failed attempts at industrialized plantation agriculture by Henry Ford in the 1930s and the billionaire Daniel K. Ludwig in the 1960s—all well-known tales of greed, naiveté, and ecological ignorance, which are described with verve by Hecht and Cockburn and others in what is sure to be a new wave of travelers' tales of horror and disaster provoked by the growing interest in the Amazon.[11] A more realistic perspective was provided in the 1920s by Kenneth Grubb, a missionary who wrote, in a sad reflection of the destruction of Indian communities, that it was possible to travel from Belém to Peru

> without seeing a distinctly tribal Indian. These rivers are silent today, except for the lap of the waters along some deserted beach, the hoarse cry of the parrots or the call of the *inambu*. The past has gone, with its people, in central Amazônia, leaving only that bitter sense of impotence, as of being present before a consuming conflagration and the same time being powerless to assist.[12]

III

The decimation of the Amazonian Indians, leaving a population of no more than 200,000 today, is only part of the story of the destruction of the

---

[11]The best book on these topics, much mined though rarely acknowledged, is that by Warren Dean, *Brazil and the Struggle for Rubber: A Study in Environmental History* (Cambridge and New York: Cambridge University Press, 1987). For a discussion of the new, or rather the revived, genre of Amazonian tales see Stephen Milk's reviews in the *TLS*, December 7–13, 1990, which examine Anthony Smith's *Explorers of the Amazon* (London and New York: Viking, 1990), Dennison Berwick's *Amazon* (London: Hutchinson, 1990), and Stephan Nugent's *Big Mouth* (Great Britain: Fourth Estate, 1990).
[12]Cited by John Hemming in *Amazon Frontier*, 246.

rain forest. Just as destruction of the forest itself brings with it the destruction of millions of unrecorded plants and creatures, so the destruction of the Amazon Indians destroys knowledge of the forest acquired over millennia. What is new since the 1980s is the scale of encroachment in the last redoubt of the Amazon's native people.

World Resources, 1990–1991: A Guide to the Global Environment, a marvelously comprehensive, well-produced handbook, cautiously estimates the yearly loss of tropical rain forest in Brazil to be somewhere between 1.7 and 8 million hectares.[13] The disparity between the figures demonstrates how tentative most calculations remain and how urgent the need for more research is. The World Resources experts believe that some 7 percent of the forested area has already been lost. Dennis J. Mahar, in his World Bank study *Government Policies and Deforestation in Brazil's Amazon Region,* estimates on the basis of Landsat satellite images that the figure is as high as 12 percent.[14] Both would agree, however, that if the present rate of clearing continues, 15 percent of all plant life in the Latin American rain forest would become extinct by the year 2000. While accurate figures are difficult to come by, Mahar argues that "because pasture has clearly been the predominant form of agricultural land use in the region, cattle ranching would appear to be the leading proximate cause of deforestation." Small farming activity has also increased, but farm plots are often sold or abandoned after only a few years of use. These areas are then converted to pasture or quickly invaded by secondary growth. Logging has also contributed to deforestation.

Hecht and Cockburn blame the generals who ran Brazil between 1964 and 1985 for the destruction of the rain forest. The generals must be held responsible for what occurred during these two decades, but like virtually all political explanations based on a single cause, this one is too simple and it may seem to imply that the solutions are simple as well, which, unfortunately, is not the case. In fact, the great push to the interior was under way well before the military coup of 1964; and, not surprisingly, it continued unabated after the military retreated to the barracks in 1985. The inauguration of the new capital, Brasília, in 1960, and the coincidental opening of two arterial roads into the forest—the two-thousand-mile dirt highway moving north between the new capital and Belém at the mouth of the Amazon and the beginning of the Brasília-Porto Velho road moving west—were the events that in many respects set the contemporary disaster in motion. Both enterprises were part of a government policy of opening

---

[13]Report by the World Resources Institute, *World Resources, 1990–1991: A Guide to the Global Environment* (New York and Oxford: Oxford University Press, 1990).
[14]Dennis J. Mahar, *Government Policies and Deforestation in Brazil's Amazon Region* (Washington, D.C.: The World Bank, 1989).

up the resources of the backlands to development—a policy broadly supported at the time by most of the different groups that make up Brazilian society. The idea of building a capital in the interior and of developing the Amazon goes back at least as far as the eighteenth century. Hecht and Cockburn do not make it sufficiently clear that the building of Brasília and the Brasília-Belém highway marked the high point of the boom under President Juscelino Kubitschek, a good democrat in his own fashion and a politician who epitomized the expansionism and optimism, as well as the pervasive corruption, of the fifties.

The approach of Kubitschek to development during the mid-1950s had very grave consequences which many authors fail to recognize, partly because they are excessively concerned with establishing continuity with the exploitative Portuguese past. But Kubitschek and the military geostrategists who took power after 1964, such as the éminence grise of the military regime, General Golbery do Couto e Silva, did something radically new; they pressed for a network of roads linking the northeast to the center and south of the country to the Amazon basin. The credits and the special favors granted to southern businessmen were intended at first to encourage them to invest in a region in which they saw few prospects for profit. But the roads to the south undermined the assumption that had dominated all previous thinking about the Amazon—the central importance of the rivers. Now land routes were to have preference over riverine communication and forest clearance over forest extraction, and water was to be considered a source of energy and not of life.

The dirt road to Belém was soon paved, and between 1960 and 1970 some 300,000 migrants went to seek their fortune along the highway. The trans-Amazonian highway intended to link the northeast and Amazônia, followed, as did the Cuiabá-Porto Velho highway in the states of Mato Grosso and Rondônia. The most severe deforestation has been concentrated along these roads and the many roads that feed into them, a process which is shown dramatically in the Oxford *Conservation Atlas*. The population of Rondônia grew by over 21 percent per annum between 1970 and 1978. In Rondônia and Mato Grosso over one-fourth of the forest has disappeared during the 1980s.

As the huge road-building programs opened up the region, government-sponsored projects to build new settlements attracted migrants from Brazil's poverty-stricken northeast as well as from its southern states, where extensive mechanization of agriculture and the spread of cash crops such as soya were displacing thousands of smallholders. The military regime encouraged cattle raising by providing special fiscal incentives, as well as easy and subsidized credit to would-be ranchers, and extensive benefits to businesses that invested in the region, exempting them from excise duties and from corporate income taxes for ten to fifteen years. Many of the ranch owners who received some $700 million in tax credits were never seriously interested in producing beef—they acquired property only to take advantage of the economic benefits. Once they received the tax credits, they sold or abandoned the projects the credits were supposed to stimulate, but not before these speculative enterprises caused extensive damage to the environment.

Businessmen from the south of Brazil, especially the São Paulo–based association of Amazon businessmen, lobbied the central government in Brasília to subsidize cattle-ranching ventures, and in 1974 the government set up the extensive Polamazonia program to encourage selective investment in production intended for export such as beef, timber, and minerals. Subsidized rural credit was extended on very favorable terms (twenty-year investment credit was made available at a nominal annual rate of 12 percent to ranchers, for example). Because a land title was required to qualify for a subsidy, Amazônia's sharecroppers, tenants, and squatters were, in effect, denied access to this capital, which served to further concentrate wealth and land ownership throughout the region. A destructive sequence was established in the early 1970s which was to repeat itself throughout the Amazon basin. Forest was cleared and opened up through the sweated labor of poor migrants whose lands were later appropriated by large estates. The forests cut down and burned for conversion to pasture during the dry season were planted with African forage grains, which seldom provided more than two to three years of good fodder. Phosphorous levels in the soil thereafter fell dramatically, and the grasses were soon overtaken by shrubs and weeds.

Overstocked, compacted, leached, and degraded, these lands will require at least one hundred years to recover. Since government credits had been used by the proprietors to offset their expenses elsewhere in Brazil, the absentee landowners were not greatly concerned by the waste of the land. The small farmers in the meanwhile were forced to push on toward new frontiers to the west—first to Rondônia, then in the 1980s to Acre and Roraima. The pattern was one of settlement and then of the settlements' failure, of land grabbing and violent protest against it, of the concentration of ownership and ecological devastation.

All of this is described in absorbing detail by Anthony Hall in his splendid book *Developing Amazonia*. Hall convincingly demonstrates that:

> the notion of Amazonia as a vast, fertile empty space ready to permanently absorb the land-hungry masses from northeastern and southern Brazil is a myth.[15]

---

[15]Anthony L. Hall, *Developing Amazonia: Deforestation and Social Conflict in Brazil's Carajás Programme* (Manchester and New York: Manchester University Press, 1989).

In his more journalistic book, Adrian Cowell, who in the early 1980s was filming the onslaught of settlers, job seekers, entrepreneurs, and speculators in Rondônia for a British TV documentary unit, describes how he became increasingly appalled by the scale and senselessness of this new phase of Amazonian development:

> The History of Amazonia may have been littered with visionaries like Ford and Ludwig who fruitlessly tried to impose some dream or vision on the forest. But here was a government and a whole society marching into the forest with the manic zest of a lemming migration, hypnotised by an obsession which was even more difficult than the lemmings' to understand. We seemed to have arrived at one of the frontier's dead-ends, where the forest mirrored the absurdity of the society confronting it.[16]

IV

The Amazon frontier soon reproduced the large landowning (*latifundia*) pattern of the northeast and south of Brazil. In 1985, 30 percent of rural properties in Brazil were less than two hectares, yet they occupied only 0.1 percent of farmland; 1.9 percent of properties of over a thousand hectares occupied 57 percent of the agricultural land. The largest 152 Amazonian estates occupied 40 million hectares, equal to the total area of cultivated land in Brazil. These estates, moreover, do not create many jobs, since lumbering and cattle ranching require few employees.

At the same time the exploration of the Amazon lands created a vast army of landless, temporary wage laborers who migrate to the urban centers and take jobs as seasonal workers or try to make a living as independent prospectors for gold (*garimpeiros*). Small farmers still produce 80 percent of the basic food crops and provide 82 percent of jobs in the eastern Amazon, but the concentration of landownership between 1985 and 1988 has caused the output of such basic staples as beans and cassava to fall by 8 percent and 14 percent, respectively.

In the eastern Amazon, and especially in the Araguaia-Tocantins region, the expansion of settlement and ranching followed the highway, and was accompanied by violent struggles over land. Until the 1950s, the economy was based on the harvest of Brazil nuts (*castanhas*) and other forest products, and controlled by a few powerful families, who shipped the nuts north to Belém. Between 1969 and 1975 the Maoist offshoot of the Brazilian Communist Party established a guerrilla campaign in the region which

---

[16]Adrian Cowell, *The Decade of Destruction: The Crusade to Save the Amazon Rain Forest* (New York: H. Holt, 1990).

fought sporadically with the Brazilian army. The guerrillas were eventually suppressed by thousands of troops.

Two other major factors came into play here, each no less dangerous to the ecology—one set in motion by mining for iron ore and the other by gold. These processes of mineral extraction and their ecological and social consequences are the subject of Anthony Hall's *Developing Amazonia*, which examines the vast complex for mining iron ore and other minerals called the Carajás project, and of David Cleary in his *Anatomy of the Amazon Gold Rush*.[17] Both books, like Adrian Cowell's *Decade of Destruction*, have the great advantage of avoiding the hyperbole that characterizes so much writing about Brazil. Cowell has chosen, as he did in his television documentaries, to follow the lives of ordinary people in the hope that these case histories will help to explain the larger story. The three books taken together re-create the fascinating history of the struggle in the Amazon as it affects people in their everyday lives.

Amazonian iron and gold could hardly have produced two more different kinds of organizations. Carajás is a huge state enterprise, regional in scope, mainly concerned with producing iron for export. To carry on the mining it has been provided with dams, hydroelectric power, railroads, and port facilities, and it has the benefit of large capital infusions from national and international investors. Prospecting for gold, by contrast, is generally an independent and uncontrolled activity, called *garimpagem* in Brazil, which is carried on by small entrepreneurs and adventurers. The large mining companies are implacable enemies of freelance prospectors, who are continually penetrating company-held territory to set up their clandestine mining operations.

Only a small portion of the gold is sold to the state, and accurate production figures, as always in the Amazon, are impossible to come by. Cleary estimates that there are hundreds of thousands of *garimpeiros*. The gold they produce was estimated in the late 1980s to be worth over one billion dollars annually. Gold mining technology is cheap, and it is easy to run, the most complex machinery needed being a small internal combustion engine. According to Cleary, in 1987 mining professionals estimated that the *garimpos* were producing around 120 metric tons of gold annually—which could place Brazil third among world gold producers, behind only South Africa and Russia—an amount equal to the great nineteenth-century gold rushes. The most dramatic *garimpo* was the one found in 1979 at Serra Pelada, about ninety kilometers from the city of Marabá in the south of Pará. At its peak in 1983, Serra Pelada produced one metric ton of gold a

---

[17]David Cleary, *Anatomy of the Amazon Gold Rush* (Iowa City: University of Iowa Press, 1990).

year and had some 100,000 *garimpeiros* and traders who removed entire hills with pickaxes and shovels.

The gold prospectors do not cut down large tracks of forest or take up large stretches of land as the ranchers do, but the ecological impact of their activities can be devastating. The most insidious and lasting damage comes from mercury, which is used to separate the gold from the ore, and poisons both the environment and the *garimpeiros*. If the *garimpeiros* were, as Cleary suggests, producing over a hundred metric tons of gold per annum in the Brazilian Amazon during the 1980s, an equivalent amount of mercury escaped into the atmosphere in the form of vapor as it was burned off during the amalgamation process.

In addition, mercury is often spilled into the ground and rivers near the *garimpo*. Testing in the Madeira River found mercury levels in fish several times higher than World Health Organization safety levels. Cleary takes a relatively benign view of the *garimpeiros*, rightly saying that they are among the few groups of poor rural Brazilians who have a chance to rise in the world. But the invasion of 45,000 *garimpeiros* into the lands of the Yanomami in the far north of Brazil is wreaking havoc among the indigenous population.[18] Lucio Flavio Pinto, a courageous Amazonian journalist whose paper, *Jornal Pessoal* (published since 1987), was almost alone in reporting in depth on Amazonian politics and corruption, points out that small-scale mining is sometimes carried on by extremely well financed operators. Pinto estimates that there were 1,200 clandestine airstrips and at least 800 small airplanes to get the gold out, while the gold business has allowed some local bosses to exercise almost medieval feudal domination over the districts.[19]

The Carajás iron project started as recently as 1967, when a helicopter with engine trouble landed in a bare patch in the forest southwest of Marabá. It was carrying several geologists who were astonished to find that they were standing on the top of a hill made up of billions of tons of high-grade iron ore, bauxite, manganese, copper, nickel, and cassiterite. The Brazilian government quickly took over the site and assigned the state-owned mining company CVRD (Companhia Vale do Rio Doce) to develop it. The Greater Carajás Project, as it became known, was granted control of a region of some 900,000 square kilometers—the size of France and Britain combined—and started an enormous concentrated effort to build roads, a railway, dams, and a hydroelectric power plant.

The Carajás program has four major components: the iron ore mine, a highly mechanized open-pit mine that began operation in 1986; two aluminum plants, one in Belém, the other in São Luís, the capital of the state of Maranhão; the Tucuruí hydroelectric complex on the Tocantins River;

---

[18]"A morte ronda os índios na floresta," *Veja*, September 19, 1990, 70–77.
[19]"Belém Pará," *Jornal Pessoal* II, no. 64 (July 1990).

and a nine-hundred-kilometer railroad inaugurated in 1985 to link Carajás and São Luís, where a deepwater port was opened a year later. Japanese corporations are the single biggest group of investors, through cheap loans of $500 billion to the Brazilian government. The European Economic Community invested $600 million. The World Bank provided $304 million, and $250 million came from U.S. commercial banks. Even the USSR provided $60 million. The CVRD contracts to supply iron to Japanese and European steel producers were tied to the loans. The CVRD is immensely profitable. Although ranked only 294th in the Fortune Global 500 in 1990, it was first in the world in profits as a percentage of sales (65 percent) and of assets (45 percent).[20]

Although within the CVRD enclave itself environmental deterioration has been carefully monitored and controlled, the company's own territory looks increasingly like a Potemkin village, surrounded everywhere by devastation. The Carajás program acted as a strong population magnet, attracting thousands of construction workers, gold panners, small farmers, and speculators into the region which until very recently had been tropical forest. The insatiable demands for the charcoal used to smelt the iron ore will eventually destroy over 70,000 acres of forest every year, and has already led to destruction of the surrounding forest in a manner recalling the insatiable demands of the sugar mills that consumed the coastal forests four centuries before. The Tucuruí hydropower complex, for which 35,000 people were displaced, has the largest dam in any of the world's tropical forests and it caused the flooding of 2,500 square kilometers of uncleared forest. The hydropower complex is central to the entire scheme—supplying electricity at subsidized prices to the iron mine, the aluminum plants, and the industries along the Carajás-São Luís Railroad.

The profitability of the Carajás project depends heavily on these huge state investments and on the cheap energy they will produce. Electronorte, the state monopoly electricity company in the Amazon, has grandiose plans for sixty-three new reservoirs in the Amazon basin, twenty-seven for the Tocantins-Araguaia region alone.[21] Road and dam building is immensely profitable, and all the major Brazilian public works and construction companies, such as Camargo Corrêa, Andrade Gutierrez, and Mendes Júnior, are involved in the projects, which absorb vast sums of government resources. Lucio Flavio Pinto estimated that those expenditures represent some 15 percent of Brazil's foreign debt.[22]

---

[20] *Fortune*, July 30, 1990.

[21] Wolfgang J. Junk and J. A. S. Nunes de Mello, "Impactos ecológicos das represas hidrelétricas na bacia Amazônica brasileira," *Estudos Avançados* 4, no. 8 (January–April 1990): 126–143.

[22] "Belém Pará," *Jornal Pessoal*, II, no. 64 (July 1990): 10.

Many of the schemes for dams and reservoirs are particularly ill considered. The Balbina reservoir near Manaus, capital of the state of Amazonas, covered an area of dense tropical forests and is, like almost all other Amazonian basin reservoirs, extremely shallow; it therefore produces a low level of energy per square kilometer flooded. Since no environmental impact studies or land survey was made before the flooding, no one really knows what potential mineral resources were submerged in the process. No programs for saving animals were set up, nor was there provision made for fish ladders at any of the dams. The deterioration of the quality of the impounded water through decomposition and absorption of organic matter can lead to a lack of oxygen in the water, cause corrosion of the hydroelectric turbines, create a buildup of sulfuric acid, and help in the proliferation of mosquitoes and the spread of intestinal diseases. Not surprisingly, an epidemic of malaria broke out in the Amazon region, rising from a reported 51,000 cases in 1970 to more than one million in 1990.

Nowhere, moreover, have small projects been developed to provide electricity to the rural populations. All the electrical power generated has been for urban and industrial use, which only serves to increase migration and to make more acute the crisis in producing food, which is largely grown by the poor and vulnerable Amazon peasants. As the small farmers and land-hungry migrants have faced the rapid concentration of land into large holdings, society and the environment have been subject to damage that Hall claims to be "unprecedented in Brazilian history."

V

The end of military rule in 1985, if anything, speeded the process of ecological depletion in the Amazon and intensified the growing confrontation between large and small landowners. In 1986 it was estimated that 64 percent of all conflicts over land in Brazil occurred in the Amazon. The Amazon frontier also showed the highest incidence of murders involving more than two victims.

After 1985 the conflict in the Amazon changed. Powerful landed interests became politically more aggressive, as the military, which had protected them, retreated and the political system became more liberal. The economic policy known as the Cruzado Plan of 1985–1986, which temporarily reduced speculative profits in the money markets, shifted investments to land and property. The new civilian government also set up a ministry of agrarian reform, and a program of land reform was announced.

The proposed reform threatened to expropriate land that was not in use and immediately caused more evictions and burning of forests as landowners avidly began to open more pastures in order to prove the land was being farmed. Peasants, too, occupied unused land on estates in the hope of acquiring titles to it. Increasingly active workers' movements emerged during the 1980s, organized by unions from the south and by the church. They began to articulate peasant demands for land reform, while their members harassed and in some cases killed landowners. At the same time a powerful organization of landowners and ranchers, the Rural Democratic Union (UDR), was formed to oppose even the mild proposals for land reform that were put forward by the administration of President José Sarney. The UDR's lobbying in Brasília was highly successful, and the constitutional assembly in 1988 voted down a proposal that would have allowed state expropriation of very large landholdings as part of a reform plan.

Many saw the hand of the UDR behind the increasing sophistication and violence of the ranchers' response to the rural workers' organizations, as well as the rising number of assassinations of union leaders, church men and women, and labor lawyers. Amnesty International's *Brazil: Authorized Violence in Rural Areas,* a report first published in September 1988, tells the story in grisly and horrifying detail. A steady increase in reported killings of peasants in rural areas had occurred throughout Brazil, more than one thousand between 1980 and 1986. Many of these killings were connected with disputes over land, and were carried out by hired gunmen (*pistoleiros*) employed by landowners; but there was also increasing participation by state policemen.

The failure to pursue serious investigations of these crimes was tantamount to complicity in them, and Amnesty concluded that the pattern of assassinations of workers' leaders was "so persistent that it facilitates fresh killings and may amount to deliberate permissiveness toward them." Amnesty could find only two cases in which hired gunmen were convicted and sentenced for politically motivated killings and not a single case in which those accused of commissioning the killing were brought to justice.

The entire Amazon region was, in the words of Anthony Anderson, "increasingly out of the control of the public sector."[23] Whereas government incentives and investment had once been a sine qua non for private activity, now ranchers, farmers, miners, loggers, and charcoal producers were working on their own. Ranchers were opening their own roads. Private gold mines were polluting the rivers. Settlements of new colonies were spreading along the southern flank of the region and overwhelming the frontier communities already in place.

By 1987, in the Cachimbo region near the center of Brazil where the Kreen-Akrore Indians had killed John Hemming's fellow explorer in 1961

---

[23]Anthony B. Anderson, ed., *Alternatives to Deforestation: Steps toward Sustainable Use of the Amazon Rain Forest* (New York: Columbia University Press, 1990).

and where in 1968 Adrian Cowell had filmed his *The Tribe That Hides from Man,* not a single Kreen-Akrore remained. Nor did most of the forest. During the 1970s two roads had joined up at Cachimbo, and hordes of prospectors had found gold in the Peixoto Azevedo River. The Kreen-Akrore had been forced from their forest redoubt by an epidemic of flu and were starving to death. With the tribe facing extinction, a handful of survivors were flown to the relative protection of the Xingú National park in Mato Grosso. The region where the vast forest had stood was now populated by the cattle of ranchers and land speculators, some living in colonists' towns close to the river. Cachimbo itself is a huge military base, used to test rocket technology that was later sold to Saddam Hussein, and it was revealed in 1990 to have housed a deep pit intended for the underground testing of nuclear weapons.

The burning seasons—whether for clearing farmland, ranch land, or charcoal burning or for mining operations—was now affecting a great arc from Acre and Rondônia along the western, southern, and eastern fringes of the Amazon rain forest. The global impact of this transformation in the Amazon and the effects of burning became dramatically evident in the mid-1980s, when satellite imaging revealed to scientists for the first time the monumental scale of the fires. In 1987 the dry season was unusually long, and as a result the forest fires in Amazônia were exceptionally intense and widespread. On August 24, 1987, Brazil's Institute for Space Research (INPE) detected 6,800 fires just in the states of Mato Grosso and a small portion of southern Pará and eastern Rondônia. Smoke from the Amazon fires lasted until December and forced the closing of most of the region's airports.

The fires in the Amazon are entirely man-made; they are not to be compared, for example, with the raging fires that strike in the American West. For trees to burn in the wet tropical forest they need to be felled and left for two or three months to dry. They are then ignited usually by people who want to clear the land, sometimes simply in the hope of selling it. That fire does not spread naturally in this region is central to the surveillance efforts of the Brazilian space institute, which began using meteorological satellites to provide four images each day of the Amazon region. Using high-resolution satellite imagery, one can obtain a good map of areas burned, pinpointing particular properties.[24]

At the peak of the burning season, from the end of August until early September, this space imaging revealed as many as eight thousand separate fires in a single day throughout the region. Since at least half the rainfall in

---

[24]Alberto Setzer, *Camões Center Quarterly* 2, nos. 1 and 2 (spring and summer 1990): 22–24. Also in *Veja*, July 5, 1989, 104.

the Amazon basin comes from water that is condensed from within the forest atmosphere itself, the scale of deforestation threatened to heavily reduce the region's rainfall. But it was the scale of the burning forest revealed by the satellites that brought home to scientists that what was occurring in Brazil was no longer only a Brazilian disaster, it was a real threat to the global climate.

The reason for this threat lay in the vital link in the carbon cycle between climate and forest. Carbon dioxide, water, and sunlight make wood and release oxygen in a process of photosynthesis. In the opposite reaction, wood decomposes or burns, producing energy and carbon dioxide. What is important is the change in carbon dioxide levels in the atmosphere. Since carbon dioxide acts as a heat-trapping gas, it keeps the earth warmer than it would normally be. The burning of the Brazilian forest dramatically shifts the balance, changing from a situation where much carbon, perhaps 150 tons, is retained in the total mass of living organisms or "biomass," to a system where only a small amount of carbon, around fifteen tons, is retained in grassland or pasture. It is because of this process, in which the forest is transformed into grassland or pasture, that Brazil becomes dangerous globally for its release of carbon dioxide.[25]

How dangerous? José Goldemberg, a renowned Brazilian physicist and former president of the University of São Paulo, estimated that the Amazon fires approximated the level of the carbon dioxide emissions from all of North America and exceeded that contributed by all of Western Europe.[26] Moist tropical forests contain approximately 35 percent of the world's living terrestrial carbon pool, according to Anthony Anderson in his introduction to the useful collection of essays by experts *Alternatives to Deforestation*. The cautious estimate by *World Resources* is that deforestation is second only to fossil fuels as a human source of atmospheric carbon dioxide, almost all of which comes from the tropics and overwhelmingly from Brazil.

The report *Environmental Damage and Climatic Change* by the Ditchley Foundation, a body not exactly famous for its extremism, states without hesitation that "global warming is . . . the ultimate environmental threat." New global measures of the surface temperature of the oceans, according to the Ditchley report, show a rise of 0.1 degrees centigrade per year for the

---

[25]Foster Brown in "The Burning of Brazil: A Discussion with Foster Brown and Alberto Setzer," *Camões Center Quarterly* 2, nos. 1 and 2 (spring and summer 1990): 20.

[26]José Goldemberg, "A Amazônia e seu futuro," *Folha de São Paulo*, January 29, 1989, A3. However, Goldemberg, who became secretary of science and technology in the Collor administration, gave much lower figures in a letter to the *New York Times* (July 28, 1990).

last eight years. This is a rate of 1.0 degrees centigrade per decade. An average global warming of 1.5 degrees centigrade would alter the climate beyond anything experienced by the planet in the past 10,000 years.[27]

There is a crude irony in this tragedy. The Brazilian politicians and military strategists who planned and promoted the march to the west did so in large part out of the desire to see Brazil make its mark on the world. They succeeded in ways they never could have imagined. Brazil was indeed being taken note of, but for causing a global environmental disaster. Out of the vortex of fire, violence, and social and political conflict in the Amazon a powerful human voice briefly but memorably emerged, that of Chico Mendes.

[27]Pearce Wright, *Environmental Damage and Climatic Change* (Oxford: Ditchley Foundation Report No. D88/4).

IN THE RAINY SEASON.

CHAPTER 12

Chico Mendes

*"What crawling villain preaches abstinence and wraps himself
In fat of lambs? no more I follow, no more obedience pay!"*
—William Blake, *America: A Prophecy*, 1793

On December 22, 1988, Francisco "Chico" Mendes, a Brazilian union organizer, was murdered at his modest house in Xapuri, a remote rubber-trad-
ing outpost of five thousand people in the Brazilian border state of Acre.
Mendes was a plump, agreeable, talkative activist who had tried to protect
the livelihood of his fellow rubber tappers, which was threatened by the
destruction of the Amazonian rain forest and the encroaching cattle
ranches. To do so he had allied himself with prominent members of the international environmental movement. He spoke the lingua franca of visiting anthropologists from Berkeley and Paris, European TV producers, and
Washington environmental lobbyists. Mendes's aim had been to protect
the forest, by persuasion if possible, by force if need be. He wanted the
Brazilian government to promote "extractive reserves," a policy by which
ecologically desirable activities such as rubber tapping and nut collecting
could continue, but environmentally destructive forest clearance would be
prevented.

Chico Mendes's assassins were gunmen of a particularly nasty ranching
clan, the Alves da Silvas. The Alves da Silva family was originally from the
state of Minas Gerais in south-central Brazil, and had moved during the
1960s to the southern Brazilian state of Paraná. In the mid-1970s they
came to Acre, on Brazil's northwestern border with Bolivia and Peru. Each
move, it was revealed later, was occasioned by the need to escape arrest for
a previous murder.

The assassination of Chico Mendes was ordered by Darly Alves da Silva and was carried out by Darci, his twenty-year-old son. An archetypal, old-time backlands boss, Darly lived on a 10,000-acre ranch with his wife, three mistresses, thirty children, and an assortment of cowboys who could have come out of the Dirty Dozen. He perfectly fit the demonology of Amazonian ecological destruction. The cattle ranchers were to a large extent responsible for the vast clearing, burning, and degradation of the Amazonian landscape that occurred throughout the 1980s in Brazil. Chico Mendes, little known within Brazil, had become through his connections with foreign ecological experts one of the best known abroad of the new generation of grassroots peasant leaders to emerge during the twilight years of the Brazilian military regime. Of the many such leaders who were selected for assassination by hired guns of the large landowners, Mendes was one of the few with influential friends abroad.

Chico Mendes became as well known internationally as Pelé and Carmen Miranda, with the difference that he is seen as a martyr from the worlds of the dark Brazilian forest and violent backlands, which seem to have special glamour for North Americans and Europeans and none at all for Brazilians. David Cleary, in his sober account of the Amazonian gold miners (*garimpeiros*), notes that there is a long tradition where "people could be enticed into believing almost anything about Amazônia,"[1] and several of the recent North American and European books about Mendes are very much of this genre. Considered together, however, they provide a revealing picture of Chico Mendes, the causes of his death, and his transformation into an international "ecology martyr."

I

Acre, the backwoods region where Chico Mendes lived, suffered heavily from the violence and destruction that swept through Amazônia in the 1980s. Once claimed by Bolivia, the region was incorporated into Brazil in 1903 during the rubber boom. In the 1940s, when the United States sought to maintain a supply of rubber after the Japanese takeover of Southeast Asia, a "war for rubber" was declared by the government of President Getúlio Vargas. Poor peasants were mobilized in the drought-plagued northeast of Brazil and sent west into the Amazon forest to tap Acre's rubber trees. But after the emergency was over, Acre once again became a remote, thinly populated federal territory, accessible almost exclusively by river from Manaus and Belém.

---

[1]David Cleary, *Anatomy of the Brazilian Gold Rush* (Iowa City: University of Iowa Press, 1990), 203.

The territory became a state in 1962. As elsewhere in Amazônia, a new highway, extending from the state of Rondônia in 1971, broke Acre's isolation from the center and south of Brazil, though the road from Rondônia remained little more than a dirt track through the forest, passable only for a few months of the year. Nevertheless, in the inexorable Brazilian process of settlement, land grabbing, ranching, and social conflict soon followed. The new state government, having high hopes for ranching, encouraged private investment inland, promoting Acre as a potential corridor to the Pacific—five hundred miles to the west with the Andes standing in between and no roads yet constructed.

This, however, was for the future—or so the government's publicists promised. One-third of the land in Acre changed hands from 1971 to 1977, much of it with forged titles. Land prices along the highway rose 2,000 percent. Financial groups from the south of Brazil bought out rubber estates and sought to evict the tappers, leading to violent fights. With the extension of another highway from the state capital, Rio Branco, to Brasiléia on the Bolivian border, Xapuri, a sleepy port halfway between the two towns, became the new cattle frontier. Between 1970 and 1984, the number of cattle in Xapuri County rose from 7,000 to 52,000 head. Augusta Dwyer, a Canadian freelance writer whose book is among the best written and most evocative of these books on the Amazon, visited Chico Mendes some months before his assassination when he told her that:

> From 1970 until 1975 or 1976 all our comrades who lived along the margin of the road to Brasiléia were expelled using the most violent means possible. Their shacks were burned down, gunmen would show up on their land, their animals were killed.[2]

Many of these dispossessed rubber tappers, some 10,000 according to the Catholic Church's land commission, crossed the frontier into Bolivia. Others migrated to the capital, Rio Branco, whose population rose from 36,000 in 1970 to 92,000 in 1980.

In the new economic situation brought about by the highway and the increase in cattle ranching, the bosses who had controlled the rubber trade and held the tappers in virtual bondage through debt found their profits declining so drastically that they were only too glad to sell off their rubber estates to the ranchers. As elsewhere in Amazônia, the new roads to the south and east broke the old riverine trading and business connections, opening up the region to the aggressive intervention of powerful economic interests from the industrial heartland of Brazil, especially São Paulo. The rubber tappers were left to look after themselves as best they could.

---

[2]Augusta Dwyer, *Into the Amazon: The Struggle for the Rain Forest* (San Francisco: Sierra Club Books, 1990).

Thus, as the rubber trade diminished, the tappers gained by default a certain degree of independence, but their livelihood also became highly dependent on the government, which imposed tariffs and taxes to keep the price of cheaper imported rubber high. This was the same government that was simultaneously handing out easy credit and tax write-offs to southern businessmen if they invested in Amazônia cattle ranching. But despite a falloff in rubber production (in the municipality of Xapuri, for instance, where 1,250 tons of rubber were produced in 1971, only 403 tons were produced in 1981), Acre remained Brazil's largest producer of natural rubber. In 1980 some 23,000 families were still directly dependent on tapping native rubber trees for their livelihood.[3]

II

Born poor in one of the most remote and backward parts of Brazil, Chico Mendes was illiterate until he was twenty years old. His grandfather had migrated from Ceará in the northeast of Brazil to Acre in the 1920s and settled near Xapuri. Mendes grew up in the forest, working as a rubber tapper from the age of nine. His family lived in a modest hut in a forest clearing at the center of a clover leaf of forest trails used by the rubber tappers. Each trail gave access to between one hundred and two hundred rubber trees over an area of seven hundred or so acres, forming part of a large tract of forest, or *seringal*. These estates were owned by well-to-do businessmen in the town of Manaus, a thousand miles downriver.

In 1962, when he was eighteen, Chico Mendes met Euclides Fernandes Távora, a Communist and former army lieutenant hiding out in the frontier jungle. Their relations remain obscure, but there seems no doubt that Távora taught Chico to read and write. He also introduced Mendes, according to Andrew Revkin in *The Burning Season*, to "the basic tenets of Marxism," giving the young rubber tapper a "mastery of the vocabulary of socialism and communism."[4] In 1965, Távora, who settled in the district for a time with a local woman, disappeared as mysteriously as he had arrived, but he had given Mendes a sense of the larger world that existed beyond the forest. Mendes himself later recalled:

---

[3]The best short introduction to the social and economic history of Acre is provided by Keith Bakx in "The Shanty Town, Final Stage of Development? The Case of Acre," in *The Future of the Amazon*, ed. David Goodman and Anthony Hall (New York: St. Martin's Press, 1990), 49–69.

[4]Andrew Revkin, *The Burning Season: The Murder of Chico Mendes and the Fight for the Amazon Rain Forest* (Boston: Houghton Mifflin, 1990). For further discussion on Euclides Távora see "Was Távora There?" *New York Review of Books*, November 7, 1991, which includes responses from Augusta Dwyer and Laura Renshaw, Grants Manager for Oxfam America, as well as research by historian Peter Beattie in the Brazilian military archives.

[Távora] gave me a lot of advice about how to organize in the trade union movement . . . Despite the defeats, humiliations, and massacres, the roots of the movement were always there, he said. The plants would always germinate again sooner or later, however much they were attacked.

Chico Mendes moved to Xapuri in 1971. He had learned enough from Euclides to teach for a year in the literacy campaign sponsored by the military regime, and he worked as a salesman in the shop of Guilherme Zaire, a local warehouse owner and rubber trader of Syrian origin. In 1975 Mendes took advantage of classes in union organizing set up by a representative of the state-sponsored Brazilian Confederation of Agricultural Workers (CONTAG). The rubber tappers, faced with the expansion of ranching and the transfer of titles to the forest where they worked, in 1976 devised an increasingly successful method of resistance, the *empate*. The *empate* was an organized showdown between the rubber tappers and the workers sent in by the ranching interests to cut down the forest. The unions claimed this was legal under the Brazilian civil code, which allows a person "to maintain or reinstate his claim through his own force, provided he does so immediately." The *empate* was not a form of Ghandhian passive resistance, but, as Cowell's TV documentaries (if not his book), Revkin's photographs, and, in particular, Dwyer's account make clear, it used tactics of pressure and persuasion. Dwyer describes it as:

In many respects, a show of class force, a large group of people, often including entire families, descending on the ill-paid workers who were slaving away to destroy the forest. Their *empate* was first an attempt to bring these fellow workers around to the other side, to make them understand that they were taking the food from the mouths of their comrades. It was also a statement, one that said to everyone: "You will have to kill us to get us out of here."

The problem with this strategy was that the right to defend land by force was also claimed by the rich landowners. In the general atmosphere of lawlessness that permeated the frontier, it is hardly surprising that the larger proprietors, reacting to the *empates*, turned increasingly to gunmen to defend their claims.

Political changes in the south of Brazil were also beginning to affect Acre during the 1970s. Brazil's military regime had maintained control partly through secret services that repressed or infiltrated dissident movements, but the regime had always been an odd hybrid that never abandoned the formalities of elections. In 1965 an artificial two-party system had been imposed after the coup. Ironically, the military thereby created an instrument for expressing antimilitary sentiment. To vote for the catchall opposition group called the Brazilian Democratic Movement (MDB) was to register dissatisfaction with the military regime. Chico Mendes had run as a candidate for the MDB in the 1977 municipal election in Xapuri. Sponsored by his then employer, the Syrian rubber trader Guilherme Zaire, Mendes was elected with two other men who also worked for Zaire.

He was not, however, particularly successful as a member of the municipal council. The chamber would empty when he launched into long, radical speeches, which even his opposition colleagues in MDB found tiresome. Chico Mendes found his period on the municipal council a disillusioning experience, but he justified his participation as well as his union work as being consistent with the lessons Távora had taught him. Távora had told him, Chico Mendes said, that "Lenin always said you shouldn't stay out of a union just because it is yellow. You must join it and use your ideas and strengthen the movement."

During the late 1970s, however, several elements came together to help the increasingly desperate cause of the rubber tappers. The church, long a bastion of landed interests, began to accept new, mainly foreign priests, who were followers of liberation theology and had experience in organizing grassroots community groups. The regime's repressive methods, including widespread use of torture, extensive surveillance and intimidation, and the restriction of political rights, and the forced exile of many political figures, had brought the Catholic Church squarely into the political and social struggle.

The church moved into the rural regions on two fronts, both of which were important to union organizing in Acre. The radical priests helped to establish grassroots communities committed to mutual assistance and political activism. By the early 1990s there were 80,000 of these CEBs (*Comunidades Eclesiais de Base*) in Brazil. The Catholic Church also set up pastoral land commissions in 1975 and soon found them in the forefront of the struggle for peasant rights. These organizations, intended to monitor land conflicts and encourage priests and lay workers to help the peasants defend their rights, became more radical as they found themselves caught up in deadly day-to-day conflict. One of the best known of the priests who became involved is Dom Pedro Casaldaliga, the bishop of São Félix de Araguaia. A Catalan with long missionary experience in the Amazon, Dom Pedro still refuses to baptize the children of some ranchers or say mass on their land. "It made no sense to go out and denounce these people for the killing of peasants and then celebrate mass in their buildings," he told Augusta Dwyer. "It would be like celebrating mass in a salon of the International Monetary Fund . . . or the UDR."

The rural workers' unions in the south also sent organizers to the new frontier who provided training, helped in union organizing, and provided legal support for what had previously been mainly isolated and spontaneous resistance. With church and union support, Mendes helped found in 1977 the Xapuri Rural Workers' Union, of which he later became president.

As the situation grew more tense, a small coterie of activist Brazilian intellectuals, social scientists, and journalists appeared in Acre. Mary Allegretti, an anthropologist from Paraná who came to Acre to study the rubber tappers of the upper Taranacá River in the late 1970s, became a close friend and adviser to Mendes. Elson Martins set up in Rio Branco a lively alternative newspaper, *Varadouro*. Between 1978 and 1981 it provided a forum for people whose views were previously unheard. At the end of the 1970s Chico Mendes, through contacts at the new federal university of Acre, established clandestine links with the Communist Party of Brazil (PCdoB), a Maoist splinter party that had taken China as its ideological model and was shifting its allegiance to Albania.

Important changes were also taking place nationally. The intrigues of the secret services began to threaten the military hierarchy itself and the generals found themselves confronted by growing pressure for change within society which they could no longer contain by force alone. Pressure from the church, unions, and other sectors of civil society, in an alliance not dissimilar to those forming in Acre, forced the regime to begin a slow process of liberalization. In 1979 the constraining and artificial two-party system was abandoned and amnesty was declared for both those accused by the military regime of political crimes and those accused of gross human rights violations. The new powerful union movement in the south, led by the metalworkers of São Paulo, whose chairman was Luiz Inácio da Silva, known as Lula, used the occasion to launch a new Workers' Party (PT): the first grassroots political movement to emerge in Brazilian history and a striking innovation in a country where political parties, including those on the populist left, were organized from the top down.

The conflict between union and ranchers in Acre, however, had by 1980 become increasingly ugly. Wilson Pinheiro, a union leader in Brasiléia, a town on Acre's border with Bolivia, was gunned down in his union's hall. Pinheiro had befriended Chico Mendes and given him advice, and many assumed that Mendes, who was traveling at the time, was also a target. The enraged rubber tappers took the law into their own hands and shot to death a rancher they suspected of being involved in the union leader's death. The reaction of the Brazilian authorities to the death of the rancher was rapid. Here was a case where "justice moved instantly," Chico Mendes told Augusta Dwyer with heavy irony. "Twenty-four hours later dozens of tappers were rounded up, tortured, their fingernails pulled out." Mendes himself was charged under the national security law in Manaus. He retreated into the forest. In 1981 he was captured and brought before a military tribunal in Manaus, where he was defended by lawyers from Lula's Workers' Party. The charges were dropped in 1984.

III

By the mid-1980s Mendes had developed links with an international network of sympathizers, some of whom could provide financial support for the rubber tappers' cause. He became particularly close to the British academic Tony Gross, who had been working for Oxfam in Brazil since 1980.[5]

In 1981 Oxfam began supporting the education programs in Xapuri run by the workers' union and aimed at bringing literacy to families in the interior of the municipality. By 1983 two producer cooperatives had been founded, located at two of the five schools then in existence. The cooperatives were supported by funds from the church's land commission. The Xapuri union, headed by Mendes, broke with the Brasiléia union, which was then close to the party of the Brazilian Democratic Movement (PMDB), the successor of the MDB, and which was working with the government's rubber agency to establish small rubber-processing plants to encourage production and improve the quality of processed rubber. In Xapuri, Mendes, who opposed cooperation with state agencies, remained affiliated with the Workers' Party. In effect, Oxfam and Mendes had chosen to support the more radical of the two opposition parties to the military regime.

Augusta Dwyer describes the differences as being between "those who want a social democratic society, such as Sweden, and those who want democratic socialism, a true workers' state. Chico belonged to this second group." The split in Acre, however, reflected the wider split then occurring nationally, leading in 1983 to the formation of an independent union organization (CUT), closely associated with the worker's party.

Tony Gross, who was now responsible for all Oxfam Amazon projects, also introduced Mary Allegretti to environmental activists in Washington. In 1985 Adrian Cowell, a British documentary producer, had, like many others concerned with the headlong destruction of the rain forest, turned his attention to Acre, where the frontier expansion which had devastated Rondônia was now threatening. For Chico Mendes, whom Cowell soon discovered, the connections with Gross, Allegretti, and Cowell were fateful ones.

Adrian Cowell was an award-winning filmmaker who had been visiting Amazonia since the late 1950s and had watched with growing resentment and exasperation the senseless destruction of the Amazon rain forest and its indigenous inhabitants. In the early 1980s he became a close friend of the Brazilian agronomist José Lutzenberger, long an outspoken critic of Brazil's development projects in the Amazon region and active promoter of the international Gaia movement to protect the world's ecology. Cowell became convinced of the need to stem the tide of destruction caused in

---

[5]Tony Gross, *Fight for the Forest: Chico Mendes in His Own Words* (London: Monthly Review Press, 1992).

large part by what he considered "phony finance," especially the credits, grants, and loans that had financed the conversion of forest to grasslands and allowed the road system to be pushed into the rain forest. He therefore, he writes, "turned towards the ultimate source of much of that finance—one of the world's controlling economic institutions—the World Bank."

In 1984, while making a film in Washington, D.C., Cowell met Bruce Rich, an environmental lobbyist leading the campaign against the banks that were financing Brazilian development, and a leading member of the Natural Resources Defense Council. It was Cowell who suggested to Bruce Rich that José Lutzenberger be invited to testify in Washington before the Congressional Subcommittee on Natural Resources. A year later, in 1985, at a strategy meeting in the United States, Cowell argued:

> [M]ost previous environmental campaigns, against whaling, for instance, had been about issues that could be decided in the First World. But as tropical forests were in the Third World, everything depended on political decisions in those countries.

At this meeting Cowell also met Stephen Schwartzman, a trained anthropologist who had worked with the Kreen-Akrore, the Indians whom Cowell had first filmed in the 1960s and whose remaining numbers had been subsequently relocated in Xingu Park. The American Beldon and Threshold Foundations later financed a visit by Schwartzman to Brazil to solicit Brazilian help in developing a campaign to oppose the activities of the banks. Cowell had doubts that the tropical forest campaign would be as successful as the one on whaling. "Tropical forests may be more important to the world," he said, "but they're less emotive, less cuddly than whales." Chico Mendes, however, was eminently "cuddly."

In 1985, Cowell and his colleagues were planning an offensive to make the fate of the tropical forests a major concern of the multinational lending institutions based in Washington with which U.S. influence was paramount. At the same time, in Brasília, the capital of Brazil, the rubber tappers' first national meeting came up with the central idea of the movement, that of "extractive reserves," the oxymoron combining the idea of preserving the forest while exploiting its products, such as latex and tropical nuts. "The extractive reserve is a form of land reform," Chico Mendes told Augusta Dwyer when she visited him in Xapuri in 1988. "The Brazilian government would be pressured to expropriate the rubber estates and designate them extractive reserves. The land would become the property of the nation with the rubber tappers holding the title to use it." The idea of "extractive reserves" could be appealing to an international audience, as Cowell immediately realized. It was at the Brasília meeting, according to Revkin, that Cowell turned his attention to the one man among the tappers who seemed smart enough, cool enough, and honest enough to take the tappers' message out of the forest and straight to the boardrooms of the banks and the halls of Congress, both in and out of Brazil. That man was Chico Mendes.

Cowell, Revkin observes, "never liked to think that he was meddling in things. He did not want to transform the movement, only to give it a louder voice." Cowell's friend, Mary Allegretti, persuaded Mendes to modify his message. Instead of the "old calls for social justice, workers' rights, and agrarian reform—standard issues of the political left . . . ," he would now call for the preservation of the Amazon. Allegretti and Cowell were now, according to Revkin, "in the middle of a three-year relationship." It was during this period that they introduced Mendes to ecological and international aid agencies in Washington, with the help of Stephen Schwartzman. Their objective was to force the international lending agencies, especially the World Bank and the Inter-American Development Bank, both highly dependent on U.S. financing and under attack by Reagan administration ideologues, to make environmental concerns central to their leading policy decisions.

There was a ready target at hand. By 1986 the road through Acre was being paved with Inter-American Development Bank funding. Allegretti and Schwartzman agreed that the time had come for an assault on the banks that were financing Brazilian roads and commitments in ranching. Through Cowell, Allegretti learned that Mendes, who was campaigning now on the Workers' Party ticket for a seat in the state legislature, had included attacks on the road paving in his campaign speeches. This had not made him very popular with local voters (he lost resoundingly), but it provided a golden opportunity for the environmental cause. "Allegretti and Cowell concluded," according to Revkin, "that Mendes would be much more effective if he left local politics behind, came out of the forest . . . and directed his criticism directly at the bank." It made for a cynical marriage of convenience.

The U.S. Treasury under Reagan was looking, as Schwartzman put it, for a "bludgeon with which to beat" the Inter-American Development bank, which the administration saw as epitomizing the evils of foreign aid. The environmental movement, or more precisely Chico Mendes, would provide the weapons. As Hecht and Cockburn observe in the *Fate of the Forest*, among the charitable foundations and environmental groups aiding the rubber tappers, "many of their constituents might have been horrified at the idea that their organizations were supporting radical unionizing efforts."[6]

---

[6]Suzanna Hecht and Alexander Cockburn, *The Fate of the Forest: Developers, Destroyers and Defenders of the Amazon* (London and New York: Verso, 1989).

In March 1987, Mendes set off on a trip to Miami to attend a meeting of the Inter-American Development Bank. Schwartzman and Cowell met him at the airport and took him to the Intercontinental Hotel. "Here we were at one of those classic meetings where everyone is saying, 'Let's have fresh raspberries, sip champagne, and talk about the poor.'" This, according to Revkin, was how Jim Bond, special assistant to Senator Robert W. Kasten Jr. (Republican of Wisconsin), described the scene when Chico Mendes arrived among the bankers at cocktail hour.

After introducing Mendes to the bankers in Miami, Schwartzman and Cowell took him to Washington, where he was introduced to Senator Kasten, who had time to shake his hand and comment: "I can promise you that our subcommittee is going to continue to put pressure on the [bank] to withhold funds—to cut off all funds possibly—if they are not more cooperative." As Revkin observes, it was the unlikeliest of alliances, a staunch conservative from a state of rolling pastures and cows and a Marxist forest dweller whose worst enemies were cattlemen.

IV

The circulation of Mendes's proposal for "extractive reserves" at the First National Rubber Tappers' Congress in Brasília in 1985 occurred at a critical moment. That year Brazil returned to civilian rule. But the birth of the "new republic," as it was optimistically called, was difficult. The civilian elected by the Congress to the presidency, Tancredo Neves, an oldtime but highly skilled politician from the opposition, died on the eve on his inauguration and the vice president, José Sarney, inherited the position. Sarney was from Maranhão, the state on the edge of the Amazon basin which provided one of the key outlets for the great mineral discoveries of Carajás. The state capital, São Luís, was the terminal of the new Carajás railroad. Sarney had headed the political party that supported the military regime. The power in the congress, however, lay with the eclectic PMDB, and after 1988 the PMDB also won twenty-two out of the twenty-three Brazilian governorships. A new plan for agrarian reform put forward by the Sarney government was eventually abandoned under intense lobbying by the large landholders, but the threat of potential expropriations was sufficient to increase conflicts throughout rural Brazil, especially in the Amazon, where both landowners and landless sought to establish title. The church and the rural union represented the peasants in this struggle, and against them were the landowners organized throughout Brazil under the banner of the UDR. Acre did not escape the conflict.

Darly Alves da Silva had moved to Acre in 1974. His ranch was not large by Acre standards. In fact, Darly's herd was so small that many supposed he had other work—smuggling goods across the Bolivian border and killing by contract. He was one of a notoriously violent family whose members had left a trail of murder behind them in Minas Gerais and Paraná. The Alves da Silva clan and Chico Mendes came into conflict over the last large section of rain forest left in Xapuri County, the Seringal Cachoeira. It included the rubber tapping estate on which Mendes had grown up, and which was now owned by four São Paulo businessmen who wanted it cleared so that they could develop the land for ranching.

A report circulated in Acre that the four businessmen had agreed to sell the land to the Alves da Silva family, but only if the Alves da Silvas would clear the tappers out of the forest. This deal was probably concluded in early 1986. Darly first tried to buy the tappers out, offering them five hundred acres of land that he said he would not touch. When they turned him down he used hired workers to drive them out by force but was met with an *empate*. He then tried legal action to enforce his title to holdings he had bought from a disgruntled tapper who did not like the union, but the union members occupied the land to prevent the transfer. Meanwhile, on a visit to Paraná where Allegretti had established a Center for Amazonian Studies, Mendes was told by members of the Pastoral Commission that there were warrants out for Darly Alves da Silva's arrest, and he used his contacts in the Acre region's newspaper to publicize the government's charges about the violent past of the Alves da Silva family. Darly's effort to take over the land failed. He eventually accepted a settlement from the federal agrarian reform office; the government expropriated the land, and paid him well for his title to it.

Worried by the union's successes, the ranchers made an effort to buy Mendes off. Although virtually penniless, he proudly rejected them. "We have all the money and all the guns. Your movement is like mosquitoes against a jaguar," Revkin quotes one of the ranchers saying. "But you don't have the people," Mendes replied.

After his unsuccessful political campaign, Mendes was almost entirely dependent on foreign financial support. The Gaia Foundation, of which José Lutzenberger was a key Brazilian member, provided several hundred dollars a month to cover his expenses until the Washington-based Ashoka Foundation took over. Mary Allegretti, Steven Schwartzman, and Adrian Cowell contributed $500 to buy Mendes and his family a house in Xapuri. The Canadian government contributed a jeep and the Ford Foundation financed travel and administrative expenses for the National Council of Rubber Tappers, of which Mendes was a member. A Ford Foundation officer introduced Augusta Dwyer to Chico Mendes at an elegant Swiss restaurant in Rio de Janeiro.

But back in Acre, the threats and violence against the tappers' union intensified throughout 1988. In June, a local union organizer and Workers' Party candidate was killed. On December 5, 1988, Chico Mendes noticed the arrival of an airplane belonging to the leader of the local ranchers' organization (UDR), João Branco, who was accompanied by two unknown men. Fearing the worst, he wrote at the time:

> I do not wish flowers at my burying, because I know they will go and root them up in the forest. I hope only that my death will serve to put an end to the impunity of the hired gunmen under the protection of the Federal Police . . . I go to Xapuri to a meeting with death. I am not a fatalist, only a realist. I have already denounced who wishes to kill me and no measures whatsoever have been or will be taken . . . [The delegate of the Federal Police] has canceled my permission to carry a gun, with the allegation that I have links to a "communizing" organization. It is the Ford Foundation of the United States, if you can believe it![7]

On December 22 he was shot in the back doorway of his house in Xapuri.

V

Fixing the blame for the assassination of Chico Mendes should have been easy. The Alves da Silvas had threatened to kill Mendes in an *anunciado*, as the Brazilians call the chilling warning given to the victim-to-be. Mendes had exposed the plans of the landowners for his assassination in a letter to the Federal Police chief in Acre, Mauro Sposito, and the state governor on October 28, 1988. He had telexed the governor and the head of the Federal Police in Brasília, Romeu Tuma, on November 29. On December 5 he had again warned Tuma, as well as President Sarney. Yet it took two years for the trial in the Mendes case to begin.

At the trial, Darci Alves da Silva unexpectedly confessed (he had done so earlier, but then retracted his statement). Many believe he confessed in order to protect his father. With the Brazilian government under international scrutiny, Darci and his father were found guilty and sentenced to nineteen years in prison. Out of almost two thousand rural assassinations the Mendes case was the first in Brazil in which the gunmen and their sponsors were tried, let alone convicted. The result, however, satisfied none of the interest groups that are in conflict over the future of the rain forest, each of which has its own, often confused, vision of the future.

The books by Revkin, Shoumatoff, and Souza, none of whom knew Mendes, are each in their different ways part of this confusion.[8] All three

---

[7]Zuenir Ventura, "O Acre de Chico Mendes," *Jornal do Brasil,* July 5, 1989, 8.
[8]Revkin, *The Burning Season*; Alex Shoumatoff, *The World Is Burning* (Boston: Little, Brown, 1990); Márcio Souza, *O Empate contra Chico Mendes* (São Paulo: Marco Zero, 1990).

books contain long summaries of recent history, but it is a history that is largely irrelevant to the story of Chico Mendes and seems for the most part culled from the same newspaper clippings and texts (or text in the case of Warren Dean's environmental history of rubber, which is extensively mined by several of these authors).[9]

Mr. Shoumatoff calls the events following Chico Mendes's death an "ecofarce." An "eco-cash-in" would be a better word. The Francisco "Chico" Mendes Foundation received nine offers for movie rights, four of them over $1 million, according to Alan U. Schwartz, the lawyer for the foundation, which is a coalition of environmentalists, rubber tappers, and family members in Acre.[10] Among the competitors for film rights were Robert Redford and Twentieth Century Fox, with Stephen Spielberg as director; Ted Turner of Turner Broadcasting System; HBO and Harmony Gold Productions; Warner Brothers; David Puttnam and Chris Menges; Goldcrest Company, with Costa-Gavras as director; and JN Film, a Brazilian company. According to Hecht and Cockburn, "Stephen Schwartzman spent a fair amount of the past few months [of 1989] in both the United States and Brazil seeking to broker a Hollywood contract for a movie about Chico Mendes and the rubber tappers that on the terms of at least one bid could net him $100,000 in consultant's fees."[11]

In addition, Little, Brown publishers reportedly paid a vast figure advance for the book by Shoumatoff, who had written a piece on Chico Mendes for *Vanity Fair*, which he hoped Redford would make into a film. The Paris publishers Plon, part of the French Group Presses de la Cité, outbid two American houses for the book by Márcio Souza, who had the cooperation of Mendes's widow, Ilzamar, in return for Plon's agreement to donate the royalties to the Mendes Foundation, of which she is president. Houghton Mifflin signed on Revkin, a senior editor of *Discover* magazine. Almost all the other books discussed here, it should be noted, are dedicated to Chico Mendes.

Shoumatoff takes a more skeptical approach than Revkin to the various parties engaged in the Acre drama. There are moments of high comedy, however, in his breathless and self-indulgent account of his Amazonian adventures, though he recounts them in all seriousness. He visited the forest with a young writer and Green Party activist called Julio Cesar from Rio de Janeiro, who had never before visited Amazônia and arrived with silk paja-

---

[9]Warren Dean, *Brazil and the Struggle for Rubber: A Study in Environmental History* (Cambridge and New York: Cambridge University Press, 1987).

[10]Edwin McDowell, "After Amazon Slaying, Deals Abound," *New York Times*, July 10, 1989, D6.

[11]Susanna Hecht and Alexander Cockburn in "Letters," *The Nation*, September 18, 1989, 292.

mas. Shoumatoff had hired Cesar to protect him from the police and the ranchers, as well as Brazilian leftists, all of whom he feared "may not have liked" his *Vanity Fair* article. Together they met Mendes's uncle Joaquim and his wife, Cecélia, "a radiant old couple," and Shoumatoff came across a rambling reflection written by Chico on a napkin that turned up after his death extolling "World Socialist Revolution." Oddly, the same napkin reflection was reproduced by Hecht and Cockburn in *The Nation* during their quarrel with Stephen Schwartzman over Schwartzman's tendency to suppress, as Hecht and Cockburn saw it, the rubber worker's radicalism. The napkin is now to be found in a small circular glass frame under a photograph of Chico Mendes on his grave in Xapuri.

Andrew Revkin's heroes are the anthropologist and activist Mary Allegretti (Mr. Revkin's translator was Ms. Allegretti's brother), the British filmmaker Adrian Cowell ("without Cowell Chico Mendes would likely have remained a small-time labor leader in the Amazonion backwater of Xapuri"), Tony Gross, the Oxfam representative, and Stephen Schwartzman, the anthropologist and Washington environmental lobbyist. This is the cast of characters of the environmental cause that Mr. Shoumatoff treats with suspicion. Mr. Souza makes them villains of his piece, though he never condescends to name them directly.

Both Revkin and Shoumatoff use many Portuguese words, presumably to create an aura of authenticity. In Márcio Souza's *O Empate contra Chico Mendes,* this device is turned on its head. His only reference in English is to "*a misteriosa* Environmental Defense Fund—EDF." This sinister, foreign-sounding EDF, as well as Mary Allegretti's "Instituto de Estudos Amazônicos (IEA)," which, Souza darkly hints, has its "headquarters in the faraway state of Paraná," are all, he says, "very good at capturing funds for environmental projects" but they "interfere with the struggle and organization of the workers . . . using funds from abroad to attack and divide the Workers' Party, the unions, and the Church." Mr. Souza believes that Chico Mendes's death, and "his mystification as Green leader and an ecologist, who defends little plants and butterflies, brought confusion and uncertainty to the movement." The colonizing mentality, he says ominously, appears "in many disguises."

Mr. Souza's left-wing rhetoric sounds surprisingly like that of the paranoid right in Brazil. The former Brazilian minister of the interior, João Alves Filho, in his testimony before the parliamentary investigation committee for the Amazon in its hearings in April 1988 following the international outcry over Chico Mendes's death, provided a thirty-nine page statement, later published in English, which contains a listing of every foreigner who ever set foot in, looked at, touched, conspired against, wrote about, or worked in the Amazon from the first arrival of the Spaniards and Portuguese in the sixteenth century until 1989. "Nowadays," the minister noted ominously, "we face new and strange plans of nations that in the past invaded, occupied, or threatened to take over the Amazon from the Brazilians. Could it be that the wolves of the past not only changed their fleece but their own natures and became harmless lambs?"[12]

"Chico Mendes, like many other popular leaders, learned to read as an adult," Mr. Souza concludes condescendingly, "and did not have a sophisticated formal education. For this reason it is not strange that he did not develop any work of theoretical investigation, no coherent project beyond that of practical necessity." But Chico Mendes himself said that "the strategic center of the movement, in terms of communications and information, is the Institute of Amazon Studies, where Mary Allegretti, Paulo Chiesa and other friends work . . ." Perhaps because he was writing a screenplay about Chico Mendes, Mr. Souza excluded or dismissed a great deal that did not fit his story line, for example, the entire notion of "extractive reserves," the central element of the rubber workers' demands after 1985, and the direct cause of Chico Mendes's murder. From his book we can imagine a Márcio Souza–Warner Brothers film in which Gross, Schwartzman, Cowell, Allegretti, et al. are portrayed as so many sinister agents of ecoimperialism. They are not, and Mr. Souza should have known better.

VI

Unlike Revkin, Shoumatoff, and Souza, Adrian Cowell knew Mendes well and in fact followed him around Brazil and the United States, filming his activities off and on over the two-year period prior to his assassination. Cowell is also as much a part of the story of Chico Mendes as he is recorder of it, yet he is very reticent in his discussion of Mendes's political views (though less reticent in claiming credit for his promotion of Mendes and his efforts to obtain for Mendes his two international awards). Only Hecht and Cockburn's book deals seriously with his ideas and only Augusta Dwyer in an account of her travels in Amazônia adequately evokes his qualities of tenacity and stubbornness or the degree to which these qualities contributed to his almost inevitable martyrdom.

Many inconsistencies in all these accounts remain unresolved. No one seems to have bothered to check the military records or otherwise tried to find the truth of Mendes's claims about the past of Euclides Távora, the former Communist and army lieutenant who befriended him when he was young. Távora told Chico Mendes that he had been part of the Prestes Col-

---

[12]Parliamentary Investigation Committee for the Amazon, statement of João Alves Filho, Minister of the Interior, Department of Communications Publication No. 27/89, Brasília, April 19, 1989, especially 16–17.

umn, the insurgent forces led by the Communist Luís Carlos Prestes in 1923 on a three-year, eight-thousand-mile odyssey through the interior of Brazil. But Távora's participation seems unlikely, since he would have been far too young at the time. When Shoumatoff interviewed Prestes shortly before his death, the Communist leader, then ninety-one, said he had never heard of Euclides Távora.

It is also odd that Távora should have been living clandestinely in 1962—the Brazilian military coup was two years later and although the Communist Party was illegal at the time (between 1947 and 1985) the Goulart regime was perceived to be sympathetic to the left (this after all was the justification put forward by the military for its overthrow). Chico Mendes, according to Cowell, also said he had met Che Guevara on his way to Bolivia, but no one else reports this claim. A former wife and daughter also turned up after Mendes's death to lay claim to the Mendes legacy, much to the surprise of Mendes's ecological colleagues from North America.

The most perplexing aspect about Chico Mendes was his relationship with Mauro Sposito, the head of the Federal Police in Acre. The Federal Police is one of the few police organizations in Brazil that are perceived to be fairly honest. (It was for this reason that President Collor appointed Romeu Tuma, head of the Federal Police, to be the chief Brazilian tax collector.) When criticized for his lack of response to the threats against Mendes, Sposito published a letter in *A Gazeta* of Rio Branco saying that Chico Mendes was a police informer—an accusation that no one apart from Augusta Dwyer, who categorically dismisses the idea, seems to want even to consider. In view of extensive surveillance to which the left was subjected by the Brazilian secret services, it seems unlikely that the Brazilian authorities would not know whether this was true. Mauro Sposito in 1991 was serving as chief assistant to the head of the Federal Police in Brasília.

It is, in any case, impossible to find a clear and consistent account of Mendes's political career in any of these books. That Mendes was a "forest ecologist" is an image rejected by Hecht and Cockburn, who see Mendes as "an extremely radical political militant" who had at the core of his program a demand "for popular control of the means of production and distribution of forest commodities, along with the provision of financial credits to producers rather than middlemen." It is obviously no accident that Chico Mendes called his daughter Elenira, "in homage to another Elenira, a young woman of courage who gave up her life in an attempt to liberate the Brazilian people," as Márcio Souza put it in his book. Elenira Rezende de Souza Nazareth was a Maoist guerrilla from the PCdoB, the splinter Communist Party of Brazil, with which Mendes had been clandestinely affiliated in the late 1970s, and she was killed in the Tocantins-Araguaia combat zone in 1972. She was "famous for her marksmanship," according to Revkin, who heard that "she invariably killed her target with a rifle shot between the eyes."[13]

Chico Mendes's son was named Sandino after the Nicaraguan guerrilla leader. Alex Shoumatoff was apparently shocked to realize that Chico Mendes was no "Albert Schweitzer, which is how the Environmental Defense Fund . . . tried to portray him in one of their fund-raising letters . . ." but a "revolutionary, a warrior . . . In the United States . . . Mendes would have been considered a pinko tree hugger and a radical labor leader." His philosophy, according to Hecht and Cockburn, "had the concrete elements of a socialist ecology—the only ecology that can save the Amazon and its inhabitants."

Andrew Revkin is the writer most taken by the idea of "extractive reserves," and he depends mainly on Mary Allegretti, Adrian Cowell, and Stephen Schwartzman for his information. Márcio Souza has only contempt for what he calls "extractives," which he dismisses as a product of the "colonizing arrogance of those who say they are the defenders of the Amazon forest but pollute and destroy the environment in Alaska or corrode the forests of Europe with acid rain." Yet here, too, the rhetoric is misleading. Souza sees the hand of the multinationals behind these disasters. So do Hecht and Cockburn. But as the Belém-based journalist Lucio Flavio Pinto points out, the recent history of American multinational investment in the economy of the Amazon is much more an example of the retreat of U.S. enterprise before the new economic power of Europe and, most especially, Japan.[14] Anthony Hall, in his excellent book *Developing Amazonia*, which I discussed in the previous chapter, argues that the foreign and especially the U.S. role in the Amazon economy has not been decisive.[15]

The emphasis of such writers as Hecht and Cockburn on the multinationals, not to mention the American government, seems somewhat misplaced when one considers the scale of the disasters the Brazilians create on their own. Hecht and Cockburn are so anxious to find American villains that they misidentify the former State Department official (and currently my colleague at the Council on Foreign Relations) Richard Murphy as the American diplomat allegedly present at the interrogation of a political prisoner who had been tortured in Recife in 1968. Ambassador Murphy, in fact, has never set foot in Brazil. Hecht and Cockburn also claim that "U.S. support for the generals remained constant," but this will come

[13]Elenira Nazareth was killed after her capture by the army. See Elio Gaspari, *A Ditadura Escancarada*, vol. 2 of *As Ilusões Armadas* (São Paulo: Companhia das Letras, 2002). Gaspari provides a detailed account of this conflict.

[14]*Jornal Pessoal*, No. 64, July 1990.

[15]Anthony L. Hall, *Developing Amazonia: Deforestation and Social Conflict in Brazil's Carajás Programme* (Manchester and New York: Manchester University Press, 1989).

as a considerable surprise to former President Jimmy Carter and Patricia Derian, Carter's assistant secretary of state for human rights, who successfully brought pressure on the Brazilian military regime to release political prisoners.

Equally odd is a passage in Shoumatoff's book quoting Robert Redford, who bought the film rights to Shoumatoff's article on Mendes in *Vanity Fair*, to the effect that Redford "wanted to play the bad guy, the ruthless American manager of a multinational project." If so, he has the wrong screenplay and would be better off speaking to Anthony Hall. In fact, the ecological and social crisis in Brazil was caused by some of the same factors that led to the ecological disasters in Russia and Eastern Europe: failed overcentralized planning, rigidly organized management, private greed and special privileges, corrupt and ineffective justice at the grass roots, as well as permeating, callous disregard by the rich for the poor. In some ways the Amazon might have been better off if the multinationals had been more heavily involved. International companies are vulnerable to pressure from environmental activists for some of the same reasons that the World Bank and Inter-American Bank are vulnerable. Brazilian corporations, especially state companies, are less subject to such pressure and because of the vast sums at stake from their involvement in road, railroad, and dam building and in mining are notoriously involved in the corruption of political decision making.

The central point about the crisis in the Amazon is that it is a story where the heroes and the villains are Brazilians; the struggle is a Brazilian struggle, and it will be resolved, if it is to be resolved, by Brazilians. The key question about the members of the Alves da Silva family who killed Chico Mendes is not whether they were the assassins; it is whether they were hired to do the job and by whom. If there was indeed an "authorized" contract to kill Chico Mendes, then it was probably his efforts to block funds for the Acre roadway that caused it. This was an action that affected large interests, the hope of the eventual linkup to the Pacific, the value of tens of thousands of acres accumulated as speculative investments. As Philip Fearnside, an ecologist and longtime resident in Amazônia, has pointed out, "Whenever a road is built or improved in Amazônia, the value of nearby land immediately multiplies by as much as a factor of 10, if not more."[16] Understandably, some of those who hoped to benefit from the new highway were among those who dismissed Mendes's death as a "personal matter," a local dispute in which neither large interests nor outsiders were involved. As Acre UDR president João Branco said, "Darly was backed into a corner; like a trapped animal. He had no choice but to kill Chico."

---

[16]Philip M. Fearnside, "A Prescription for Slowing Deforestation in Amazônia," *The Environment* 31, no. 4 (May 1989): 18.

This in effect was the opinion of the court that convicted the Alves da Silvas in December 1990.

Zuenir Ventura, one of Brazil's best journalists, visited the only witness to have heard the Alves da Silva family talk of plans to kill Mendes, a boy named Genesio, then thirteen years old, who was virtually unprotected when Ventura found him, although supposedly under police protection. "It seemed to me," Ventura concluded, "that Xapuri was like the town in the movie *Mississippi Burning* but without the resources of the FBI, and a crazy idea occurred to me: why, instead of bringing in two environmentalists, not bring instead the two Federal agents?"[17] Ventura in fact took upon himself the protection of the child until the trial took place. Genesio's evidence was crucial to the guilty verdict.

VII

Márcio Souza is right, however, when he insists on the need to see the Amazônia crisis in its wider Brazilian political and social setting. The international attention that Chico Mendes case has received grew in part from the links he had forged with the environmentalists. But the Chico Mendes story also leaped to international attention because his death coincided with the vast holocaust of 1988 throughout the Amazon basin, where the brutal burning season was graphically pictured by satellite photography at a time when the Northern Hemisphere was also experiencing forest fires on an unprecedented scale. The outcry brought results. The Brazilian government cut back on the credits that had fueled the vast conversion to pasture, and began to use the satellite images provided by the Brazilian Institute for Space Research (INPE) to pinpoint fires and find those shown to be burning illegally.

But these were palliatives. The forestry patrols had a handful of helicopters and aircraft, whereas the ranchers and *garimpeiros* had hundreds. Still it was a beginning. In 1989 Brazil held its first popular election for the presidency in almost thirty years and the campaign pitted the leader of the Workers' Party, Lula, against a young governor of the northeastern state of Alagoas, Fernando Collor de Mello. Lula, backed by an alliance of unions, church-based communities, and intellectuals, came close to victory, but he was defeated in the second round by Collor. The leader of the UDR, the ranchers organization, had come in in tenth place, with fewer votes than the candidate of the Brazilian Communist Party.

During his presidential campaign, Collor dismissed the ecological complaints against Brazil as outside interference, but on his European tour before his inauguration he was shocked by the depth and anger of world

---

[17]Ventura, ibid.

opinion on the question of the Amazon—criticism he ran into everywhere, including a public rebuke from Prince Charles two days before his visit to London. The ending of government loans and tax credits diminished the burn off, and climatic consideration may also have improved the situation since there seem to have been fewer fires after 1988. The figures from the Brazilian Institute for Space Research (INPE) in 1991 showed a 25 percent drop in burning in the period of July to September 1990 in comparison with the same period in 1989, though the diminution has been less impressive in Acre and in Rondônia, where the number of fires actually increased.[18]

Collor then appointed the most outspoken and famous of Brazil's ecological activists, José Lutzenberger, to be the secretary of state for the environment. He also appointed another outspoken critic of Brazil's development policies, the rector of the University of São Paulo, the Brazilian physicist José Goldemberg, to become secretary of science and technology. In this position, Goldemberg sent shock waves through the military establishment by publicly acknowledging Brazil's nuclear program and opening up to the press the deep pits at Cachimbo in the central Amazon, pits intended for testing nuclear weapons. These moves prompted Adrian Cowell, Lutzenberger's good friend and promoter, to proclaim the 1990s to be "the decade of the environment in Brazil." Cowell's television series *The Decade of Destruction*, which was shown in Europe and North America in 1990, concluded on a very optimistic note portraying Collor as a born-again hero of the environment.[19]

In 1992 Brazil hosted the United Nations Conference on Environment and Development. This gave some incentive to environmental good behavior. But the decline in the rate of forest destruction may also be a result of a general economic downturn in Brazil. The Brazilian government was then in the midst of bitter negotiations with private banks over Brazil's vast foreign debt, and the favorable comments on the environment from Brazilian officials who a year before were attacking the environmentalists as foreign mercenaries might have been part of a deliberate policy to seek allies in the attempt to reach a more favorable settlement with foreign creditors.

There is a danger in romanticizing the idea of extractive reserves and the power of an alliance of "forest people." The market for Brazilian forest-extracted rubber now depends entirely on government price supports.

---

[18]"Chamas apagadas," *Veja*, January 9, 1991, 44–45. According to figures in *Veja*, April 7, 1999, 111, forest destruction in 1992 was 13,786 square kilometers; 14,896 in 1994; 29,059 in 1995; 18,161 in 1996; and 13,277 in 1997. Another alarming five-year high was reached in 2000; INPE figures released in May 2001 show that nearly 20,000 square kilometers of forest were cleared in 2000; see: http://www.inpe.br/.
[19]Adrian Cowell, *The Decade of Destruction: The Crusade to Save the Amazon Rainforest* (New York: H. Holt, 1990).

With the opening up of the Brazilian economy and the encouragement of plantation rubber elsewhere in Brazil, such subsidies will do no more than artificially prop up a system that until the last decade was universally condemned as highly exploitative of the workers involved.[20] The key promoters of the idea are not unaware of this vulnerability. Mary Allegretti herself recognizes that "because long-term prospects of wild rubber in the Brazilian economy are not bright . . . the establishment of extractive reserves should be accompanied by policies aimed at . . . promoting exploitation of other rain forest products."[21] To concentrate exclusively on the reserves also diverts attention from the scale complexity, and grave global consequences of the ecological disaster elsewhere in the region.

The Carajás region of the eastern Amazon, for example, absorbs vast sums of money, and huge construction companies and powerful political interests are determined to see it enlarged at great environmental cost. Armies of public relations professionals and lobbyists are deployed both within Brazil and outside it on behalf of these interests. Here the problems are less easily reduced to the primary colors of a "Chico Mendes story," since they are the result of the vast expansion of a frontier that is no longer under government control and that is driven by the hunger for land and for gold, each of which promises opportunities to the landless and poverty stricken. These inescapable circumstances make solutions to the ecological problems of Amazônia all the more difficult.[22]

The bishop of Acre was not hopeful:

> Once the trial [of Mendes's assassins] is over the issue will be seen by the public to be resolved and the attention will move on. The world must realize that there are thousands of Chico Mendeses.[23]

The 1991 Americas Watch report on rural violence was a sad reminder of how little changed since the 1988 Amnesty International report, which

---

[20]See comments by Mac Margolis in "False Visions of the Amazon," *Journal of Commerce*, July 28, 1990.

[21]Mary Allegretti, in Anthony B. Anderson, ed., *Alternatives to Deforestation: Steps toward Sustainable Use of the Amazon Rain Forest* (New York: Columbia University Press, 1990), 259.

[22]An excellent listing of over a hundred organizations concerned with the ecology of the Amazon, describing their objectives, programs, special needs, and resources, including addresses for them in both South and North America and in Europe, is provided by the Rainforest Action Network in *Amazonia: Voices from the Rainforest: A Resource and Action Guide*, ed. Angela Gennino, (San Francisco: Rainforest Action Network; Amazonia Film Project, 1990), 398–404.

[23]Cited by Christina Lamb in "The Forest Martyr," *Weekend Financial Times*, December 8–9, 1990.

described how cheap life remained in the Brazilian backlands.[24] The warnings of Amnesty preceded by three months Chico Mendes's assassination. The Americas Watch report's publication in January 1991 coincided with the killing of a union leader whose life Americas Watch had specifically warned was in danger.

Ironically, the road Mendes opposed has now been rerouted through Xapuri and Brasiléia and on to the Peruvian frontier, much to the delight of the rubber tappers who control much of the land in the region and hope to benefit from it. And Mendes's widow has used some of the money she received for the film rights to *The Chico Mendes Story* to buy a small ranch, notwithstanding the criticism of ranching and its ecological effects by Mendes and his environmentalist allies.[25] It is here, regrettably, that the mystification of the Mendes case, the view that the situation has improved as a result of his martyrdom, and the sordid squabbles over the Mendes legacy create a smoke screen that obstructs rather than encourages any resolution of the incalculable disaster that is unfolding inexorably in the Amazon.[26]

---

[24]*Rural Violence in Brazil: January 1991, An Americas Watch Report* (New York: Human Rights Watch, 1991).

[25]Jan Rocha, "Mendes and His Murderers," *TLS*, January 11, 1991, 7. See also "A vida nova de Ilzamar" in *Veja*, December 12, 1990, 34.

[26]In the government of Luiz Inácio Lula da Silva which took office on January 1, 2003, Marina Silva, who was co-founder with Chico Mendes of the CUT affiliate in Acre, became minister of the environment.

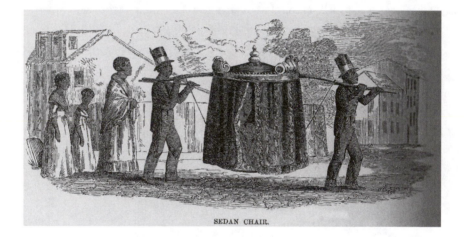

SEDAN CHAIR.

CHAPTER 13

The Two Brazils

"We progress at night when the politicians sleep."
—Brazilian saying

As 1998 began, Brazilians were full of confidence that their country was poised to surge into the twenty-first century, that perhaps it was finally on the road to becoming the great power many had long imagined it would be. In 1994, Finance Minister Fernando Henrique Cardoso, a former Marxist professor of sociology turned neoliberal reformer, had masterminded a sweeping currency reform—the Real Plan—which joined other liberalizing measures and thrust Brazil, with the world's eighth-largest economy, into the forefront of the global trend toward open markets and free trade. Not only were Brazilians prospering but their decade-old democracy had found solid footing. Later in 1994, Cardoso was rewarded for his efforts as finance minister with the presidency, becoming Brazil's second directly elected civilian chief executive since the military surrendered power in 1985.

I

Then came the global economic crisis, beginning with the currency collapses in Southeast Asia in 1997, escalating with the Russian defaults in August 1998, and landing with a crash on Brazil shortly after. Having failed, despite its many other successes, to get its fiscal house in order, Brazil found itself dangerously dependent on infusions of foreign capital to finance its trade and government deficits, struggling to stay afloat even as nervous investors fled with their dollars.

President Cardoso, who won a second term in October of 1998 in the midst of the crisis, was forced to take drastic measures to cut government spending, increase taxes, and reduce indebtedness. In return, Brazil won a $41.5 billion bailout orchestrated by the International Monetary Fund (IMF)—and the guarantee of more painful measures to come, as well as a recession that promises to be long and deep. Cardoso, who was, in his Marxist days, a high priest of dependency theory—the notion that the developed capitalist nations would forever hold the less developed economies in thrall—must have wondered if he had been so wrong after all.

Yet Brazil's decade of political and economic success changed the country in certain irreversible ways. And the changes will, paradoxically, complicate its recovery. Prosperity, the opening up of political life, and the expansion of educational opportunities brought with them a deeper political engagement by the population, and the emergence of unions, political parties, and a variety of grassroots organizations. To a degree that is unprecedented in the country's history, Brazilians found their political voice, and they began to rethink what it means to be Brazilian.

IMF-mandated policies thus risk bringing about headlong confrontation between the Brazil of bankers and businessmen and a new Brazil of political and social activism. One thing is certain: the Brazilian government can no longer rule by dictate or from the top down, whatever it promises the IMF.

How successfully these two Brazils work out their collective future will be one of the most dramatic stories of the first decade of the twenty-first century, and not only for Brazil. Failure in this South American giant will profoundly affect the reforms under way throughout Latin America as well as the assumptions on which the new international economic order has been founded. It is precisely for this reason that then U.S. Treasury Secretary Robert Rubin declared that Brazil is "too big to be allowed to fail."

Brazil for many foreigners is still the land of the bossa nova and "The Girl from Ipanema," but Brazilians themselves are becoming irritated with their country's willful folkloric self-image as forever young, bronzed, and beach bound, oblivious to the past and giddily committed to a future as ephemeral as the country's torrid *telenovelas*. Antonio Carlos Jobim, author of that great lyrical celebration of Ipanema beach and the graceful passing beauty of its denizens, once said that Brazil is "not for beginners." And he was right.

Brazilians still want to have fun, to be sure, and no one is proposing the abolition of Carnival. Yet as Brazil has embraced democracy, bringing new voices into the political and social arenas, Brazilians are beginning to recognize that getting to the future involves understanding the past.

This new concern with history is reflected in the recent vogue for restoring colonial architecture—some of the most extraordinary examples in the Americas—which was once allowed to rot or was simply swept away to make room for modern buildings. In Bahia and São Luís in Maranhão, splendid baroque churches and eighteenth-century townhouses have been magnificently restored; old forts and ruins of Jesuit missions along the southern frontier have become popular tourist attractions. But these buildings are artifacts of the traditional Brazilian history, while the past that Brazil is rediscovering is replete with contradictions.

Brazil's transition to national independence in 1822, unlike that of its Spanish American neighbors, preserved great continuity in institutions— the military, the law, and administration. It was led, after all, by the eldest son of the Portuguese monarch, who promptly named himself Emperor Pedro I. Portuguese-speaking America, unlike its Spanish-speaking neighbors, also avoided fragmentation into numerous new republics. Independent Brazil emerged as a monarchy with its huge territory intact. The state as it developed was, as a consequence, highly centralizing, and the national mythology it spawned depicted the country as a product almost exclusively of the coastal Portuguese and the imperial inheritance.

But today Brazilians are learning a new history. It brings into focus the unruly Brazil of the escaped slaves who held out for decades in the backlands of what is today the state of Alagoas against the Portuguese in the seventeenth century; the bloody uprisings in the Amazon, Pernambuco, and the southern borderlands of Rio Grande do Sul against the Brazilian Empire in the early nineteenth century; and the extraordinary messianic communities of the semiarid interior of Bahia brutally suppressed a century ago and immortalized by the great Brazilian essayist Euclides da Cunha in his *Rebellion in the Backlands*, and more recently by the Peruvian novelist Mario Vargas Llosa in his *War at the End of the World*. The historian Laura de Mello e Sousa calls this the Brazil of the "unclassified ones"—the majority of the Brazilian population, neither white nor black, neither slave master nor slave in origin, not landowners but squatters and smallholders, not only Portuguese but Italians, Germans, Japanese, Arabs, and Jews, as well as mestizos, mulattos, Indians, and Africans, not only bankers but small entrepreneurs and shopkeepers, not just bishops but African *orixás* and Pentecostal pastors.

The recognition of the "unclassified ones" has been accompanied by the emergence of movements among the landless, the indigenous peoples, industrial workers, Protestants, and others. African Brazilians are perhaps the most important group now finding a political voice.[1] For centuries,

---

[1] Racial self-definition is a complex matter in Brazil, where a very wide range of racial categories between black and white has traditionally been recognized. The count of "African Brazilians" varies from a high of 120 million, using a U.S. definition that includes all persons with some degree of African ancestry, to Brazil's official 1991 census estimate, which listed only 7 million blacks (*pretos*) and classified 62 million Brazilians as browns (*pardos*). Essentially in stark contrast to the traditional U.S. classification, being black in Brazil means having no white ancestors. Brazil was the foremost recipient of African slaves in the Western Hemisphere.

they retained a resilient pluralistic religious and cultural presence at the core of Brazilian society, but one barely recognized in the corridors of elite power until very recently. São Paulo elected its first black mayor, Celso Pitta, in 1996, and President Cardoso brought Edson Arantes do Nascimento, the great Brazilian soccer star universally known as Pelé, into his cabinet as minister of sport. The secretary of social welfare in the government of Luiz Inácio Lula da Silva which took office in January 2003, Benedita da Silva, is an African Brazilian born in a Rio favela (shantytown). As more Afro-Brazilians have moved into the middle class, black faces have also appeared more regularly in advertisements and the press.

Brazil's rediscovery of history challenges above all the peculiar legacy that has since the eighteenth century allowed the country's rulers to graft the imperative of authoritarianism onto their vision of the future. It was this mind-set that made the French positivists so attractive to the military officers who overthrew the monarchy in 1889, and to the generals who seized control in 1964. It is perfectly summed up in the motto emblazoned across Brazil's national flag: *Ordem e Progresso* (Order and Progress). Democracy in Brazil has all too often been seen as the enemy of progress, the harbinger of anarchy, disunion, and backwardness. That, it seems clear, will no longer do.

Brazil's transformation grows in part out of its recent prosperity. When I first came to Rio de Janeiro as a student in the mid-1960s, the country was still largely rural, with short life expectancy, large families, low per capita income, and a high illiteracy rate. By the 1990s, Brazil, with a population of more than 160 million, had become one of the world's largest economies, with a per capita income of more than $5,000. Family size dropped dramatically, from 6 children per family in the 1970s to 2.5 in the mid-1990s. It had become a largely urban country. Brazil's two million cars in 1970 increased in number to twenty-six million, its TV sets from four million to thirty-one million. Infant mortality decreased from 118 per 1,000 in 1970 to 17 per 1,000, and illiteracy greatly diminished.

The Brazilian states of São Paulo and Rio Grande do Sul, if they stood alone, would be numbered among the richest forty-five nations on earth. The economy of Rio Grande do Sul, the southernmost state, abutting Argentina and Uruguay, was built on European immigration and cattle. The state of São Paulo has a gross national product larger than Argentina's, and São Paulo City is a megalopolis with a population of 15 million and a vibrant financial, cultural, and business life; the state-supported university of São Paulo is a world-class institution. Like several of Brazil's larger cities, São Paulo has a lively press; dailies such as the *Folha de São Paulo*, the grand old *Estado de São Paulo*, the business-oriented *Gazeta Mercantil* and the new *Valor Econômico* are as articulate, critical, and influential as any quality newspaper in Europe or North America. Brazil also boasts one of the world's most successful television networks, TV Globo, and one of its most aggressive publishing empires, Editora Abril, proprietor of the mass-circulation newsweekly *Veja*, which reaches more than four million readers, all of them full-fledged members of the emerging global consumer order.

II

A large segment of the population, perhaps 40 million people, however, remains in poverty, with incomes below $50 a month. Brazil's income disparities are among the worst in the world. The most impoverished 20 percent of Brazilians receive a mere 2 percent of the national wealth, while the richest 20 percent receive 60 percent. Festering shantytowns surround the large urban centers, and Rio's favelas are especially notorious for crime and violence. This is the Brazil of half-starved children playing outside makeshift shacks in dusty northeastern villages and smudge-faced urchins knocked out by glue sniffing, huddled together under benches in São Paulo's principal downtown squares. But extreme poverty is now concentrated in the semiarid northeast of Brazil, where drought and disease have long been curses of biblical dimensions. Both were greatly aggravated in 1998 by the effects of El Niño. Brazilians are proud to call themselves a racial as well as a political democracy, and are irritated when scholars and activists point out that poverty is disproportionately concentrated among the Afro-Brazilian population. In fact, whites on average earn two and a half times as much as blacks. As veteran Brazil watcher Ronald Schneider notes, out of 14,000 priests, 378 bishops and archbishops, and seven cardinals, the Brazilian Catholic Church has only 200 nonwhite priests. Similar disproportions can be seen in Brazil's diplomatic service and military officer corps.

Nevertheless, the poor did see their lives improve during most of the 1990s, with large numbers of people moving up from the bottom ranks of society into the emerging middle class. The credit for this change belongs to Cardoso's Real Plan, introduced in 1994 while he was finance minister under President Itamar Franco. Confronted with economic chaos and feverish inflation, Cardoso created a new currency, the real, linked to the U.S. dollar, with its value pegged to permit only minimal depreciation. Inflation plunged from more than 2,000 percent annually to single digits, with instant tonic effects felt throughout the country.

As the currency stabilized, Brazilians had money to spend for refrigerators, televisions, and clothing. Analysts looking at consumer trends over the first six years of the Real Plan reckoned that some 19 million people moved from basic subsistence into the lower level of the Brazilian middle class, which by the year 2000 embraced some 58 million people. Those who remained poor benefited as well, finding more money in their pockets for meat, chicken, eggs, corn, and beans. Their income increased by 30 percent during 1995–1996 alone. In earlier decades, poverty pushed millions of Brazilians from the hinterlands into São Paulo and Rio de Janeiro and out into the frontier on the western fringes of the Amazon basin. During the 1990s, prosperity allowed many of the smaller cities in the interior of Brazil to flourish, attracting some five million mostly middle-class people searching for a better quality of life.

The spread of prosperity and population over the face of Brazil has made it both a more homogenous and a more complex society. For four and a half centuries, most of Brazil's population remained around key seaports close to the zones where sugar, cotton, cacao, coffee, and other major export commodities are grown. Brazil's first historian, Friar Vicente do Salvador, writing in 1627, said that the Portuguese settlers and their African slaves "scratched at the seacoast like crabs." The first Europeans to penetrate the vast interior were intrepid missionaries, explorers, and ruthless Portuguese frontiersmen traveling up the Amazon River and the tributaries that run south into the La Plata basin. This huge geographical area, larger than the contiguous United States, remained for centuries a hollow frontier, incorporating vast unexplored territories and many thousands of indigenous peoples unknown to the Portuguese governors and viceroys who ruled until 1808, or to the Portuguese monarchs who held court in Rio de Janeiro between 1808 and 1821, or to the Brazilian emperors Pedro I and Pedro II, who succeeded them after the declaration of Brazil's independence from Portugal in 1822, or to the generals and civilian politicians who established the United States of Brazil in 1889.

Yet slowly and inexorably the hollow frontier was filled in, as cattle ranchers moved inland from the coast and squatters established themselves between the plantation-dominated littoral and the backlands. These independent-minded mixed-race families lived largely outside the juridical formulas that elsewhere defined and contained both Portuguese masters and African slaves, but they helped root Brazilian society in the Brazilian landscape.

In the eighteenth century, the first great modern gold rush brought European settlers, slaves, and, belatedly, government, into the mountainous interior of what is today the state of Minas Gerais. Today the spectacular churches and mountain towns they constructed are among Brazil's most precious colonial heritage; here the magnificently carved figures of the Apostles by the crippled mulatto sculptor Aleijadinho stand as marvels of this age of extravagance and piety. In the nineteenth century, large-scale coffee bean plantations were developed in São Paulo and Paraná in the south, reviving the demand for African slaves. After the abolition of slavery in 1888, immigrant laborers poured in from Italy and southern Germany, joined in the 1920s by newcomers from Japan. By the early twentieth century, a cotton textile industry was established in São Paulo, augmented in the 1960s by steel and automobile industries, creating an industrial urban working class and a powerful business elite.

Both civilian and military rulers saw the development of the interior as the means to Brazil's future greatness. In the late 1950s, President Juscelino Kubitschek forced through the extraordinary plans for the futuristic new capital and federal district of Brasília, set down like a spaceship on the largely uninhabited high plateau of Goiânia in the center-west of the country. Modernistic bowls, towers, and upturned cups contained the Congress and its functionaries, dwarfed against a backdrop of enormous sky and red earth. Soon thereafter, the generals who ousted Kubitschek's successor, President João Goulart, and established one of Latin America's longest-lived military regimes (1964–1985) embarked on a series of grandiose schemes to develop the Amazon. Ignoring the established river-based lifelines, they drove roads straight through the tropical rain forest and built huge dams to tame the Amazon's tributaries and flood the river plains, often with disastrous ecological consequences. The highways brought with them economic exploitation and its predictable companions, greedy speculators and corrupt and callous bureaucrats, as well as a plague of infectious diseases. The forced contact with the outside world was disastrous for the remaining 250,000 Brazilian Indians, the majority living in the Amazon forests. The long-isolated Yanomami were hard hit with malaria as 10,000 prospectors invaded their territory in the late 1980s.

The military regime also poured money into the expansion of higher education, substituting more pragmatic American approaches for the old French-influenced disciplines that had produced Cardoso and other scholars. But this only created a new generation enamored of democracy as well as technology. Purging and exiling Cardoso (who was seen as a dangerous Marxist despite the fact that he was the son and grandson of generals) and other professors from the University of São Paulo and other major institutions also had paradoxical consequences. It provoked U.S. foundations, notably the Ford Foundation, to invest heavily in a parallel system of private research centers in Brazil that would later provide a haven and political base for the democratic opposition.

Meanwhile, the exiles were welcomed on American campuses. Cardoso, who lived in Chile, and later in France, became a visiting professor at the University of California, Berkeley, and Stanford University, and spent two years at the Institute for Advanced Study in Princeton, New Jersey, working closely with that wise and brilliant pragmatist, the veteran economist and proponent of reform by "muddling through," Albert O. Hirschman. When he returned to Brazil in 1970, Cardoso, like many of the other upper-middle-class exiles of his generation, had become thoroughly cosmopolitan, skeptical of Marxism, well connected in the wider world, and thoroughly knowledgeable about the workings of the U.S. political and economic systems.

III

Momentous changes were also taking place at the grass roots within Brazil. Throughout the late 1970s and early 1980s, trade unions that had been founded in the 1930s during the dictatorship of Getúlio Vargas on an Italian fascist model as syndicates dependent on the state shook off government control. Most formidable was the metalworkers' union in São Paulo. The unions nourished the emergence of a new Workers' Party (PT) in 1980 and a National Trade Union Confederation (CUT) in 1983. Together they provided a base for the charismatic Luiz Inácio da Silva, popularly known as Lula, who rose through union ranks from the shop floor and awakened hopes that he would become a Brazilian Lech Walesa. Lula ran three times unsuccessfully for the presidency, but in 2002 made a historic breakthrough, and by 61 percent of the popular vote, a full 22.5 percentage points more than the government candidate, former health minister José Serra, was decisively elected Brazil's leader.[2]

The Workers' Party thrives in the industrialized south of Brazil, and by the 1998 election had gained control of the important governorship of Rio Grande do Sul with the election of PT candidate Olívio Dutra. But the organization of workers was not restricted to the industrial zones. Threatened by the encroachment of cattle ranchers and loggers, rubber tappers on the Amazon frontier began to mobilize in the 1980s to protect their livelihood. Like the metalworkers in São Paulo, these poor workmen produced a formidable grassroots leader from among their ranks, Chico Mendes. His rubber tappers' organization linked up with Brazilian social activists and international environmental groups to pressure the Brazilian government for recognition of their grievances and to carve out ecological reserves to protect the forests on which their way of life depended. They also developed critical networks of international supporters in Europe and the United States who were able to pressure international lending agencies such as the Inter-American Development Bank and the World Bank to incorporate ecological concerns into their decisions about loans to Brazil.

---

[2]See Kenneth Maxwell, "Brazil: Lula's Prospects," *New York Review of Books*, December 5, 2002. For the early years of the PT see Margaret E. Keck, *The Workers' Party and Democratization in Brazil* (New Haven: Yale University Press, 1992).

The indigenous communities, facing a life-and-death struggle for survival as the outside world pressed in on their remaining refuges in the Amazon basin, also found a voice during the 1980s. With the support of international organizations such as the Cambridge, Massachusetts–based Cultural Survival, tribes such as the Kayapó and Xavante pressed for recognition and protection against the freelance gold prospectors who were invading their forests and polluting their rivers with deadly mercury. A Xavante chief, Mário Juruna, was elected federal deputy in 1983, and Ailton Krenak became well known in Brasília and among the international human rights networks.

While the hierarchy of the Catholic Church was divided on its approach to political activism, grassroots clergy strongly influenced by liberation theology provided organizational support to Brazil's many new reform movements. Protestant fundamentalists have also emerged as a force in the Brazilian social and religious landscape. Small, impeccable, white Pentecostal meeting houses now dot the landscape. The Universal Church of the Kingdom of God, founded in 1977 by a Pentecostal pastor, Edir Macedo, claims more than 3.5 million members and receives more than $700 million in annual donations. It owns Brazil's third-largest TV network and thirty radio stations. As it is often said in Brazil: "Catholics opted for the poor; the poor opted for the evangelicals."

Many Protestant converts come from the lower levels of the new urban middle class. Protestant evangelicals practice a faith of personal salvation and promote a frugal lifestyle emphasizing thrift and family. They are seen as a conservative force; at the local level, however, their organizations have quickly shifted to municipal activism, seeking improved water supplies and better services, which has propelled them increasingly into politics. The evangelical caucus in the Brazilian Congress had reached thirty-five by 1998, and an evangelical bishop in Rio de Janeiro, Carlos Rodrigues, has consistently received a huge vote in congressional elections. The former governor of the state of Rio de Janeiro and presidential candidate in 2002, Anthony Garotinho, is also an evangelical. Responding to the evangelical challenge, the Catholic Church in Brazil is now encouraging a powerful charismatic movement that is galvanizing many of the faithful in Brazil's cities. The charismatics, like the evangelicals, place a strong emphasis on family values, but they, like the Catholic hierarchy, are also critical of the harshness of Brazil's capitalist system.

Most threatening to Brazil's political elite and to its large rural landowners in particular has been the emergence of a powerful rural movement of the landless. Founded in Rio Grande do Sul in the mid-1980s, the Movimento dos Trabalhadores Rurais Sem Terra (Movement of Landless Rural Workers, MST) now has some five hundred thousand members, including all sorts of people from the margins of Brazilian society: the unemployed, migrant agricultural workers, the illiterate, slum dwellers, all people the traditional left believed it was impossible to organize, stimulated by Brazil's total failure for centuries to break the power of the great latifundios and bring about any meaningful land distribution. Less than 1 percent of farms, all over five hundred acres in dimension, account for 40 percent of all occupied farmlands in Brazil. The movement was also energized by the expulsion of many smallholders from their plots, especially in Rio Grande do Sul, Paraná, and Santa Catarina, by the mechanization of large-scale soya and wheat production in the 1980s. The MST is now the largest and best-organized social movement in Latin America, with successful cooperatives, a website, and extensive international contacts. Its members often take the law into their own hands, invading properties and setting up squatter settlements, sacking warehouses to obtain food, and challenging landowners. Almost as often they provoke violent reactions from *fazendeiros* (large landowners), local police, and hired gunmen.[3]

What the MST seeks is access to land and the breakup of the large estates, many of which remain undeveloped and unproductive, or are held for tax purposes or to draw government subsidies. Its ideology is an eclectic mix of revolutionary socialism and Catholic activism, as befits an organization built in large part by itinerant priests. Its most prominent leader is an economist named João Pedro Stédile, who did postgraduate work in Mexico and takes inspiration from the Mexican Zapatistas. He argues that the Brazilian elite is too "subservient to foreign interests"—an obvious swipe at the IMF and the forces of global capitalism as well as the former *dependentista*, Fernando Henrique Cardoso, while he was lodged in the futuristic presidential palace in Brasília.

Finally there is the Brazilian environmental movement, composed of some 800 organizations stirred into being by the uncontrolled destruction of the Amazon rain forest, ecological disasters in the grotesquely polluted chemical complex at Cubatão in São Paulo state, and rampant encroachment on the remnants of the once-lush Atlantic forests.

In 1998 forest fires in the Amazon region, aggravated by the impact of El Niño, were the worst on record, but the Cardoso administration did little to respond until the extent of the catastrophe became difficult to hide. The devastating drought in the northeast, another predictable consequence of El Niño, also received scant attention until famished peasants organized by the MST raided warehouses and occupied bank agencies and police stations. This finally caught the attention of the indifferent bureaucrats in the surreal world of Brasília, preoccupied with the purchase of expensive Oriental carpets for their offices so that "foreign visitors could be more ele-

---

[3]On the MST see Bernardo Mancano Fernandes, *A formação do MST no Brasil* (Petrópolis, R.J.: Editora Vozes, 2000).

gantly received," as a spokesman for the minister of communication explained to the *New York Times*. Not surprisingly, all these movements strike a raw chord with the "owners of power," as the brilliant Brazilian lawyer and social critic Raymundo Faoro so aptly put it. Owing to the overseas support the environmental movement receives, the Brazilian military views it as a pawn of foreign interests, part of a thinly disguised effort by the United States to take the Amazon away from Brazil. The military intelligence network closely monitors the activities of the MST, and President Cardoso's ministers often dismissed the movement as "enemies of modernity." It was similar attitudes that a hundred years ago led to the repression and slaughter in the backlands so brilliantly immortalized by Euclides da Cunha and Mario Vargas Llosa.

The great twentieth-century Brazilian historian Sérgio Buarque de Holanda defined a Brazilian as a "cordial" individual, and Brazilians are people of great and infectious charm. But where politics and social conflicts meet, their country can be a very violent place. It has many martyrs to prove it, among them Chico Mendes, gunned down in 1988 by cattle ranchers threatened by his rubber tappers' movement. More than a thousand labor leaders and grassroots peasant activists have been assassinated in Brazil since the mid-1980s. In much of the country the murderers of activists act with impunity. In November 1998, Miguel Pereira de Melo, the crusading Brazilian photojournalist, was killed by gunmen. He had recorded the 1996 massacre of landless peasants by military police and was about to testify at the trial of those officers.

IV

The subtler obstacles to pluralism may prove the hardest to overcome. Reform will require changing an oligarchic style of politics and an entrenched bureaucracy that have both skillfully deflected challenges for centuries. Indeed, the deals made to bring about the transition from military to civilian rule during the 1980s guaranteed the persistence in power of many old-line politicians, including preeminently the powerful Bahia political boss, former state governor and president of the Senate, Antônio Carlos Magalhães. ACM, as he is universally known, is a gregarious, tough, and single-minded political operator who proudly professes his admiration for Napoleon. Through most of the Cardoso administration he was as influential as ever, a pivotal figure in the coalition that supported Cardoso—an odd but very Brazilian twist of fate since Cardoso was precisely the sort of upper-class intellectual that Antônio Carlos Magalhães and other power brokers under the military regimes of the past most distrusted.

The bosses and bureaucrats have plenty to protect. The welfare and pension system, for example, does virtually nothing for the poorer workers but vastly benefits state functionaries. In 1996, Brazil had twenty-nine four-star generals on active duty and 5,000 people drawing generous pension checks at the four-star level, including far-flung relatives of dead and retired officers.

Brazil's formal political structure also makes reform excruciatingly difficult. It has twenty-seven state governors and more than 5,500 municipal mayors (*prefeitos*), many of whom have run up massive deficits which by tradition the federal government is expected to cover. The 1988 constitution obliges the central government to transfer a large share of tax revenues to the state governments and municipalities but without a commensurate shift of responsibility for government programs. The idea was to devolve power and encourage democracy. The result was to strengthen parochial interests and the local political bosses. These problems were aggravated by the Real Plan's success, since, during the years of high inflation, government deficits had miraculously disappeared as delayed payments wiped out obligations. But after 1994 such flimflams no longer worked, as money retained its value. The opening of the economy and the stabilization of the currency had some perverse effects as well. Many industrial workers were displaced as imports flooded the consumer market. Not only did the service sector expand, but many industrial workers were forced into the informal sector. Subsequently, unemployment increased dramatically.

Cardoso hoped to pass a half-dozen ambitious reform measures during his first term—from cutting public payrolls to rewriting tax laws—and, not surprisingly, all fell victim to constant dilution and delays. His major success, altering the constitution to allow for his own reelection, was bought at the high cost of also allowing state and local political bosses to run for reelection. They promptly opened the spending spigots to ensure victory at the polls, swelling public-sector debt to more than $300 billion in early 1998 and leaving Brazil pitifully vulnerable when the international crisis hit.

President Cardoso found it difficult to sustain the momentum of reform in his second term. Arrayed against him were the old corporatist interests, eager to protect the past and their own privileges, as well as the newly assertive groups such as the MST, which opposed Cardoso's policies.

Cardoso's popularity, though great enough to have reelected him with a clear majority in the October 1998 presidential election, was based almost entirely on the success of the Real Plan. He saw himself as a man of the center-left, an adherent of the new "third way" of Bill Clinton and Tony Blair, but was perceived by the public as being a political leader decisively of the center-right, the friend of bankers, industrialists, civil servants, and politicians rather than workers and the landless. As the realities of IMF-imposed austerity begin to hit home—Brazil's economy was already shrinking by the end of 1998—Cardoso found his popular support waning. He self-consciously steered away from the heady rhetoric of populism, avoided demagoguery, and preferred persuasion and compromise to executive decree, but his resolve was increasingly tested as his term in office drew to a close.

Lula lost the 1998 election in part because he chose to attack the Real Plan. But the 1998 elections also saw the emergence of middle-class Workers' Party leaders who spoke a language closer to that of the new social democrats of Europe, consciously avoiding the radical rhetoric of the shop floor. These Workers' Party representatives in Congress provided solid opposition to Cardoso's IMF-inspired policies over the course of his second term. The center-left political allies within Cardoso's own political family were alienated by his orthodox economic retrenchment, which cut deeply into the social programs Brazil so desperately needs. The president also found less support from powerful governors, especially since they were forced to bear the brunt of the budget cuts. Particularly troublesome was the newly elected governor of the important state of Minas Gerais, former president Itamar Franco, under whom, as finance minister, Cardoso implemented the Real Plan. The erratic Franco was still deeply resentful that Cardoso and not he got all the credit. In fact it was his repudiation of the debt of Minas Gerais with the federal government that provoked a major crisis in Brazil's international financing and the devaluation of the Real that shook Brazil in early 1999.[4] Nor will the protests of landless rural workers go away. Stédile in particular made no secret of his desire to "finish off the neoliberal model." Over the course of his second term the MST laid siege to the family rural estate of President Cardoso several times, going so far on one occasion as to invade the main house itself.

It is ironic that in the charged international economic climate in which Fernando Henrique Cardoso began his second term as president in 1999, the protection of the Real Plan, by plunging Brazil into recession, posed the greatest threat to the benefits it brought to many Brazilians. Yet posing one of the greatest challenges to the IMF-mandated program to satisfy the international markets are groups and forces within Brazil that barely existed before political and economic liberalization began in the early 1990s. The travails of the Brazilian economy—no matter where they lead—should not obscure the significant success story the rise of these new voices represents.

---

[4]See Kenneth Maxwell, "Brazil in Meltdown," *World Policy Journal* (Spring 1999), 25–33.

SCENE ON A COOLIE SHIP.

CHAPTER 14

Macao
Shadow Land

"Wishing to speak ill of their adversary, the Chinese will say:
'He's a man who makes a habit of going to Macao.'"
—Father Matteo Ricci, Peking, 1605

Fifty miles across the Pearl River estuary from Hong Kong lies the ancient city of Macao. First settled by the Portuguese in the 1550s, it was handed back to China on December 20, 1999. This tiny European enclave on the South China Sea played a small and long-forgotten role in U.S. history; on July 3, 1844, the first Chinese-American treaty, known as the Treaty of Wang Xia, was negotiated and signed here. In 1997 the Chinese made much of the fact that their recuperation of sovereignty over Hong Kong marked the final abrogation of the 1842 Chinese-British Treaty of Nanjing, whereby China had ceded Hong Kong to Queen Victoria "in perpetuity" and was forced to pay $12 million for having "obliged" the British to wage war on them, as well as compensation to the tune of an additional $6 million for the cost of the opium seized from British merchants and destroyed by the Chinese authorities—the original casus belli of the "Opium War."

In contrast, the Treaty of Wang Xia was not punitive; and the United States—with its own anticolonial past strongly in mind—acquired the same "most favored nation" status in China that the British enjoyed, not by force of arms but by convincing the Chinese that it sought no unfair advantage and, above all, did not seek territory.

In July 1844, Caleb Cushing, a congressman from Massachusetts and a forceful advocate for the China trade merchants of his state, and the Imperial commissioner Qiying met at the old Temple of Kun Iam, which today faces onto a busy avenue toward the center of the small peninsula on which Macao stands. At that time, the temple lay within the Chinese village of Wang Xia, just outside the seventeenth-century walls of Macao city but well inside the territory controlled by the Portuguese. Kun Iam, as she is known in Macao, is the Buddhist Kwan Yin, Goddess of Mercy and Queen of Heaven. The image of the goddess, dressed in the robes of a Chinese bride, is set above the altar table in the smoky inner third chamber of the temple, where, on a side wall, a long glass case contains the gold lacquer figures of eighteen Chinese wise men, including Marco Polo—whose statuette has bulging round eyes, a largish nose, and a small curly beard intended to denote his European origin. Beyond the temple's maze of shrines lies a garden with a round stone table, four simple granite stools, and a plaque written in Chinese that mark the spot where the treaty of "peace, amity, and commerce" was signed by Caleb Cushing and Qiying.

The Treaty of Wang Xia gave American cargo ships access to the five Chinese treaty ports, only recently forced open to foreigners as a result of the Opium War, and it also gave Americans the right to construct hospitals, churches, and cemeteries in China, a privilege the missionaries who served as Caleb Cushing's translators in Macao were especially anxious to obtain. The Imperial commissioner Qiying had been China's representative at the acrimonious Nanjing negotiations, and his large entourage of soldiers, servants, officials, and advisers was lodged at the Temple of Kun Iam during the negotiations with Cushing.

The Treaty of Wang Xia, which governed the American relationship with China until 1905, committed the United States and China "to a perfect reciprocity" and was concluded with the utmost cordiality in less than two weeks. As Qiying wrote to Cushing when inviting him to take "fruit and tea" at the temple of Kun Iam: "This conduct is vastly different from that of the English taking and keeping possession of Hong Kong. . . ."[1]

The British officials based in Hong Kong had implied that the Chinese could not be trusted to police their own agreement since it was insinuated in London that they had signed one document with the British, but then published a different version for the use of their own customs officials. Cushing thought it "a harsh construction to suspect the Chinese of such an act." The problem, he thought, had more to do with the "want of care on the part of the English translators." Daniel Webster, the U.S. secretary of state, had given Cushing careful instructions: "You are a messenger of peace, sent by the greatest power of America to the greatest empire in Asia to offer re-

---

[1]The Sino-American Treaty and documents can be found in Hunter Miller, ed., *Treaties and Other International Acts of the United States of America*, 4 (Washington, D.C.: GPO, 1934), 647–662.

spect and good will and to establish the means of friendly intercourse." It is a pity that no senior U.S. public official in recent decades has taken the short helicopter flight to Macao across the Pearl River estuary from Hong Kong and stopped by at the Kun Iam Temple. It would do no harm at all to think back to the Treaty of Wang Xia once in a while, or to the goodwill the United States could once count on, in its less bellicose days.

I

The territory of Macao today consists of a tiny, densely populated peninsula of just over two square miles and two islands: Taipa, of 2.2 square miles, and Coloane, of 3 square miles. Its population is about 430,000, of which 97 percent are Chinese. Lisbon had wanted the transfer of Macao to China to take place in 2007 and mark the four hundred and fiftieth anniversary of their settlement on the south China coast, but the Chinese wished to have the matter settled before the end of the millennium.[2] The British mandarins of Whitehall, who could not come to terms with the fact that the Portuguese flag would fly over Macao longer than the Union Jack flew over Hong Kong, and smarting from accusations that they blundered in their reading of Chinese intentions and "lost" Hong Kong prematurely, were quick to claim that the Portuguese had sold out to the Chinese long ago.[3] Sir Percy Craddock, former British ambassador to Beijing and adviser to Margaret Thatcher on China policy while she was prime minister, called Portuguese authority in Macao "a ghostly sham." The Portuguese in Macao, however, have been long used to such snootiness from the British, who often forget that they arrived in China as drug dealers, not democrats. The British inhabitants of Hong Kong in the 1850s called Macao "an unrecognized and unpermitted, but unchallenged squatting, on an undefined portion of Chinese territory."

In many ways they were right. Lisbon was always very far away and the Chinese very close at hand. Yet Macao had been most convenient to the British for the century before their own forceful annexation of Hong Kong. Prior to that date, the Chinese denied foreign merchants the right to remain year-round at the great trading city of Guangzhou (Canton), and Macao was absolutely essential to British merchants, or to any other European or American merchants for that matter, if they wanted an entrepôt from which to sell Indian opium and purchase Chinese tea. The ambiguity of Macao's status suited all parties.

---

[2]See Geoffrey C. Gunn, *Encountering Macau: A Portuguese City-State on the Periphery of China, 1557–1999* (Boulder, Colo.: Westview, 1996).
[3]"Did Britain's Diplomats Blunder?" *Economist*, May 17, 1997, 47–48.

The Portuguese arrived in the Pearl River estuary as early as 1513, although Macao itself was not settled by them until 1557. The initiative for its founding came from the merchants of Malacca, seized by Afonso de Albuquerque in 1511, giving the Portuguese a stronghold on the critical sea passage between the South China Sea and the Bay of Bengal. Initially, Macao's prosperity rested on its strategic location on the trade route from Goa through Malacca to Japan. No less important was access to Guangzhou, the great outlet for South China silk, porcelain, and lacquerware, a three-to-five-day voyage some eighty miles up the Pearl River from Macao.

Climatic conditions were also important for Macao. As the Northern Hemisphere tilts on its axis toward the sun in the early spring, the Asia landmass warms and the rising heated air creates a low-pressure zone, drawing the cooler, denser air from the ocean, creating the southern monsoon, which blows up the Indian Ocean and eastward and northward along the China coast. In the autumn the process is reversed. For centuries, seaborne traders took advantage of the monsoons, moving north and east to arrive off the southern coast of China in the spring and summer and departing for South and Southeast Asia in the winter. The Canton fairs of January and June were held to coincide with the monsoons.

The Portuguese, who saw Macao always from the seaward end of the peninsula, named it after the seaward-facing temple of A Ma. The Chinese, looking out to the peninsula from the mainland, named the narrow sand spit and the hills of the peninsula beyond after the stem and bud of a lotus flower. The Chinese found the Portuguese both peculiar and fearsome. "They are white and black," one Chinese observer noted. "The faces are pink, and their hair is all white. Even the young appear as white as snow." The Chinese were impressed by the European's "beaklike noses, deep-set green eyes, piercing and unblinking like a cat's." The African slaves the Portuguese brought with them the Chinese claimed were "generally similar to humans." The Chinese believed that the Portuguese were cannibals, kidnapped children, and were quickly roused to anger and violence, at which time they ceased to be human and became wild animals.[4] The Chinese also had a healthy respect for Portuguese firepower and fighting ability, and wanted to confine them to a remote place where they could be observed, monitored, and, if need be, learned from. The technological wonders and curiosities to be observed in Macao especially intrigued the Chinese. One Chinese observer found a "particularly obscene device," the inflatable naked woman made of leather and silk some Portuguese travelers carried with them in a case to be taken to bed when needed.

---

[4]There was truth to the charges of kidnapping. See C. R. (Charles Ralph) Boxer, *Fidalgos in the Far East, 1550–1770* (The Hague: Martinus Nijhoff, 1948), 223.

Chinese dislike and suspicion of Westerners remained strong throughout the Ming period and beyond. The Italian-born Jesuit Matteo Ricci, who had entered China in 1582, writing to the general of the Jesuit Order Claudio Acquaviva, noted that those wishing to speak ill of their adversaries say, "He's a man who makes a habit of going to Macao."[5] To keep out such influences, in 1573 the Chinese district magistrate ordered the construction of a barrier gate surmounted by a small gatehouse at the midpoint of the sand spit between the Macao peninsula and the mainland. Here Chinese troops were stationed to control the flow of people and goods across the border.[6]

When, in 1684, after a period of prohibition, China resumed foreign trade contacts, Macao was incorporated in China's system of port control, and in 1688, the Chinese established a customs office (*hoppo*) in Macao. Chinese bureaucratic oversight was increased in the eighteenth century, when the Portuguese-Macanese fleet was strictly limited to twenty-five vessels. In 1736, a local mandarinate was established, and at midcentury the district magistrate moved his residence to the Chinese village of Wang Xia within the Macao peninsula itself.[7] In effect, Macao lived under an overlapping mixed Portuguese-Chinese jurisdiction, and the Portuguese paid tribute to the Chinese emperor for the right to reside there.

The link with Lisbon was always tenuous. The distance between Portugal and Macao by sea was immense, a voyage of some 10,000 to 15,000 miles that began south and west across the Atlantic to Brazil, then east to the Cape of Good Hope and north to Madagascar, across the Indian Ocean to the Malabar Coast, on from Goa, Cochin, and Calicut and around India to the Coromandel Coast and Malacca, and from there past Java and the Malay Peninsula to Macao. Macao lived by commerce, and it was pivotal to the trade network between Japan, South China, and Southeast Asia and India. From the 1550s until the 1640s, it became prosperous on the silks exported from China to Japan and the silver brought back from Japan in payment. Silver was also used to purchase exports in Macao and Canton for reexport to Southeast Asia, India, and Europe.

---

[5]Jonathan D. Spence, *The Memory Palace of Matteo Ricci* (New York: Viking Penguin, 1984), 193.
[6]The district or county office was the lowest level in the Chinese imperial bureaucracy. The major responsibility of this low-level bureaucrat in Macao was to make sure that the Portuguese paid their annual rent and customs duties to the Chinese imperial authorities. See Jonathan Porter, *Macau: The Imaginary City* (Boulder, Colo.: Westview, 1996). Porter's is by far the best recent book on Macao in English.
[7]Angela Guimarães, *Uma relação especial: Macau e as relações luso-chinesas, 1780–1844* (Lisbon: Edição Centro de Investigações e Estudos de Sociologia, 1996.)

Macao's prosperity depended in the early years on an inter-Asian commerce where the Portuguese had established themselves as intermediaries, partly because of their superior gunpower but also because of the political decision of the Chinese not to take part in overseas commerce and maritime exploration, despite the success of their voyages into the Indian Ocean in the preceding century.[8] Goa, the administrative heart of all the Portuguese settlements from East Africa to Japan, was at the western end of this interoceanic commercial system. Every two or three years, the "Japan ship" set out from Goa carrying cotton cloth from India, glassware, silver, ivory, Spanish velvet and scarlet cloth, olives, olive oil, and wine. At Malacca, pepper, cloves, and aromatic woods were taken on for sale in Japan and China.

At Macao, the carrack remained sometimes for up to a year before making for Nagasaki with white silk, red silk, porcelain, musk, white and black sugar, and other precious commodities. The Japanese called these vessels *Kuro-fune*, or "black ships," a name revived for Commodore Perry's vessels three centuries later. Beginning in 1571, a prosperous if unauthorized trade between Manila and Macao was financed by the silver flowing across the Pacific from the mines of Peru and Mexico.

The Portuguese administration of Macao reflected this seasonal, oceanic, and inter-Asian trade. Executive authority was held not by a Portuguese resident official but by the captain-major who commanded the Japan-bound carrack, and he was only in Macao while en route to India or awaiting the monsoon for the onward voyage to Japan. The "Great Ship of the Amacon," as the English called it, was an enormous vessel of 1,600 tons or more, the largest in the world at the time; only the Manila galleon that plied the Pacific between the Philippines and Acapulco was comparable.[9] The illustrious figure of the captain major is depicted in the Japanese *Namban-byobu* screens of the period, where he is often shown sitting on a folding chair on the ship's deck, surrounded by cases of trade goods, or he is seen arriving on land in Japan with his retinue, accompanied by black

---

[8]For a discussion of the seven great Chinese voyages of the Grand Eunuch Zheng He between 1405 and 1433, see K. N. Chaudhuri, *Trade and Civilization in the Indian Ocean: An Economic History from the Rise of Islam to 1750* (Cambridge: Cambridge University Press, 1985), especially 34–62.

[9]C. R. (Charles Ralph) Boxer's *The Great Ship of the Amacon: Annals of Macao and the Old Japan Trade, 1555–1640* (Lisbon: Centro de Estudos Históricos Ultramarinos, 1963) is one of the great works on the Portuguese in Asia and is still unsurpassed for its pithy detail and original research. More recently, the Indian historian Sanjay Subrahmanyam has written an excellent overview, *The Portuguese Empire in Asia, 1500–1700: A Political and Economic History* (London and New York: Longman, 1993).

slaves and acrobats, Arabian steeds, cages of hawks, peacocks and tigers, to be greeted by black-garbed Jesuits.[10]

To govern in the absence of the captain major, the citizens of Macao formed an elected body, the Senado de Camara, in 1586. This included a chief judge, a secretary, and a procurador, whose job was to represent the city government with the Chinese authorities, which recognized his right to do so. The Macao Senate thus became the first representative institution established in Asia, occasionally removing Portuguese officials it disapproved of, and by running the day-to-day operations of the city.[11]

The impressive building of the Loyal Senate still dominates the colonnaded central square of Macao. The walls of its council chamber are hung with the portraits of the senators who have held office since the sixteenth century; they have recently been joined by a portrait of Ho Yin, the rich Chinese senator who ran the Chinese Chamber of Commerce in Macao and was the unofficial link between the Chinese in Macao and Beijing in the 1960s and 1970s. His son Edmund Ho Hau Wah became the first chief executive of Macao when the enclave returned to China.

The threats to Macao for most of its history came less from the Chinese, in fact, than from other Europeans, especially the Dutch. The Jesuits built the first fortification on the Monte, the central strong point of the peninsula; and the Jesuits as well as the fortress helped defend Macao from a naval assault by the Dutch in 1622, when they laid siege to the city with thirteen men-of-war carrying a force of 1,300 men. A large cannon mounted on the São Paulo Church and manned by Father Jeronimo Rho, a Jesuit of Italian origin and a mathematician, fired a shot that landed directly on the Dutch magazine. It was John the Baptist Day, and he was promptly dubbed patron saint of the city. It was claimed that the African slaves in Macao took the reference to John the Baptist too literally and to celebrate the feast beheaded the unfortunate Dutch captives.[12]

In 1641, however, a key link in the trade chain that underpinned the city's prosperity was broken when Malacca fell to the Dutch. Even more catastrophic for Macao was the expulsion of the Portuguese from Japan in 1639, and the end of the profitable Japan commerce. The Senate of Macao

---

[10]Yoshitomo Okamoto, *The Namban Art of Japan* (New York and Tokyo: Weatherhill and Heibonsha, 1972). See also Luiz Carlos Lisboa and Mara Rúbia Arakaki, *Namban* (São Paulo: Aliança Cultural Brasil-Japão, 1993).

[11]C. R. (Charles Ralph) Boxer, *Portuguese Society in the Tropics: The Municipal Councils of Goa, Macao, Bahia, and Luanda 1510–1600* (Madison: University of Wisconsin Press, 1965).

[12]For these events, see Boxer, *Fidalgos in the Far East*, 72–92; and Jonathan Israel, *The Dutch Republic and the Hispanic World, 1606–1661* (Oxford: Clarendon Press, 1982), 119–120.

sent a delegation to plead with the Japanese to reverse their prohibition. As a final warning that they meant what they said, the Japanese executed sixty-one of the delegates; only the servants were spared to relay the message back to Macao.

Portugal's assertion of its own sovereignty in the revolution against Spanish rule in 1640 also meant that Macao's lucrative trade with Manila collapsed. In China, the Manchus had overthrown the Ming dynasty and were consolidating their power. With Manila and Japan gone, the Macao merchants no longer had the silver with which to finance their trade. "We are living proof of the fable of Midas who died of very hunger at a table of golden dishes," wrote one Macao merchant, João Marques Moreira, in 1644. "Such is happening to us now, for having seen our tables replete with gold, silver, diamonds, rubies, pearls and seed pearls, we are dying by inches."[13] The Jesuit priest Gabriel de Magalhães drew an equally discouraging lesson. "Can God forget the piety of such a city," he wrote to the Macao Senate from Peking in 1656. "Where is the refuge and sanctuary of religion but in this city, which is gloriously called after the name of God. Can God forget his promises? He hath promised tribulations and a hundredfold for the suffering of his saints; and a hundredfold will He pay."[14]

After 1640, Macao turned to Indochina, Macassar, and Timor, and many of its merchants became commission agents for Cantonese businessmen who continued to trade with the Japanese in Chinese junks. In fact, Macanese merchants were often front men, or compradores, for wealthy Chinese merchants and slipped easily into the role of intermediaries selling their names to both Chinese and Europeans to allow them to do business through Macao.

II

It was during the period of economic decline and isolation, however, that the "Macanese" acquired a distinct identity. This identity was reflected, in part, in their ethnic makeup through racial intermarriage or concubinage between European men and Malay, Indian, Japanese, and Chinese women. A Creole Macao patois developed, a mixture of Portuguese and Chinese with Malay words and phrases, which facilitated communication between Europeans and Chinese merchants and shopkeepers as the Macanese became important intermediaries to both Chinese and Europeans. Macao's domestic architecture and decoration reflected this eclectic mix, with large roomy houses built around Chinese-styled central courts, shuttered European windows on upper stories, with doors opening onto an interior space

---

[13]Boxer, *Great Ship from Amacon*, 19.
[14]Ibid.

graced with carved, painted columns, ornate railings, interior lanterns, and shrines. Macao's houses were painted yellow, green, and pink, soon faded by the sun and stained with mildew from the subtropical rain.[15]

In the eighteenth century, English, and other European merchants who were engaged in the Canton trade, prohibited from living permanently in Canton by the Chinese, established year-long residences and trading companies along the beautiful semicircular bay of Macao's Praia Grande. Among the most important of their establishments was the headquarters of the English East India Company, whose directors occupied a house close to the Camões Grotto, which is now the offices of the Orient Foundation. Through an archway still boasting the East India Company name stands Macao's Protestant church and a leafy Protestant cemetery, where the gifted painter of the South China coast George Chinnery (1774–1852) is buried, as well as many young New England seamen, their names recorded on simple headstones "raised by their messmates."[16]

Opium was first imported to China from India for medical uses, principally to relieve pain and dysentery. But the traffic in opium escalated exponentially after the English East India Company's tea monopoly was abolished in the 1830s, and the tea market in Britain expanded by 40 percent. The Chinese tried unsuccessfully to prevent the imports of opium, provoking the aggressive intervention of British gunboats to protect opium traders. Prosperity returned to Macao's waterfront, crowded now with opium-laden vessels, its warehouses full of disguised crates awaiting transshipment upriver to Canton.

The founding of Hong Kong, however, struck at Macao's prosperity no less than had the loss of Malacca and the destruction of the Portuguese presence in Japan two centuries before. Macao was no longer needed to house merchants engaged in the commerce of Canton. Macao's shallow, easily silted harbor was no competition for Hong Kong's deepwater anchorage on the other side of the Pearl estuary. Macao's merchants thus turned to less savory enterprises, creating an underworld specializing in drugs, slavery, and prostitution. From the 1850s to the 1870s, the notorious "coolie trade" to Peru and Cuba flourished in Macao; the conditions under

---

[15]The most accessible Chinese text on this period is the report by two officials, Tcheong-u-Lam and Ian-kuong-Iam, *Ou Mun Kei-Leok: monografia de Macau,* trans. Luís Gonçalves (Macao: Imprensa Nacional, 1950). Boxer reproduced the remarkable illustrations of Chinese and Portuguese inhabitants of Macao contained in the original manuscript in his *Fidalgos in the Far East.*
[16]This period has been skillfully evoked in the romanticized histories of Austin Coates's *City of Broken Promises* (Hong Kong: Oxford University Press, 1967) and *A Macao Narrative* (Hong Kong: Oxford University Press, 1975). For the opium trade, see Martin Booth, *Opium: A History* (New York: St. Martin's Press, 1998), 103–137.

which the rural Chinese were transported as indentured workers to the New World were as bad as those of the recently suppressed African slave trade. Poverty and instability at home, and economic opportunities overseas, led to increasing mainland emigration to the Philippines, Cochin China, Malaysia, Singapore, and Indonesia, as well as to Hawaii, the United States, Canada, and South Africa. Most of the emigrants came from the coastal districts of the Canton delta, which made Macao, more porous than Hong Kong, an important conduit for remittances of the overseas Chinese to their families at home.

The political consequences followed quickly as well. The establishment of Hong Kong inspired the Portuguese to seek a similar status for Macao. Until the 1840s, the dual sovereignty exercised over Macao was of mutual convenience to China and Portugal. But this balance of power was to change dramatically. Encouraged by the example of the British, an aggressive Portuguese governor, João Ferreira do Amaral, was determined to imitate them. He imposed taxes on the Chinese fishermen, expelled the Chinese customs agents, suspended the annual tribute payments to the Chinese emperor, and took control of the barrier gate that had always been under Chinese control.

The Chinese reacted with fury. Governor Amaral, while inspecting the new construction of the gate, was pulled from his horse and assassinated, his head and left hand chopped off and taken back to China. When the Chinese sent additional forces to garrison their fort outside Macao, a young Macanese lieutenant, Mesquita by name, set out with thirty-six Macanese soldiers and routed them. He became an instant hero to Macao's residents, and his statue was raised in the square outside the Loyal Senate, where it stood until it was destroyed by Maoist student rioters in 1966. But the avenue that today cuts through what was once the old Chinese village of Wang Xia still bears his name, and Governor Amaral is commemorated by the road leading up to the old barrier gate, and did so at least until December 20, 1999.

The Chinese returned Governor Amaral's head and hand in 1850, and his remains were later shipped to Lisbon to be buried in the curiously named Cemitério dos Prazeres (cemetery of the pleasures) in that city. But symbols remain potent in this world of shadow play. Governor Amaral's statue in Macao was removed in 1991 and sent back to Lisbon at the insistence of the director of Beijing's Office of Hong Kong and Macao Affairs.

III

In the sixteenth century, the Portuguese named Macao the "City of God in China." Later on, they added the phrase, "There Is No Other More Loyal," in recognition, it is said, of Macao's support of Portuguese independence from Spain in 1640 despite the fact it was threatened by Spanish troops from Manila, a city with which it enjoyed a profitable commerce. In fact, the title was given in the early nineteenth century, when Macao resisted British attempts to "protect" it from the French by sending in an occupation force during the Napoleonic Wars. The Portuguese were wont to name their overseas settlements in such a grandiloquent manner, but such names rarely stuck in popular usage. "Macao" is a bastardization of a Chinese name, and referred to the bay of the goddess A Ma (A-Ma-Gao). Her temple, the oldest in Macao, faces out at the seaward end of the peninsula. It is set tight against the rocks of the steep hillside, as a Chinese temple usually is to placate the dragon who lived in such places. A Ma is holy to fishermen and is daily thronged with worshipers, unlike Macao's largely empty Catholic churches.

I was in Macao at the time of the A Ma festival, and all day long the temple was filled with the endless staccato concussion of firecrackers, to which the sampans and high-decked Pearl River fishing junks responded as they rounded the headland on their way to and from Macao's inner harbor, turning their prows toward the temple and paying a noisy obsequiousness to the goddess. A modern maritime museum, built on landfill in front of the temple gate, and where both Chinese and Portuguese navigational exploits are celebrated, was closed for the day in homage to a more ancient presence, entirely hidden behind the intricate bamboo latticework and colorful banners of a traveling Chinese opera.

At times, Macao certainly was the "City of God in China," home to many zealous Jesuits and saints-to-be. The Spanish-born Francis Xavier died on the nearby island of Shangchuan, awaiting the call to Peking that never came, and the chapel named after him on Coloane Island contains part of the left arm of the saint as well as the venerated bones of Vietnamese and Japanese Christian martyrs. By the seventeenth century, it was claimed that Macao had more convents and monasteries than Vatican City. Speculative landfills and high-rise buildings have today almost obliterated the old Macao of fortresses and churches, a skyline recorded by George Chinnery in the nineteenth century, and which had remained largely unchanged from the mid-seventeenth century until the late 1980s.

In the eighteenth century, this remarkable cityscape often reminded sailors arriving from the seaward side of the Macao peninsula of the bay of Naples. Some part of this atmosphere still remains toward the end of the Praia Grande, where the grand old Bela Vista Hotel, scene of much intrigue over the decades, still sits high on the hillside. The Bela Vista, much to the dismay of many, became the Portuguese consulate after Macao returned to China. This area of Macao, with its curving seaside boulevard and old shade trees and the remaining musty nineteenth-century palaces of the great Macao merchants of that time, recalls the Urca district under the Sugar Loaf Mountain in Rio de Janeiro, or the port of Cannes in the 1950s. Here motorized rickshaws ply their trade, neatly uniformed Chinese children play happily in the gardens outside the Matteo Ricci School, and Macao's old folks quietly exercise each morning before the sticky subtropical heat rises with the sun.

The Praia Grande was traditionally the "European" or "Christian" quarter of Macao. The Chinese quarter lay over the hill, around the inner harbor, and beyond the old city wall. To reach the inner harbor from the Praia Grande is a brief walk past Government House, up past the empty Saint Joseph's Seminary, which holds in its cluttered rooms the paintings of the Christian martyrs crucified by the Japanese in 1596, past a remarkable square onto which faces the colonnaded facade of the oldest European Theater in China, and beyond a quiet stucco building that houses a magnificent Chinese library, bequeathed to Macao by a Hong Kong Chinese tycoon in gratitude for Macao's role in harboring his family and many other Hong Kong residents during the Japanese occupation of the British colony.

The inner harbor lies below, a bustling commercial and industrial waterfront with old warehouses, a gaudy floating casino, long sidewalks under arches onto which face a jumble of narrow open entranceways housing the occasional dark interior of a Buddhist temple, metal workshop, food store, and fish shop, peopled by straggling bleary-eyed gamblers and worn-out prostitutes on their way home, and busy shoppers and old men chatting. The inner harbor itself is crowded with craft of all sizes and shapes, and at a very short distance beyond is China proper.

The cornerstone of Macao's most famous Jesuit Church of São Paulo was laid in 1601. Only its facade now stands at the top of its wide staircase beside the great seventeenth-century fortress of the Monte, also built by the Jesuits and a critical bastion for the defense of Macao. The first Jesuits settled permanently in Macao in 1563. By the end of the 1570s, a spacious residence had been constructed between the Monte and the hilly garden within which lies the grotto named after the Portuguese epic poet Luís de Camões, who may or may not have lived in Macao (the two leading historians of Macao, Father Manuel Teixeira and Charles R. Boxer, vigorously disagreed on the subject).[17] The garden is still a beautiful place, and a bust of Camões, under which are carved the first three verses of the first canto of *The Lusiads*, now sits within the grotto. Here, under the shade trees, old

---

[17]For a discussion on Charles R. Boxer (1904–2000) see chapter 15. Father Teixeira (1924–) left Macau in May 2001; see Father Manuel Teixeira and José Hermano Saraiva, *Camões Was in Macau*, Portuguese/Chinese bilingual edition (Macau: Macau Foundation; International Institute of Macau, 2001).

Chinese men bring their caged birds each morning to chirp and warble. It is fortunate that less than 2 percent of Macao's population can read Portuguese, hence few can understand Camões's somewhat disparaging reference in his second verse about the "*terras viciosas de África e de Ásia.*" The oratory for St. Martin, built in 1580 by Michele Ruggieri as a center for Chinese and Japanese converts, also housed the school where he, and then Matteo Ricci, could learn Chinese. The Jesuit college founded in 1594 subsequently developed Chinese studies, Latin, mathematics, and music, and, eventually, with its printing press and extensive library, became one of the great centers of Chinese studies in Asia.

The famous church of São Paulo itself was financed by the city of Macao, from which the Jesuits had obtained a fixed share of profits from the Japan trades. A Chinese narrative of the seventeenth century described the "Mother of Heaven" on the altar as a goddess who "wears curious cloths and a veil made of glass beads; her hair appears lifelike." I was struck by the relative simplicity of the Catholic churches in Macao, almost Calvinist in their lack of ornamentation and strikingly plain in comparison to the baroque effervescence of churches in Brazil or Spanish America of the same period. But having visited the incense-laden interior of the temple of Kun Iam, this made more sense, as did the seventeenth-century Chinese references to the virgin set above the altar of São Paulo.

The great facade of São Paulo, still one of Macao's most prominent landmarks, reflects the vision of its Chinese and Japanese craftsmen. A broad flight of steps leads up to the front of the church where the facade rises in four tiers; the second containing the four Jesuit saints, with Loyola and Francis Xavier at the center; a dragon and a Portuguese great ship in full sail are on the third tier, to the left and right of which are admonitions in Chinese; on the fourth is Jesus and the instruments of the crucification, and at the top a bronze dove between the sun and the moon. The steps of São Paulo are usually thronged with Japanese tourists amazed at the work of their seventeenth-century ancestors. To the extreme left of the facade are two stone slabs that once held the flags indicating that the Jesuits were granted the rank of mandarin by the Chinese emperor.

Francis Xavier had failed in his attempt to enter China. But Alessandro Valignano, Father Visitor of the order in the East Indies, while spending ten months in Macao on his return from Japan, developed a new and far more effective strategy to "open the rock," as he put it.[18] He found the Chinese, with "their love of learning, their neat dress, their delicate eating habits, their banning of weapons in public places, the shyness of their women, their good government," in every way superior to the Japanese. Valignano

---

[18]On Valignano, see Spence, *Memory Palace of Matteo Ricci*, 40–41. For the Jesuits in Macao and China, see also Porter, *Macau*, 104–116.

decided, in effect, that to convince the Chinese of Christianity's validity, it was necessary to impress the educated elite, to dazzle them with the Jesuits' own education and skills. In order to do so, the Jesuits must learn the language and traditions of China.

Michele Ruggieri was the first new recruit under this dispensation to arrive in Macao, via Goa in 1578, but he encountered enormous difficulty himself in mastering Chinese and requested that Matteo Ricci be sent from Goa to join him in Macao. Ricci was to be much more successful and went on to establish, in 1601, the Jesuit mission in Peking. Here his skill and what Ricci called his *cosette*, bits and pieces, metallic spheres, sundials, prisms, and, above all, clocks, were much appreciated. Ricci and his followers attempted to show that the moral doctrine of Confucius in no way conflicted with Christian morality, and that the ritual observances were purely secular. The remarkable Cologne-born Johann Adam Schall von Bell, who arrived in Macao in 1619 in response to Ricci's call for true scientists to meet the Chinese demand for competent mathematicians and astronomers, succeeded brilliantly in fulfilling Valignano's surmise that scholars more than mendicants would win the way to Peking. He studied Chinese in Macao and helped defend the city from the Dutch in 1622; a year later he was in Peking and accurately predicted the lunar eclipse with great impact on the court, beginning an extraordinary career. He eventually became the first director of the Imperial Astronomical Bureau under the Manchus, from 1644 to 1655, and was permitted to build a mission compound and church close to the imperial palace, a place, to the surprise of the Chinese hosts, the Portuguese president Jorge Sampaio sought out during a visit to Beijing in 1998. The Peking Jesuits dressed and behaved like Confucian literati, but they also brought ingenious gadgets and clever maps, which allowed them to survive the transition from Ming to Qing dynasties, providing protection for the Christian mission in China and obstructing other Europeans in their attempts to reach the Chinese court.

The Jesuits, despite their dominant role, were not the first Catholic order in China, nor were they the only order in Macao. The Augustinians, Dominicans, and Franciscans had little love for the Jesuits, or for each other. In 1613, Jesuits and Dominicans and their respective partisans fought pitched battles in the streets with guns and swords, much to the consternation of the Chinese authorities, who put the Canton armed forces on alert and banned food sales to the Portuguese.[19] It was not the Chinese who in the end undermined the Jesuits' position in China and made impossible the continuation of their experiment in cultural adapta-

---

[19]The Macao Senate had to calm the Chinese with a lengthy memorial explaining that no anti-Chinese plot was involved in the fracas.

tion pioneered by Valignano; it was contention within the Catholic Church over the question of how far the church should go in accommodating Chinese traditions. The bitter controversy over Chinese rites was eventually resolved against the Jesuits by papal decree in 1742. The Jesuit Order was itself expelled by the Portuguese from its overseas possessions in 1759 (1762 in Macao) and suppressed by the papacy in the 1770s.[20] The vast riches the Jesuits were supposed to have hoarded in secret tunnels between their church and the Monte were never found; but old myths die hard, and the archaeologists accompanying the building of a new historical museum to present Macao's history beyond 1999 told me they are again searching for these hidden chambers.

Portugal suppressed the monastic orders in the 1830s, converting the monasteries and convents to other uses. When in 1835 fire destroyed the old Jesuit college, which once housed one of the great Western centers of Chinese scholarship, it was no longer a place of worship but the kitchen for the local garrison. In the narrow street that leads from the base of the steps at São Paulo toward the grotto garden I noticed a shop window overflowing with porcelain statuary. Here many small fat Chinese buddhas were lined up beside several "mothers of heaven" or "Our Lady of Fatima," fairly interchangeable in these parts apparently depending on the season, as well as miniature Red Guards raising a flag much in the style of the U.S. Marines at Iwo Jima, and Mao holding up his little book, even Joseph Stalin looking much as I remember seeing him in Moscow some weeks before he was removed from the Lenin Mausoleum in Red Square. In the end, it seems most things can be commercialized.

By the early nineteenth century, Macao had become a home base for earnest Protestant missionaries, many of them Americans, doing good works and building hospitals and anxious to proselytize the Chinese masses. They were of course deeply suspicious of their Catholic hosts—a suspicion returned in good measure by Macao's numerous Catholic priests. The bishop of Macao's enormous palace, now empty, sits atop the hill on the landward side of the Penha peninsula, of which the A Ma Temple marks the seaward end, just where the Chinese dragon might have been supposed to live.

The current bishop of Macao, Dom Domingos Lam, the first Chinese to head the diocese since its founding in 1576, is turning the palace into a university business and management school, and prefers to live elsewhere.

---

[20]On the expulsion of the Jesuits from Portugal and its empire, see Kenneth Maxwell, *Pombal, Paradox of the Enlightenment* (Cambridge and New York: Cambridge University Press, 1995), 71–86; on the Jesuits within the Portuguese Empire, see Dauril Alden, *The Making of an Enterprise: The Society of Jesus in Portugal, Its Empire and Beyond* (Stanford: Stanford University Press, 1996).

Bishop Lam is a small, chain-smoking, energetic cleric. His door "is open to all comers," he told me when I called on him at his office next to the cathedral in downtown Macao. He is a great enthusiast for the World Wide Web and its potential for his work in Macao, as well as for communication beyond it.

There are fewer than twenty thousand Catholics in Macao today, but the church's role is much more important than these numbers suggest. Over forty thousand children, for example, are enrolled in Catholic private schools. He "never talks politics," the bishop told me. "We do what we have to do regardless, and I don't much worry if people like it or not; they can draw their own conclusions." His position is a sensitive one given what he calls "the bad relationship between the Chinese government and the Vatican." In an elliptical way, the bishop was saying something very important about Macao: look at actions and not words.

The Catholic schools and religious expression are both explicitly protected in Macao's Basic Law (Article 34), to which China formally committed itself in 1993. The Basic Law became the constitution of Macao after December 1999. The status of the enclave is that of a "special administrative region" (SAR) of China like Hong Kong, under the formula invented by the late Deng Xiaoping of "one country, two systems." It is an arrangement intended, as with Hong Kong, to leave the territory to run its own internal affairs while preserving its special Sino-European character and capitalist system.[21]

Yet even before the ink was dry on the Basic Law, doubts emerged as to how much autonomy this particular special administrative region would have. Bishop Lam's commitment to establishing a new interuniversity institute with a school of business and management in collaboration with Portugal's Catholic University quickly became subject to intense pressure from Beijing, which made it clear that China will not accept an institution subject to the control of a "foreign state," by which China means the Vatican.

Bishop Lam made no direct reference to this dispute in his conversation with me, but he did make a point of handing me the brochure for the university institute and its planned curriculum, as well as calling up on his computer and printing out for me a listing of the Christian missions supported by his bishopric, including the construction in 1992 of a church at Ta-huang, the largest church built in the Pearl River delta region in the past fifty years. Given the historical role of Macao in Christian missionary en-

---

[21]The Basic Law is printed in full in Steve Shipp, *Macau, China: A Political History of the Portuguese Colony's Transition to Chinese Rule* (Jefferson, N.C.: McFarland, 1997), 143–171. There is also a good description of the negotiations and legal background in R. D. Cremer, ed., *Macau: City of Commerce and Culture*, 2d ed. (Hong Kong: API Press, 1991), especially 261–353.

deavors in the Far East and China, how the Beijing Communists deal with this part of Macao's heritage will be a vital indication of their willingness to abide by other protections embedded in Macao's Basic Law.

The bishop's resistance to attempts to manipulate him provoked some criticism on the Portuguese side too. A number of Portuguese officials find him "very Chinese," tending to place "community values over individual values." My own sense of the bishop is that he is a man of great personal strength and conviction, and that he will be a key player at one of the most sensitive points of potential confrontation in the coming years. Bishop Lam walked me past the faded portraits of his predecessors as I left his residence. They stretch back four centuries. But as the great Jesuit polymath António Vieira noted in the 1640s: "The preachers took the Gospel and the merchants took the preachers." Macao's raison d'être after all was commerce, and it remains so: only the commodities have changed over the centuries.

IV

Macao, despite its godly aspirations, was no less often a city of sin, a nether zone of concubines and prostitutes, an opaque shadow world of shady deals and opium dens, well known for its corruption. One shocked visitor in the 1930s saw Macao as the playground of the "riffraff of the world, the drunken shipmasters; the flotsam of the sea; the derelicts, and more shameless, beautiful, savage women than any part of the world." W. H. Auden in a memorable phrase called it "a weed from Catholic Europe."

This is the Macao thousands of eager Hong Kong residents hope for as they crowd aboard the jet hydrofoils that rush back and forth across the Pearl River estuary between the two cities. Owned by Macao's casino king, Stanley Ho, these speedy vessels bring gamblers to the Hotel Lisboa and the casino "VIP rooms," where they rub shoulders with Communist cadres from the mainland, dropping their ill-gotten gains at the card tables. Six million visitors cross to Macao each year; 80 percent of them are Hong Kong Chinese, most of whom head straight for the gambling. The rich pickings of Macao's casinos are swiftly reinvested in China, Europe, and New York, in Hong Kong enterprises, and Lisbon real estate, as well as in payoffs to Chinese party officials, local administrators, and Portuguese bureaucrats, and in campaign contributions to Portuguese politicians—and in 1996, it seems, to U.S. politicians as well—who can provide favors. The casinos provide over 60 percent of Macao government revenues.

Stanley Ho has held the gaming monopoly since 1962 through his Macao Tourism and Entertainment Corporation (STDM) in which he holds a 25 percent personal stake, although his gambling monopoly was due to expire in 2001. Ho's net value was placed in 1992 at well over a billion dollars and his gambling interests now extend to Europe through the

Portuguese-based Sol Estoril group. He is the head of the Shun Tak shipping company, which dominates the transportation routes between Hong Kong and Macao. There are very few enterprises or developments in Macao in which Stanley Ho is not a major participant.

Ho, now in his late seventies, was born in Hong Kong to a well-to-do Eurasian family and educated at the University of Hong Kong. He made his fortune during the Japanese occupation. Macao, as a Portuguese territory, retained its neutrality during the Second World War and became a refuge for many from Hong Kong. Ho developed a profitable trade between Japan, Macao, and occupied Hong Kong. After the Communist takeover of China and during the Korean War, he supplied the Chinese with gold and airplanes and other embargoed materials.

It is sometimes said of Stanley Ho's role that Macau it is the only place in the world where a "casino king" owns his own colony. As one might expect, the Macao casino king is not himself a gambler; he does "not have the patience for it," he says. Stanley Ho and the Portuguese governor open the gambling season on the eve of the Chinese New Year. Ho arrives in his green Rolls Royce and the governor in a black Mercedes Benz to place the first stakes at the roulette table at Ho's flagship, the "Casino Lisboa."

The final years of Portuguese administration saw increasing gang violence around the edges of Ho's empire. He stepped up security and hired Gurkhas demobilized by the British in Hong Kong to provide protection. The triads, Chinese secret societies and criminal brotherhoods, have played a key role in the Chinese underworld for centuries and are at war again in Macao, with two Hong Kong–based gangs, the 14K and the Wo On Lok (the latter through its Macao affiliate, the Shui Fong) pitted against each other. These triad organizations are believed to number about 400,000 members worldwide, from corporate executives to street corner thugs.[22]

The upsurge of gang-related shootings, knifings, arson, and bombings in Macao is also partly attributed to the drying up of illegal shakedowns from the construction business in the territory. The speculative property boom in Macao, fueled by hot money flowing in from China in the early 1990s, burst after China clamped down in an attempt to cool off its economy. Property values in Macao collapsed, leaving more than thirty thousand apartments, or a quarter of the total housing stock, empty and unsold. Clampdowns on the triads in China, Taiwan, and Hong Kong forced them to shift their operations to Macao.

The triads are not subtle when they go to war. One of the first victims, the general manager of the Macao Holiday Inn, Gerhard Kropp, tried to

---

[22] *South China Morning Post*, May 12, 1997.

keep prostitutes and their pimps out of his lobby. He was ambushed at his home by three assailants who hacked at him with knives and choppers. He nearly lost three fingers and left for a new posting. "Choppings," an assault with a cleaver, are the triads' favorite means to settle scores. The triads then took their war to the elegant Praia Grande Avenue. Most blatant was a pointblank and deadly fusillade unleashed by two motorcyclists brandishing 7.62-mm Chinese military issue semiautomatic pistols, who ambushed a car carrying a former officer of the Hong Kong police and a bodyguard of the 14K's leader.

The killings were believed to be in retaliation for the murder on Macao's Taipa Island of a rich businessman and Kong Lik triad member from Hong Kong who was a shareholder in one of the enclave's franchised VIP gambling rooms and a gambling-tour operator for wealthy clients from Indonesia, Hong Kong, and Thailand.[23] Breaking a long unwritten convention against attacking senior government officials and expatriate Portuguese, the gangs then attempted to murder the chief of Macao's gambling secretariat, who was shot twice in the head and, despite a remarkable recovery, was called back to Lisbon for his own safety.

Macao's lone prodemocrat legislator, Antonio Ng Kuok-cheong, says police corruption and triad membership by officers have caused the crisis. He blames the casino regulations that allow individuals to operate VIP rooms for high rollers.[24] After several police raids on suspected triad safehouses failed, the director of the judiciary police, António Marques Baptista, confiscated his officers' mobile phones and pagers and immediately met with a striking success. He now never leaves his office without a bodyguard, and his car is flanked by armed motorcycle outriders. A very nervous Macao public was not reassured by Baptista's statement that for law-abiding men, women, and children "the streets were safe because these attacks were carried out by professional killers who never miss their targets."[25]

The question of what constitutes a threat to "public order" has serious political implications. Recurrent claims in the press that the "situation is out of control" can provide an excuse for more Chinese intervention. Article 18 of the Basic Law provides that: "In the event that the standing committee of the national People's Congress decides to declare a state of war or, by reason of turmoil within the Macao Special Administrative Region, which endangers national unity and is beyond the control of the government of the region, decides that the region is in a state of emergency, the

---

[23]Ibid., April 19, 1997.
[24]Reuters World Service, May 12, 1997.
[25]*South China Morning Post*, April 19, 1997; and Foreign Broadcast Information Service (FBIS), Chi-92–082, April 27, 1997.

central people's government may issue an order applying relevant national laws in the region."[26]

As the owner of a furniture store near the landmark facade of the old São Paulo Church told Peter Stein of the *Wall Street Journal*: "If Macao's police can't solve the problem, China will."[27] The Xinhua News Agency, China's official mouthpiece, has urged tougher measures and asserted that the Guandong authorities will help if need be.[28]

Given the multiple layers of motivation on all sides in Macao it is worth noting that the professional hit men brought in from China by the triads—and who slip back across the border in ten minutes on foot or by boat across the narrow inner harbor—are believed to be members of the Chinese security forces. All the recent hits have been carried out with People's Army–issue firearms. The struggle over ownership of the new Grandview Hotel on Taipa Island involved the Anran Company owned by the Chinese Ministry of State Security, which is also believed to be trying to obtain a slice of the casino monopoly.[29]

Indeed, almost on cue, before the Portuguese could bring in sophisticated eavesdropping devices, the bigwigs of the local Chinese community, together with Stanley Ho and the representative of the Chinese central government in Macao, the head of the Xinhua News Agency, acted with the authorities across the border in Guandong Province to cut triad money-laundering sources and bring the warring factions to an agreement. The Beijing government has used the argument of public order to justify the stationing of army troops in Macao after its retrocession to China on December 20, 1999.

V

The last Portuguese governor of Macao, General Vasco Rocha Vieira, whom I met at the pink-and-white colonial-style Government House (which houses both his office and the Macao legislature), told me that he believes the English press in Hong Kong has greatly exaggerated the problem of gang violence in Macao and that the streets of Macao are among the safest in the world. Statistically, he may be right. I was certainly able to walk anywhere in Macao. But gang-related mayhem has a life of its own. Gory pictures of murdered hoodlums have already badly dented Macao's vital tourist business. The number of gamblers visiting Macao from Hong

---

[26]Shipp, *Macau, China*, 146.
[27]*Wall Street Journal*, May 6, 1997.
[28]FBIS, Chi-93–139, May 19, 1997, A6.
[29]FBIS, Chi-92–127, daily report, May 7, 1997; FBIS, Chi-97–128, May 8, 1997; and *Far Eastern Economic Review*, September 26, 1996, 30.

Kong, who are big spenders and are vital to Macao's prosperity, has fallen precipitously since gang violence first broke out. And Macao's competitors for Hong Kong dollars in the gambling business have been quick to take note of its troubles. Hong Kong's shrewd business leaders not only have recently signed a deal with Disney for a vast new theme park, but also have been visiting Las Vegas and dropping hints that Hong Kong might establish its own casino. Like the loss of the Japan trade in the seventeenth century, or the establishment of Hong Kong in the nineteenth century, such a move would be a disaster for Macao, and Stanley Ho has been quick to condemn the idea.

General Rocha Vieira is a quiet but determined individual. He believed, as the Portuguese who dealt with Macao generally did, that it is essential to work with the Chinese and not against them. They see this as the best way, as the general told me, "of making possible a continuing and effective presence of European culture in this important Chinese region." He was a general without troops. The last Portuguese military units withdrew from Macao at the end of 1975. After the fall of the dictatorship in Lisbon in 1974, the Macao governorship became a revolving door for Portuguese politicians, and the instability of the governments in Lisbon in the early years of the new democracy did not help Portuguese credibility or enable Portugal to become a serious player in the real power games in Macao.

The dominant role played in Lisbon by the pro-Moscow Portuguese Communist Party between 1974 and 1976 was also viewed with great suspicion by Beijing. General Rocha Vieira, however, came with impeccable credentials in that respect. Not only had he served in Macao in the 1970s, but he played a critical role in Lisbon during the anti-communist coup of November 1975, which in effect sent the Portuguese Communists packing.

His head of security in Macao, Brigadier Manuel Monge, an early member of the armed forces movement that overthrew the right-wing regime in Portugal in 1974, like General Rocha Vieira, had also fallen afoul of the Portuguese Communists. While the democratic credentials of both these military officers are impeccable, more important from Beijing's perspective was the fact that both had opposed the Moscow-inspired power grab in Lisbon.[30]

In Macao, General Rocha Vieira, who was appointed governor in 1991, brought both stability and integrity to an office that had been severely tainted previously by accusations of corruption. Universally and unsolicitedly, people I spoke with in Macao testified to his honesty. But I also detected in General Rocha Vieira a sense of determination that the

---

[30]For this period in Portugal, see Kenneth Maxwell, *The Making of a Portuguese Democracy* (Cambridge and New York: Cambridge University Press, 1995).

Portuguese in Macao avoid at all costs the disasters that followed their withdrawals in Africa and East Timor, and that if the Portuguese politicians and functionaries have notoriously sticky fingers, then the Portuguese military at least will withdraw with honor.

Macao's formal institutional structure, where the Portuguese presence in Macao is most pronounced, has many of the trappings of a Western society: law courts, an elected legislature, formal protection of free speech and assembly. Most of these rights in Macao preceded the liberalization in Hong Kong and were a direct consequence of the Portuguese Revolution of 1974, which provided the constitutional means on the Portuguese side for reexamining sovereignty and reforming Macao's institutions. In 1976, wide autonomy was granted to Macao by the new democratic Portugal under an "organic statute" that established a wide range of civil rights and set up the Macao Legislative Assembly. Election to the legislature was by means of a restricted franchise with only one-third of the seats open to direct election. (The remaining representatives were either indirectly elected by professional and neighborhood organizations or appointed by the Portuguese governor.) Nevertheless, the Portuguese residents and a minority of the Chinese population have participated in direct elections in Macao since 1976.

The Macao legislature was no rubber stamp. In the early years, the Macanese legislators, who had centuries of experience bucking the authority of Portuguese governors through their domination of the Loyal Senate, became so outspoken in their opposition to the executive that a governor dissolved the legislative assembly and called new elections in 1984. The system of proportional representation used in Macao as in Portugal also helped to assure a voice for the small liberal minority in Macao, which has consistently obtained at least one of the directly elected seats since the assembly was first instituted. In the hotly contested 1996 election, for example, one seat went to a prodemocracy candidate. The eight indirectly elected members of the assembly come from the traditional probusiness, pro-China sector.

Beijing did not object to direct elections in Macao as it had in Hong Kong, and the legislature continued in office through the transfer of sovereignty in 1999 until 2001, unlike that of Hong Kong, which was dissolved at the time of the handover. Since 1992, Macao has had its own court of final appeal.

The Basic Law also includes some significant concessions on China's part; there is no restriction on foreign passport holders taking important posts in the administration after 1999, except those of chief executive and chief justice, a reassurance to the large number of Macao Chinese who qualify for Portuguese passports. The 10,000 Macanese Eurasians retain access to the civil service, where they have traditionally sought official careers, and over a quarter of Chinese residents of Macao hold Portuguese, hence EU, passports. Both China and Portugal are aware that if they mishandle the transfer, Macao could easily lose much of its Eurasian and Macao-born Chinese and end up as an empty shell and suburb of the Chinese border city of Zhuhai.

Portuguese authority in Macao, however, was essentially broken in 1966, when the balance of power in Macao between the Portuguese and Chinese shifted dramatically during the turmoil unleashed by the Cultural Revolution. Maoist militants rioted in Macao's streets, and the Portuguese governor, after some initial armed clashes, capitulated to their demands, which included the closing of the offices of the Nationalist Kuomintang in Macao and the ending of Macao's use as an exit point for dissidents fleeing China. The Portuguese governor was obliged to sign the agreement in the office of the Chinese Chamber of Commerce under a huge portrait of Mao Zedong, with Ho Yin presiding. But Beijing did not want the Portuguese facade destroyed. It was useful to the Chinese Communists to preserve a place where the appearance of separation from the regime could provide a gray area for deals and contacts, a place with enough ambiguity to permit a degree of separation and plausible deniability.

To the surprise of the Salazar regime, China did not seek to expel the Portuguese administration from Macao in 1966; and when in the mid-1970s the Portuguese twice tried to give Macao back to China, the offer was politely refused, with Ho Yin telling the Portuguese that the time was not ripe.[31]

But this in many ways was the traditional use the Chinese had made of the Portuguese enclave. Professor Fok Kai Cheong, an American-trained historian at the University of Macao, calls this arrangement the "Macao Formula," a type of implicit acquiescence in each other's claims to overlapping areas of sovereignty.[32] Premier António de Oliveira Salazar's wily foreign minister, Franco Nogueira, said that after 1967 the Portuguese in Macao remained as "a caretaker of a condominium under foreign supervision."[33]

In effect, the modus vivendi after the Maoist riots reestablished the old de facto system of overlapping authority, with the head of the Xinhua

---

[31]China thus demanded that the United Nations exclude Macao from the list of territories "under colonial rule." As far as China was concerned, Macao was "part of China" and a domestic question. The Portuguese acquiesced in this definition and described Macao thereafter as "a Chinese territory under Portuguese administration."

[32]Fok Kai Cheong, *Estudos sobre a instalação dos portugueses em Macau* (Lisbon and Macao: Gradiva, 1996).

[33]Franco Nogueira, *Salazar: estudo biográfico*, 6 vols. (Coimbra: Atlántida Editora, 1977), III, 393.

News Agency representing the interests of the central government, much as the local mandarins had done prior to the 1840s, which the historian Charles R. Boxer called a matter of "give and take." And while it has been true from the sixteenth century onward that China could disrupt Macao's food supply at any moment and impose its will by force, China never sought to do so.

Unlike the other ancient Portuguese enclaves in Asia, Goa, invaded by India in 1961, and East Timor, bloodily annexed by Indonesia in 1975, in the case of Macao the Chinese chose stealth. As the director of the Xinhua News Agency's Hong Kong branch said, quoting Sun Tzu's *The Art of War*, "defeating the enemy without going to war is the utmost success."[34] The Chinese waited for the moment that suited them.

VI

The largely European superstructure of Macao is embedded in a politics and society rooted in a complex network of powerful interconnecting Chinese clans whose collaboration is essential if anything is to be done at all in Macao. These Chinese networks of individuals and business interests are closely tied to the mainland and to Beijing. The Nam Kwong trading company was China's official political and economic representative in Macao for thirty-five years until 1984, when these functions were split into political and trading arms, with the Xinhua News Agency and its Macao head becoming China's spokesman and unofficial representative in the territory. Today, China is the leading investor in Macao, with two hundred companies in the territory controlling 50 percent of finance and insurance and 70 percent of the tourism business.[35]

Overlapping memberships in Chinese and Portuguese institutions is typical of Macao, as is the continuity within the leadership of the Macao Chinese community. The venerable Macao Chinese Chamber of Commerce, founded in 1912, became the central mediator between Portugal and China between 1949 and 1979. From 1950 until his death in 1983, its chairman and the undisputed leader of the Macao Chinese was the aforementioned Ho Yin, a very rich businessman with interests in hotels, restaurants, banks, buses, and utility companies. Two-thirds of the Chinese members of the legislative assembly are also members of the Board of Directors of the Chamber of Commerce. The current chairman is also a

---

[34]FBIS, Chi-97–086, daily report, May 2, 1997, A11. C. R. (Charles Ralph) Boxer, "Dares-e-tomares nas relações luso-chinesas durante os sécules XVII e XVIII através de Macau," *Boletim do Arquivo Histórico de Macau* 1 (January 1981): 3–13.
[35]*Economist Intelligence Unit*, Country Report: Macau, May 13, 1997.

member of the standing committee of the National People's Congress in Beijing.

Ho Yin's son, Edmund Ho Hau Wah, the then forty-four-year-old executive director and general manager of the Tai Fung Bank, half of which is owned by the Bank of China, became chief executive of the Macao SAR after the Chinese takeover in December 1999. The Tai Fung Bank is the second-largest bank in the territory and Edmund Ho is chairman of the Banking Association and was a member of the Basic Law drafting committee and of the Sino-Portuguese Joint Liaison Group. He was then also vice chairman of the All China Federation of Industry and Commerce.

I met with Edmund Ho—who is Canadian educated—in his wood-paneled third-floor office at the Tai Fung Bank, which sits off Macao's busy Central Avenue. His major concern, he said, is how Macao positions itself for the challenges of the new century by diversifying its economic base to enable it to sustain a real autonomy, especially from the neighboring Chinese mainland development areas. He sees a need for urgently enhancing technical and scientific education and believes the city is too small to be viable.

Macao's per capita income, at $15,010 in 1995, was the fifth-highest in Asia, after Japan, Brunei, Hong Kong, and Singapore, and higher than Taiwan and South Korea. But like Hong Kong, its manufacturing industry is crossing the border to find cheaper labor. When I met with Edmund Ho, he had just returned from Brazil, where he had accompanied Governor Rocha Vieira on a mission to promote Macao as a bridge to China for Brazilian businesses.

The Chinese print media in Macao tends to follow the Beijing line, under the ever-watchful eye of the Xinhua News Agency. The lively Portuguese language press has a small circulation and is focused on the internecine intrigues of Portuguese politics, something the Chinese find entirely impenetrable and confusing, with the Portuguese endlessly and needlessly complicating their own lives. Several Macao Chinese leaders told me they find Portuguese politics as obscure as those of the old men of the Central Committee in Beijing. The local television station, TDM, is 50.5 percent owned by the government and by Stanley Ho's STDM, the Nam Kwong Group, and Edmund Ho. The electronic media in Macao take a more independent line than the Chinese print media, but the Portuguese-language station tends to broadcast the metropolitan news program of no special interest to most of the residents of Macao, who cannot understand the language, let alone the content. Much of the population watches the Hong Kong English-language and Cantonese-language stations, and many have access to international cable and satellite television services.

The Chinese population of Macao is of quite diverse origins. Tanka boat people constitute the oldest elements of the population, though most today have left their boats and live in city apartments. In the past there was a strong Fukanese component, but now 50 percent of the Chinese in Macao are of rural Guandongese origin. These longtime residents have not lived under the Communist regime and retain many of the practices of an Old China, long destroyed on the mainland by war and revolution. Many hold Portuguese passports. The leadership of the Chinese community rests principally in this group, families with more than two generations of residence in Macao, influential in the world of business and the secret societies. They are extremely conservative socially and pro-Beijing politically. Their children, often educated overseas, tend to be English-speaking, are strongly influenced by developments in Hong Kong, and are more liberal than their parents.

About 40 percent of the Chinese population of Macao are more recent immigrants, many having come clandestinely from the mainland since the 1980s. There is a smaller but important group that came from the Chinese diaspora, returning to Macao from Southeast Asia in the 1960s. These tend to be middle-class people with a high level of education.

Several significant figures in Macao arrived from China after 1979, including intellectuals as well as underworld figures and a contingent of Chinese from Southeast Asia. Some had played key roles in Beijing in the past, and now hold important positions in Macao's financial and intellectual circles. One of the most prominent of these is the multilingual Gary Ngai, from a Chinese family that spent five generations in the former Dutch East Indies and, later, Indonesia. Formerly a close confidant of Deng and his personal translator, he was until recently vice president of Macao's Cultural Institute and then became executive director of the Sino-Latin Foundation.

The Eurasian population of the city, known as the "Macanese," is a tightly knit group numbering until recently between 10,000 and 15,000; but extensive out-migration means that today the Macanese dispersed throughout the world probably equal or surpass the number of Macanese at home. The Macanese community integrates genetic elements from across Asia, its ancestors including principally Malays, Japanese, Indians, Timorese, Chinese, and Koreans as well as Portuguese. In the local Cantonese argot they are referred to as "sons and daughters of the soil," that is, people "born in the land" and not "foreigners" to the Chinese, as the Portuguese were and remain. Macanese culture was a rich Creole mix, and they spoke and wrote in a local patois. The Loyal Senate, Macao's de facto government during much of its first three centuries, was dominated by elected Macanese representatives. The Macanese also dominated the middle levels of the colonial administration and were important in the merchant and legal communities.

The Maoist riots of 1966 were a profound shock to this group. The Macanese had always identified themselves with the ruling Portuguese, and their sense of betrayal at Portugal's capitulation to Chinese demands was profound. The Macanese had formerly distanced themselves from Chinese elites in Macao in everything except business; after 1966 this changed, especially with respect to marriage patterns, religion, and politics.[36] The estrangement of the Macanese from the Portuguese was also aggravated by the fact that Macao's bureaucracy became more, not less, "colonial" in the 1980s, its higher ranks filled with short-term Portuguese expatriate appointees whom the Macanese deeply resent. Unlike Hong Kong where expatriate British officials made up a very small percentage of the civil service prior to the handover, in Macao the Portuguese participation increased as the end neared and with an inevitable consequence: the Portuguese administration became more isolated from Macao's daily realities and more dependent on the collaboration of the long-entrenched leadership of the Chinese community.[37] Gary Ngai calls these officials the "full stops," individuals who have no real interest in the future of Macao but a great deal of interest in enriching themselves at Macao's expense.

VII

But in an economy fueled by vast flows of cash, by casinos and sex; with institutions isolated by language and procedure from the vast majority of the population; where for centuries intermediaries provided the contacts, bribes, and special knowledge that produced results; an ambiguous place where the wheels could be greased by kickbacks or favors, where money could be laundered and commodities as well as people slipped in and out without great supervision; where entrepreneurs lived by providing what was prohibited elsewhere in their neighborhood—it is hardly surprising that Macao, like other free cities with multiple and overlapping sovereignties, should be a place ready-made for espionage and fund transfers for the broader but clandestine political purposes of the great powers that chose to keep Macao the way it is in the first place.

So when Ron Brown, the late U.S. secretary of commerce, held a private dinner party at the Hong Kong Island Shangri-La Hotel in October 1995, to which "a Macao property businessman and his wife, a Macao banker and legislative councilor, a Macao entertainment magnate and members of several illustrious Hong Kong families" were invited, they were met by Yah

---

[36]There is an excellent account of the Macanese in "The Macanese: Anthropology, History, Ethnology," *Review of Culture* (Instituto Cultural de Macau), no. 20, 1994.
[37]For a forceful analysis of the problem of corruption in Macao, see Lo Shiu-hing, "Bureaucratic Corruption and Its Control in Macao," *Asian Journal of Public Administration* 15 (June 1993): 32–58.

Lin Trie, a Chinese American, co-owner of a Chinese restaurant a few blocks from the Arkansas State Capitol and a favorite watering hole of Bill Clinton while governor, and Trie's partner Antonio Pan, a former executive of the Lippo Group, and Ernest Green, a Clinton crony and Arkansas fundraiser for the Democratic Party. The guests quickly got the message. After all, they were well used to similar requests from Portuguese presidential candidates.[38] Brown himself, of course, had been the party's chief fundraiser before his appointment as secretary of commerce. In early 1996, despite State Department objections, new rules permitting the export of high-speed computers to Chinese companies went into effect. According to a comprehensive investigative report by Jeff Gerth and Eric Schmitt in the *New York Times* in 1998, "the Central Intelligence Agency and other Federal agencies concluded that at least some of those computers [were] being used by the Chinese military. . . ."[39]

"Charlie" Trie was to become a central if illusive figure in the inconclusive Senate investigation of campaign abuses, the House Select Committee's report on Chinese "theft of nuclear secrets," as well as a federal prosecution and conviction, all related to laundered Chinese contributions to the 1996 presidential campaign. And most of these contributions were laundered through Macao. Charlie Trie visited the White House twenty-three times, at least, between 1993 and 1996, taking with him several casino barons from Macao—more times to be sure than Congressman Caleb

---

[38]Hong Kong Sing Tao Jim Pao (in Chinese), FBIS, Chi-96–236, daily report, December 5, 1996, A16 (translated text). The veil that closely covers the role of Macao and its money in domestic Portuguese politics was partially lifted by the "tell all," or at least part of the "all," in a remarkable book by Rui Mateus, the former confidant, translator, and political bagman for Mário Soares. Mateus was caught up in allegations of corruption in the contracting of Macao's new international airport, and former President Soares quickly dumped him; as a result, Mateus's book reveals a good deal of the seamy side of Portuguese politics, including the extraordinary tale of the murky proposed deals over the use of Macao as a base for a television franchise aimed at the Hong Kong market and southern China, involving Soares and, at various stages, the late Robert Maxwell, Rupert Murdoch, and Stanley Ho. See Rui Mateus, *Contos proibidos: memórias de um PS desconbecido* (Lisbon: Dom Quixote, 1996). Soares, when asked about the Mateus book, said that he "had not read it. . . . He did not wish to disturb himself or waste time uselessly." See Maria João Avillez, *Soares, democracia* (Lisbon: Público, 1996), 272. Martin Booth in his book *Opium, A History* (New York: St Martin's Press, 1998) pointed out how convenient gambling casinos can be for money laundering—or, as he writes, for "money cleaning facilities." According to Booth up to $2 billion may be laundered monthly through Macao (see 336–337). This seemed a very high dollar figure to me; but when I asked a former high-level U.S. government official who was directly involved in international narcotics control, she said this was entirely plausible.

[39]*New York Times*, October 19, 1998.

Cushing did in the late 1840s, when Macao was last on the White House's agenda at the time of the Treaty of Wang Xia.[40]

Macao was also the front for the purchase for $20 million by a local company (Chong Lot, incorporated in Macao for a mere $125,000 at a nonexistent address on the Praia Grande) of a partially built Ukrainian 67,000-ton aircraft carrier. Vasyl Hureyev, Ukraine's industry minister, said it was to be used as "a discotheque." Other reports said it would be used as a floating casino. The problem no one noticed was that Macao cannot harbor deepwater ships. One of the central reasons Hong Kong boomed after it was founded in the 1840s, and Macao did not, is that Macao is situated on the side of the Pearl River estuary that silts up. In a very peculiar comment, Portuguese Prime Minister António Guterres, who visited Macao in April 1998, said that Macao's crime rate "compared favorably to the Ukraine's," a remark even the Chinese government found complacent in the extreme, and told him so privately in Beijing a few days later.[41]

Rui Afonso, a Macao lawyer and former member of the legislature, took a much more sober view, saying that the security situation in Macao was desperate, that a culture of private justice by execution had emerged, and that the Portuguese had lost the stamina to rule.

But the gangs went too far when they embarrassed both the Portuguese and the Chinese in the run-up to the December handover, which each side wanted to look as smooth as possible. The sensational and much-delayed

---

[40]U.S. Senate, *Final Report of the Committee on Governmental Affairs, Investigation of Illegal or Improper Activities in Connection with 1996 Federal Election Campaigns, together with additional and minority views, March 10, 1998.* 105th Cong., 2d sess. (Washington, D.C.: GPO, 1998), 2497–2904, 5270–5413; and U.S. House of Representatives, *Report of the Select Committee, U.S. National Security and Military/ Commercial Concerns with the People's Republic of China,* 105th Cong., 2d sess. (Washington, D.C.: GPO, 1999). The most comprehensive discussion on Yah Lin "Charlie" Trie's role as a direct source or solicitor of the second-largest volume of contributions returned by the Democratic National Committee is to be found in the testimony of Jerry Campane, special agent, Senate Governmental Affairs Campaign Finance Investigation, on July 29, 1998. This testimony was not in the six-volume Senate committee report, but is available through the Federal Document Clearing House. Charlie Trie was charged by the Justice Department's Campaign Finance Task Force. He pleaded guilty and was sentenced to eighteen months of home detention, three years' probation, and a $5,000 fine (*Wall Street Journal,* November 10, 1999). Ron Brown's tragic death in a plane accident on April 3, 1996, the obsessive attention devoted to President Clinton's affair with Monica Lewinsky and the consequent impeachment battle, powerful business interests who wanted deals with the Chinese government, as well as the general lack of enthusiasm of key politicians on both parties in the Senate and House of Representatives for any close scrutiny of campaign contributions, combined to blunt the investigations of the Chinese money connection in the 1996 election, and Macao's central role in the scandal. In this, as in so much else, Clinton was lucky.

[41]*Economist Intelligence Unit,* Country Report: Macau, April 27, 1998.

trial of Wan Kuok-koi, alias "Broken Tooth," alleged head of the 14K triad in Macao, ended (to the surprise of many in Macao) in his conviction on November 23, barely a month before the handover ceremonies were scheduled to occur. The Macao court found Wan guilty of being a member of a triad group, loan sharking, illegal gambling, and interfering with a local telecommunications network, and sentenced him to fifteen years. Two days later, a former police officer and gang member was also sentenced and jailed. Wan's mistake was to have emerged too blatantly from the shadows, boasting about his gangland prowess in newspaper interviews. He was arrested while attending a gangster movie called *Casino*, purportedly based on his life history, which he had financed. And in a risky challenge to the soon-to-be sovereign power, a well-known pro-China Macao legislator had been attacked and wounded leaving the offices of the Xinhua News Agency, no less.

But these last-minute tidy-ups cannot disguise the fragility of the legal system and the administration, where language and procedure are incomprehensible to 90 percent of the population, where laws have only recently been hastily and often badly translated into Chinese, and where a supreme court only created in 1993 has judges with less than a year's experience in charge. The University of Macao only graduated its first class of lawyers in the mid-1990s, and locally trained magistrates have little practical court experience. Despite the hoopla, the sprucing up and repainting of public buildings, and the construction of new museums, the fact remains that after almost four and a half centuries in Macao, the Portuguese had spent only the past half decade preparing Chinese officials to assume the critical bureaucratic roles that would assure not only the continuation of Portuguese institutions in Macao but also, and more important, help guarantee that the statutory rights that legally protect Macao's special status within China after the handover are respected and upheld.

I asked a Hong Kong Chinese tycoon I had breakfast with what he thought about all this. He replied elliptically. In Shanghai, he said, where he was born, the police were also totally, irretrievably corrupt, so the army had invited them to a banquet. Then, while they were eating and drinking, the army set up sand bags and machine guns, and when the police were allowed out, mowed them all down. It was not an encouraging answer.

VIII

Macao, in addition to the rich veneer of an old Europe, also retains much of traditional China, isolated as it has been from the turmoil that devastated China over the past century. Many ancient religious practices survive in Macao, where hardly a street or corner or niche does not house a small shrine, candle, incense stick, or offering to a rich diversity of dieties. A wide range of religious and civil groupings have long lived there in mutual tolerance. Partly as a consequence, the population of Macao is not as apolitical as it appears. After the Tiananmen Square bloodbath in 1989, over 150,000 people—a very significant proportion of Macao's population of half a million—protested, in an unprecedented rebuke to Beijing.

The 1996 legislative elections saw workers in the tourist and gambling sectors organize politically and join forces with the prodemocracy representative, Antonio Ng Kuok-cheong, in complaining of vote buying by the big business interests. Workers in manufacturing jobs also complained that the powerful pro-Beijing union confederation was more interested in politics than in workers' rights and wages.[42] Macao human rights activists complain that procedural changes may vitiate any guarantees of judicial independence guaranteed by the Basic Law because of new rules limiting tenure of judges to three years (they had lifetime tenure under the Portuguese system) and the dominant role of the government in the selection of magistrates and judges.[43]

Legislation to create a press council galvanized the usually self-censoring press into vociferous protest. The president of the Macao Journalists Club complained that the government proposal was "very dangerous" and that any press watchdog body should be "a genuinely independent body which protects press freedom. Macao is a very small community, interpersonal relations are very close and it is very difficult to find someone who is totally independent, free of influence and unaffected by the people around him."[44]

Macao's Chinese and Macanese intellectuals are also beginning to realize that Macao's special blend of Asia and Europe risks being engulfed by the burgeoning economic growth of the Pearl River delta and the self-interested philistinism of the odd coalition of capitalist magnates, Communist Party commissars, and short-term Portuguese bureaucrats who together have set the agenda in construction and real estate in recent years. An important motivation behind the cultivation of the Chinese central authorities in Beijing by Macao's Chinese leaders and their belated embrace of Macao's rich Sino-Portuguese cultural history is their growing anxiety

---

[42]Lo Shiu-hing, "Comparative Political Systems: The Cases of Hong Kong and Macau," *Journal of Contemporary Asia* 25, no. 2 (1995): 254–271, and his "Aspects of Political Development in Macao," *China Quarterly*, no. 120 (December 1989): 837–851.

[43]These questions are discussed in detail in U.S. Department of State, *Macau Country Report on Human Rights Practices for 1996*, released January 30, 1997.

[44]*Asian Wall Street Journal Weekly*, September 23, 1996.

about the activities of the neighboring special economic zone of Zhuhai. This relationship has turned extremely competitive—"malignant and vicious" is how Gary Ngai describes it—and has led to a failure to collaborate on waste disposal, delays in a proposed Macao-Canton rail and highway connection, the construction of duplicative international airports, and even to Zhuhai's preemption of Macao's famous grand prix auto race with a grand prix of its own held a week earlier. There are now two grandiose schemes afoot to construct duplicative bridges across the Pearl River estuary. And Macao has also become aware that its income from gambling would be greatly diminished if China or Hong Kong were to permit casinos. Should this occur, Macao could face a fatal blow to its prosperity.

As Gary Ngai told me, turning Macao from "a city of gambling to a city of culture is the best way for Macao to survive in the future, turning it from a shadow of Hong Kong in tourism to a dragon head of cultural tourism in the Pearl River delta." Macao's business leaders have come to realize that it is in their own interest to persuade Beijing that Macao has a special role to play precisely because of its unique European-Chinese mix, and they have started to aggressively develop links to the European Community as well as the Portuguese-speaking world.[45] Preserving the "City of God in China" has thus by a strange historical reversal now fallen to the Chinese of Macao, rather than to the Portuguese. The local Chinese elite's own power and influence rest to a considerable degree in persuading Beijing that cultural preservation in this case is an asset to China and in convincing the local "nationalists" that this heritage is not "colonial trash" to be thrown overboard.

Gary Ngai, along with Professor Fok and other scholars from Macao and Portugal, have formed a new Sino-Latin Foundation. "It is precisely Macao's history and cultural identity which distinguished it from Hong Kong and other Chinese coastal cities, a Sino-Latin identity; formed over four centuries of its existence," is the way Ngai puts it. Funds have been provided by Stanley Ho and local entrepreneurs who launched the foundation with the blessing of the Portuguese governor and the head of the Xinhua News Agency. It is not an ignoble effort among the triad wars and the real estate deals and the shadowy world of espionage and money laundering.

One can only wish them luck, recalling of course the admonition of Bishop Lam that nothing in Macao is ever what it appears to be, and the shrewd observation of that wise old historian Charles Boxer that it is es-

---

[45]For the economic situation at the time of the transition, see International Monetary Fund, Public Information Notice No. 99140, May 7, 1999; Article IV Consultation held in 1998 with Portugal-Macau.

sential to remember, for better or worse, that "in Macao, if anywhere, East and West did meet."[46] So it is not inappropriate that at this tiny, ambiguous, and opaque spot, the great adventure that took Europe more than 500 years ago to Asia in search of the riches of Cathay ended, just before the end of the millennium as the Chinese had wanted, and very much on their terms.

---

[46]Boxer, *Fidalgos in the Far East*, 288.

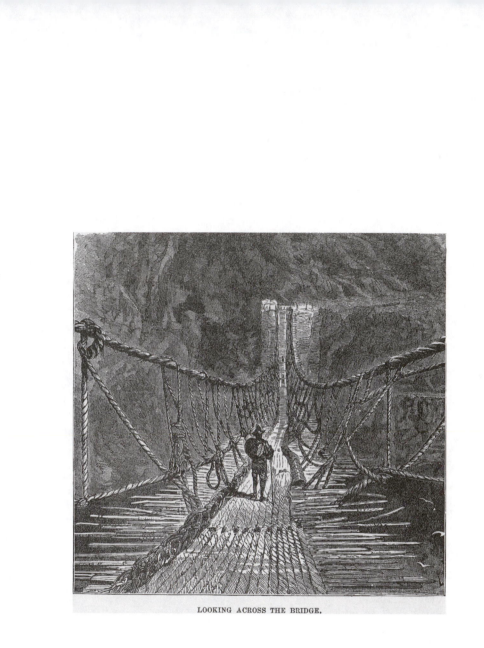

LOOKING ACROSS THE BRIDGE.

CHAPTER 15

Heroes and Traitors

"Home is where I hang my hat."
—Charles Boxer, Camões Center, 1989

Heroes come cheap these days. The word is bandied around so promiscuously for high-priced sports stars and short-lived celebrities that when a real hero appears he or she makes people uncomfortable. The 2000 U.S. presidential election saw a real hero enter the competition—Senator John McCain—not a popular figure among his fellow senators but a truly exceptional man who survived long years of solitary confinement and torture as a POW in Vietnam to emerge as a leading advocate of reconciliation with his former tormentors. Charles R. Boxer was such a man, both a victim and an admirer of the Japanese, and resented, like Senator McCain, by some of his former colleagues for his magnanimity. But if heroes come cheap, so do accusations of treachery. This is the rub of the C. R. Boxer *affaire*, a concoction of old resentments, gossip, and jealousies from a lost colonial world served up now to impinge the reputation of a truly remarkable and complex individual.

I

"Charles Boxer was a fine soldier and a brilliant historian. But . . . was he also a traitor whose information prolonged the Second World War?" So began the headline of an article in the British newspaper *The Guardian* on February 24, 2001, by Hywel Williams. In his article Williams asserts that Boxer "may" have been a "traitor" who betrayed ". . . his fellow officers in a Japanese-run POW camp in Hong Kong in a way that undermined the entire British intelligence system in south east Asia." Boxer, Williams goes on, was "a globalist intellectual before his time" whose work "framed the assumptions of the post-colonial and anti-western elites in Brazil, west Africa and Japan, where he was read, translated and feted."

Williams claims that Boxer had fallen "under the spell of the Japanese cultural style, its combination of intellectual-aesthetic refinement and power politics." It was, he continues, just like "the Philby-Burgess-Maclean-Blunt generation of English intellectuals [who] embraced Marxist communism in Soviet form." Boxer, he says, like "other members of his [social] class had found another country and another cause in the east." After the war "collaborators everywhere got off lightly." Boxer's case, writes Williams, could be "a spectacular example of wartime temptation."

These were dramatic charges against one of the twentieth century's greatest historians, coming in one of Britain's most respected newspapers. Once known as the *Manchester Guardian*, this newspaper since its founding in 1821 has been Britain's strongest liberal voice, independent, nonconformist, and a stalwart champion of unpopular causes. It is the one British newspaper I have read diligently over the years, and I have long admired its writing and reporting. Its pioneering *Manchester Guardian Weekly* incorporates selections from *Le Monde* and the *Washington Post*.

Charles R. Boxer died in 2000 at the age of ninety-six. This protects the newspaper from the risk of a charge of libel. In its March 10, 2001, edition *The Guardian* published a detailed refutation of Williams's accusations against Boxer by the American historian Dauril Alden. Fortuitously, Alden had just finished a biography of Boxer.[1] Professor Alden is a meticulous scholar of the old school for whom solid documentation is the core of historical scholarship. His detailed rebuttal of Williams's charges against Boxer can be read on *The Guardian*'s website, www.guardianunlimited.co.uk, where the newspaper originally posted Williams's attack.

Curiously, however, the Williams article itself was removed from the website archive. Such stealth in cyberspace is despicable—if *The Guardian* is ashamed of what it published in the first place, it should say so. It is hard to understand the lapse of editorial judgment that led *The Guardian* to lend its pages to such a scurrilous attack, filled with innuendo, inaccuracies, and undocumented aspersion on the honor of the most honorable of men. And it in no way relieves *The Guardian* from the moral obligation to apologize to Boxer's family and its readers for this grotesque breach of its own high journalistic standards. One assumes that under English libel law if any of the individuals attacked in the Hywel Williams article were still alive, *The Guardian* would be facing the probability of funding several academic chairs in Portuguese imperial history named in Boxer's memory.

---

[1]Dauril Alden, *Charles R. Boxer, An Uncommon Life: Soldier, Historian, Teacher, Collector, Traveller* (Lisbon: Fundação Oriente, 2001).

To generations of historians of the Portuguese-speaking world C. R. Boxer was a true colossus. His highly original, pithy, and path-breaking books, monographs, and articles flowed forth with seeming effortlessness. Boxer's works covered the history of early European intrusions into Japan and China during the sixteenth century, and splendid accounts of the opulence and decline of Goa, seat of Portugal's empire in Asia. In over 350 publications, all of the highest order of scholarship, Boxer wrote on sixteenth-century naval warfare in the Persian Gulf, the tribulations of the maritime trading route between Europe and Asia, a sparkling overview of Brazil during the eighteenth century in the age of gold strikes and frontier expansion, magnificent syntheses of both Dutch and Portuguese colonial history, race relations, and social mores, as well as many pioneering comparative studies of local municipal institutions in Asia, Africa, and South America. Famously in the 1960s at the height of Portugal's colonial wars in Africa, he took on the "Luso-tropicalist" propaganda of the Salazar dictatorship by unraveling its roots in Gilberto Freyre's assertion of Portuguese colonial nonracialism and was thoroughly vilified for it by the regime and its apologists.

In my view Boxer's magnificent account of the career of Salvador Correia de Sá Benevides (1602–1686) is one of his very best books. This "notable old stickler," as Sir Robert Southwell called Salvador de Sá in a letter to Lord Arlington in 1667, played a decisive role in the titanic seventeenth-century struggle between the Iberian powers and the Dutch for hegemony in the South Atlantic. The inscription for his now lost tomb at the Lisbon convent of the bare-footed Carmelites praised Salvador de Sá as "the Restorer of the Faith of CHRIST in the Kingdom of Angola, Congo, Benguela, São Tomé and conqueror of the Dutch." As Boxer demonstrated, to this accolade should have been added the savior of Portuguese-speaking Brazil.

Remarkably, Boxer had only formally entered academic life when middle-aged. Without a university degree, but on the strength of his outstanding scholarship, he was appointed in 1947 to the prestigious chair at King's College, London, named in honor of the great Portuguese poet Luís de Camões, author of *The Lusiads*. He got the job at King's College, he said, because there was no real competition: "it's like the duckbilled platypus. I'm the only one of my kind."

Boxer's attainments were so intimidating that when I wrote to him from Lisbon in 1963 to ask how one should prepare for the field I was then thinking of entering, he almost stopped me in my tracks. The basic qualifications, he said, for anyone studying the Portuguese empire were a combination of languages that encompassed Dutch and French and Italian on the European side, in addition to Portuguese and Spanish, and for studying Asia, Japanese and Chinese at the minimum and the paleographic skills to be able to read archival documents in as many of these languages as possible from 1500 on. A strong foundation in the classics was advisable as well, as was a thorough knowledge of the religious literature and theological controversies within the Catholic Church, and between Catholics and Protestants since the Restoration. He said this not to boast: he had no tolerance for pretension. He was only reciting some part of skills he possessed himself and used so effectively to do his work. Boxer despite his eminence was extraordinarily generous with his time and advice to those of us with lesser attainments.

II

Although it was well known that Boxer had been a soldier until his forties, there was another Boxer about whom we—or at least I—knew very little. This was Boxer the spy and Boxer the lover. Father Manuel Teixeira, the veteran Portuguese priest who is Macao's premier historian, once asked Boxer about his religion. It was well known that as a prisoner of war of the Japanese for almost four years in Hong Kong and later Canton (Guangzhou to the Chinese), he had rejected the Bible in preference for the complete works of Shakespeare, a decision that troubled the redoubtable old priest, with whom Boxer had long retained a friendly rivalry. Boxer, whose penchant for bawdy jokes and barrack-room doggerel was notorious, answered: I am an Episcopalian from the waist up and a Mormon from the waist down. In the case of the Mormons, he was evidently thinking of polygamy and not the Salt Lake City Tabernacle Choir. Boxer's Hong Kong affair with the American journalist Emily Hahn was one of the twentieth century's most publicized romances. For seventy years Hahn, known to her friends and family as "Mickey," was one of *The New Yorker*'s most prolific contributors. Like Boxer, her literary output was astounding—52 books and hundreds of articles, short stories, and poems. Their wartime affair in Hong Kong was fully laid out by Hahn herself in the best-seller *China to Me: A Partial Autobiography.*[2] She predeceased Charles Boxer in 1997 at the age of ninety-two.

To many who had followed her adventures over the years, Emily Hahn was the star and Charles Boxer was the handsome military bit player. Her U.S. obituaries hardly mentioned him or his achievements as a scholar. For Emily Hahn's public Charles Boxer was forever the British major from Hong Kong who became her lover, father of her children, and then her

---

[2]Emily Hahn, *China to Me, A Partial Autobiography* (New York: Doubleday, Doran, 1944). Also see Emily Hahn, *No Hurry to Get Home: The Memoir of the New Yorker Writer Whose Unconventional Life and Adventures Spanned the Twentieth Century* (Seattle: Seal Press, 2000) and Ken Cuthbertson, *Nobody Said Not to Go: The Life, Loves, and Adventures of Emily Hahn* (New York: Faber and Faber, 1998).

husband for over fifty years. Boxer and Hahn settled down at his country seat in Dorset in the late 1940s, but Hahn was ill suited to the role of chatelaine in a drafty English manor during the pinched conditions of the postwar British countryside. Her all-too-accurate commentary on British mores and foibles in *England to Me* published in 1949 was not appreciated by her adopted countrymen. After 1950 her marriage to Boxer became a transatlantic commute. Hahn avoided taxes in Britain by brief sojourns, while Boxer, after a stint at Yale University, when in the United States checked into the Yale Club on Vanderbilt Avenue behind Grand Central Station in New York City.

Emily Hahn was born of Jewish-German ancestry in St. Louis, Missouri, in 1905. In 1926 she earned the first degree in mining engineer awarded to a woman by the University of Wisconsin. During the early 1920s she had driven across America in a Model T Ford dressed as a boy and settled briefly in Santa Fe, New Mexico. Her letters to friends in Chicago, where her family had moved, provided the material sent to but initially rejected by *The New Yorker*. She worked as a screenwriter in the early days of Hollywood, took graduate studies in geology at Columbia University in New York, and had her first *New Yorker* piece published in 1929. When a California love affair went wrong, she took off in 1930 for Africa, settled among the pigmies in the Belgium Congo and became attached to gibbons. At least one of these slender-bodied long-armed arboreal apes thereafter accompanied her everywhere perched on her shoulder.

In 1935 she stopped off for a few days at Shanghai. "It had become clear to me from the first day in China that I was going to stay forever," she wrote later. In China she met the Soong sisters. The eldest was wed to Dr. W. H. Kung, a wealthy Shanghai banker and China's prime minister in the late 1930s. Another Soong sister had married Sun Yat-sen, founder of the Chinese republic, still revered by both Nationalists and Communists as the founder of modern China. The third sister married Chiang Kai-shek, the Nationalist leader.

Hahn wrote the stories of these remarkable women in her book *The Soong Sisters*, published in 1941. In Shanghai Hahn had a long affair with one of China's leading intellectuals and poets, Zau Sinmay, and became an opium addict. She was a friend of such luminaries of the Shanghai scene as Sir Victor Sassoon and C. V. Starr, publisher of the American *Shanghai Evening Post and Mercury* and backer of Sinmay's abortive attempts to establish a bilingual literary journal. She met the young Communist insurgent leaders Mao Zedong and Zhou Enlai. All the while she was filing reports for *The New Yorker* as its China correspondent, recording in vivid autobiographical detail life in China against a background of civil war and revolution and the Japanese invasion.

When Emily Hahn became Charles Boxer's lover in Hong Kong in 1940 he was already "an old Asian hand," as the saying went in British colonial circles. Boxer, who was working with British military intelligence, had in 1939 married Ursula Tulloch. Hywel Williams, in his article in *The Guardian*, claims Tulloch, known as the "most beautiful woman" in Hong Kong, was also one of the most promiscuous. Her ambition, Williams asserts, "was to sleep her way through the entire intelligence community in the far east." A marvelous English euphemism the word "sleep" in this context. Sleep was presumably the last thing, Williams implies, that Ursula Tulloch, Boxer, or anyone else was thinking of when they went to bed in Hong Kong. Boxer and Tulloch were the colony's prime "swingers," Williams asserts.

Alf Bennett, one of Boxer's old friends, arrived in Hong Kong in 1939 to join the Far East Intelligence Bureau and after the headquarters was moved to Singapore later that year, remained in Hong Kong and worked in adjacent offices to Boxer and saw him every day. Alf Bennett was kind enough to share with me his reaction to *The Guardian* article. He says that "whatever the author wished to convey by 'swingers,' not a word of that time, this is complete nonsense." Boxer was a hard drinker and enjoyed a good party, but as Alf Bennett says, "Charles was soon back to his books to write an erudite article."

Ursula Tulloch was also evacuated from Hong Kong to Singapore. It had been assumed, inaccurately as it turned out, that Singapore would be safer from attack by the Japanese and was in any case impregnable. When this confidence proved disastrously misplaced, she managed to escape when Singapore fell to the Japanese in 1942, making her way to Ceylon (now Sri Lanka) where she chose to stay working as a cryptographer. In 1947, after divorce from Boxer, she married I. A. R. Peebles, a journalist at the *London Sunday Times* and a well-known sportsman. Following Peebles's death she married again. Ursula Tulloch, of course, like Charles Boxer and Emily Hahn, is no longer around to refute Williams's assertions. She died in 1996 at the age of eighty-six.

Boxer had met Hahn first in Shanghai, startled when first greeted at the offices of Sinmay's magazine by "an enormous ape . . . wearing a red cap . . ." This was Emily Hahn's companion, the gibbon "Mr. Mills." Boxer told her he too was a writer, of "historical works, very dull." But he had been given to understand that Emily and Sinmay "were actors in one of the great love stories of the world, so naturally I didn't want to intrude." Hahn found Boxer a "brilliant, amusing, mad man, who had insisted on talking to me about the latest Chungking politics, of which I knew nothing, and harping on the approaching dissolution of the British Empire." After Hahn congratulated him on his marriage he said, "It always happens when one lives in Hong Kong. One either becomes a hopeless drunkard or one marries. I did both."

When Emily Hahn came to Hong Kong with Sinmay, "the Major," as she invariably called Boxer, took the direct approach. At a dinner he overheard Hahn say she could not have children. Well, Boxer told her, I do not believe that, let's see, and the child can be my heir. The subsequent birth of Carola in November 1941 took place six weeks before the Japanese surprise attack on Pearl Harbor. The Japanese assault on Hong Kong itself came shortly thereafter. After holding out for sixteen days, the British surrendered on Christmas Day 1941, the centenary of the British annexation of Hong Kong island from the Chinese Empire during the Anglo-Chinese Opium War of 1839–1842. Boxer, who had rejected two Japanese demands for surrender on behalf of the British governor, had been severely wounded.

The task of conveying the formal rendition of Hong Kong to the Japanese thereby fell to his friend Alf Bennett, a Japanese-speaker who had also served in Japan. He was very unhappy to have been handed this unpleasant duty. But Emily Hahn gave a notable description of Alf Bennett in 1940:

> Alf was an RAF officer, at once deliberately comic and knowingly glamorous. He had an incredible mustache, curled at the ends like Father's in the Clarence Day play. He had high blood pressure and a growling voice; he roared, and drank, and knew poetry, and fancied himself a picturesque figure, as he was. Picturesque and privileged. Everybody knew Alf, and women were wistful about him, but a little afraid.

Boxer himself had no doubt about the outcome of the war, even as he lay gravely wounded in the hospital as Hong Kong fell. "In the end they can't win. I don't see how they can, do you? Against America, and England, and Holland and China. We must try to survive, that's all."

III

Boxer came from a family with a long military tradition, and was born in 1904 on the Isle of Wight. He was educated at Wellington College, named after the Duke of Wellington, victor over Napoleon at Waterloo, and at the Royal Military Academy at Sandhurst. He was commissioned into the Linconshire Regiment as a lieutenant in 1923. Boxer's father, who also served in the Linconshire Regiment, had been killed at Ypres in 1915. His was a typically heroic and needless death, as were so many on the dreadful killing fields of the Western Front in World War I. Seriously wounded while serving with General Kitchener in Egypt. Boxer's father had, however, insisted on returning to active duty when the world war broke out. At Ypres he had led his men up out of the trenches into withering machine-gun fire, propped up on his walking stick and resting on the elbow of his batman.

Following language and intelligence training, Charles Boxer was seconded to the Japanese army in 1930 for three years as part of an exchange of Japanese and English officers. He was assigned to the 38 Infantry in Nara. "Usually in armies the smart people were in the cavalry, but in Japan the cavalry was regarded as a lot more stupid and upper class and not nearly as good as the infantry," Boxer said in 1989 in an interview we recorded at the Camões Center at Columbia University. Boxer enjoyed Japan: "When you are young and lusty as an eagle and with a lot of money you do." He took up the Japanese fencing called kendo—"Everyone does it now, but in 1930 all the foreigners did *jujitsu*. I was the first one to do *kendo*." Boxer explained, "I was very pro-Japanese anyway and the older generation was still very pro-British . . . it was a man's country and if you learned Japanese, which I did, you were fine." Not that women were absent from Boxer's Japanese life. His housekeeper concubine was a northerner from Kakoadati on the island of Kakkaido. "There was no secret about it. She had been someone else's concubine before and was very reliable."[3]

It was in Japan that he expanded his interest in Portuguese imperial history, concentrating his attention on the first disastrous experiment of European incursion into Japan and its catastrophic ending when Tokugawa closed off the country to outside influence in the 1640s. The Japanese literally crucified hundreds of Christian missionaries and converts and for good measure executed a delegation of anxious envoys sent out from the Portuguese China enclave of Macao in order to make it entirely clear to the European outsiders that they meant what they said. This was the subject of Boxer's book *The Christian Century in Japan, 1549–1650* (1951).

Boxer returned to London for a two-year posting from 1935–1936 to the military intelligence section of the War Office. Here, he told us in 1989, "I had something to do with Anthony Blunt or Anthony Burgess—one of those traitors who was in the Foreign Office because we had to liase with each other over the phone." I am glad Mr. Hywel Williams did not see this reference to the notorious Soviet moles within the British establishment— it would undoubtedly have provided more grist to his conspiratorial mill. In midwinter 1937 Boxer was sent to Hong Kong, traveling by way of the Trans-Siberian Railroad, Manchuria, Korea, Japan, and Shanghai. In Hong Kong he worked with the Far East Combined Bureau, a military intelligence unit, and traveled widely in China on his spy missions as well as returning several times to Japan.

The center of Hywel Williams's charge of collaboration against Boxer focuses on the period of the Japanese occupation of Hong Kong and secret

---

[3]"Boxer on Boxer: A Conversation," *Camões Center Quarterly* I, no. 2 (June 1989): 11–22.

transmissions between prisoners of war held at the Argyle Street camp in Kowloon for British officers and the British Army Aid (BAAG) operating out of Chongqing, former capital of Sichuan Province and the base of Chiang Kai-shek's Nationalist army. The discovery of the "transmitter" by the Japanese in July 1943, Hywel Williams implies, was a result of Boxer's treachery. Only a handful of officers knew of the transmitter at the time, he claims, and all were executed except Boxer.

Professor Alden takes apart these charges systematically in his March 10, 2001, refutation of Hywel Williams's article. As Alden proves, far from being responsible for "prolonging" World War II, Boxer was the one who warned that "there could be no greater error than to assume, as is so often done, that Japan's military is too bogged down in China to prevent it being turned against us . . ." It was the British War Office and Foreign Office that ignored and underestimated this threat. As Alden also points out, Boxer was shot in the back by a sniper trying to rally leaderless troops against the invasion. At the Argyle Street camp in Kowloon the control of information became critical to morale as the tides of war shifted against the Japanese. For a time this news was accessible through a secret shortwave radio receiver (not transmitter). After the Japanese found it, Boxer and others were arrested, interrogated, and condemned to hard labor. Alden quotes Ralph Goodwin, a camp escapee who wrote that Boxer's prison companions "never ceased to marvel at [his] amazing fortitude and calmness of spirit."

After the war Boxer declined a decoration from the British government (an MBE–Member of the British Empire) since he said he "had done nothing to deserve the honor." Later in 1975 he declined an honor a second time, a Commander of the British Empire (CBE). There was, he said, no empire left to be a Commander of. Boxer himself rarely, if ever, spoke of his imprisonment; nor did he want to write an autobiography. To have experienced torture, he told a colleague, was to "share the experience of many helpless people in the past." Colleagues looking at his personal files found his folders empty. "Ever the intelligence officer" was the reaction of a long-time colleague at King's College. When pressed on this period during the Camões Center interview in 1989 and asked if he was surprised or apprehensive when Hong Kong fell, he said,

> No, I knew the Japanese and I saw clearly that would happen to us. I knew damned well that if they treated their own people badly why should they treat us better. The Japanese army's discipline was very severe, even when they made the slightest mistake. We had seen all this in Japan and I had no illusions.

Emily Hahn was less reticent about the events in Hong Kong during the Japanese occupation. Her voluminous writings and correspondence give a richly detailed account of these years. Her book, *China to Me*, published in 1944 while Boxer was still held in a POW camp in Hong Kong, dealt explicitly with the whole cast of characters—Japanese, British, Chinese, and American—Hahn met in this period. Her activities and subterfuges, negotiations and hardships, and her relationship with Boxer was shared with the over seven hundred thousand readers who bought her best-seller. The "collaboration" Hywel Williams imputes to Boxer and Hahn was no mystery at all, nor did it involve betrayal by any stretch of the imagination.

In fact it was Hahn's identification papers, showing her to have a Chinese husband, Sinmay, that saved her. And with the connivance of the Japanese consul in Hong Kong, Mr. Shiroshici Kimura, who knew Boxer and Hahn before the war. Hahn registered their exchange in *China to Me*:

> "You know I'm an American. Everyone knows that. I have an American passport; you know that too."
>
> "I know."
>
> "According to American law this Chinese marriage does not make me Chinese."
>
> "According to Japanese law," he said, "it does."
>
> "And you know that's Boxer's baby, don't you?"
>
> "Of course. Your—uh—private life does not alter the law. You will not be interned, Miss Hahn. Indeed, you cannot be interned. We are ejecting all Chinese subjects from the internment camps."

One of Williams's more bizarre inaccuracies is his "charge" that Hahn was a "feminist and a communist sympathizer," doubtless intended to reinforce his innuendoes that Boxer was like the Soviet moles within the British establishment, a man with the proclivities for treachery because of his relationship with such a woman. Ironically this McCarthy-like smear, and in *The Guardian* no less, parallels the suspicions of U.S. military intelligence when Hahn eventually got back to New York with Carola in December 1943, and was interrogated by eight panels of military intelligence officials and the FBI. Why had she not been interned? Had she been a Japanese spy? Why had she fraternized with such high-ranking Japanese officers? Why had she received "favors" from the Japanese?

Hahn kept replying:

> the comparative freedom I had got out of the lie was important. It was not only that the very idea of being herded behind barbed wire was revolting. Outside, I was able to carry food and medicine to the military camp where Carola's father was incarcerated. We all did, every week, a draggle-tailed group of women whose men were locked up. Chinese women, and Swiss and French and Danish and Eurasian and Russian, and me.

Hahn was without question a women ahead of her time in very many ways, but she scoffed at the idea of being a feminist: "[F]eminists belong to clubs. They collect money for causes. I wish feminists well but I've never wanted to be one." She was too much the individualist for such collective causes, and as the late William Maxwell of *The New Yorker* pointed out, though it hardly needed emphasis for anyone who read what she wrote over the years: she liked men. She was also no leftist, far from it: during the increasingly bitter divisions in the United States over China during the late 1940s she spoke up for the Nationalists of Chiang Kai-shek and criticized the Communist propaganda many Americans she claimed had "fallen for." She dismissed as "stay at home experts" those American leftists and liberals who supported the Chinese Communists. In fact it is probably precisely because she was not a feminist nor a leftist in the fashionable New York manner that even today Emily Hahn is not recognized as the amazing and very American original that she undoubtedly was.

Boxer also trespassed beyond the narrow bounds of British colonial etiquette and ingrained racism. As Hahn had written about Shanghai,

> The British were not aware of the Chinese as a people. Oh I don't mean the British didn't *see* the Chinese. They did. They mentioned them often as peasants, dwellers in the picturesque villages we saw when we went houseboating or shooting. They spoke of them as servants, quaint and lovable. . . . The British community, however, reserved its social life for itself and those among the Caucasian groups that could be considered suitably upper class.

Boxer and Hahn were just the opposite. They moved in multiracial circles. Hahn had a Chinese lover. And she was an American. All these elements upset and obsessed and disgusted British Hong Kong. And the resentments have evidently not diminished over the years. It is doubtless from these poisoned roots that the tittle-tattle and gossip arose, which landed up on the pages of *The Guardian*. As Hahn notes at one point in *China to Me*, "Nobody English thought of inviting Chinese people to 'informal parties.'" Boxer had no tolerance for racism, Portuguese or British. A Japanese interrogator at the fall of Hong Kong paid him an unwitting tribute when he told Hahn, "Everybody say British bad; Boxer okay. No proud."

IV

I asked Boxer in 1989 about how the British Army had reacted to his scholarly interest. "Provided you hunted and had a horse and that kind of thing then you were regarded as more or less all right," he replied. "Whether you took any interest in history didn't matter at all. If you were interested in

Portuguese or Dutch that was regarded as mildly eccentric, but as long as you hunted and had a horse those were the main things." In Hong Kong hunting was not enough. His Japanese connections were also no mystery: this was precisely the reason for his intelligence posting to Hong Kong in the first place. His Japanese regiment had in fact been one of those which seized Hong Kong from the British in 1941. The Japanese knew Boxer and he knew them, and he used this understanding to help his fellow prisoners survive.

Unlike Blunt, Burgess, and the Soviet moles, Boxer was no cynic. His closest friends saw him as a stoic. In his personal copy of the *Meditations* of Marcus Aurelius he had marked the passage on what it is to die, how ". . . he can conceive of it not otherwise, than as a work of nature, and he that fears any work of nature, is a very child." And this stoicism sustained him through the ordeal of over three years in captivity, torture, and solitary confinement. Was he afraid, we asked in 1989. "No, there was no reason to be afraid. It was part of life. I feel sorry that a lot of people who died never lived to see the end of the war. My friends never lived to see this, because they were shot and killed. I was one of the lucky ones." Boxer was no traitor, nor in his own mind was he a hero. He was, as his friend Professor Peter Marshall of King's College called him, a person of "granite integrity." When offered decorations he rejected them. But a title Charles Boxer might just have accepted was the one he liked to quote about Salvador Correa de Sá. For whatever else Boxer may or may not have been, he was undoubtedly like his seventeenth-century Luso-Brazilian hero: "a notable old stickler." A stickler is defined in my dictionary as a tenacious and persistent person in search of the truth. This is something once upon a time the *Manchester Guardian* also used to be.

THE AQUEDUCT.

CHAPTER 16

Orfeu

*"Rio de Janeiro/My joy and my delight!
By day I have no water/By night I have no light."*
—Anonymous Samba lyric, 1965

I first saw *Black Orpheus* (1959) by Marcel Camus in the early l960s in a crowded and cold old movie palace on the outskirts of Cambridge, England. It was a dull and dismal winter evening and I was barely twenty years old: so I suppose I was ripe for romance; the more exotic and erotic the better, even if on celluloid. It was powerful enough to make me determined to set out to see Brazil for myself.

The new *Orfeu* (1999) directed by Carlos (aka "Cacá") Diegues I saw in São Paulo, in a rush, on a hot afternoon. The nearly empty theater off the Avenida Paulista was shiny and new with an electronic entrance gate I had great difficulty navigating until assisted by a sleepy attendant—and the air was conditioned to English chilliness. I got there late and the film had begun, so I missed the beginning.

Euridice was the wife of Orfeu, the legendary Thracian poet and musician who could cast charms and spells by his singing and who was permitted by Pluto to follow her out of Hades provided that he refrain from looking back at her. Orfeu did, and Euridice was doomed to return. But the new resilient Orfeu of the cinema has little to do with this Greek provenance, set as his story now is within a Western Roman Catholic festival, his music and its spell rooted in samba, speaking Portuguese with Brazilian inventiveness, and located in a favela close to the sky, high up above the sweeping arcs of Rio's beaches.

As I arrived, the spectacular Rio backdrop was still there on the screen, and very occasionally, almost apologetically, the old music in the background. But the scene I happened in upon was more *Lethal Weapon* than Vinícius de Moraes. A flabby, terrified middle-aged white man, surrounded by a largely nonwhite crowd, was about to have his head blown off. It was. His body was subsequently dumped over the edge of the morro (slum), into a festering rubbish dump. I have no idea what the poor man had done. Raped a little girl? Cheated on a drug deal? Was he a stand-in that represented the Brazilian establishment, indifferent as ever to the plight of the favelas, unless reminded, violently, that this is where millions of Brazilians live out their daily lives, and not only during Carnival, and most without "a room with a view"?

Brazilian movie critics never seemed to have much liked the rendition by Camus. It is too "exotic tourism" as the phrase goes. But foreigners should be forgiven for enjoying it. In 1962, I certainly took *Black Orpheus* for what I saw on the screen: the fantasy, the cityscape, the magnificent setting, and the human grace and musicality. But I also subsequently had the suspicion that what many middle-class Brazilians objected to about *Orfeu* was precisely the fact that it was not *Orfeu do Carnaval* as it was entitled in Brazil (based on the original 1956 play *Orfeu da Conceição* by Vinícius de Moraes), but very much *Black Orpheus,* and that their unconscious reaction was much like the Bahian police in the 1900s who would confiscate the cameras of European photographers in Salvador when they were seen taking pictures of nonwhites. This was not the Brazil foreigners were supposed to see, much less propagate abroad by means of images. It represented after all that "archaic" Brazil, so deeply embarrassing to Brazilians enamored by the idea of "progress," as in many ways it still does in some illustrious circles who should know better.

Some of the music, grace, and fantasy survive in the new version of *Orfeu.* But I was struck by the Americanization, (or is it the "globalization"?) of Brazilian popular culture over the past thirty years—Toni Garrido's dreadlocks more Afro-Caribbean than Afro-Brazilian; the Pentecostal pastor replacing the ritual of macumba; in place of the rattling bondes crossing atop of Rio's eighteenth-century aqueduct, shining subway cars full of revelers that could just as well have been rumbling under New York's Eighth Avenue, transporting back uptown from Greenwich Village the bejeweled and extravagantly attired denizens of the "Wigstock Parade," the annual extravaganza of New York drag queens and transvestites. The Carnival sequences were more flamboyant and spectacular and costly than before, but curiously self-contained within the concrete shell of the *sambódromo* (samba stadium); the rich spectators more voyeurs than participants, separated and packaged and commercialized well away from the action, and totally protected from the streets where Carnival once predominantly took place, even in my time in the midsixties. Was Cacá Diegues's telescopic gunsight view of the desfile, the setup for the would-be assassination of Orfeu, intended to demonstrate this? Or is Carnival now mainly for TV only?

I had in the mid-1960s been dropped off along the Vidigal road and climbed up some steep steps in the hillside to a small enchanting *chácara* (country cottage) where a Swedish couple working for the UN lived. As the dusk gathered, far away in the distance between the leafy canopy of the mata Atlântica lay the twinkling lights of Leblon, and below a sparkling purple-hewed South Atlantic Ocean. When I was in Rio a few days before I saw the new *Orfeu*, the main sewer pipe from the favela (shanty-town) that now covered the hillside had broken and was spewing sludge into the ocean from much the same location we had looked down over Rio that evening thirty-five years ago. It seemed that this was just the spot Diegues had set the most grotesque and memorable image of his film, the Hades where the drug gangs threw the bodies of their victims, and where the detritus of the globalized favela rotted, and the body of Euridice fell so decorously on a tree limb.

Not that violence and greed did not lurk behind the facade in the 1960s anymore than it does today. I heard afterward that my hosts of that evening were hounded out of their bucolic paradise some year or so later by the hired *pistoleiros* (gunmen) of a Brazilian politican who wanted the land, and were hurriedly flown thoroughly terrified back to Stockholm for their own safety. It was a pity. They were sweet, good-hearted people who only wanted to change the world for the better, and Brazil was the worse off for losing their contribution. It would be sad to think they had been moved out so rudely to provide space for a rubbish dump and a broken sewage pipe.

With its concrete blockhouses and narrow Moorish alleys and steep winding staircases and small open squares the Rio favela in Diegues's film looks much like old Lisbon of the Alfama; an ironic historical throwback to emerge just as Brazil's cultural bureaucrats, or should I say *servidores públicos* (public servants) as they are so inappropriately called, ensconced within their sanitized office blocks on the high plateau in Brasília, squabbled over how to spend the public money on a suitable celebration of Cabral's accidental stopoff at Porto Seguro on his way to India in 1500.

But these "jump cuts" permeated my reaction to Diegues's *Orfeu*. Poor Cabral and his Portuguese companions were shocked at the nakedness of the people they encountered on the Brazilian beach, and even more by their lack of self-consciousness about it—their lack of "shame" as they put it. I was struck by how overdressed all the characters in the new *Orfeu* had become—poor Euridice must have sweltered, swaddled in what looked like a discarded wedding gown, or the traficante Lucinho and his bizarre woolen hat with his affected mannerisms, more Chicago in winter than Rio in summertime. Even Orfeu was decked out in an American gigolo undershirt and baggy pants—though we did get to see his naked bottom briefly. This was not a very sexy movie despite the fact that sex or at least unrequited love was what the story was all about. There was no spark to this tragic triangle, and the life came more from the minor characters (the marvelous Mary Sheila as the traficante Be Happy—how more American can you get than that—and Isabella Fillards as Mira) than from the principals, who seemed self-absorbed and narcissistic, more in love with themselves than each other.

But I suppose all of this just reflects the passing of time and nostalgic remembrances of things past. Today more Brazilians after all live in a context that is more urban than rural, more international than national. Carnival is more marginal than ever from the life of those who can afford to consume culture and who are more distant and fearful of the underclass than that time long ago when the romanticized and populist interpretations of the culture brokers who once frequented the cafés of the Zona Sul of Rio de Janeiro held sway. I was struck by this very forcibly the afternoon I went to see *Orfeu* off the Avenida Paulista, and again while on my way to the airport later that evening, stuck in interminable traffic with the taxi driver warning me to hide my bag to avoid the attention of thieves.

The night before, a Chilean who had married a Brazilian and lived in Brazil many years said in passing that the real Gotham City was not in Manhattan but here in São Paulo. I could not get this marvelous insight out of my head, looking up at the odd 1950s style antennae on top the skyscrapers, the deeply sunken highways and buttressed overpasses, the underilluminated public streetlights, the cars skimming past the red stoplight to avoid the armed gunmen at the intersections, the screaming sirens, the ugly stucco churches wedged between the gray housing blocks, and the raucous neon-lit brothels and the aggressive pimps banging on the car windows along the Rua Augusta. What Brazil really needed as the twentieth century ended was a Fellini who would set the Greek tragedy down in the realm of Batman. Where Orfeu would be trapped in an interminable bus ride from the periphery of the city, Euridice would be taking tickets at the air-conditioned theater off the Avenida Paulista, and the gunman would be lurking in Hades behind a concrete support for the highway above waiting to press his revolver against the closed window, thinking of crack not sex, and whose life would end far too early to see any sparkling ocean in the distance.

But I had after all missed the beginning of the movie, so perhaps I missed the whole point. This is an old story for a foreigner to Brazil, and especially for historians. At the best of times, they can only see fragments of a mosaic, sometimes they can make sense of it; more often they cannot. So I plead guilty to being unduly influenced by my early Orfeu, and certainly I do not regret it. Unfortunately, these days I do not think undergraduates at Cambridge even go out to see exotic foreign films, let alone in old movie palaces on cold winter nights. So I doubt they have the opportunity to be inspired as I was to set out on a long trek south to see for myself what the movie screen promised. Perhaps like the mythological Orfeu (the original, that is, not the version of Camus or Diegues) I should not have looked back to see if Euridice was following.[1]

---

[1] The Brazilian singer, songwriter, and author Caetano Veloso, who composed the soundtrack to Diegues's movie, took strong exception to my comments on the film and especially on race in Brazil, and responded with a sharp attack in the lead article in the *New York Times* Sunday "Arts & Leisure" section on August 20, 2000, which coincided with the film's New York City premiere. New York film critics and, more important, New York audiences reacted much as I did; the film had a very short run. In any case, I was not writing a review when I wrote my piece.

Sources of Publications

Note: The chapters in this volume have been updated and edited where appropriate. Orthographic inconsistencies reflect original usage.

1. "Encontros Iniciais de um Viajante," *Folha de São Paulo* (December 28, 1997), MAIS!, 8–10.
2. "¡Adiós Columbus!," *New York Review of Books* 40, no. 3 (January 28, 1993).
3. "The Road to Kisses," *New York Review of Books* 53, no. 14 (September 19, 1996).
4. "Pirate Democracy," *New York Review of Books* 56, no. 4 (May 6, 1997).
5. "The Atlantic in the Eighteenth Century: A Southern Perspective on the Need to Return to the 'Big Picture,'" *Transactions of the Royal Historical Society* (London, 1993), 209–336.
6. "The Spark: Pombal, the Amazon and the Jesuits," *Portuguese Studies* 17 (November 2001): 168–183.
7. "The Generation of the 1790s and the Idea of the Luso-Brazilian Empire," in *The Colonial Roots of Modern Brazil,* ed. Dauril Alden (Berkeley and London: University of California Press, 1973), 107–144.
8. "Why Was Brazil Different? The Contexts of Independence," John Parry Memorial Lecture, Harvard University, April 25, 2000, *Working Papers on Latin America* (Cambridge: David Rockefeller Center for Latin America Studies, 2000).

9. "Uma Dupla Incomun," *Folha de São Paulo* (October 7, 2001), MAIS!, 14–19.

10. "Yale Naked: A Story of Slavery, Sex and Mannon," *Notícia e Opinião* (August 24, 2001).

11. "The Tragedy of the Amazon," *New York Review of Books* 38, no. 5 (March 7, 1991): 24–29.

12. "The Mystery of Chico Mendes," *New York Review of Books* 38, no. 6 (March 28, 1991): 39–48.

13. "The Two Brazils," *The Wilson Quarterly* XXIII, no. 1 (winter 1999): 50–60.

14. "Macao: The Shadow Land," *World Policy Journal* XVI, no. 4 (winter 1999/2000): 73–95.

15. "The C. R. Boxer Affaire: Heroes, Traitors, and the Manchester Guardian," *Notícia e Opinião* (March 16, 2001).

16. "Um Fellini que Leve 'Orfeu' ao Reino de Batman," *Folha de São Paulo* (October 28, 1999), Seção Ilustrada.

Abbreviations

ABNRJ, Anais da Biblioteca Nacional do Rio de Janeiro

ADIM, Actas da Devassa da Inconfidência Mineira (1st edition)

AHU, Arquivo Histórico Ultramarino, Lisbon

AMI, Anais do Museu da Inconfidência

ANRJ, Arquivo Nacional, Rio de Janeiro

BNL, Biblioteca Nacional, Lisboa, Fundo Geral

BNLCP, Biblioteca Nacional, Lisboa, Coleção Pombalina

BT, Board of Trade, PRO, London

CUT, Central Única dos Trabalhadores

CVRD, Companhia Vale do Rio Doce

DH, Documentos Históricos, Biblioteca Nacional, Rio de Janeiro

DISP, Documentos Interessantes para a História e Costumes de S. Paulo, São Paulo

FO, Foreign Office Papers, PRO, London

IHGB, Arquivo do Instituto Histórico e Geográfico Brasileiro, Rio de Janeiro

INPE, Instituto Nacional de Pesquisas Espaciais

MHPB, Memórias históricas e políticas da província da Bahia do Coronel Ignácio Accioli de Cerqueira e Silva; mandadas reeditar e annotar pelo governo deste estado . . . annotador dr. Braz do Amaral . . . (6 vols.)(Bahia: Imprensa Official do Estado, 1919–1925)

MST, Movimento dos Trabalhadores Rurais Sem Terra

PMDB, Partido do Movimento Democrático Brasileiro

PRO, Public Record Office, London

PT, Partido dos Trabalhadores

RAPM, Revista do Arquivo Público Mineiro

RHDI/MdeP, Revista Histórica das Idéias; O Marquês de Pombal e o seu tempo (2 vols.) (Coimbra, 1982)

RHSP, Revista Histórica, São Paulo

RIHGB, Revista do Instituto Histórico e Geográfico Brasileiro

TLS, The Times Literary Supplement, London

UDR, União Democrática Ruralista

Index